Communicating a World-in-Crisis

GLOBAL CRISES AND THE MEDIA

Simon Cottle
General Editor

Vol. 31

Communicating a World-in-Crisis

Edited by

Simon Cottle

PETER LANG
New York - Berlin - Bruxelles - Chennai - Lausanne - Oxford

Library of Congress Cataloging-in-Publication Data

Names: Cottle, Simon, editor.
Title: Communicating a world-in-crisis / edited by Simon Cottle.
Description: New York : Peter Lang, [2025] | Series: Global crises and the media, 1947-2587 ; volume 31 | Includes bibliographical references.
Identifiers: LCCN 2024040005 (print) | LCCN 2024040006 (ebook) | ISBN 9783034354097 (hardback) | ISBN 9781636671888 (paperback) | ISBN 9781636671864 (ebook) | ISBN 9781636671871 (epub)
Subjects: LCSH: Climatic changes in mass media. | Environmentalism in mass media. | Communication in climatology. | Communication in the environmental sciences. | Climatic changes–Social aspects. | Environmental disasters–Social aspects.
Classification: LCC P96.C58 C66 2025 (print) | LCC P96.C58 (ebook) | DDC 363.701/4–dc23/eng/20241016
LC record available at https://lccn.loc.gov/2024040005
LC ebook record available at https://lccn.loc.gov/2024040006
DOI 10.3726/b22368

Bibliographic information published by the Deutsche Nationalbibliothek.
The German National Library lists this publication in the German National Bibliography; detailed bibliographic data is available on the Internet at http://dnb.d-nb.de.

Cover design by Peter Lang Group AG

ISSN 1947-2587 (print)
ISBN 9781636671888 (paperback)
ISBN 9783034354097 (hardback)
ISBN 9781636671864 (ebook)
ISBN 9781636671871 (epub)
DOI 10.3726/b22368

Published by Peter Lang Publishing Inc., New York, USA
info@peterlang.com – www.peterlang.com

This publication has been peer reviewed.

CONTENTS

Afterword

LIST OF FIGURES

LIST OF TABLES

PREFACE

Nature of Things, the arresting image on the front cover of this book, was drawn by the artist Guno Park. I am personally grateful to him for granting permission for his exquisite artwork to be reproduced here. The original drawing standing over six feet tall, is an impressive and perfectly executed drawing of the entanglement of human life, and death, with nature. It powerfully symbolises, I think, the interwoven dependence of human life with nature, of how we are ourselves inextricably part of nature and symbiotic with it – and how we forget this at our peril.

Today's world-in-crisis generates multiple and deeply entangled crises where not only human existence but the web-of-life itself has come under assault and is becoming dangerously degraded. Think: biodiversity loss, the sixth mass extinction, climate change, toxic and plastic waste, land, water and air pollution, soil degradation, zoonotic diseases, food and freshwater precarity, nuclear weapons and the ecological impacts of war. And yet, as we are forced to recognise the damage being caused to not only human life but the web-of-life itself, so the way to a sustainable and survivable world begins to come into clearer view, even if through a veil of tears. It is apparent that an 'overshooting' world addicted to incessant growth, materialist ideas of progress and human exceptionalism have – almost – run their course and that a new way of collective being must be found. A way in which practices of social justice and ecological sustainability and custodianship become foundational and collectively enacted in symbiotic relationship with all life forms and surrounding ecosystems. Ideas and practices that have long been at the heart of indigenous communities, their ways of life, cosmologies and traditional wisdom.

Communicating a World-in-Crisis is not preoccupied with the prospects of mass death or societal collapse, but with the communicative possibilities of helping to ensure life's continuity in the web-of-life and into the future. This demands however that we must all wake up to the all too real existential threats generated by today's world-in-crisis and how they continue to converge and deepen, taking us to a planetary cliff edge preceded by 'endless emergency' and potential-possible-probable extinction. The contributors to this volume expertly and insightfully explore different mediums and creative practices within and across today's communication ecology, broadly conceived, seeking out to what extent and how each can make a positive contribution to wider understanding of not only our current planetary predicament but also the cultural flourishing of new ideas and regenerative practices that variously embody imagined futures and the politics of active hope. Guno Park's beautifully crafted drawing of nature's entanglement in human life, and death, helps remind us all, communicatively and powerfully, of the necessity to recognise and live symbiotically in the web-of-life as the positive antidote to today's otherwise terminating world-in-crisis.

Simon Cottle

· 1 ·

INTRODUCTION: COMMUNICATING A WORLD-IN-CRISIS

Simon Cottle

Today we are waking up to a *world-in-crisis* and its unfolding in real time. A world in which crises *caused* by the inexorable and ecologically destructive advance of human society and its predominant economic system, are finally reaching their planetary nadir – or endgame. The world it seems, notwithstanding its gross inequalities, multipolar politics and pluriverse of cultural identities and outlooks, is universally ensnared by human history's most globally rapacious, economically extractive, and ecologically devastating system of production and consumption yet devised and set loose by the human species. A system underpinned by a normative worldview wedded to ideas of incessant growth, material progress and human exceptionalism.

Climate change straddles the Earth as the most precipitous threat to humanity, but it is sadly mistaken to think that this is the only existential catastrophe now bearing down on life on planet earth. Climate change is a symptom or expression of a deeper underlying malaise that manifests simultaneously across a range of interconnected crises. Pandemics, biodiversity loss, the sixth mass extinction, energy, water and food insecurity, soil degradation, toxic pollution, weapons of mass annihilation and AI (Artificial Intelligence), amongst others, all now pose further threats to existence. Entangled within and precipitating many of them are global financial crashes and deepening inequality, increasing political polarisation and instability, failing supply chains, world population growth and mass population movements and, inevitably, increased humanitarian disasters. The latter, moreover, are no longer *spatially* confined 'over there' in the global South but take root 'at home' in the global North and *temporally* threaten to become permanent emergencies everywhere. It is imperative that we recognise the increasingly entangled and compounding nature of global crises today and address these holistically as endemic to a *world-in-crisis* (Cottle, 2023).

Communicating a World-in-Crisis deliberately sets out to explore how today's accelerating and deepening global crises are communicated in and through diverse media and forms of communication, broadly conceived. We live in a world suffused with and enacted through communication: from digitised broadcasting, newspapers and magazines to photography, film and computer games; from street posters, street protests and spectacular advertising to social media and sporting events; from the cultural practices of writing, art and theatre to the classrooms of education and training; and from music's cacophony of sounds and the pedagogic displays of museums to our own communicative embodiment in gesture, speech, and social performativity. In all these and other ways, we live out most of our lives *communicatively*. Indeed, anything capable of sending, responding and adapting to 'information' or being ascribed with meaning and read semiotically 'communicates' – and that's everything!

This book deliberately, if unusually, throws its communicative net widely. It does so to better explore how today's world-in-crisis is *variously* being communicated in and across different communicative fields, media and practices. How global crises become communicated proves critical to how we come to know, understand and situate them within the world as well as how we could or should respond – whether cognitively, emotionally, intellectually, morally or politically (Cottle, 2009a, b, 2014, 2022). With the help of academic and activist voices, and here these distinctions need not be so distinct, the chapters not only question the evident silences and failings of different media and communicative practices to fully engage in the systemic complexity and existential gravity of today's crisis-generating world, but also, importantly, they seek to recognise, broaden and/or deepen the characteristic modes of different media and communicative practice to better align them with processes of future imagining and pathways of transition and societal change.

Today's communication systems and fields of creative practice constitute a complex of institutional and cultural formations, forms and flows that variously interconnect and/or inform each other and communicate today's deepening global crises. An encompassing communications ecology that is expansive both in space and time, is situated in the vortices of culture and power, and which variously helps to suture social relations within everyday as well as public life. All are, of course, also materially implicated in those extractive processes that deplete our planet's resources and impact natural environments, as well as, sometimes, shining a powerful light on the forces and effects of environmental destruction. And so too, sometimes, can their depictions of ecology capture our sense of awe and wonderment at the natural world and even encourage us to recognise our relational interdependence in the web-of-life.

When we approach communication broadly and as richly differentiated fields, then, so can we better discern how each *variously* encompasses and deploys different communicative dimensions and appeals. These can range across, for example, the informational and imagistic, analytic and aesthetic, expositional and expressive, cognitive and cultural, factual and fictional, deliberative and dramatic, propositional and performative, phenomenologically embodied and, with the advent of immersive technologies, the practically extended and virtually experienced. How these and other dimensions of communication find prominence in and across different communication fields and in respect of today's crisis-ridden world, and how they exert possible consequences for understanding, feeling and action is explored by many of the contributors to this volume.

This introductory chapter sets the scene for the contributions that follow. First it sets out some of the latest indices and research evidence documenting the trajectories of decline and potential collapse that now position human society and planetary biosphere in existential jeopardy. Second, we briefly review more conceptually and theoretically some of the different perspectives on world collapse and the constellation of different traditions of intellectual thought and practice that coalesce under the mantle of overarching ideas of the Anthropocene (Crutzen and Steffen, 2003), Capitalocene (Moore, 2015) and Symbiocene (Albrecht, 2019) or Ecological Civilisation (Korton, 2021; Lent, 2021). Together these prove heuristically useful for understanding the complex and systemic nature of today's world-in-crisis. Third, the chapter provides a brief route map of the book's structuration and an overview of the chapters that follow.

Indices of a world-in-crisis

We live in a world where systemic global crises now cascade and converge, deepening existential threats to humanity and the planet's biosphere. Climate change is wreaking havoc around the globe, with extreme weather events including unprecedented heatwaves and megafires, storms and flooding, and melting glaciers and icecaps destroying lives and livelihoods and rendering some places in the world uninhabitable and some traditional ways of life unsustainable. The year 2023 became the world's hottest year since records began in 1850; the ten hottest years in this 174-year history have all occurred during the last decade (2014–2023). In this same year our planet witnessed unprecedented levels of ocean warming, glacier melting, and a catalogue of devastating climate-related disasters across all the world's continents. These have predominantly impacted societies and communities least responsible (IPCC, 2022). As this book goes to press, the years ahead only look set to continue the now annual catalogue of accelerating and deepening climate-related catastrophes.

Carbon emissions continue year on year to rise to new levels, as they have done in contra-agreement to the Paris Accords goals of 2015 and every UN COP (Conference of the Parties) thereafter. This seemingly inexorable trajectory continues the steep upward J patterns of growth and carbon emissions unleashed over centuries by industrialised and extractive societies (Steffen et al., 2015). On current trends temperature rises of 2.4°C to 2.8°C can be anticipated by 2100 or earlier, resulting in even more devastating extreme weather events, sea level rises, species extinctions, mass human migrations, and mass deaths and suffering. As ecosystems become impacted and destabilise, so biodiversity, soil quality, freshwater supplies and food production and human health are all also in decline (Borrelli et al., 2020; UNEP, 2023; FSIN, 2023). But it is not only climate change of course that bleeds into other global crises, whether famine, water scarcity, disease, mass migrations or conflicts.

Since 1970, and this still numbs me to say it, over two-thirds of all the world's population sizes of all mammals, reptiles, amphibians, birds and fish have been lost (WWF, 2022) and an insect apocalypse, including pollinators so crucial to food production, has also taken place, in large measure caused by pesticides, toxic pollution and monocultural agriculture (Goulson, 2021; Millman, 2022). The number of species going extinct all together continues to rise year on year in today's human-induced sixth mass extinction (Kolbert, 2014; Erlich, 2017; Cowie et al., 2022). The world death toll from Covid-19 at its height is estimated to have caused between 15 million (WHO, 2022) and 18 million (Wang et al., 2022) excess mortality deaths. And the rise of zoonotic diseases and global pandemics caused by the relentless encroachment of human society on biodiverse environments, expansion of monocultural agriculture and trade in wildlife, is set to continue in the foreseeable future (WWF, 2020; Lawler et al., 2021; Vidal, 2023).

Soil depletion, with 90 per cent of Earth's topsoil at risk by 2050 (UN News, 2022), alongside freshwater scarcity and food insecurity (FSIN, 2023) also pose existential threats to a world population that has increased exponentially from 1 billion in 1800 to 8.1 billion people today. Increased conflicts, wars and mass population movements as well as political polarisation and the rise of populist authoritarianisms have all become exacerbated by socioeconomic and ecological system destabilisation and processes of collapse.

Conditions for violence and atrocity crimes, including genocide, have also become exacerbated by the impacts of climate change, biodiversity loss and other environmental pressures. Moreover, 'Not only are these factors a source of conflict in themselves, but they can also severely hinder a society's capacity to prevent atrocity crimes' (GCR2P, 2023). In a world where eight states currently have nuclear weaponry including Russia and Israel, which, as I write, are both prosecuting wars that threaten regional and international escalation, and with other nuclear powers also holding deep-seated geopolitical enmities, the risks of a world nuclear conflagration and subsequent 'nuclear winter' remain ever-present. The Bulletin of Atomic Scientists has positioned the world doomsday clock in 2023 and 2024, at 90 seconds to midnight – the closest it has ever been (Toon, 2018; FAS, 2022; Starkey, 2024).

In its *2024 Global Humanitarian Overview*, the UN notes how armed conflicts, the climate emergency and collapsing economies are 'taking a devastating toll on the most vulnerable communities on all continents, resulting in catastrophic hunger, massive displacement and disease outbreaks'. It goes on: 'One child in every five lives in, or has fled from, conflict zones in 2023. Some 258 million people face acute hunger. One in 73 people worldwide is displaced – a doubling in 10 years. And disease outbreaks are causing preventable deaths in all corners of the world' (OCHA, 2024).

Six of the world's nine life system boundaries, including freshwater change, biosphere integrity, land system change, and biogeochemical flows are now being overshot and are impacting, along with climate change, the world's biodiversity, food security, human health, and water quality (See Figure 1.1 below, Stockholm Resilience Centre, 2023, see also Raworth, 2017, and DEAL https://doughnuteconomics.org/).

Potentially catastrophic tipping points in Earth systems (for example, ocean warming, melting glaciers, rainforest density) can now be anticipated. A risk tipping point has been defined as 'the point at which a given socioecological system ceases to buffer risks and provide its expected functions, after which the risk of catastrophic impacts to the system increases substantially' (UN IEHS, 2023). Tim Lenton, from the Global Systems Institute and based on the latest detailed analyses, is unequivocal: 'Negative tipping points show that the threat posed by the climate and ecological crisis is far more severe than is commonly understood and is of a magnitude never before faced by humanity. Currently, there is no adequate global governance at the scale of the threats posed by negative tipping points. The world is on a disastrous trajectory' (Lenton et al., 2023, p. 5). Future scenarios, post-tipping point, include the loss of whole ecosystems and the capacity to grow staple crops, leading to mass population displacement, political instability and financial collapse.

A new lexicon: From global crises to a world-in-crisis

In a world of interconnected and interacting complex systems, global crises as we have heard, are not only systemically *endemic* and potentially globally *encompassing*, but also increasingly *entangled* and thereby mutually *exacerbated* (Cottle, 2009b, 2011). They have become 'wicked problems' (Rittel and Webber, 1973), but now played out at planetary scale. Here system complexity combined with lack of knowledge and difficulties of prediction, can undermine remedial responses to crises, and can even exacerbate them or cause related crises.

The recent proliferation of terms naming the recent cascade of global crises speaks to a world-in-crisis or a 'new age of catastrophe' (Callinicos, 2023). *Planetary emergency* (Club of Rome, 2019; Thunberg, 2023), for example, is a politically powered term that has the merit of combining climate and ecological crises into one planetary crisis, thereby avoiding the widespread tendency (in much of academia and elsewhere) to divorce climate change from other ecological system breakdowns as set out above (Figure 1.1). As a term it also, however, condenses the historically long durée of economic growth and deepening ecological collapse into seemingly an emergency event, rather than signalling its deep-seated, systemic and enduring nature.

The term *Permacrisis*, in contrast, has the advantage of emphasising 'an extended period of instability and insecurity' and 'especially one resulting from a series of catastrophic events' (Collins Dictionary 2022). In practice, it can nonetheless prove both selective and somewhat eclectic when applied to very

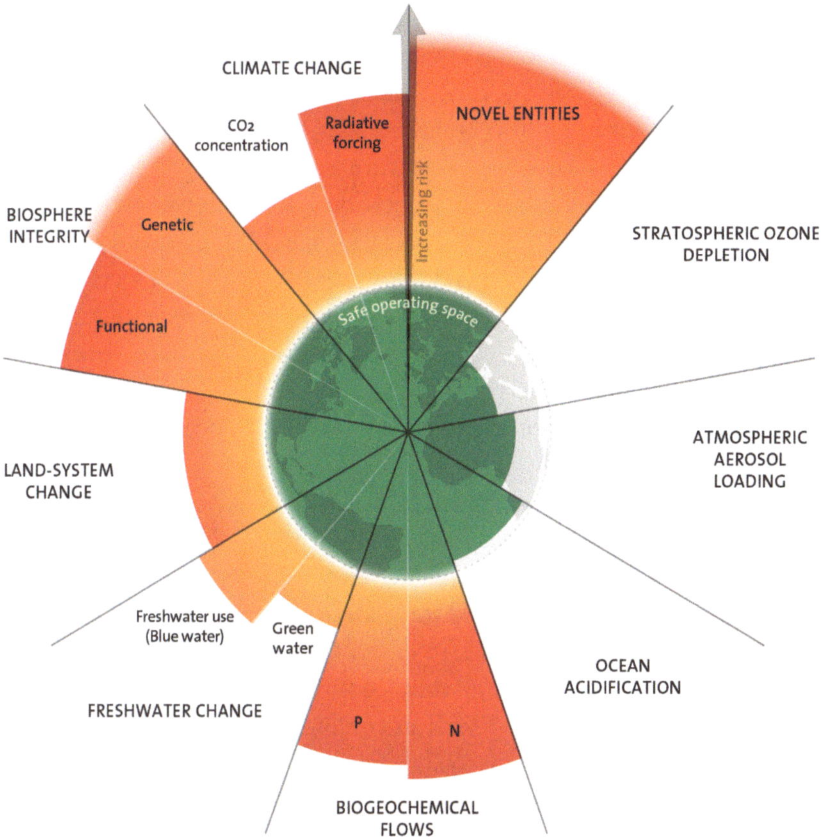

Figure 1.1. 2023 Planetary Boundaries (Stockholm Resilience Centre) Licensed under CC BY-NC-ND 3.0

different catastrophic events. It lacks explanatory depth, for example, when confined to 'broken approaches' to growth, economic management and governance (Brown et al., 2024), rather than exposing the contradictions posed by the continuing pursuit of growth (including Green growth) and finite planetary boundaries and a sustainable biosphere.

The term *Polycrisis* (Miller and Heinberg, 2023; WEF, 2023), or *Global polycrisis* (Lawrence et al., 2022) and *Planetary Polycrisis* (Albert, 2024), for their part, productively draw attention to how 'crises in multiple global systems become causally entangled in ways that significantly degrade humanity's prospects' (Lawrence et al., 2022, p. 9). The conceptualisation of polycrisis is sensitive to the complex system interconnections and cascade effects between environmental and social breakdown and, as suggested in the terms above, at different national, regional, global and planetary scales (Miller and Heinberg, 2023). When used descriptively, however, 'polycrises' can become separated from their fundamental economic underpinning as well as the history of geopolitical power (World Economic Forum, 2023, cf. Miller and Heinberg, 2023) and its current hegemonic configuration (Callinicos, 2023). When used in its plural form, it sometimes thereby also distances itself from a more encompassing world-system perspective and theorisation of today's planetary demise, whether formulated in terms of limits to growth (Meadows et al., 1972), the juggernaut of late modernity (Giddens, 1990), world-risk society (Beck, 2000), or the modern history of today's world-system of nation states (Wallerstein, 2004). (But exceptionally see Michael Albert's recent theorisation *Navigating the Polycrisis*; Albert, 2024).

Others today signal more explicitly the multiple and entrenched dynamics of *civilizational collapse*, whether historically (Tainter, 1988; Diamond, 2011; Ophuls, 2012; Harper, 2017), or currently (Read and Alexander, 2019; Servigne and Stevens, 2020; Bendell and Read, 2021; Servigne et al., 2021; Bendell, 2023). When addressing dynamics of civilisational or societal collapse, these can unfold over years, decades or even centuries and need not be taken to imply a sudden 'event'. This said, nuclear conflagration, a cascade of Earth system changing tipping points, the slowing of the AMOC (Atlantic Meridional Overturning Circulation), or overall failed energy return on energy investment (EROEI), could reduce the time scale of 'collapse' considerably. As can the Achilles heel of democratic systems dependent on winning votes whilst seeking to implement unpopular but necessary policies of transition, and insufficient political subsidiarity and governance at local to planetary levels (Blake and Gilman 2024).

These and other analyses inform the growing schools of *collapsology* (Servigne et al., 2021), which not only collate and extrapolate findings from the latest world reports of different systems now experiencing destabilisation and breakdown, but are also concerned with processes of 'deep adaptation' (Bendell and Read, 2021), including processes of collective and personal resilience. Heightened sensitivity to the psychological feelings of grief and dismay when witnessing the seemingly unstoppable juggernaut of economic growth and ecological degradation increasingly permeate these academic and other interventions (Albrecht, 2019; Macy, 2021; Bendell, 2023).

All the positions above have their differing semantic emphases, but all seek to name and thereby draw attention to the multiple, complex and interacting crises that are now shaping the state of the planet. And this, as we have heard, is so much more than climate change. I prefer nonetheless the term *World-in-Crisis* not because many of the emphases signalled in the terms above are wrong, but simply because this term helps to better encapsulate and grant emphasise to the globalised and ontological underpinning of the world today that is now both defined by and ensnared in complex systems producing an unsustainable state of crisis (Cottle, 2022, 2023). The term '*meta-crisis*' is similar in this respect perhaps, but 'world-in-crisis' signals this socio-ecological ontology of crisis and does so explicitly within world parameters.

Our world-in-crisis is enveloped, then, in the complex systems of globalised human society, a world society (notwithstanding its differences) that is now seemingly locked into exponential growth, ecological exhaustion, energy entropy and excessive complexity (Meadows et al., 1972; Ophuls, 2012; Rifkin, 2022; Bendell, 2023), fundamental drivers of civilisational collapse in the past, and today turbo-charged by global financialised capitalism (Frazer, 2022, Foster, 2022). And all underpinned in the continuing desacralisation of nature formed on the altar of material progress, instrumental rationality, and human speciesism (Eisenstein, 2018; Matthews, 2023; Lake, 2024). It is these emphases that I seek to signal in the term world-in-crisis. We inhabit a pluriverse world of different political cultures and cultural epistemologies or ways of knowing, certainly, but also share a world now globally conditioned by universal socio-ecological threats played out at planetary scale (Beck, 2006; Escobar, 2020; Chakrabarty, 2021).

The growing acceptance of our world as fundamentally out of kilter because of the global expansion and encroachment of Western society's rapacious economic system, is also encapsulated in the epochal conceptualisations of the Anthropocene (Crutzen and Steffen, 2003) and Capitalocene (Moore, 2015), and, in mirror reversal, the Symbiocene (Albrecht, 2019). Though the exact periodisation of the Anthropocene is still disputed along with the extent to which earth systems continue to exert more-than-human agency (Clark, 2014; Haraway, 2016; Ghosh, 2022), through 'feral ecologies', for example (Tsing et al., 2022), most Earth scientists generally agree that the evidence of the 'great acceleration' of human society's footprint on earth systems and the biosphere since the Industrial Revolution is undeniable, and has proved ecologically devastating at planetary scale (Steffen et al., 2015; Lewis and Maslin, 2018).

When approached through the lens of critical political economy, the Anthropocene may be better conceived as the Capitalocene (Moore, 2015). In contrast to historical descriptions and depoliticised claims of 'human society', the Capitalocene invites a more historically nuanced explanation for the ecological devastation wrought by successive waves of capitalism and the colonisation and commodification of nature (and people). 'The crisis today', argues Moore in his treatise on world ecology, 'is not multiple but singular and manifold. It is not a crisis of capitalism *and* nature but of modernity-*in*-nature' (Moore, 2015, p. 4).

At root and driving most of today's global socio-ecological crises is a globalised economic system, recently labelled as 'cannibal capitalism' (Frazer, 2022), that is fundamentally based on unending (unsustainable) economic growth. Historically and contemporaneously, this has always involved extractivism and the exploitation of nature, even up to its complete destruction and disappearance (Foster, 2022; Frazer, 2022; Saito, 2022). This is buttressed through a normative culture based on materialist ideas of progress and a hubristic Enlightenment faith in human exceptionalism outside of the web-of-life (Eisenstein, 2018; Lent 2021; Rifkin, 2022; Girardet, 2023) coupled with a religious, predominantly Christian, view of nature as humankind's 'dominion' (Armstrong, 2022). These ideas have been written on at length by others and inform, in mirror reversal, much that is written – and felt – under the mantle and sensibility of the Symbiocene (Albrecht, 2019) and formative ideas of ecological civilisation (Korton, 2021; Lent, 2021; Matthews, 2023; Rifkin, 2022).

Here voices both inside and outside of the traditional academy are heard referring to the 'Great Unravelling' (Macy, 2021) and the 'Great Turning' (Kelly and Macy, 2021), as well as the 'Great Dying' (Haque, 2021) and the 'Great Awakening'. Powerful currents of ideas and sentiments now swirl within and around the loose sands of an emergent, if still inchoate, *zeitgeist* for a new age. An ecological age based on symbioses, regenerative culture and planetary stewardship, and with an increased emphasis on localism, social justice and the re-sacralisation of nature and the web-of-life. These currents are found in pantheistic ideas of spirituality, in Buddhism and Taoism for instance, and the increased recognition of our ecological interdependency and (inter)being (Tolle, 2016; Hanh, 2021; Lent, 2021; Loy, 2019; Macy, 2021). They also resonate in psychological feelings of eco-grief, anger and despair (Gillespie, 2020), as well as new Earth emotions such as solastalgia and terrafurie prompted by the destruction of our planet and the collective efforts to resist this (Albrecht, 2019), and in the 'gift' from impending catastrophes to re-vision our sense of self and relationship to others and recognise our place in the natural world (Macy, 2021).

In recent years a powerful intellectual bridge has helped ease the way for such disparate outlooks, sentiments, and philosophies to coalesce under a more encompassing and ecologically centred view of impending civilisational collapse. The new philosophy of science, better attuned to complex systems (Meadows, 2008) that are holistic, open, emergent, interdependent and autopoietic, challenges the hold of traditional Western science and Enlightenment thinking with its linear, closed, mechanistic, atomistic and reductionist approach to inquiry and laws of causality (Capra and Luisi, 2014; McGilchrist, 2021; Theise, 2023). It is from here as well as from the legacy of Romanticism (Sayre and Lowry, 2021), deep ecology (Naess, 2021), traditional indigenous wisdom (Kimmerer, 2013, 2022; Pascoe, 2016; Yunkaporta, 2020; Lake, 2024) and even evolutionary neuropsychology (McGilchrist, 2021) that ideas of 'ecological civilization' (Lent, 2021) and the re-sacralisation of nature (Armstrong, 2022) are now posited as a necessary antidote to the unsustainable ecological and human degradations wrought by the planetary-encompassing Anthropocene and/or Capitalocene.

When approached through a lens on communications and culture it is important to recognise that to be concerned, as we must all be, with the demise of our world, does not necessarily imprison us in a state of hopelessness or worse, nihilism, and that nothing can be done. As we have heard above, there is already a powerful confluence of traditions of thought and practices, some of them rekindled and revitalised in the contemporary encounter with crises and catastrophe and the purposeful pursuit of active hope (not to be confused with complacent optimism) (Macy and Johnstone, 2021), which together hold out the promise of 'emergence' from 'emergency' (Wahl, 2016; Korton, 2021; Adnan, 2021; Girardet, 2022).

The social theorist Ulrich Beck who positioned ecology at the heart of his formulations of 'world risk society' and today's world 'civilisational community of fate' (Beck, 2000, 2009) spoke of 'enforced enlightenment' and 'emancipatory catastrophism'. *The Metamorphosis of the World* (2016), his last book, also invited us to recognise how 'Global risk comes as a threat' but it also 'brings hope'. In the context of climate change, for example, the growing 'anticipation of global catastrophe violates', he says, 'sacred (unwritten) norms of human existence and civilization', and feelings of 'anthropological shock' can produce wide-ranging processes of 'social catharsis'. In such circumstances, 'new normative horizons as a frame of social and political action and a cosmopolitized field of activities emerge' (Beck, 2016, pp. 117–118).

The progressive as well as repressive potentiality of crises and disasters, especially when staged in the cultural eye of the media, has also been noted by others (Alexander, 2006; Klein, 2007; Cottle, 2014; Bennett, 2021). This book sets out to explore, then, not only some of the diverse ways in which different media and communication practices, communicate and invite us to attend to a world-in-crisis, but also how we may yet find resources for active hope, imagined futures and collective action.

Book structuration and chapter summaries

Communicating a World-in-Crisis is structured over seven sections and comprises 20 chapters including this Introduction and an Afterword by the editor. *Section I: Mainstream Journalism and the Planetary Emergency* includes three chapters each of which addresses mainstream journalism and its performance in respect of reporting today's planetary emergency. *Chapter 2: Reporting a World-in-Crisis: On Silence, Silos and the Symbiocene* by Simon Cottle, builds on the Introduction above and focuses on the evident and widespread failures of mainstream journalism to recognise today's world-in-crisis and report this in holistic terms and in global context. This disaggregated and ultimately dissimulating news portrayal in an axial age of change constitutes, he argues, an epochal crisis of perception. This is explained in relation to many of the shaping determinants of news as well as the distinctive spatial and temporal nature of today's world-in-crisis and associated psychological and phenomenological responses to existential challenges. The potential of mainstream journalism however, to report in ways that could yet help serve pathways of transition and even processes of societal transformation is also recognised. This is addressed in the context of increasing societal and ecological destabilisation and anticipated processes of enforced enlightenment.

Chapter 3: Evaluating Reporting Roles in Climate Disasters written by Victoria Fielding explores the different roles performed by journalists when reporting natural disasters and their link to climate change. These range from traditional monitorial roles to the newer styles of advocacy and engaged commentary. Based on detailed empirical study of twelve Australian online news sites, the chapter documents how these roles are performed in and across different news media and with what consequences for the public representation and elaboration of climate change.

Chapter 4: Reporting Protests and the Planetary Emergency by César Jiménez-Martínez, examines how mainstream UK news media report on ecological protests staged by the new wave of protestors such as Extinction Rebellion, Just Stop Oil and Insulate Britain and how these reports compare with those disseminated by the groups themselves. Martinez asks and examines what are the key differences – visually, propositionally and argumentatively – and how these impact considerations of protest legitimation or de-legitimation in the news media?

Section II: Community Activism Harnessing Media and Hope includes three chapters each of which identify and reflect on the culturally meaningful and progressive ways in which media and communication can encourage participation and sustain local and community relations in collective endeavours centred on climate and ecological issues. *Chapter 5: From Climate Crisis to Environment(al) Hope: Community, Affect and Local Television* by Elke Weissmann and Belinda Tyrrell, explores through the production of television programmes centring on local communities and climate actions how these are often rooted in local conditions and everyday cultures. It is here, it is suggested, that inspiration and examples of collective hope are often to be found and this calls for a rebalancing of the media's depiction of disaster narratives and crisis events and those emerging positive stories of community action at the local level. The latter all too often remain publicly invisible in national media but could yet promise a grassroots pathway of transition in the future.

Chapter 6: First Nations Community Media and the Climate Crisis: Prospects for Radical Ecological Democracy by Kerrie Foxwell, Bridget Backhaus, Troy Meston and Wilcannia River Radio, also explores the progressive prospects of engaging local communities in climate actions. Here the focus shifts to the mostly indigenous remote Australian town of Wilcannia, located in the traditional lands of the Barkindji people. Wilcannia River Radio, along with other First Nations community media outlets, it is argued, provides communication that is both participatory and embedded in local knowledges, story and the relationality between community and Country. In such ways an alternative to dominant narratives and climate coloniality is enacted and, importantly, this holds the seeds for radical eco-communicative democracy in a reimagined future.

Chapter 7: Green Festivals and Re-figurative Politics: Communicating Resilience and Hope is written by Steve Muggeridge, a long-term director of the Green Gathering festivals. Based on an insider account of the historical evolution of green festivals, their informing traditions and their collective embodiment of alternative, life-affirming, ecological practices, green festivals can be seen as powerful incubators for communicating ideas and feelings for possible transitions to a socially just and ecologically sustainable society. Green festivals have long offered a point of connection, with others, with nature, and with imagined futures that becomes even more necessary and urgent in a world confronting ecological collapse. They have much to teach mainstream society as it embarks on processes of transition.

Section III: Photography, Documentary and Film: Visualising Change reflects on and explores different mediums of photography, documentary and cinema and how they communicate contemporary ecological concerns. *Chapter 8: Fantasies in Visual Spectacles of Climate Change* by Niina Uusitalo invites us to look at climate change visuals from the point of view of spectacles and fantasy as means of understanding the affective power of spectacular images. Most catastrophic dystopian images and utopian technological images, she argues, evoke emotive responses but at the same time allow for the viewing subject to remain in their preceding subjectivities. With the help of examples, the chapter addresses how visual climate spectacles can sometimes be interrupted and progressively reordered using fantasy's affective power.

Chapter 9: Earthship Freo: A Case Study of the Potential and Limitations of Participatory Documentary Filmmaking by Michelle Johnston and Mignon Shardlow, explores the potential and limitations of participatory documentary filmmaking in fostering active hope and transformative action. Their chapter focuses on the production of a feature documentary, *Earthship Freo*, and describes how the filmmakers navigated their passion for environmental advocacy, ethical considerations, truthful representation, and a desire to tell a story that appeals to an audience.

Chapter 10: The New Weird: Independent Cinema as an Ecosophical Response to Climate Change by Kingsley Marshall, reviews the development of differing approaches of film and cinema to climate change and ecology with the help of distinguishing concepts of *ecocritical*, *ecocinema*, *ecological cinema*, and the *ecosophical*. As he does so, the chapter reflects on different films and the diverse ways in which independent filmmakers particularly, freed from corporate constraints, have depicted and narrativised the complexity of climate change and created new modes of seeing and of representation – including the repurposing of fantasy and horror tropes.

Section IV: Literature, Theatre and Art: Expressing and Embodying Affect, moves across environmental literature, radical theatre and ecoart with three discussions identifying distinctive modes of expression and forms of ecological engagement in each. *Chapter 11: 'There's Something You Need to Hear': The Literature of Environmental Crisis* by Pippa Marland, reflects on the potential of literature to represent the complexity of the Anthropocene by exploring three recent and contrasting novels all of which have centred on environmental concerns. By this means, Marland explores different formal and conceptual literary strategies for dealing with the complexity of Anthropocene and how different narratives may reveal rather than conceal the conditions of our time and whether these novels, even as they narrate examples of devastation and loss, leave room for hope, radical or otherwise.

Chapter 12: From Hidden Wars to Hidden Theatre: Embodying a World-in-Crisis by Carrie Westwater, explores the evolution of radical theatre and how a contemporary theatre company, Hidden Theatre, aims to bring the 'hidden' back into view through direct mediation of the experiences and consequences of living in crises by ordinary citizens. Through a radically different approach to theatre that is journalistic, the company seeks to create a space in which voice can be granted to the media voiceless. In such ways the stories of those positioned at the sharp end of crises and trauma – whether refugees and asylum seekers in Italy or Palestinians living in the West Bank and Gaza – can become symbolically rehabilitated and re-humanised as their stories are retold, listened to, embodied, and felt.

Chapter 13: Visionary Ecoart: Stories for Regenerative Ecologies, by Ruth Wallen, situates her discussion of ecological art in a period that Joanna Macy has termed 'The Great Turning'. Here ecoart is seen as purposefully committed to regenerating systems in an unravelling, high-energy entropy society, whilst also cultivating creativity and cultural flourishing. Through an appreciative review of selected ecoart works described and illustrated in her chapter and informed by ecosophical ideas, Wallen reflects on their distinctive 'stories'. In this way we encounter some of the different threads of ecoart and how their multiple narratives can variously contribute to 'regenerative economies where all beings can thrive' and how ecoart can 'help restore relationships with a living earth'.

Section V: Music and Museums: Immersive Experience comprises two chapters that seek to relay and reflect on how music and museums, respectively, have sought to engage audiences with climate change and the planetary emergency. *Chapter 14: Music in an Era of Planetary Discontinuity: What Music Can and Can't Do in This Crisis*, by Simon Kerr, explores with the help of examples, music's contribution to understanding and responding to deepening ecological crises. He argues that music's strength in the context of deepening crises is not fundamentally conceptual but emotive. Music's superpower is based in its possessing a 'unique capacity to emotionally replenish and support people in crisis'. With a focus mainly on popular music and the communication of the planetary crisis, music is found to be not so much about educating people about the climate predicament and its surrounding politics but in helping us to cope with it.

Chapter 15: Communicating 'Stories that Matter': Activist Museography and Immersive Practice in the Climate Emergency, by Jenny Kidd and Salsabilla Sakinah, explores how museums have sought to engage with planetary issues in the past before attending in detail to museums' more recent use of immersive approaches to 'tell stories that matter'. The discussion is situated in the recent 'immersive turn' in museums and by heritage sites and reflects on several examples that have aimed to engage with the climate emergency. The chapter argues that there are both challenges as well as, potentially, progressive benefits associated with museums' use of immersive experiences, not least of which their capacity to stimulate visitors to experience and feel the human and other consequences of climate change.

Section VI: Education and Training: Pedagogies for a Sustainable World provides two contributions reflecting on the importance of training and education in the communication of climate and sustainability. *Chapter 16: Communicating Sustainability: Science Literacy and Transformative Pedagogies*, by Ron Johnston critically appraises the developing approaches and educational pedagogies focussed on transition towards a more ecologically aware and sustainability orientated local and global society. Both the evident deficiencies and continuing value of evolving pedagogies are teased out before a case is made for an ethically oriented and multidisciplinary pedagogical approach to the complex nature of today's world of interconnected socio-ecological crises. An approach in which science literacy is granted increased recognition as part of the democratisation of knowledge.

Chapter 17: 'All Journalists Will Be Environmental Journalists Tomorrow': On Problems, Pedagogy and Prospects, by Chris Paterson, explores issues in the reporting of climate change and how this is explained to students, including trainee journalists. As the climate emergency unfolds so journalists will become increasingly involved in climate reporting, argues Paterson, and there are compelling reasons why journalism educators should embed climate change in their teaching. This chapter based on journalism education practice and climate research, sets out both issues and pedagogic ideas designed to better equip journalists of tomorrow with the necessary understanding and analytical tools to report the climate emergency. And to do so competently, assuredly, and responsibly.

Section VII: Communications and Intelligence for a World-in-Crisis comprises two chapters and returns to fundamental questions of communication and what it is to communicate intelligently in a world that is increasingly characterised by strife, destabilisation and potential collapse. *Chapter 18: Communicating Whole Intelligence to Regenerate the Living Human World*, by Malcolm Parlett, sets out the multiple dimensions of self-reflexive, inter-personal communication that are needed for humane, empathetic, eco-sensitive and practically engaged communications – and which are increasingly needed in a world waking up to the need for transformative, regenerative, change. Parlett's reflective exposition of 'whole intelligence' based on 'responding to the situation', 'interrelating', 'embodying', 'self-recognising' and 'experimenting', brings together and advances some of the most persuasive ideas and practices for better understanding ourselves, our communicative encounters with others, and how to intervene within a world of change.

Chapter 19: Beyond Artificial Intelligence: Toward Integrated Intelligence for a World-in-Crisis by Jeremy Lent, incisively reflects on the deficiencies of much current thinking and debate about Artificial Intelligence (AI) when it is modelled on an insufficient understanding of human intelligence as conceptual, instrumental and controlling. Artificial intelligence if modelled on these or similar attributes can only take us to a world that is equally misaligned with human society and the web-of-life as the instrumentality, rationality and hubristic faith in human superiority has brought us to our current planetary demise. Jeremy Lent, in this concluding contribution, succinctly reminds us of the importance of integrative intelligence that incorporates both conceptual and animate intelligence, reason and emotion, analytical acuity and embodied knowing and how this is essential for relational, reciprocal, and ecologically responsive living.

Finally, in an *Afterword*, 'Cultural Response and Creative Resilience: A Personal Reflection' the editor draws the volume to a close and reflects on the feelings of despair as well as the creative flourishing of ideas and pursuit of active hope, that can sometimes accompany the endeavour to communicate a world-in-crisis. He shares a few thoughts and experiences on how he has personally sought to live with and communicate not only ideas of planetary *emergency* and the *endgame*, but also *emergence* and how in his own communicative and cultural practices, including as a musician and songwriter, it is still possible to find some solace, enjoy a sense of solidarity with others, and even help (albeit in a small way) to instantiate active hope – not despite but precisely because of the enormity of the planetary emergency that now threatens to engulf us all.

References

Adnan, I. (2021) *The politics of waking up*. London: Perspectiva Press.

Albert, M.J. (2024) *Navigating the polycrisis*. Cambridge, MA: MIT Press.

Albrecht, G. (2019) *Earth emotions*. London: Cornell University Press.

Alexander, J. (2006) *The civil sphere*. New York: Oxford University Press.

Armstrong, K. (2022) *Sacred nature*. New York: Penguin Random House.

Beck, U. (2000) *World risk society*. Cambridge: Polity.

Beck, U. (2006) *Cosmopolitan vision*. Cambridge: Polity.

Beck, U. (2009) *World at risk*. Cambridge: Polity.

Beck, U. (2016) *The metamorphosis of the world*. Cambridge: Polity.

Bendell, J. and Read, R. (2021) *Deep adaptation*. Cambridge: Polity.

Bendell, J. (2023) *Breaking together*. Bristol: Good Works.

Bennett, L. (2021) *Communicating the future*. Cambridge: Polity.

Blake, J.S. and Gilman, N. (2024) *Children of a modest star*. Stanford: Stanford University Press.

Borrelli, P., Robinson, D.A., Panagos, P., et al. (2020) 'Land use and climate change impacts on global soil erosion by water (2015–2070)', *Proceedings of the National Academy of Sciences*, 117(36), pp. 21994–22001.

Brown, G., el-Erian, M. and Spence, M. (2024) *Permacrisis: A plan to fix a fractured world*. London: Simon & Schuster.

Callinicos, A. (2023) *The new age of catastrophe*. Cambridge: Polity.

Capra, F. and Luisi, P.L. (2014) *The systems view of life*. Cambridge: Cambridge University Press.

Chakrabarty, D. (2021) *The climate of history in a planetary age*. Chicago: University of Chicago Press.

Clark, N. (2014) 'Geo-politics and the disaster of the Anthropocene', *Sociological Review*, 62(1), pp. 19–37.

Club of Rome (2019) *Planetary emergency plan*. https://www.clubofrome.org/publication/the-planetary-emergency-plan/, accessed 5 March 2024.

Collins Dictionaries (2022) *English dictionary complete and unabridged*. Glasgow: HarperCollins Publishers.

Cottle, S. (2009a) *Global crisis reporting*. Maidenhead: Open University Press.

Cottle, S. (2009b) 'Global crises in the news: Staging new wars, disasters, and climate change', *Journal of International Communication*, 3, pp. 494–516.

Cottle, S. (2011) 'Taking global crises in the news seriously: Notes from the dark side of globalization', *Global Media and Communication*, 7(2), pp. 77–95.

Cottle, S. (2014) 'Rethinking media and disasters in a global age: What's changed and why it matters', *Media War & Conflict*, 7(1), pp. 3–22.

Cottle, S. (2022) 'Peace and conflict reporting in a world-in-crisis' in Orgeret, K. (ed.), *Insights on peace and conflict reporting*. London: Routledge, pp. 10–31.

Cottle, S. (2023) 'Reporting civilisational collapse: Research notes from a world-in-crisis', *Global Media and Communication*, 19(2), pp. 269–288.

Cowie, R., Bouchet, P. and Fontaine, B. (2022) 'The sixth mass extinction: Fact, fiction or speculation?', *Biological Reviews*, 97(2), pp. 640–663.

Crutzen, P. and Steffen, W. (2003) 'How long have we been in the Anthropocene era?' *Climatic Change*, 61(3), pp. 251–257.

Diamond, J. (2011) *Collapse*. London: Penguin.

Eisenstein, C. (2018) *Climate: A new story*. Berkeley, CA: North Atlantic Books.

Erlich, P. (2017) *Biological extinction*. https://www.youtube.com/watch?v=1j7TpoLmR60&t=567s, accessed 6 March 2024.

Escobar, A. (2020) *Pluriversal politics*. Duke University Press.

Federation of American Scientists (FAS) (2022) *Status of world nuclear forces*. https://fas.org/issues/nuclear-weapons/status-world-nuclear-forces/, accessed 6 March 2024.

Food Security Information Network (FSIN) (2023) *2023 Global Report on Food Crises*. https://www.fsinplatform.org/report/global-report-food-crises-2023/, accessed 5 March 2024.

Foster, J. (2022) *Capitalism in the Anthropocene*. New York: Monthly Review Press.

Frazer, N. (2022) *Cannibal capitalism*. London: Verso.

Ghosh, A. (2022). *The nutmegs' curse: Parables for a planet in crisis*. London: John Murray.

Giddens, A. (1990) *The consequences of modernity*. Cambridge: Polity.

Gillespie, S. (2020) *Climate crisis and consciousness*. Milton Park: Routledge.

Girardet, H. (2022) 'Biosphere and technosphere.' *Ecologist*. 1 December 2022 https://theecologist.org/sites/default/files/2022-11/Technosphere_0.pdf, accessed 19 September 2024.

Girardet, H. (2023) 'The future – what future?' *Ecologist*. 1 August 2023. https://theecologist.org/sites/default/files/2023-08/futurewhatfuture.pdf, accessed 19 September 2024.

Global Centre for the Responsibility to Protect (GCR2P) (2023) *Summary of the UN Secretary-General's 2023 Report on R2P*. https://www.globalr2p.org/publications/summary-2023-report/#, accessed 8 March 2024.

Goulson, D. (2021) *Silent earth*. London: Jonathan Cape.

Hanh, T. (2021) *Zen and the art of saving the planet*. London: Penguin.

Haque, U. (2021) 'The age of the Great Dying', *Eudaimonia*, 9 July. https://eand.co/the-age-of-the-great-dying-is-beginning-651b1a210432, accessed 5 March 2024.

Haraway, D. (2016) *Staying with the trouble*. Durham, NC: Duke University Press.

Harper, K. (2017) *The fate of Rome*. Princeton: Princeton University Press.

Kelly, S. and Macy, J. (2021) 'The great turning' in Bendell, J. and Read, R. (eds.) *Deep adaptation*. Cambridge: Polity, pp. 197–208.

Kimmerer, R. (2013) *Braiding sweetgrass*. London: Penguin.

Kimmerer, R. (2022) 'Ancient green: Moss, climate and deep time', *Emergence Magazine*, April. https://emergencemagazine.org/essay/ancient-green, accessed 5 March 2024.

Klein, N. (2007) *The shock doctrine*. York: Allen Lane.

Kolbert, E. (2014) *The sixth extinction*. London: Bloomsbury.

Korton, D. (2021) *Ecological civilization: From emergency to emergence.* https://www.clubofrome.org/publication/ecological-civilization-from-emergency-to-emergence/, accessed 13 September 2024.

Lawrence, M., Janzwood, S. and Homer-Dixon, T. (2022) *What is a global polycrisis?* Version 2.0. Discussion Paper 2022–4. Cascade Institute. https://cascadeinstitute.org/technical-paper/what-is-a-globalpolycrisis/, accessed 5 March 2024.

Lake, O. (2024) *The story is in our bones: How worldviews and climate justice can remake a world in crisis.* Gabriola Island: New Society Publisher.

Lawler, O.K., Allan, H.L., Baxter, P.W.J., et al. (2021) 'The COVID-19 pandemic is intricately linked to biodiversity loss and ecosystem health', *The Lancet*, 5(11), E840–E850.

Lent, J. (2021) *The web of meaning.* London: Profile Books.

Lenton, T., McKay, D., Loriani, S., Abrams, J., Lade, S., Donges, J., Milkoreit, M., Powell, T., Smith, S., Zimm, C., Buxton, J., Bailey, E., Laybourn, L., Ghadiali, A. and Dyke, J. (eds.) (2023) *The Global Tipping Points Report 2023.* University of Exeter, Exeter, UK. https://global-tipping-points.org/, accessed 5 March 2024.

Lewis, S. and Maslin, M. (2018) *The human planet.* London: Penguin Books.

Loy, D.R. (2019) *Ecodharma.* Somerville, MA: Wisdom Publications.

Macy, J. (2021) *World as lover, world as self.* California: Parallax Press.

Macy, J. and Johnstone, C. (2021) *Active hope.* California: New World Library.

Matthews, F. (2023) *The Dao of civilisation.* London: Anthem Press.

McGilchrist, I. (2021) *The matter with things.* London: Perspectiva Press.

Meadows, D. (2008) *Thinking in systems.* Vermont: Chelsea Green Publishing.

Meadows, D., Meadows, D., Randers, J., et al. (1972) *The limits to growth.* Ticehurst: Earth Island.

Miller, A. and Heinberg, R. (2023) *Welcome to the great unraveling: Navigating the polycrisis of environmental and social breakdown.* Oregon: Post Carbon Institute.

Millman, O. (2022) *The insect crisis.* London: Atlantic Books.

Moore, J. (2015) *Capitalism in the web of life.* New York: Verso Books.

Naess, A. (2021) *There is no point of return.* London: Penguin.

Ophuls, W. (2012) *Immoderate greatness: Why civilizations fail.* Scotts Valley, CA: CreateSpace Independent Publishing Platform.

OCHA. (2024) *Global Humanitarian Overview 2024.* https://www.unocha.org/publications/report/world/global-humanitarian-overview-2024-enarfrsp, accessed 26 March 2024.

Pascoe, B. (2016) *Dark Emu.* Broome: Magabala Books.

Raworth, K. (2017) *Doughnut economics.* London: Penguin.

Read, R. and Alexander, S. (2019) *This civilization is finished.* Melbourne: Simplicity Institute.

Rittel, H. and Webber, M. (1973) 'Dilemmas in general theory of planning', *Policy Sciences*, 4(2), pp. 155–169.

Rifkin, J. (2022) *The age of resilience.* London: Swift Press.

Saito, K. (2022) *Marx in the Anthropocene.* Cambridge: Cambridge University Press.

Sayre, R. and Lowy, M. (2021) *Romantic anti-capitalism and nature.* Milton Park: Routledge.

Servigne, P. and Stevens, R. (2020) *How everything can collapse.* Cambridge: Polity.

Servigne, P., Stevens, R. and Chapelle, G. (2021) *Another end of the world is possible*. Cambridge: Polity.

Starkey, S. (2024) 'Press release: Doomsday clock remains at 90 seconds to midnight', *Bulletin of Atomic Scientists*, 23 January 2024. https://thebulletin.org/2024/01/press-release-doomsday-clock-remains-at-90-seconds-to-midnight/

Steffen, W., Broadgate, W., Deutsch, L., et al. (2015) 'The trajectory of the Anthropocene: The great acceleration', *The Anthropocene Review*, 2(1), pp. 81–98.

Stockholm Resilience Centre (2023) *The nine planetary boundaries*. https://www.stockholmresilience.org/research/planetary-boundaries/the-nine-planetary-boundaries.html

Tainter, J. (1988) *The collapse of complex societies*. Cambridge: Cambridge University Press.

Theise, N. (2023) *Notes on complexity*. New York: Spiegel and Grau.

Thunberg, G. (2023) *The climate book*. Penguin Random House.

Tolle, E. (2016) *A new earth*. London: Penguin Books.

Toon, B. (2018) 'I've studied nuclear war for 35 years – you should be worried', TEDxMileHigh. https://www.youtube.com/watch?v=M7hOpT01PGI, accessed 26 March 2024.

Tsing, A., Deger, J., Saxena, A., et al. (2022) FERAL ATLAS; The more-than-human Anthropocene. http://FERALATLAS.ORG/#, accessed 26 March 2024.

United Nations Environment Programme (UNEP) (2023) *Climate Change 2023: Synthesis Report*. https://www.unep.org/resources/report/climate-change-2023-synthesis-report#, accessed 26 March 2024.

United Nations Institute for Environment and Human Security (2023) *Interconnected Disasters Risk Report 2023*. https://interconnectedrisks.org, accessed 26 March 2024.

United Nations News (2022) *FAO warns of 90% of Earth's topsoil at risk by 2050*. https://news.un.org/en/story/2022/07/1123462, accessed 13 September 2024.

Vidal, J. (2023) *Fevered planet*. London: Bloomsbury.

Wahl, D.C. (2016) *Designing regenerative cultures*. Axminster: Triarchy Press.

Wallerstein, I. (2004) *World-systems analysis*. Durham, NC: Duke University Press.

Wang, H., Paulson, K. and Murray, C. (2022) 'Estimating excess mortality due to the COVID-19 pandemic', *The Journal-Lancet*, 399(10334), pp. 1513–1536.

World Economic Forum (2023) 'We're on the brink of a polycrisis, how worried should we be?' *Global Risks Report*. https://www.weforum.org/agenda/2023/01/polycrisis-global-risks-report-cost-of-living/, accessed 26 March 2024.

World Health Organization (WHO) (2022) '14.9 million excess deaths associated with the COVID-19 pandemic in 2020 and 2021. May 5, 2022', News release. https://www.who.int/news/item/05-05-2022-14.9-million-excess-deaths-were-associated-with-the-covid-19-pandemic-in-2020-and-2021 accessed 16 September 2024.

WWF. (2020) *Nature and pandemics*. https://www.wwf.org.uk/nature-and-pandemics, accessed 26 March 2024.

WWF. (2022) *World Wide Fund for Nature Living Planet Report 2022*. https://www.wwf.org.uk/our-reports/living-planet-report-2022, accessed 26 March 2024.

Yunkaporta, T. (2020) *Sand talk*. Singapore: Collins.

Section I:

Mainstream Journalism and the Planetary Emergency

·2·

REPORTING A WORLD-IN-CRISIS: ON SILENCE, SILOS AND THE SYMBIOCENE

Simon Cottle

There is an *axial crisis of perception* at the core of world society today, and journalism is positioned at its heart. A *crisis of perception* that includes a failure of imagination and which turns on how all of us become aware of and attend to, if at all, the multiple existential threats now converging in today's world-in-crisis. (1) It is historically *axial* because depending on how we collectively perceive, understand and respond to the shared anthropogenic threats to humanity and nature, so the very existence of life on Earth as we know it hangs in the balance. (2) This is our new Axial Age. An interregnum between the preceding age of fossil-fuelled industrialism and rapacious capitalism based on economic growth, materialism and speciesism, an age that is now visibly exhausted and failing, and an embryonic new age that has yet to be fully imagined much less realised, an age promising increased social justice, ecological consciousness, regenerative culture and planetary custodianship. As outlined in the preceding chapter, our world is reeling from systemic, deepening and mutually entangled global crises that for the most part are spawned from an unsustainable socio-ecological world (dis)order. A world where finite planetary limits are being overshot and the incessant pursuit of economic growth trashes nature and the biosphere, as well as human well-being and human rights.

So how does news journalism attend to the onward crush of systemic socio-ecological crises now converging in a world-in-crisis and situate them in world context? What resources for understanding and potential action are provisioned within journalism agendas and story framings that can facilitate necessary planetary vision and pathways for transition and processes of societal transformation? How are we to account for journalism's current performance in response to today's world-in-crisis, and how *should* we expect journalism to perform in response to those trajectories of breakdown and collapse already unfolding, and into the foreseeable future? Is journalism in all its different formations and forms destined to reproduce the axial crisis of perception, or can it perform its part in wider processes of cultural flourishing and the growing awareness for the need for societal transformation – from local and national to bio-regional and planetary scale?

The following explores these concerns based on what is already known about the practices and performance of journalism in respect of global crisis reporting and set against the overwhelming evidence of today's world-in-crisis and planetary emergency (Chapter 1). With few exceptions, mainstream news media, I maintain, provide an impoverished if not entirely dissimulating view of today's planetary emergency, and the reasons for this will be elaborated. Based on this critique and explanation, the discussion then moves to consider some of the ways in which mainstream journalism could yet be cultivated (and increasingly compelled by events) to better meet its obligations in respect of world-in-crisis reporting and how this could meaningfully align with and better support pathways of transition.

Reporting a world-in-crisis: News Silence

Journalism in its different forms occupies a pivotal role in today's complex media ecology and in the communication of global crises. Journalism serves to frame disasters and crises in different ways but it can also enter into them and their subsequent unfolding when influencing political, social and cultural responses and how they reverberate around the world (Cottle, 2009a, b, 2011, 2022; Keen, 2023). Historically journalism has assumed the responsibility of raising the alarm and *signalling* the latest catastrophic events and informing civil society of their magnitude, repercussions, and onward trajectory (Carey, 1996; Defoe, 2003/1704; Cottle, 2014). And so too can journalism culturally *symbolise*, dramatise and narrate the human stories and emotions of global crises (Pantti et al., 2012; Cottle, 2013, 2024; Smith and Howe, 2015). In these and other ways it both breathes and oxygenates the cultural air of sense-making and helps orient society to the world we live in. Journalism also variously helps to *stage* public debates and political deliberation that give vent to the stakeholder disagreements that flow in, through and around crises, their political prescriptions, and wider responses (Cottle and Rai, 2006).

In all these ways, then, journalism has been and continues to perform an integral part in the communication and understanding of different crises. However, as evidence of our world-in-crisis grows, so the necessity to move beyond thinking and reporting about global crises as separate issues to a holistic view of today's unprecedented and unravelling world, becomes ever more apparent (Cottle, 2023a). Only then will we be able to grasp the enormity of the systemic, compounding and deepening existential threats now confronting human society and the biosphere, understand their complex underpinnings and conceive of socially just and ecologically sustainable ways to better align human existence *inside* the web-of-life.

Mainstream journalism, that is, public service and commercial broadcast news media and most newspapers, with very few exceptions only (see below), is proving exceedingly slow to recognise, contextualise and represent the severity and compound nature of those existential crises now confronting world society and the biosphere. It continues for the most part to report through nationally inflected (globally myopic) news lenses, and it generally does so in 'existentially averse' ways, preferring not to join up the dots of a world-in-crisis or foresee, and thereby help to forestall, immanent and imminent processes of breakdown and collapse.

The BBC's climate editor in interview with John Simpson publicly states, for example, 'If you gave up hope I mean what would, what would be the story you are telling? It would be a story, a tragic story of, you know, decline' (BBC, *Unspun World*, 15.6.22). This deliberate distancing from anything that could be called 'doomerism' – let's name this as 'existential aversion' – helps to account for BBC reports such as the one below. This reported on the failure of world governments, following the Paris Agreement and COP 21 to limit the global temperature increase to 1.5 degrees above pre-industrial levels. Global average temperatures exceeded this for a full 12-month period in 2023. The BBC flagship news programme *News at Ten*, reported this as its fourth news item, describing the rise in global temperature with helpful graphs and accounted for this with reference to the 'vast quantities of greenhouse gases caused by human activities' (BBC *News at Ten*, 8.2.24). As it did so, the presenter also commiserates with Italian 'ski resorts which now have a severe lack of snow', before handing over to the BBC's climate editor who quickly and enthusiastically proceeds to celebrate the construction of 'the biggest engineering project in the Scottish Highlands since the 1940s' which 'will store excess renewable power'.

The global catastrophe of rising world temperatures, and what it means for life on the planet (IPCC, 2022) is thereby quickly passed over in this report, and attention is returned to a relatively small, techno-fix, national piece of the global energy jigsaw and without any further analysis of the world's year-on-year failing pledges to limit greenhouse gases or what this will mean for life on planet Earth in the years and decades ahead. Too often journalism ducks the hard reality detailed in the accumulating scientific reports and experienced by those now living in vulnerable communities around the world, and quickly moves on to perceived stories of 'hope', not wishing to demoralise its audience. But real hope, 'active hope' (Macy and Johnstone, 2022), not spurious optimism founded on a disaggregated view of the world, can only be based on a holistic and honest picture of the perilous state of the planet and the systemic drivers that are now causing destabilisation and possible collapse, including exponential growth, ecological exhaustion, expedited energy entropy and excessive global system complexity (Ophuls, 2012, see also: Club of Rome, 2019; McGilchrist, 2019; Bendell and Read, 2021; Servigne et al., 2021; Rifkin, 2023; Miller and Heinberg, 2023; Bendell, 2023; Hagens, 2023).

Journalism still regards crises for the most part as newsworthy aberrations from the norm, rather than as the new catastrophic norm of a faltering planet and declining biosphere. Journalism's default position, it seems, is set to an unquestioned world of 'business-as-usual' and 'life-as-normal'. When reporting on the endemic, deeply enmeshed and enduring global crises that manifest in today's world-in-crisis, this not only proves deficient but dangerously dissimulating. Consider, for example, recent reporting of climate change, Covid-19, and war. How has each been reported in global context and sought to draw out the complex underpinning and entanglements of today's world-in-crisis?

Reporting of the latest IPCC (International Panel on Climate Change) reports and COP (Conference of the Parties) conferences, has generally sought to incorporate and relay scientific warnings about the inexorable advance of climate change. But this reporting is at best institutionally intermittent and event-dependent, whether on the release of the latest IPCC reports, the public staging of COP events, or major protests. Extreme weather events and the relentless breaking of new weather records can also create opportunities for recognising and signalling the onward march of climate catastrophes, though this is not always followed through.

Noticeably mainstream media quickly retreat after such news events to their preferred 'business as usual', 'life as normal' reporting. Climate change in this conventionalised outlook becomes compartmentalised as a particular news 'issue' and is granted periodic news interest only, rather than as the ever-present and deepening existential threat that should demand extensive and intensive journalism engagement. It is generally not reported as an existential threat warranting daily exposure and multifaceted in-depth reporting on par, say, with previous collective fights for survival in times of total war. A war in which an 'existential stocktake' needs to regularly frame climate and ecological news in respect of current and cumulative global and national CO2 emissions as well as national performance in respect of average per capita CO2 output, wealth and consumption patterns (Wadleigh, 2023). Only then can citizens hold governments to account. And rarely is it reported from the global to the local in its complex entanglement within today's world-in-crisis – whether collapsing ecosystems, biodiversity loss, growing food and water scarcity or increased prevalence of disease and impacts on human health, conflicts and forced migration (OCHA, 2024). There is more to today's world-in-crisis than climate change and the latter cannot be adequately reported, much less adequately understood and responded to, when disaggregated and decontextualised from today's world-in-crisis and the systemic, unrelenting pursuit of economic growth (Eisenstein, 2018; Bendell and Read, 2021).

Unlike climate change the reporting of the Covid pandemic in most liberal democracies *was* granted daily prominence and, exceptionally, became characterised by daily updates, elite briefings, and mediated dispatches from the frontlines of health care, as well as from the home front of lockdown (Cottle, 2022). Unlike the slow-burn of climate change, COVID-19 visibly impacted health and mortality, economies, and everyday life in dramatic ways. The world of journalism generally failed, however, to explore probable connections between this global public health disaster and its likely ecological underpinnings as a zoonotic disease, generated and exacerbated by deforestation, mono-culture agriculture, the trade in wildlife and urbanisation (WWF, 2020; Vidal, 2023). And the liminal period of the economic slow-down and personal lockdown of behaviour was also not used to seriously reappraise and rethink the world of work, well-being or our relationship to the natural world and opportunity to cut back on carbon emissions through shifts to homeworking, travel and changed consumption patterns.

Reporting of the Russian invasion of Ukraine, in contrast, has been compelled to recognise and report on the entanglement of European economies, the continuing high dependency on hydrocarbon fuels, and the implications of restricted supplies on country plans to transition to clean energies and nuclear power in the context of climate change. The forced migrations of millions of people, precipitation of a world food crisis, shortage of fertiliser and rising prices and the renewed fears of nuclear escalation have also all featured in the reporting of this devastating Russian invasion. However, Western news reporting has tended to report such global system complexity and interdependency through a normative and nationally inflected news lens. This focused initially on the mass exodus of refugees amidst the daily military updates and political responses, and then on concerns over national economic instability, energy sovereignty and the impact on consumer prices in the UK and Europe. The reporting did not contextualise and examine the Ukraine crisis as part of a preceding world-in-crisis including the urgency of COP26 commitments to reduce carbon emissions, and it ignored the military carbon footprint of the war and routinely dissimulated the devastating ecological impacts of contemporary warfare (Cottle, 2023b).

With the advent of the Israeli attack on the Occupied Territories in Gaza 2023, following the Hamas massacres on October 7, Western news attention has shifted its news gaze somewhat from the Russian invasion of Ukraine to the Israeli bombardment and mass destruction of Gaza and unfolding humanitarian disaster. The ramifications of contemporary warfare in the context of the planetary climate and ecological emergency once again are eclipsed as is the continuing Western security and energy interests in the Middle East and complicity of Western governments in Israeli mass slaughter through weapons provision and UN Security Council spoiler diplomacy.

At the core of mainstream journalism, then, is a deafening silence about the entangled nature of today's world-in-crisis and how this both expresses and often exacerbates processes of breakdown and collapse. Given the existential nature of today's combined socio-ecological crises, or polycrisis, as well as their continuing trajectory and future consequences, it is reasonable to expect journalism to both explore and deliberate their underpinning drivers and potential responses. In times of total war, when civil society as well as states are threatened, journalism, we know, actively seeks to rally communities and mobilise collective efforts on the home front. Where are journalism's networks and communicative bridges to the plethora of local-to-global initiatives by NGOs and others now striving to engage and energise collective efforts in response to the systemic nature of today's planetary threats?

Reporting a world-in-crisis: News Silos

To understand and help explain the crucial silences of mainstream journalism in response to today's world-in-crisis, we need to understand its deep structuration into various silos – its siloed thinking in respect of surrounding and dominant normative outlooks, its siloed positioning within the wider corporate media marketplace and differentiated global news ecology, and its siloed practices and professional cognitive mapping of news into distinct subject categories and self-contained issues.

In a normative worldview where economic growth is regarded by most mainstream news media as well as by most political elites, as an unquestioned public (and private) good, and where rising GDP is routinely used as a taken-for-granted measure of national success, the long-term consequences of exponential growth and the fundamental causes of ecological exhaustion are routinely overlooked. As are the inherent entropy of energy systems, the failings of complex systems of governance, and the human insufficiency of a culture wedded to consumer sovereignty rather than cultural citizenship and ecological custodianship. Through such taken-for-granted assumptions journalism enacts and circulates the prevailing normative outlooks of late modern capitalist society.

It is compelled to report on the accelerating interruptions of megafires and melting icecaps, of forced migrations and failing supply chains, of pandemics and emaciated polar bears, but its default position is to report daily life and business as usual, accommodating these incursions into the established worldview rather than seeing them as the basis of a planetary wakeup call, much less as a profound nudge to reassess and reinvigorate news reporting in response to the world's biggest, possibly last, news story. Instead, it compounds the axial crisis of perception and contributes to the 'Great Derangement' of our times (Ghosh, 2016). A time of seeming collective insanity, of displacement, denial and disavowal, as human society sleepwalks to the cliff edge.

Today's corporate news media giants, as with their entertainment big brothers, are failing to perceive and convey how global crises are mutually entangled, ecologically enmeshed and endemic to a world premised on unstoppable economic growth, materialist ideas of the 'good life', and presumptions of human exceptionalism outside the web-of-life. Journalism it seems is located not only in news silos in the wider media ecology but also in siloed thinking in respect of its cognitive reporting stance to separate news stories and news issues. How can we account for this?

We know that corporate mainstream news providers are shaped by political economy determinants (concentrated ownership, market competition and pursuit of profits), that they operate in a field of strategic power and vested interests, and as we've heard, they give expression to historically and culturally prevailing worldviews. This both shapes and delimits news agendas and public discourse (Cottle, 2006, 2009a; Schudson, 2019; Bennett, 2021). News agendas and story framing are further influenced by the operation of basic news values (Harcup and O'Neil, 2017), routine reliance on elite sources (Bennett et al., 2006), and professional codes of objectivity, impartiality and balance (Boykoff and Boykoff, 2007). The event orientation of news is also out of synch with planetary and crisis temporalities (Bødker and Morris, 2022), whether slow-burn disasters or permanent emergencies (see also Zelizer, 2017). And the division of journalist labour into 'news beats' and specialist correspondents (Robbins and Wheatley, 2021), can further reinforce the cognitive splintering of the world into seemingly distinct 'issues'.

These all help to account for the diluted, disaggregated and dissimulating nature of much of today's reporting. In addition, however, the world of journalism and journalist sense-making is enacted and embodied in the wider socio-cultural world where phenomenological and psychological dispositions are also apt to be 'at work'. The phenomenological hold of taken-for-granted background expectations about life, work and daily routines plays into habituated journalist thinking and reporting outlooks. This can be rooted in the temporalities of everyday life, in its routinised practices and, to borrow Marx's phrase, the 'dull compulsion of the economic' (the day-to-day necessity of working to pay bills and to live). It is also knitted into private life worlds and family commitments which, together, conspire to reproduce the phenomenological sense of life's ongoing daily continuity, rather than its immanent disruption or even destruction. This phenomenological distancing, embodied in everyday feelings of affect, emotional ties, and lived expectations of continuity is at odds with fully recognising and reporting with full gravitas warnings of civilisational and biosphere destabilisation and possible collapse.

The psychology of denial and disavowal (Gillespie, 2020) can also be at work when explaining journalism's existential reporting aversion. An emotionally discomforted psychology will be differently enacted by journalists who variously, for example, either (1) reluctantly accept and know the scale and depth of the world's unravelling, (2) prefer to defer this to some distant horizon, or (3) blatantly deny the coming planetary apocalypse. These personalised responses are further reinforced and institutionalised in different editorial stances or decrees from corporate leaders. It is well known for example that former CEO of News Corp, Rupert Murdoch, dictated his denialist views on climate change from on high and expected adherence to these by his news editors (Redfearn and Morten, 2023).

Reporting a world-in-crisis: Toward the Symbiocene?

With few exceptions only and for the reasons indicated, mainstream journalism is generally oriented to reporting through a dominating worldview of economic growth, materialist ideas of progress, and unspoken presumption of human exceptionalism – mutually reinforcing premisses that are antithetical to an ecological sensibility and sustainable future way of life. Journalism and its world-news ecology (Cottle, 2012; Reese, 2016; Chadwick, 2017) are predominantly shaped in a force-field of strategic power, vying interests and economics (Bennett, 2021). But journalism is also capable of giving expression to and sometimes channelling the changing concerns and moral horizons of the civil sphere (Alexander, 2006; Cottle, 2019) – and these are now on the move (Read, 2022). As societies increasingly confront the destructive climate and ecological fallout from the juggernaut of late modernity (Giddens, 1990), or today's insatiable world 'superorganism' (Hagens, 2023), so new social movements like Extinction Rebellion, Just Stop Oil, and Fridays for Future, have taken to the streets and national surveys indicate widespread and growing climate and eco-anxiety (Hickman et al., 2021; Whitlock, 2023). As outlined in Chapter 1, these disparate ecological ideas and sensibilities coalesce in emergent ideas of ecological civilisation (Club of Rome, 2019; Korton, 2021; Lent, 2021; Matthews, 2023) or the Symbiocene (Albrecht, 2019), in part a reversed mirror image of today's world-in-crisis when viewed through an ecological and social justice lens on the Anthropocene (Crutzen and Steffen, 2003) or Capitalocene (Moore, 2015).

Journalism is critically positioned to not only report on and deepen understanding about the accelerating trajectory of existential crises – global, systemic, and complexly intertwined – and needs to do so with an overriding sense of daily urgency, but also to report extensively on today's growing ecological consciousness and the forging of pathways to transition and transformation. A new 'journalist imagination' or 'journalistic imaginary' is needed and may well be increasingly compelled by the onward crush of deepening economic and ecological crises now defining our new, potentially Axial, age. Such a journalistic imaginary would be re-oriented in at least eight distinguishable ways, though each would often overlap in practice. Some are already emergent as green shoots; others will need to be cultivated in dialogue as cultural and political shifts in society unfold.

First, a culture of reporting today's world-in-crisis or planetary emergency needs to take root across mainstream news media as well as outside it, and with an enhanced sense of planetary urgency. This needs to be comparable perhaps to reporting in times of 'total war', where a societal ethos of 'we're in this together' is established both in the field of reporting and mobilised beyond. An 'existential stocktake' (Wadleigh, 2023) needs to increasingly frame news reporting, documenting (1) both global and national patterns of cumulative and current CO2 and other greenhouse gases emissions, (2) patterns of country-based consumption/resource depletion, and (3) differentials of country wealth, all measured in total and average per capita.

Second, reporting needs to increasingly recognise the complex entanglement of seemingly distinct crises in a world-in-crisis. Such reporting must be undertaken with expanded vision on how accelerating and deepening global crises originate and reverberate around the world, and not solely viewed through nationally parochial, globally myopic, news glasses (Beck, 2009; Cottle, 2011; Berglez, 2013).

Third, news presentism and journalism's preferred temporality of 'here and now' reporting (Zelizer, 2017), must be expanded to fit the unfolding temporalities of potential extinction. A temporality, in other words, in which future imaginaries, whether premised on predictions of collapse or the politics of transition, are deemed to be legitimate timescapes for news reporting. Exceptionally, for example, Jon Snow, presenter of Channel 4 News, was 'turned into a 'hologram' to report on potential climate impacts over the course of the next century in a new project for Channel 4 News ahead of the COP climate conference in Glasgow' (C4 News 19.10.2021). Subsequently posted on their *Climate Futures* website, it describes how:

> Jon Snow takes audiences on a journey from a gigantic wind farm off the east coast of England in 2035, to the site of irreversible loss of the Amazon rainforest in 2080 and to scenes of the flight from China's coastal ghost towns in 2100. He is joined by climate scientists from the University of Oxford and The Grantham Institute for Climate Change to give audiences a glimpse into possible futures that they will likely live through – based on the latest research and UN projections. (https://www.channel4.com/news/our-climate-futures)

Such innovative use of presentational technology and creative expansion of journalism's usual reporting temporality can only be welcomed and encouraged in the years ahead.

Fourth, journalism must give increased recognition to, and communicatively enhance, the public elaboration of pathways of transition and societal transformation and deepen its critical reporting of policy initiatives at transnational, national, sub-national and, importantly, local levels. It must also recognise and give voice to the cultural flourishing of ideas and pre-figurative politics of deep adaptation, regeneration and growing ecological awareness. An ecological sensibility implies affective, experiential and emotional engagement and this, we know, can be sustained through the cultural and symbolic resonance of images, 'moving' film and close-up, personal experiential storytelling, as well as informational and deliberative forms of news presentation (Cottle and Rai, 2006; Cottle, 2024).

Fifth, journalism will need to seek to creatively deploy, innovate and expand its established communicative architecture and traditional modes of reporting when visualising and dramatising, narrating and telling, expressing and deliberating stories that speak to our world-in-crisis (Cottle and Rai, 2006; Parks, 2020). And to do so in and through the digital affordances currently available and in and across today's interconnecting 'world news ecology' (Cottle, 2012, 2014). In today's digitised world-news ecology this includes multiple news sites and advocacy groups, such as, for example, *Client Earth*, *Resilience*, *The Climate Journal*, *HotNews* or *Imagine* who are dedicated to ecological projects of recognition and change and compile original reports based on independent expertise and delivered with editorial skills of storytelling. Ways of enhancing communicative interactions between alternative sites and mainstream news providers should be pursued, helping to sensitise journalists to compelling new stories, lived experiences and new sources of expertise.

Sixth, journalistic reflexivity needs to be encouraged in ways that are better aligned to the reporting of planetary existential threats. Here the possible promise of various alternative and/or complementary models of journalism practice and orientation need to be explored in the journalist imaginary and context of global crisis reporting, whether public/civic journalism (Rosen, 1999), development journalism (Waisbord, 2009), peace journalism (McGoldrick and Lynch, 2005), humanitarian journalism (Scott et al., 2023), engaged journalism (Nettlefold and Pecl, 2022), and constructive or solutions-based journalism (McIntyre, 2019). Examples of industry 'good practice' should be professionally recognised and publicly valorised and where possible expanded across mainstream news outlets and platforms. This includes, for example, *The Guardian* newspaper's Environment Pledge (2023), and its ongoing commitment to ecological reporting; the *The Independent's* 'weekly round-up on the climate crisis, and the solutions being deployed to tackle it'; and those rare broadcasting news moments when reporting the synchronous and entangled nature of global crises (e.g. see Berglez, 2013; Cottle, 2023b).

Seventh, journalism as with the rest of society needs to participate in a grown-up and ongoing conversation about the C-word, and how runaway financial and corporate capitalism and the elective affinity of normative ideas of incessant growth, material progress and human speciesism, have brought the planet to its current demise. To borrow the words of UN Secretary-General Antonio Guterres 'It's time to say: enough. Enough of brutalizing biodiversity. Enough of killing ourselves with carbon. Enough of treating nature like a toilet. Enough of burning and drilling and mining our way deeper' (Opening speech of the UN Climate Change Conference COP26, Glasgow, Scotland, 1.11.21). Journalism is positioned to become a political crucible of contention and opposing ideas, as well as a cultural forum for the expression and flowering of sentiments toward ecology and its degradations. This is often lived and enacted at the local level, and local news providers have an obligation to give expression to local initiatives and projects for change, though currently this remains underdeveloped (see Weissmann and Tyrrell, Chapter 5 for a promising exception).

Eighth, more compassionate forms of journalism will be required that recognise the collective and psychological trauma of people experiencing the sharp end of catastrophe and the legitimate fears of all those now waking up to the planetary emergency and its impacts not only on human society but the ecological web-of-life (Gillespie, 2020; Macy, 2021) and, increasingly, this will involve journalists themselves. Glenn Albrecht, originator of the Symbiocene concept, has identified a range of psychoterratic Earth emotions, including new emotional responses both negative and positive to our changing planet (Albrecht, 2019). These include, for example, *solastalgia* (felt loss of home or destroyed environment), *terrafurrie* (extreme anger at ecological devastation), *soliphilia* (love of place and preparedness to protect) and *eutierria* (positive feeling of oneness with the Earth). The communication and elaboration of these and other Earth emotions within world-in-crisis reporting needs to become increasingly recognised and expressed in the years ahead (Cottle, 2024).

Journalism's future imaginary: Cultivated and/or compelled?

When read through the prism of current understanding of journalism organisation and constraints such a journalistic imaginary will seem to many, well, just that, imaginary! Naïve, flawed and/or hopelessly idealistic may also come to mind. When based on what we already know from political economy, the sociology of news and sources, and culture of journalism practice and performance (Cottle, 2006, 2009a, b, 2011), this is understandable. But we are no longer living in 'normal times', whatever historically they are, and the trajectories of decline and collapse only look set to accelerate and deepen in the years ahead. As in historical times of 'total war', it is possible to anticipate and indeed to collectively demand that journalism better orients itself, and us, to the world and its existential demise. Journalism need not always be assumed to be historically static or intransigent to change (Carey, 1996; Zelizer, 2017; Schudson, 2019). The juggernaut of late modernity (Giddens, 1990) or the planetary superorganism of economic growth and ecological exhaustion (Hagens, 2023) can also give birth to its nemesis. It's in the ecological air we breathe as much as the compelled politics and changing social relations forced to adapt to an increasingly catastrophised world. This is the terrain of Ulrich Beck's societal metamorphosis (2016) that complexly, in myriad and often understated ways, reaches down into everyday life, into institutions and ways of doing things, and begins to form an 'epochal change of horizons' (Beck, 2015, p. 77).

Journalism historically has the proven capacity to recalibrate and readjust its cultural sights, its collective moral compass, though not always for the better it is true. But we should not overlook or downplay the part played by modern means of communication in the deepening of democratic expectations (Scannell, 1989) and in the advance of progressive movements of change (Cottle, 2004; Alexander, 2006): whether in respect of the civil rights movement challenging racism, gender inequality and new identity politics, or the universal recognition of human rights and struggles for animal welfare and environmental justice around the world.

Journalism takes its cue not only from owners and powerful vested interests, but professionally and culturally from the metaphorical winds of change blowing through wider society. In hot-housed times literally blasted by winds of change, in times of 'anthropological shock' and 'enforced enlightenment', the politics of 'emancipatory catastrophism' finds a foothold and may even be set loose (Beck, 2015). In such circumstances, journalism may become increasingly compelled to not only acknowledge but also grant expression to views and voices challenging the business as usual, life as normal, worldview, a view long past its sell-by-date in a visibly dying world.

Journalism's future imaginary need not be assumed to be a sudden and unlikely moment of ideological conversion. Rather it may be anticipated as an ongoing process of societal metamorphosis in the fading dusk of world civilisation and in the gathering vortex of demands for transition and societal transformation to a more ecologically sustainable and socially just world.

Conclusion

Our life chances and indeed the continuing chance of Life itself on planet Earth, has become a race to planetary ecological consciousness. Journalism can yet perform an indispensable and vitalising role in (1) *signalling*, (2) *symbolising*, and (3) *staging* the inescapable necessity for deep adaptation and pathways of transition. It can do so by (4) *scrutinising* and exploring the credibility of government and corporate policies, and by (5) *seeking out* and giving expression to the flourishing of ideas and pre-figurative practices built on imagined futures and compelled new horizons in the civil sphere and across the pluriverse of different cultures and communities around the globe.

The axial crisis of perception is at the core of today's world-in-crisis, and journalism occupies a key position in either continuing to reproduce a fossil-fuelled, materialist worldview that has brought the world to probable collapse or help furnish an ecological sensibility and consciousness (as well as *future imaginaries*) that could yet build pathways of transition and transformation to a more socially just and ecologically sustainable way of being inside the web-of-life. This is not to suggest an easy path of transition. Struggles over material standards of living and protecting established ways of life, the rise of authoritarian populism and 'post-truth' politics, and widely circulating conspiracy claims in the digital sphere all now pose considerable obstacles to change. These will no doubt become exacerbated and mobilised in opposition to pathways of transition in the turbulent times ahead, even as the necessity for such pathways become ever more pressing.

Journalism is not outside of society, culture and crises, as you and I are not outside of the web-of-life. The prospects for journalism stepping up to the great existential challenges of our time will conceivably become *compelled* by the onward crush of crises, catastrophes and system breakdowns, but journalism's response will also have to be *cultivated* in the wider awakening to the necessity for change and transformation informed by a growing ecological sensibility and consciousness. In respect of the axial crisis of perception, journalism, in all its different guises is not destined to always reproduce the Great Derangement of our times, and some alternative offshoots and occasional mainstream exceptions, as signalled above, are beginning to show a more productive way forward. Journalism more generally could yet become both compelled and cultivated to become an integral part of the solutions to surviving beyond our world-in-crisis and thereby, necessarily, better attuned to reporting on sustainable living in the web-of-life.

Notes

1. This chapter develops on previous publications, including Cottle (2014, 2022, 2023a, 2023b, 2024).
2. By 'world society' and indeed 'world-in-crisis', it is not being suggested that our world is not also composed of pluriverse cultures and diverse communities, histories, narratives, discourses, cosmologies and epistemological standpoints (Escobar, 2020), or that communities and cultures do not experience world crises from different vantage points and positions of precarity and are thereby impacted and able to respond in different ways. It is nonetheless also the case that our shared world is now universally, ontologically, under stress, as its predominant socio-ecological system manifests as a world-in-crisis (or, if preferred, 'meta-crisis', 'polycrisis', 'permacrisis', 'planetary emergency' or 'civilisational collapse' see Chapter 1). This is rooted in fundamental contradictions between economic growth and ecological exhaustion, global inequality and social justice, ego-consumerism and eco-custodianship and philosophic and psychological pattens of reductionism and control and reciprocity and care. A late modern, capitalist system, originated in 'the West' and imposed violently through slavery, colonialism and imperialism and now financialised and globalised with universalising impacts on world human society and the planet's biosphere. This position compels recognition of both the universal and the particular, but not as an incommensurable binary based on adopting a position of *either/or*, but rather as a beneficial polyvocal and dialogical communicative nexus based on the global cosmopolitan principle of *both/and* (Beck, 2006, see also Chakrabarty, 2021).

References

Albrecht, G. (2019) *Earth emotions*. New York: Cornell University Press.
Alexander, J. (2006) *The civil sphere*. New York: Oxford University Press.
Beck, U. (2006) *Cosmopolitan vision*. Cambridge: Polity.
Beck, U. (2009) *World at risk*. Cambridge: Polity.

Beck, U. (2015) 'Emancipatory catastrophism: What does it mean to climate change and risk society?', *Current Sociology*, 63(1), pp. 75–88.
Beck, U. (2016) *The metamorphosis of the world*. Cambridge: Polity.
Bendell, J. (2023) *Breaking together*. Bristol: Good Books.
Bendell, J. and Read, R. (2021) *Deep adaptation*. Cambridge: Polity.
Bennett, L. (2021) *Communicating the future*. Cambridge: Polity.
Bennett L, Lawrence, G. and Livingston, S. (2006) *When the press fails*. Chicago, IL: University of Chicago Press.
Berglez, P. (2013) *Global journalism*. New York: Peter Lang.
Boykoff, M.T. and Boykoff, J.M. (2007) 'Climate change and journalistic norms: A case-study of US mass-media coverage', *Geoforum; Journal of Physical, Human, and Regional Geosciences*, 38(6), pp. 1190–1204.
Bødker, H. and Morris, H. (2022) *Climate change and journalism*. Milton Park: Routledge.
Carey, P. (1996) *The faber book of reportage*. London: Faber and Faber.
Chadwick, A. (2017) *The hybrid media system*. New York: Oxford University Press.
Chakrabarty, D. (2021) *The climate of history in a planetary age*. Chicago: University of Chicago Press.
Club of Rome (2019), *Planetary emergency plan*. https://www.clubofrome.org/publication/the-planetary-emergency-plan/, accessed 26 March 2024.
Cottle, S. (2004) *The racist murder of Stephen Lawrence: Media performance and public transformation*. Westport: Praeger.
Cottle, S. (2006) *Mediatized conflict*. Maidenhead: Open University Press.
Cottle, S. (2009a) *Global crisis reporting*. Maidenhead: Open University Press.
Cottle, S. (2009b) 'Global crises in the news: Staging new wars, disasters, and climate change', *Journal of International Communication*, 3, pp. 494–516.
Cottle, S. (2011) 'Taking global crises in the news seriously: Notes from the dark side of globalization', *Global Media and Communication*, 7(2), pp. 77–95.
Cottle, S. (2012) 'Global crises and world news ecology' in Allan, S. (ed.) *The Routledge companion to news and journalism studies*. Milton Park: Routledge, pp. 473–484.
Cottle, S. (2013) 'Journalists witnessing disasters: From the calculus of death to the injunction to care', *Journalism Studies*, 14(2), pp. 1–17.
Cottle, S. (2014) 'Rethinking media and disasters in a global age: What's changed and why it matters', *Media War & Conflict*, 7(1), pp. 3–22.
Cottle, S. (2019) 'Journalism coming of (global) age. II', *Journalism*, 20(1), pp. 102–105.
Cottle, S. (2022) 'Peace and conflict reporting in a world-in-crisis' in Orgeret, K. (ed.) *Insights on peace and conflict reporting*. London: Routledge, pp. 10–31.
Cottle, S. (2023a) 'Reporting civilisational collapse: Research notes from a world-in-crisis', *Global Media and Communication*, 19(2), pp. 269–288.
Cottle, S. (2023b) 'Reporting the war in Ukraine: Ecological dissimulation in a dying world' in Mortensen, M. and Pantti, M. (eds.) *Media and the war in Ukraine*. New York: Peter Lang, pp. 195–214.
Cottle, S. (2024) 'Reporting a world-in-crisis: It's going to be emotional!' in Sanfiel, M. and Salojarvi, V. (eds.) *Handbook of journalism and emotion*. London: Routledge.

Cottle, S. and Rai, M. (2006) 'Between display and deliberation: Analyzing TV news as communicative architecture', *Media Culture & Society*, 28(2), pp. 163–189.

Crutzen, P.J. and Steffen, W. (2003) 'How long have we been in the Anthropocene era?' *Climatic Change*, 61(3), pp. 251–257.

Defoe, D. (2003 [1704]) *The storm*. London: Penguin Classics.

Eisenstein, C. (2018) *Climate: A new story*. Berkely: North Atlantic Books.

Escobar, A. (2020) *Pluriversal politics*. Duke University.

Ghosh, A. (2016) *The great derangement*. Chicago, IL: University of Chicago Press.

Giddens, A. (1990) *The consequences of modernity*. Cambridge: Polity.

Gillespie, S. (2020) *Climate crisis and consciousness*. Milton Park: Routledge.

Guardian, The. (2023) Guardian environment pledge 2023. *The Guardian*. https://www.theguardian.com/environment/2023/nov/28/guardian-environment-pledge-2023 Accessed 16 September 2024.

Hagens, N. (2023) *The superorganism and the future*. https://www.youtube.com/watch?v=mN87PWfj7LA, accessed 26 March 2024.

Harcup, T. and O'Neill, D. (2017) 'What is news? News values revisited (again)', *Journalism Studies*, 18(12), pp. 1470–1488.

Hickman, C., Marks, E., Pihkala, P., Claydon, S., Lewandowski, R. and Mayall, E. (2021) 'Climate anxiety in children and young people and their beliefs about government responses to climate change: A global survey', *The Lancet*, 5(12): E863–E873. https://doi.org/10.1016/S2542-5196(21)00278-3, accessed 26 March 2024.

Keen, D. (2023) *When disasters come home*. Cambridge: Polity.

Intergovernmental Panel on Climate Change (IPCC) (2022) *IPCC sixth assessment report: Impacts, adaptation and vulnerability*. https://www.ipcc.ch/report/ar6/wg2/, accessed 26 March 2024.

Korton, D. (2021) *Ecological civilization: From emergency to emergence*. https://davidkorten.org/wp-content/uploads/2021/11/Korten-EcoCiv-11032021.pdf, accessed 26 March 2024.

Lent, J. (2021) *The web of meaning*. London: Profile Books.

Macy, J. (2021) *World as lover, world as self*. California: Parallax Press.

Macy, J. and Johnstone, C. (2022) *Active hope*. Novato, CA: New World Library.

Matthews, F. (2023) *The Dao of civilization: A letter to China*. London: Anthem Press.

McGilchrist, I. (2019) *The master and his emissary*. New Haven: Yale University Press.

McGoldrick, A. and Lynch, J. (2005) *Peace journalism*. Stroud: Hawthorn Press.

McIntyre, K. (2019) 'Solutions journalism', *Journalism Practice*, 13(8), pp. 1029–1033.

Miller, A. and Heinberg, R. (2023) *Welcome to the great unraveling: Navigating the polycrisis of environmental and social breakdown*. Oregon: Post Carbon Institute.

Moore, J. (2015) *Capitalism in the web of life*. New York: Verso Books.

Nettlefold, J. and Pecl, G.T. (2022) 'Engaged journalism and climate change', *Journalism Practice*, 16(1), pp. 19–34.

Organisation for Humanitarian Affairs (OCHA) (2024) *Global Humanitarian Overview 2024*. https://humanitarianaction.info/document/global-humanitarian-overview-2024, accessed 26 March 2024.

Ophuls, W. (2012) *Immoderate greatness: Why civilizations fail.* Scotts Valley, CA: CreateSpace Independent Publishing Platform.

Ophuls, W. (2013) *Plato's revenge.* Cambridge: MIT Press.

Parks, P. (2020) 'Researching with our hair on fire', *Journalism & Mass Communication Quarterly*, 97(2), pp. 393–415.

Pantti, M., Wahl-Jorgensen, K. and Cottle, S. (2012) *Disasters and the media.* New York: Peter Lang.

Read, R. (2022) *Do you want to know the truth?* Melbourne: Simplicity Institute.

Redfearn, G. and Morton, A. (2023) '"Climate villain": Scientists say Rupert Murdoch wielded his media empire to sow confusion and doubt', *The Guardian*, 23 September 2023. https://www.theguardian.com/media/2023/sep/23/rupert-murdoch-climate-change-denial accessed 16 September 2024.

Reese, S. (2016) 'The new geography of journalism research', *Digital Journalism*, 4(7), pp. 816–826.

Rifkin, J. (2023) *The age of resilience.* London: Swift Press.

Robbins, D. and Wheatley, D. (2021) 'Complexity, objectivity, and shifting roles: Environmental correspondents march to a changing beat', *Journalism Practice*, 15(9), pp. 1289–1306.

Rosen, J. (1999) *What are journalists for?* New Haven: Yale University Press.

Scannell, P. (1989) 'Public service broadcasting and modern public life', *Media Culture & Society*, 11(2), pp. 135–166.

Schudson, M. (2019) 'Approaches to the sociology of news' in Curran, J. and Hesmondhalgh, D. (eds.) *Media and society.* London: Bloomsbury, pp. 139–165.

Scott, M., Wright, K. and Bunce, M. (2023) *Humanitarian journalists.* Milton Park: Routledge.

Servigne, P., Stevens, R. and Chapelle, G. (2021) *Another end of the world is possible.* Cambridge: Polity.

Smith, P. and Howe, N. (2015) *Climate change as social drama.* Cambridge: Cambridge University Press.

Vidal. J. (2023) *Fevered planet.* London: Bloomsbury.

Wadleigh. M. (2023), *Existential Stocktake.* https://existentialstocktake.org/about/, accessed 26 March 2024.

Waisbord, S. (2009) 'Rethinking development journalism' in Allan, S. (ed.) *The Routledge companion to news and journalism.* Milton Park: Routledge, pp. 148–158.

Whitlock, J. (2023) 'Climate anxiety in young people', *Nature Mental Health*, 1, pp. 297–298.

WWF. (2020) *Nature and pandemics.* https://www.wwf.org.uk/nature-and-pandemics, accessed 26 March 2024.

Zelizer, B. (2017) 'Thinking temporally about journalism's future' in Zelizer, B. (ed.) *What journalism could be.* Cambridge: Polity, pp. 239–262.

· 3 ·

EVALUATING REPORTING ROLES IN CLIMATE DISASTERS

Victoria Fielding

In 2007, the BBC cancelled their planned day-long television programme 'Planet Relief', implying it would be politically biased to educate their viewers about the global crisis of catastrophic climate change. In justifying the cancellation, a *BBC* editor said 'It's absolutely not the job of the BBC to save the planet' (Cottle, 2008, p. 88). This begs the question, whose job is it?

Scientists can reach consensus identifying climate change, can argue action is needed, and can suggest and appraise solutions. But in a democratic society, they cannot implement climate policies. That must be done through political consensus. This is why climate change is both an environmental and political issue. Democratic consensus for action cannot happen without news media informing audiences about the problem, and policies to solve it.

Despite the centrality of politics to climate action, climate change news reporting is regularly studied as a form of environmental or science reporting (Brüggemann and Engesser, 2014; Schäfer and Painter, 2021; Brüggemann et al., 2022). Studies have shown, however, that climate change has been politicised and polarised in media, including in Australia (Asayama et al., 2017; Chinn et al., 2020; Holmes and Star, 2018). Politicisation is regularly considered problematic in climate reporting, suggesting that when science is politicised, it is not useful to the public (Chinn et al., 2020). There is concern that when politicians are quoted in climate stories, they may 'directly contradict scientific consensus or cut against the interests of organized science' (Schäfer and Painter, 2021, p. 3). It could also be argued, however, that now that science has convincingly reached consensus about the existence of climate change, and the urgency to act, the issue should be turned over to democratic political debate – not about *if* something should be done, but *what*.

Journalists play a key role in promoting understanding of climate change by facilitating a vibrant public debate, a marketplace of ideas about policies the public can support for action on climate change (Asard and Bennett, 1997). Journalists also underpin a healthy democracy as watchdogs holding political leaders to account by scrutinising whether they are appropriately following the science and taking action on climate change (Christians et al., 2009). Alongside these traditional journalism roles, new styles of advocacy journalism, melding reporting with commentary, have appeared. These are influencing climate change reporting, with radical advocates supporting climate action, and conservative advocates opposing action (Fielding, 2023).

In this chapter, online news reporting and commentary about the role of climate change in exacerbating the 2019/2020 Australian bushfire crisis and 2022 floods is evaluated in relation to these journalistic roles in democracy. This analysis gauges whether Australian journalists as a collective are informing a healthy democracy by facilitating a 'pluralistic search for consensus' (Fahy, 2018, p. 855) through majority support for much-needed climate action, or whether they are contributing to a deadlock of never-ending debate.

Politicised bushfires and floods: The Australian political and media context

Australia's climate change politics has a long and complicated history. Over the last 16 years, the rise and fall of two centre-left Labor Party Prime Ministers and four right-wing Liberal Party Prime Ministers was influenced by climate politics (Baker, 2022). Liberal Prime Minister Scott Morrison won the 2019 election after 'weaponising climate action' against the Labor Party opposition (Murphy, 2022).

The political battle over climate change action became an international spectacle when Australia experienced catastrophic bushfires in the summer of 2019–2020 and unprecedented floods in 2022. During the bushfire crisis in five states, 33 people were killed and 11 million hectares burned (BBC, 2020).

Australia's Climate Council, a non-profit climate communication organisation, warned climate change was creating more dangerous bushfire conditions, lengthening the fire season, and reducing opportunities to do fuel reduction burning (Climate Council, 2019). From February to April 2022, flooding in southern Queensland and northern New South Wales caused the deaths of 23 people and flooded over 32,000 homes and businesses (Center for Disaster Philanthropy, 2022). The Climate Council advised the floods were 'climate change-driven' and 'the most extreme disasters in Australian history' (Rice et al., 2022).

During the bushfire crisis, polling showed the environment was for the first time ranked Australians' number one concern, but the COVID-19 pandemic in early 2020 displaced it and concern has remained low ever since (Ipsos, 2023). Polling has shown moderate increasing acceptance in Australia of anthropogenic climate science with 15 per cent believing climate change is entirely caused by humans and 35 per cent mostly caused by humans. There remains a stubborn 15 to 20 per cent of the country who do not believe in climate change or do not believe it is impacted by humans and 27 per cent who believe humans only partly cause climate change, a belief incompatible with scientific consensus (Ipsos, 2023).

Mixed acceptance of climate change is related to a lack of bipartisan calls for action. Before the 2022 election, only 22 per cent of Liberal and National Party voters wanted more climate action, compared to 64 per cent of Labor Party voters (Ipsos, 2022). Although Morrison's government adopted a net zero emissions target by 2050, it only offered an emissions reduction target of 26 to 28 per cent below 2005 levels by 2030, compared to the Labor Party's 43 per cent, and did not establish any 'credible policy mechanisms to deliver emissions reduction' (Chandrasekhar and Gabbatiss, 2022; Murphy, 2022). The democratic will for climate action influenced swings towards candidates calling for such action at the 2022 election, after which the Labor Party formed a slim majority government (Morton and Murphy, 2022).

Australia's political contestation over climate change policy is reflected in Australian media reporting. Australia has the most concentrated media industry in the world, with print and online media outlets dominated by Rupert Murdoch's News Corp Australia, which owns 57.5 per cent of newspapers (Dwyer and Muller, 2016; Gaber and Tiffen, 2018, p. 34). News Corp's papers have been described as exhibiting 'overt conservative bias' (Gaber and Tiffen, 2018, p. 33). On the issue of climate change, particularly, *The Australian*, News Corp's national masthead, has a long history of platforming sceptics (Bacon, 2013), has been criticised as waging a 'protracted war on climate science' (Manne, 2011), and for making no distinction between climate science and political advocacy (McKnight, 2010). Between April 2019 and March 2020, 45 per cent of articles in four News Corp mastheads 'rejected or cast doubt' on scientific consensus on climate change (Bacon and Jegan, 2020, p. 93).

Another important news outlet is Australia's public broadcaster, the *ABC*. Although legally required to provide impartial and balanced coverage, it has been criticised in the past for platforming climate change sceptics (Chubb and Nash, 2012). *The Guardian* entered the Australian digital news industry in 2013 and has continued its UK tradition of prioritising science-based reporting to highlight climate change in news reporting (Painter et al., 2021), and newer forms of media advocacy (Forde, 2018).

The news media's coverage of the consensus on climate change and its link to national crises like bushfires and floods has implications for the public's understanding of climate change and their will to support action. Cottle says climate reporting has evolved through the phases of science, then scepticism, and now that the world is experiencing climate-driven disasters like heatwaves, droughts, bushfires and floods, is entering a phase of spectacle (Cottle, 2008). Although media images of climate-driven disasters play an important role in 'bringing home' the dangers of climate change, this spectacle is not necessarily used by journalists to communicate potential political actions to address climate change (Cottle, 2008, p. 91).

Evaluating climate change reporting using a model of journalism's role in a democracy

Much scholarly research traces the evolving standards and practices of journalism as it responds to the global issue of climate change (Schäfer and Painter, 2021). Droughts and heatwaves are increasingly linked by journalists to climate change (Boykoff et al., 2020; Osaka et al., 2020; Painter et al., 2021). Studies have found that broadly, left-wing media give climate change more coverage than right-wing media (Brüggemann and Engesser, 2017; Painter et al., 2021).

This chapter builds on this scholarship by evaluating news media's representation of climate change during the Australian 2019/2020 bushfires and 2022 floods by applying a model of journalists' influence on democracy (Figure 3.1, Fielding, 2023, p. 2).

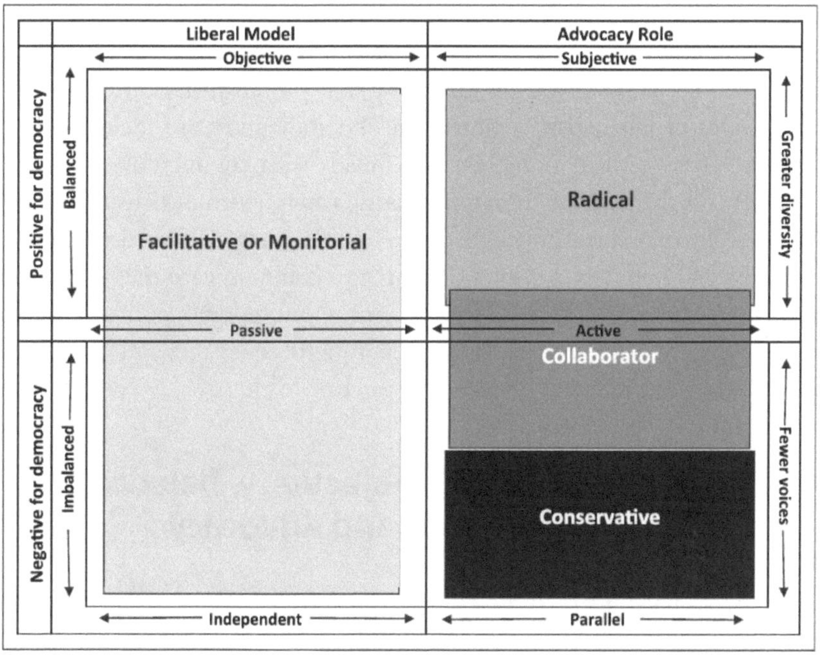

Figure 3.1. A Model of Journalism's Influence on Democracy (Fielding, 2023, p. 2)

This model delineates five potential roles for journalists and theorises about their positive or negative influence on democracy. The two roles most discussed within the western Liberal Model of media are the facilitative and the monitorial. These are defined in line with Christians et al.'s (2009) normative roles of journalists as: facilitators of a vibrant and diverse public debate which gives citizens democratically valuable information; and monitoring power by scrutinising the actions of the powerful (Fielding, 2023). These roles also fit with Keane's (2009) concept of monitorial democracy which positions media as one of many institutions responsible for scrutinising power and empowering citizens to hold power accountable. The top left-hand quadrant is positive for democracy; journalists who are objective, balanced and independent from special interests are serving democracy effectively (Fielding, 2023). The three other roles are described as advocacy, which is defined as journalists subjectively taking a position on social, political or environmental issues (Fielding, 2023). Collaborator advocacy is rare in Western media systems and is characterised by journalists collaborating with the state. Radical advocacy plays a positive role in democracy by giving voice to those who struggle to be heard in the news marketplace of ideas, and who challenge dominant powers (Fielding, 2023). Conservative advocacy is negative for democracy because it reduces the number of voices, and advocates for the already powerful (Fielding, 2023).

Instances of journalism, editorials and commentary are included in this analysis because hard news increasingly melds with commentary or opinion, particularly on the issue of climate reporting where journalists use more interpretative styles of reporting (Brüggemann and Engesser, 2017). Australia's News Corp's editorial policy also allows reporting to communicate the 'publication's standpoint' (Muller, 2023, p. 8). By combining online news and commentary, this research provides a holistic and meaningful assessment of the content available to news audiences on the issue of climate change.

Climate reporting: Objectivity, balance, independence, and advocacy

The model of journalists' influence on democracy (Figure 3.1) encompasses objectivity, balance, independence, and advocacy in climate change reporting. Objectivity is considered a cornerstone of journalistic professionalism in Western news institutions (Skovsgaard et al., 2013). Journalistic objectivity is defined by Schudson as fair representation of facts separated from values and without intentional 'shaping' or 'slanting' (Schudson, 2005, p. 19). Studies of climate change reporting have found objectivity is still considered important. However, it is being actively rejected or redefined in response to concerns that non-scientific information, or even lies, are regularly published in the name of objective practice (Hiles and Hinnant, 2014; Strauss et al., 2022). Objectivity has been adapted to include interpretative methods where journalists use their judgement to appraise sources in line with the 'weight of evidence' (Hiles and Hinnant, 2014; Fahy, 2018; Mocatta et al., 2023). Interpretative styles have resulted in journalists using their monitorial role to exclude or critique climate sceptics (Brüggemann and Engesser, 2014; Schäfer and Painter, 2021), reducing the number of sceptical voices in climate reporting (Schmid-Petri et al., 2017; McAllister et al., 2021). Sceptics, however, are still found in right-wing media (Brüggemann and Engesser, 2017), particularly in anglosphere countries including USA, UK and Australia (Painter et al., 2023).

Objectivity is related to balance in reporting, which requires inclusion of diverse voices so audiences can make up their own minds (Skovsgaard et al., 2013). Boykoff and Boykoff's (2004) study of US coverage of climate science found the practice of balancing climate science against scepticism biased information and misinformed audiences. Such false balance distorted public acceptance of expert consensus (Koehler, 2016). More recent studies find journalists moving on from problematic 'balance as bias' reporting about the existence of climate change (Hiles and Hinnant, 2014; Schmid-Petri et al., 2017). However, when reporting the political element of climate change – climate action and policies – journalists across left-wing, centrist and right-wing outlets continue to balance pro-action sources against response sceptics (Painter et al., 2023), also referred to as impact sceptics (Schmid-Petri et al., 2017). Response scepticism is used by conservative political and economic groups who were traditionally science sceptics and have now pivoted to reject or contest climate action policies (Lamb et al., 2020; Painter et al., 2023).

Changing practices of objectivity and balance have also raised questions about whether journalists are becoming advocates for environmental causes. Environmental advocacy in journalism is perceived by many journalists as problematic because it is subjective and requires them to take a position (Hiles and Hinnant, 2014; Robbins and Wheatley, 2021; Mocatta et al., 2023). A minority of journalists, however, see climate advocacy as acceptable because 'it's OK to advocate for saving the planet' (Hiles and Hinnant, 2014, p. 444; Painter et al., 2021). There are outlets like *The Guardian* which transparently advocate for climate action, including a campaign called 'Keep It In the Ground' (Forde, 2017). Brüggemann et al. (2022) suggest journalists' concerns about the inadequacy of their old reporting practices have led to a new type of advocacy journalism: 'transformative journalisms', differentiated from political advocacy for particular interests because the planet is the 'ultimate public good' (Brüggemann et al., 2022).

Method and findings

The model of journalisms' influence on democracy (Fielding, 2023) is used to evaluate how reporting about climate change in the context of the 2019/2020 Australian bushfire crisis and 2022 flooding disaster contributed to public understanding of scientific consensus and the need to act. Twelve popular Australian online news sites were chosen, owned by Australia's six major new organisations (Table 3.1). Since many of these organisations own television, radio or printed newspapers, and content is syndicated across platforms, this study broadens analysis outside of the usual print newspaper studies (Schäfer and Painter, 2021).

Table 3.1. Online News Sites, Owner and Related Offline Outlets

Online news site	Owner	Related outlets
ABC News Online	ABC	ABC Television and Radio (National)
Daily Mail Australia	Daily Mail and General Trust	
The Guardian	Guardian Media Group	
Sky News	News Corp	Sky News Cable Television News (National)
Herald Sun	News Corp	Herald Sun Newspaper (Victoria)
The Australian	News Corp	The Australian Newspaper (National)
News.com.au	News Corp	
Daily Telegraph	News Corp	Daily Telegraph Newspaper (New South Wales)
Nine.com.au	Nine Entertainment Co.	Nine Commercial Television News
The Age	Nine Entertainment Co.	The Age Newspaper (Victoria)
Sydney Morning Herald	Nine Entertainment Co.	The Sydney Morning Herald (New South Wales)
7News	Seven West Media Limited	Seven Commercial Television News

Google Search was used to identify articles about the bushfires, including those mentioning bushfires and climate change or global warming, during the bushfire crisis from 31 December 2019 to 7 January 2020. Stories about flooding, including those mentioning climate change during the floods were sourced during the period of 1 March 2022 to 15 March 2022. Once duplicates were removed, of the total, 168 stories about bushfires and 92 stories about floods mentioned climate change.

Each article was manually coded by a single researcher to allow for quantitative and qualitative content analysis. This interpretive method explored whether and how the five roles in the model of journalisms' influence on democracy manifested, including sources used, positions taken, and how power was scrutinised. Coding also measured the number of words per code to identify its magnitude in the text.

The volume and proportion of each outlet's bushfire and flood stories to those which mention climate change during the sample period is depicted in Figure 3.2.

Figure 3.3 shows articles mentioning climate change grouped by media organisation, with syndicated content removed, indicating significant coverage, where climate change is only mentioned, or where climate change's link

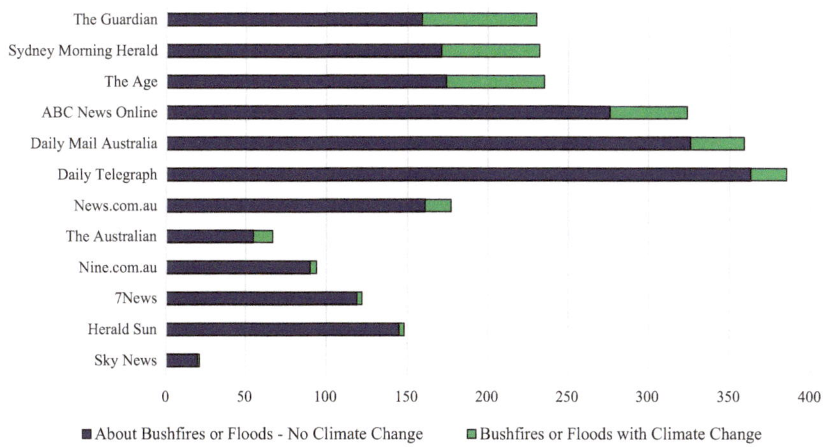

Figure 3.2. Number of Articles Total by Outlet About Bushfires and Floods with or without Climate Change

to bushfires or floods is downplayed. The *Guardian* has the most articles about climate change, Seven West Limited the fewest, followed by News Corp, which also published six articles downplaying or denying the link between climate change and bushfires or floods.

The majority of the 260 articles mentioning climate change facilitated voices taking positions for or against climate change's existence and action (220, bushfires 142, floods 78). A substantial number contained evidence of monitorial journalism with the majority of these scrutinising the Morrison government's climate change record (132, bushfires 90, floods 42).

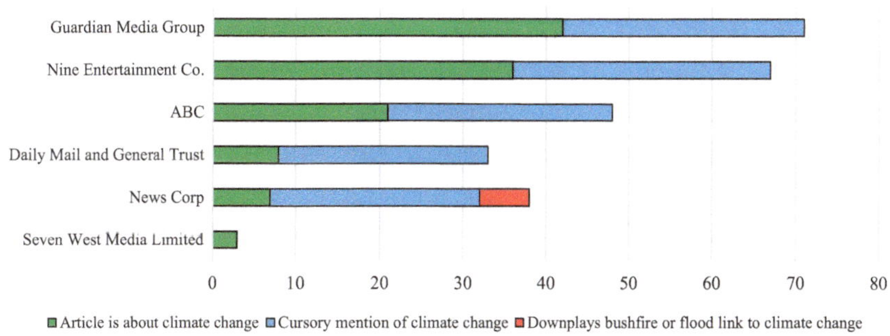

Figure 3.3. Number of Articles about Climate Change in Context of Bushfires and Floods by Outlet.

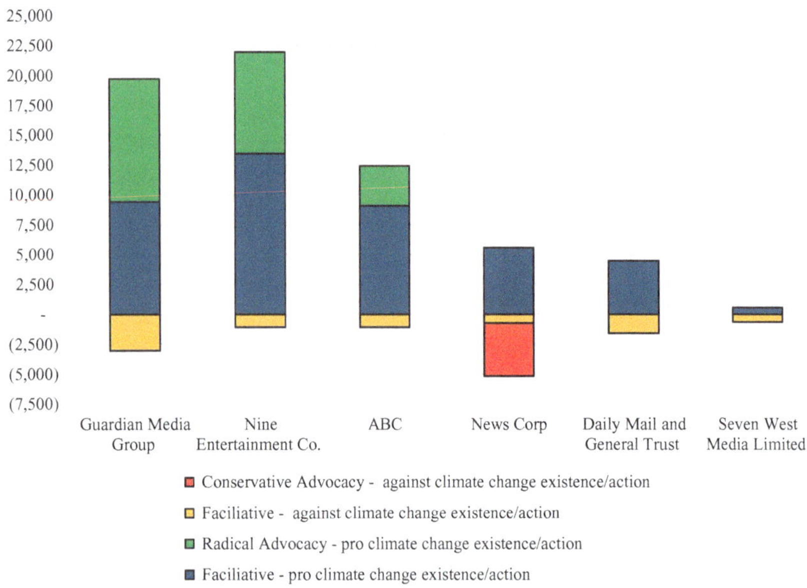

Figure 3.4. Pro and Anti-climate Change Positions by Number of Words by Media Organisation, by Roles Facilitative, Radical and Conservative Advocacy

Thirty-five articles fit the definition of radical advocacy because the author advocated for climate change existence or action (bushfires, 23, floods, 12). These were published by *The Guardian* (22), Nine Entertainment Co. (8); and *ABC* (5). Five articles fit the definition of conservative advocacy because the authors advocated against climate change existence and/or action (3 bushfires, 2 floods). All were published by News Corp's *The Australian* (4) and *Sky News* (1). There was no evidence of collaborative advocacy between the media and the state.

Figure 3.4 depicts the climate science positions published by the six media organisations, by number of words. The majority of facilitative and advocacy content affirms the existence of climate change and need for action.

Figure 3.5 depicts the balance between the number of positions held (not the number of words), across different roles. Eighty-five per cent of facilitated positions accept the existence of climate change and its link to bushfires and floods, with 12 per cent against. Similarly, 84 per cent of advocacy positions for climate change and action are radical, and 16 per cent conservative. The content is, however, more balanced when it comes to arguments for and against climate action. In the facilitative debate, 60 per cent are pro-action, and 40

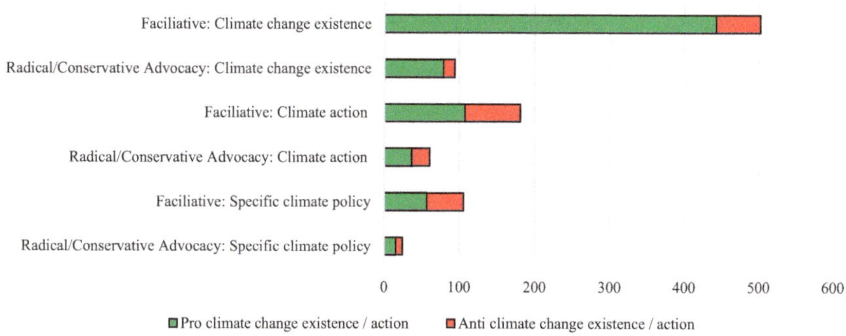

Figure 3.5. Number of Positions across all Articles for Climate Existence, Action and Specific Policies

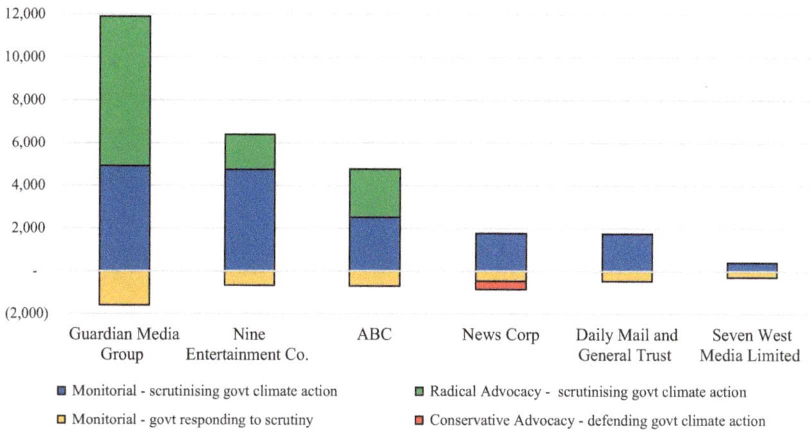

Figure 3.6. Scrutiny of Government Climate Action by Number of Words: Monitorial, Radical and Conservative Advocacy Roles

per cent against. Radical advocacy for climate action represents 61 per cent of positions and conservative 39 per cent. The split between facilitated debate for and against specific policies is even more balanced with 54 per cent for and 46 per cent against. There is little discussion of specific policies in radical and conservative advocacy, with 16 positions (64 per cent) pro-specific climate policies and 9 (36 per cent) against.

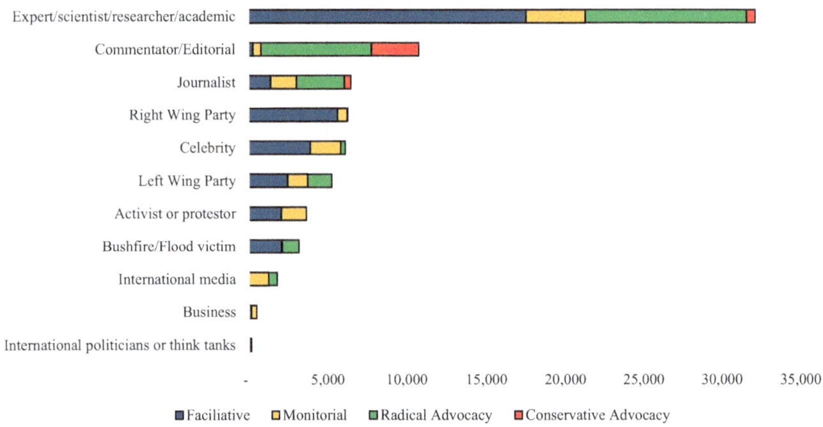

Figure 3.7. Voices and Sources Included by Words Across Four Journalism Roles

Figure 3.6 shows how many words were used to scrutinise the Morrison government about climate change action by each media organisation across the four journalistic roles. This shows there is large variation across outlets, with News Corp doing very little scrutiny of the government, but also using conservative advocacy to defend the government's climate change position. *The Guardian* stands out as having done the most scrutiny, particularly in radical advocacy content.

The voices and sources used across all types of roles are shown in Figure 3.7. Experts, usually climate scientists, were given most space across outlets, particularly in a facilitative role, but also to scrutinise the government and to do radical advocacy.

Discussion

This research identifies that all outlets analysed except News Corp are making the link between climate change, and bushfires and floods. Experts, particularly scientists, are the most used source and they present compelling scientific consensus of climate change existence. However, while there is near consensus about the role climate change played in fires and floods, when it comes to the political element of climate consensus – the need to take climate action and consider specific actions to reduce emissions – Australian media remains locked in a partisan debate.

In the seven years after the Australian 2009 Black Saturday bushfires, only 2.9 per cent of 418 stories about bushfire risk and protection referred to climate change worsening bushfires (Anderson et al., 2018). Climate attention has increased; 14 per cent of stories sampled about the 2019/2020 bushfires and 2022 floods mentioned climate change. Of these stories, 45 per cent were about climate change, 53 per cent mentioned climate change and 2 per cent downplayed or denied the link between natural disasters and climate. Four media outlets contributed 72 per cent of the articles: *The Guardian* (21 per cent), *Sydney Morning Herald* (18 per cent), *The Age* (18 per cent) and the ABC (14 per cent). Thirteen articles across *The Guardian* and Nine Entertainment Co. were written by specialist climate change reporters. As found in other studies, *The Guardian* frequently publishes about climate change (Carvalho, 2007; McAllister et al., 2021), and specialist reporters increase coverage quantity (Brüggemann and Engesser, 2014; Schäfer and Painter, 2021).

The *Daily Mail* contributed 10 per cent of coverage, mostly mentions of climate change with little meaningful coverage. The two commercial broadcast news websites produced very little coverage (*7News* 1 per cent, *Nine.com.au* 1 per cent), suggesting their broadcast stations also gave scant coverage of climate. Five News Corp outlets – *The Australian*, *News.com.au*, *Daily Telegraph*, *Herald Sun* and *Sky News* collectively contributed only 16 per cent of climate change coverage, mostly just mentions, including all the articles downplaying climate change. *The Australian* and *Sky News* also had low coverage of bushfires and floods as compared to other outlets, with *The Australian* contributing 3 per cent of total coverage, and *Sky News* 1 per cent (Figure 3.2). This finding aligns with Painter et al.'s (2023, p. 8) suggestion that News Corp's editorial policy is 'denialism by silence' in climate reporting. Analysis of News Corp climate reporting also found the organisation produces a large volume of sceptical content but leaves out the impacts and consequences of climate change – consequences like bushfires and floods (Bacon and Jegan, 2020).

Evaluation of journalists' facilitating role found climate sceptics (Figure 3.5) were mostly excluded (Hiles and Hinnant, 2014; Strauss et al., 2022). As in other studies, when sceptical voices were included, they were mostly contextualised and criticised (Brüggemann and Engesser, 2014; Schäfer and Painter, 2021). For example, during the bushfire crisis, Liberal MP Craig Kelly denied the link between climate change and bushfires during an interview on Good Morning Britain and was criticised by hosts Piers Morgan and Laura Tobin, a meteorologist. Coverage of this interview fit the monitorial role because it led journalists to ask Prime Minister Scott Morrison whether he accepted the link between climate change and bushfires. Although he said he did, he also said the bushfires were not caused by Australia's emissions, in line with his argument that Australia should delay action.

Morrison's downplaying of the need for action affected the amount of what Painter et al. (2023) call 'response scepticism' in reporting. As per Figure 3.5, reporting across the five outlets was much more balanced when it came to including positions for and against action, and discussing climate policies. The 40 per cent of voices against climate action were mostly Morrison responding to journalists' scrutiny of his passive climate change position (Figure 3.6). Morrison explained this stance using arguments similar to those identified in Lamb et al.'s (2020) study of discourses of climate delay, including prioritising technology rather than market-driven policies and suggesting Australia's emissions, and therefore action, is insignificant to a global problem. Painter et al. (2023, p. 6) similarly found Morrison's response scepticism was reported in stories about the IPCC's 2021 report where journalists quoted Morrison arguing for 'technology not taxes'.

Despite journalists scrutinising Morrison's position on climate science, his response scepticism was rarely examined. Journalists thus appear unconcerned about quoting response sceptics who are contradicting scientific consensus about the need for action (Schäfer and Painter, 2021, p. 3). This suggests when it comes to balancing political, as opposed to scientific, voices in climate reporting, 'the old rule' of traditional routines of objectivity and balance still apply (Hiles and Hinnant, 2014, p. 442). Schmid-Petri et al. (2017) make the point that scientific consensus is based not just on the existence of climate change, but the urgency to do something about it. They suggest the balancing of response scepticism represents the dangerous emergence of a new form of information 'balance as bias' (Schmid-Petri et al., 2017). This balance, they say, helps legitimise voices opposed to action beyond those who overtly deny science (Schmid-Petri et al., 2017, p. 508). This study agrees that climate change reporting about Australia's bushfires and floods represented climate change as real, but still legitimised a debate about whether something should be done about it.

Radical advocacy articles were markedly different from those considered facilitative and monitorial. Not only did they give no coverage to science sceptics, but response sceptics were absent, and Morrison's inaction was far more regularly and harshly criticised. Radical advocacy gave voice to climate scientists (9), a left-wing former politician (1), bushfire or flood victims (4), and a celebrity (1), as well as commentators (11) and journalists (7). Despite these pieces subjectively advocating for climate change existence and action and thereby challenging traditional notions of objectivity, none misrepresented reality by distorting the facts of scientific consensus. Subjectivity can thus still be underpinned by 'actual scientific facts', and these facts can effectively be used to communicate truth, and to speak truth to power (Eide and Kunelius, 2020, p. 169). Radical advocacy involves journalists and other authors adopting interpretative styles of reporting in line with the weight of evidence on the need for climate action, which means crossing the line between traditional liberal models of facilitating voices by advocating in their own voice (Hiles and Hinnant, 2014; Brüggemann and Engesser, 2017).

Although radical advocacy is useful to the public's understanding of climate change, journalists in mainstream outlets are likely reluctant to adopt this reporting style. Response sceptics may not be scrutinised because journalists fear accusations of bias (Brüggemann and Engesser, 2014), or being branded activists (Lester, 2013). The perception of advocacy as 'political' is at the heart of the journalism versus advocacy divide. Brüggemann et al. (2020, p. 11) suggest journalists and scientists are increasingly accepting of climate advocacy because, they imply, unlike political advocacy, it is not advocating for 'self-interest or partisan politics'. As forthrightly as the radical advocates writing about bushfires and floods implored their readers to endorse climate action, there was indeed a distinct lack of discussion of the stark choices between the government and opposition polices, even months before the 2022 election. Furthermore, despite other studies finding climate change reporting is dominated by political sources (Chinn et al., 2020), across all reporting roles, political voices apart from Morrison's had very little coverage which meant there was little opportunity for Morrison's political opponents to discuss their alternative climate policies. This suggests that even in the three major Australian news organisations where radical environmental advocacy is published, political advocacy for climate action is 'too hot to handle' (Cottle, 2008, p. 88).

Conservative advocates at News Corp, however, had no such qualms about conservative political advocacy, nor about the accuracy of their coverage. News Corp's conservative advocacy gave voice to their insiders – powerful commentators and a journalist and thus did not extend or diversify the marketplace of ideas. As per Figures 3.4 and 3.6, within facilitative and monitorial journalism, News Corp discussed climate change less, included sceptical voices more, and scrutinised the government less about climate action. One of the rare places where scrutiny of the government was found amongst News Corp outlets was an article published by *News.com.au* which reported the scathing analysis of

Morrison's climate inaction in international media. Perhaps such scrutiny is permissible when done by distant proxies. News Corp outlets also contributed the only content defending Morrison's climate policies. As per Painter et al.'s (2023) finding, people concerned about climate change were attacked by News Corp conservative advocates as 'catastrophists'. A piece in *The Australian* criticised *The Guardian* and the ABC for reporting too much about the link between climate and natural disasters. Particularly at *The Australian* and *Sky News*, News Corp's coverage was reminiscent of Muller's characterisation of 'hyperpartisan campaigning without regard for truth or consequences' (2023, p. 12). Similar to other studies, News Corp was found to publish the least useful information about the link between climate change and natural disasters, and instead sowed doubt (Manne, 2011; Bacon, 2013).

Where Brüggemann and Engesser (2017) found niches of denial still exist in climate reporting, the size of Australia's News Corp means their continued denial of climate science and action cannot be considered niche. Considering News Corp's climate reporting, it is hardly surprising that only 32 per cent of right-leaning news consumers are concerned about climate change, compared to 81 per cent of left-leaning ones (Park et al., 2022). This left-leaning concern about climate change has led younger and educated audiences to accept journalist advocacy for climate action (Park et al., 2022). However, these outlets are preaching to the climate converted and not necessarily helping Australians reach pluralistic consensus about the need for action (Fahy, 2018, p. 855).

Conclusion

The model of journalisms' influence on democracy (Fielding, 2023) is a useful way to evaluate the complex environmental and political nexus of climate change reporting. Traditional news media roles of facilitator and monitor, where carried out, have been found to mostly inform the public accurately about the link between climate change and natural disasters and to hold the government accountable for accepting this link. The model's objectivity continuum helps to explain more interpretative judgements made by journalists in avoiding 'balance as bias' by leaving out science sceptics or holding them to account. Such evolution of these roles is, however, mostly reserved for reporting science. When it comes to politics, the old balance rules apply and thus the debate over whether action should be taken, or what specific action is needed continues to legitimise response sceptics like Morrison who argue against action, despite scientific consensus. Furthermore, the journalistic disconnect between scientific and political reporting is itself problematic since climate action is both a scientific and a political story. Indeed, scepticism about the science of climate change has always been politically motivated, just as is response scepticism.

Journalists' interpretative style of reporting is also found to cross the line into radical advocacy at some outlets. This changes the rules of reporting, allowing for sceptical voices – including response sceptics – to be excluded and powerful sceptics harshly critiqued. Crucially, the subjective style of radical advocacy does not undermine the accuracy of reporting, but rather is unashamedly informed by scientific consensus. Conservative advocacy, on the other hand, is a form of subjectivity which is not informed by science, but regularly misrepresents and even attacks science, and still hosts sceptical voices. Despite this, many studies find journalists are careful to avoid radical advocacy. Yet, conservative advocacy at right-wing outlets is identified, though not named, by many studies and is treated as legitimate. Just as it is dangerous to present a climate scientist's views on climate change as equally legitimate as a sceptic's, it is wrong to suggest left-wing outlets doing radical advocacy by faithfully reporting science are equivalent to right-wing outlets misrepresenting scientific consensus for political gain. These outlets use their power to degrade democratic consensus on climate action.

References

Anderson, D., Chubb, P. and Djerf-Pierre, M. (2018) Fanning the blame: Media accountability, climate and crisis on the Australian 'fire continent'. *Environmental Communication*, 12(7), pp. 928–941.

Asard, E. and Bennett, W.L. (1997) *Democracy and the marketplace of ideas: Communication and government in Sweden and the United States*. Cambridge, UK: Cambridge University Press.

Asayama, S., Lidberg, J., Cloteau, A., Comby, J.-B. and Chubb, P. (2017) 'Who captures the voice of the climate? Policy networks and the political role of media in Australia, France and Japan' in Kunelius, R., Eide, E., Tegelberg, M. and Yagodin, D. (eds.) *Media and global climate knowledge: Journalism and the IPCC*. New York: Palgrave Macmillan, pp. 171–192.

Bacon, W. (2013) *Sceptical climate. Part 2: Climate science in Australian newspapers* [Record #2782 is using a reference type undefined in this output style].

Bacon, W., & Jegan, A. (2020). Lies, debates and silences: How NewsCorp produces climate scepticism in Australia. In: An independent report commissioned by GetUp.

Baker, N. (2022) 'The recent history of Australia's climate change wars', *SBS News*. https://www.sbs.com.au/news/article/the-recent-history-of-australias-climate-change-wars/ss9nn2yd6

BBC. (2020) 'Australia fires: A visual guide to the bushfire crisis', *BBC News*. https://www.bbc.com/news/world-australia-50951043

Boykoff, M., Katzung, J. and Nacu-Schmidt, A. (2020) *A review of media coverage of climate change and global warming in 2019. Media and climate change observatory*. Boulder: Center for Science and Technology Policy Research, Cooperative Institute for Research in Environmental Sciences, University of Colorado. Retrieved from https://bit.ly/3hw83Rg

Boykoff, M.T. and Boykoff, J.M. (2004) 'Balance as bias: Global warming and the US prestige press', *Global Environmental Change*, 14(2), pp. 125–136.

Brüggemann, M. and Engesser, S. (2014) 'Between consensus and denial: Climate journalists as interpretive community', *Science Communication*, 36(4), pp. 399–427.

Brüggemann, M. and Engesser, S. (2017) 'Beyond false balance: How interpretive journalism shapes media coverage of climate change', *Global Environmental Change*, 42, pp. 58–67.

Brüggemann, M., Frech, J. and Schäfer, T. (2022) 'Transformative journalisms: How the ecological crisis is transforming journalism' in Hansen, A. (ed.) *Routledge handbook of global environmental politics: Second edition 2022*. London: Taylor & Francis. https://doi.org/10.4324/9781003008873

Brüggemann, M., Lörcher, I. and Walter, S. (2020) 'Post-normal science communication: Exploring the blurring boundaries of science and journalism', *Journal of Science Communication*, 19(3), A02.

Carvalho, A. (2007) 'Ideological cultures and media discourses on scientific knowledge: Re-reading news on climate change', *Public Understanding of Science*, 16(2), pp. 223–243.

Center for Disaster Philanthropy (2022) *2022 Australian flooding*. Center for Disaster Philanthropy. Retrieved 14 July, from https://disasterphilanthropy.org/disasters/2022-australian-flooding/

Chandrasekhar, A. and Gabbatiss, J. (2022, May 24) 'Q&A: What does the new Australian Labor government mean for climate change?', *Carbon Brief*. https://www.carbonbrief.org/qa-what-does-the-new-australian-labor-government-mean-for-climate-change/

Chinn, S., Hart, P.S. and Soroka, S. (2020) 'Politicization and polarization in climate change news content, 1985–2017', *Science Communication*, 42(1), pp. 112–129.

Christians, C.G., Glasser, T.L., McQuail, D., Nordenstreng, K. and White, R.A. (2009) *Normative theories of the media: Journalism in democratic societies*. Urbana: University of Illinois Press.

Chubb, P. and Nash, C. (2012) 'The politics of reporting climate change at the Australian Broadcasting Corporation', *Media International Australia*, 144(1), pp. 37–48.

Climate Council (2019, November 13) *The Facts about Bushfires and Climate Change*. https://www.climatecouncil.org.au/not-normal-climate-change-bushfire-web/

Cottle, S. (2008) *Global crisis reporting: Journalism in the global age*. Maidenhead: McGraw-Hill Education.

Dwyer, T. and Muller, D. (2016) 'FactCheck: Is Australia's level of media ownership concentration one of the highest in the world', *The Conversation*. https://theconversation.com/factcheck-is-australias-level-of-media-ownership-concentration-one-of-the-highest-in-the-world-68437

Eide, E. and Kunelius, R. (2020) 'Climate reporting: Challenges and opportunities' in Holmes, D.C. and Richardson, L.M. (eds.) *Research handbook on communicating climate change*. Cheltenham: Edward Elgar, pp. 164–182.

Fahy, D. (2018) 'Objectivity as trained judgment: How environmental reporters pioneered journalism for a "post-truth" era', *Environmental Communication*, 12(7), pp. 855–861.

Fielding, V. (2023). Conservative advocacy journalism: Explored with a model of journalists' influence on democracy. *Journalism*, 24(8), 1817–1835.

Forde, S. (2017) 'Alternative approaches to environment coverage in the digital era: The Guardian's "Keep it in the Ground" campaign' in Hackett, R.A., Forde, S., Gunster, S. and Foxwell-Norton, K. (eds.) *Journalism and climate crisis*. Oxford: Routledge, pp. 167–187.

Forde, S. (2018) 'Journalism as an advocate for social change and public engagement: Reporting environmental crisis in the digital era' in Schapals, A.K., Bruns, A. and McNair, B. (eds.) *Digitizing democracy*. London: Routledge, pp. 73–87.

Gaber, I. and Tiffen, R. (2018) 'Politics and the media in Australia and the United Kingdom: Parallels and contrasts', *Media International Australia*, 167(1), pp. 27–40. https://doi.org/10.1177/1329878x18766721

Hiles, S.S. and Hinnant, A. (2014) 'Climate change in the newsroom: Journalists' evolving standards of objectivity when covering global warming', *Science Communication*, 36(4), pp. 428–453.

Holmes, D. and Star, C. (2018) 'Climate change communication in Australia: The politics, mainstream media and fossil fuel industry nexus' in *Handbook of climate change communication: Vol. 1: Theory of Climate Change Communication*. Cham: Springer, pp. 151–170.

Ipsos (2022) *The IPSOS Climate Change Report 2022* (Climate Change Report, Issue). https://www.ipsos.com/sites/default/files/ct/publication/documents/2022-04/Ipsos%20Climate%20Change%20Report%202022.pdf

Ipsos (2023) *The IPSOS Climate Change Report 2023* (Climate Change Report, Issue). https://www.ipsos.com/sites/default/files/Ipsos_ClimateChangeReport_2023.pdf

Keane, J. (2009) *The life and death of democracy*. New York: Simon and Schuster.

Koehler, D.J. (2016) 'Can journalistic "false balance" distort public perception of consensus in expert opinion?', *Journal of Experimental Psychology: Applied*, 22(1), p. 24.

Lamb, W.F., Mattioli, G., Levi, S., Roberts, J.T., Capstick, S., Creutzig, F., Minx, J.C., Müller-Hansen, F., Culhane, T. and Steinberger, J.K. (2020) Discourses of climate delay. *Global Sustainability*, 3, e17.

Lester, E. (2013) 'On flak, balance and activism: The ups and downs of environmental journalism' in Tanner, S. and Richardson, N. (eds.) *Journalism research and investigation in a digital world*. South Melbourne: Oxford University Press, pp. 221–231.

Manne, R. (2011) 'Bad news: Murdoch's Australian and the shaping of the nation', *Quarterly Essay*, 43, pp. 1–119.

McAllister, L., Daly, M., Chandler, P., McNatt, M., Benham, A. and Boykoff, M. (2021) 'Balance as bias, resolute on the retreat? Updates & analyses of newspaper coverage in the United States, United Kingdom, New Zealand, Australia and Canada over the past 15 years', *Environmental Research Letters*, 16(9), p. 094008.

McKnight, D. (2010) 'A change in the climate? The journalism of opinion at News Corporation', *Journalism*, 11(6), pp. 693–706.

Mocatta, G., Mayes, E., Hess, K. and Hartup, M.E. (2023) 'The trouble with "quiet advocacy": Local journalism and reporting climate change in rural and regional Australia', *Media, Culture & Society*, 45(1), pp. 157–177.

Morton, A. and Murphy, K. (2022) 'Climate concern the main reason voters swung to independents at federal election, study finds', *The Guardian*. https://www.theguardian.com/australia-news/2022/nov/28/climate-concern-the-main-reason-voters-swung-to-independents-at-federal-election-study-finds

Muller, D. (2023) 'News Corp's policy on the separation of news and comment contradicts a core Press Council principle', *Australian Journalism Review*, 45(1), pp. 7–14.

Murphy, K. (2022) 'Australia's rightwing government weaponised climate change – now it has faced its reckoning', *The Guardian*. https://www.theguardian.com/australia-news/2022/may/22/australia-rightwing-government-weaponised-climate-change-reckoning-scott-morrison

Osaka, S., Painter, J., Walton, P. and Halperin, A. (2020) 'Media representation of extreme event attribution: A case study of the 2011–17 California drought', *Weather, Climate, and Society*, 12(4), pp. 847–862.

Painter, J., Ettinger, J., Doutreix, M.N., Strauß, N., Wonneberger, A. and Walton, P. (2021) 'Is it climate change? Coverage by online news sites of the 2019 European summer heatwaves in France, Germany, the Netherlands, and the UK', *Climatic Change*, 169(1–2). https://doi.org/10.1007/s10584-021-03222-w

Painter, J., Ettinger, J., Holmes, D., Loy, L., Pinto, J., Richardson, L., Thomas-Walters, L., Vowles, K. and Wetts, R. (2023) 'Climate delay discourses present in global mainstream television coverage of the IPCC's 2021 report', *Communications Earth & Environment*, 4(1).

Park, S., McGuinness, K., Fisher, C., Lee, J.Y., McCallum, K. and Nolan, D. (2022) *Digital news report: Australia 2022* (1740885295).

Rice, M., Hughes, L., Steffen, W., Bradshaw, S., Bambrick, H., Hutley, N., Arndt, D., Dean, A. and Morgan, W. (2022) *A supercharged climate: Rain bombs, flash flooding and destruction*. https://www.climatecouncil.org.au/resources/supercharged-climate-rain-bombs-flash-flooding-destruction/

Robbins, D. and Wheatley, D. (2021) 'Complexity, objectivity, and shifting roles: Environmental correspondents march to a changing beat', *Journalism Practice*, 15(9), pp. 1289–1306.

Schäfer, M.S. and Painter, J. (2021) 'Climate journalism in a changing media ecosystem: Assessing the production of climate change-related news around the world', *Wiley Interdisciplinary Reviews: Climate Change*, 12(1), e675.

Schmid-Petri, H., Adam, S., Schmucki, I. and Häussler, T. (2017) 'A changing climate of skepticism: The factors shaping climate change coverage in the US press', *Public Understanding of Science*, 26(4), pp. 498–513.

Schudson, M. (2005) 'The emergence of the objectivity norm in American journalism' in Høyer, S. and Pöttker, H. (eds.) *Diffusion of the news paradigm 1850–2000*. Sweden: Nordicom, University of Gothenburg, pp. 149–170.

Skovsgaard, M., Albæk, E., Bro, P. and de Vreese, C. (2013) 'A reality check: How journalists' role perceptions impact their implementation of the objectivity norm', *Journalism*, 14(1), pp. 22–42. https://doi.org/10.1177/1464884912442286

Strauss, N., Painter, J., Ettinger, J., Doutreix, M.-N., Wonneberger, A. and Walton, P. (2022) 'Reporting on the 2019 European heatwaves and climate change: Journalists' attitudes, motivations and role perceptions', *Journalism Practice*, 16(2–3), pp. 462–485.

· 4 ·

REPORTING PROTESTS AND THE PLANETARY EMERGENCY

César Jiménez-Martínez[1]

Due to declining participation levels in traditional civic organisations such as political parties and trade unions, protests have become in liberal democracies a way for citizens to mobilise identities, strengthen collective solidarity and make visible their concerns and demands in the hope of securing social change. Protests are expressions of contentious collective action, and aim to reconfigure public discourse boundaries by outlining what is possible and appropriate to see and say (Lester and Cottle, 2022). They are especially relevant for groups that lack both time and material resources to channel their claims institutionally, who perceive themselves as far from the centres of power, and who are suspicious of state bureaucracy (Stokes, 2020).

Although governments, politicians and academics often talk about the 'right to protest' as an essential component of civic life, that right is not absolute. Authorities restrict it using excuses such as maintaining public order, protecting national security, and preventing crime. Those in power consequently hold that protests are a valid method of political expression as long as they are 'peaceful' (Butler, 2020; Wall, 2023). Some scholars have echoed this view, arguing that non-violent demonstrations have proved to be more successful than violent ones, and that the latter undermine long-term structural change, discourage potential supporters' engagement and crystalise opposite positions (Fishman, 2024).

The contingent nature of collective action, and the attempts by governments to control and deactivate it, nonetheless make it difficult to objectively agree on what 'peaceful' or non-violent protests are, especially when activists rely on a 'logic of damage' to make their grievances visible (Della Porta and Diani, 2006). Such logic encompasses an array of often law-breaking actions, from traditional non-violent civil disobedience to more radical deeds (Scheuerman, 2022). Complicating matters further, authorities usually ignore 'peaceful' expressions of dissent and draw on ever-expanding definitions of 'violence' to clamp down on civil liberties (Doran, 2017; Moss, 2022). As Butler notes, '[s]tates and institutions sometimes call 'violent' any number of expressions of political dissent, or of opposition to the state or the authority of the institution in question' (Butler, 2020, p. 2). Are consequently marches, sit-ins and strikes a disruption to everyday life or a valid political expression? Is blocking traffic, gluing oneself to a road or throwing soup at a work of art a crime or the exercise of a right? And if these actions are crimes, should only law-abiding demonstrations, previously coordinated with the police – but also predictable and easy to contain – be allowed?

Recent discussions on this topic have looked closely at environmental movements (e.g. Moss, 2022; Scheuerman, 2022; Berglund, 2023). In the UK, groups such as Extinction Rebellion (XR), Insulate Britain and Just Stop Oil – all formed between 2018 and 2022– have been both celebrated and condemned for their reliance on 'non-violent civil disobedience' to call for governments and corporations to urgently act on the climate crisis. Their actions have included slow marching, blocking traffic, gluing themselves to bridges or buildings, vandalising works of art in museums and galleries, interrupting media events, tunnelling under construction works, and being arrested by the police, among others (Berglund, 2023; Fagerholm, Göransson, Thompson and Hedvall, 2023). Recent conservative British governments were highly critical of these activists, calling them 'shameful', 'attention seekers' and 'irresponsible crusties', and expanded police powers to criminalise many of their tactics (Moss, 2022; Cristiano et al., 2023).

'Peaceful' or not, protests are essentially acts of communication, with individuals publicly gathering to direct attention to a cause (Wall, 2023). Failure or success to communicate grievances therefore happen not only on the streets but also in and through forms of media. Yet the media – understood as technologies and organisations – are a contested field, where authorities, activists, journalists, corporations and other actors construct and circulate competing frames and understandings about the legality and legitimacy of collective action, as in the case of environmental activism (Lester and Cottle, 2022; Russell, 2023). The media are consequently an arena where the goals and aims of social movements are supported, discarded or ignored, as well as a space where 'the discursive battle about what is defined as "peaceful" and what as "illegal" or "violent"' (Terwindt, 2014, p. 165) occurs.

This chapter examines these tensions by looking at the visibility of protests by XR, Insulate Britain and Just Stop Oil on legacy and social media in the UK. Drawing on 74 television reports and 1,112 Instagram posts from between 2019 and 2023, the chapter scrutinises the different frames employed by news organisations and environmental activists to represent collective action. The findings show that both news organisations and activists emphasised disruption and depicted protesters as the main source of disorder, thereby stressing the *form* rather than the *content* of protests. This is an important limitation, which risks obscuring more complex debates on the climate crisis. Despite this shortcoming, the fact that activists provided visibility to – and acknowledged responsibility for – their own disruptive actions, sheds light on important questions about the limits of collective action in liberal democracies, especially in a context in which states are increasingly criminalising and restraining public expressions of dissent and defiance.

The contested legitimacy of collective action

The right to protest is considered a cornerstone of liberal democracy but its boundaries are difficult to outline. In the case of the UK, there is no explicit right to protest, yet the European Convention of Human Rights – incorporated into UK law through the 1988 Human Rights Act – protects freedom of assembly and expression (Moss, 2022). In practice however, the legitimacy and legality of collective action is highly contingent, and depends on a combination of factors, such as grievances, political opportunities, protesters' tactics, as well as demonstrators' ability to direct and sustain visibility to their causes (Della Porta, 2008; Cammaerts, 2015; Zlobina and Gonzalez Vazquez, 2018). Protests and state responses to them have also become increasingly complex. Activists have expanded their *repertoires of contention*, relying not only on marches, boycotts and strikes, but also on symbolic tactics and digital self-mediation (della Porta, 2023). In parallel, the *repertoires of containment* of the police have become multifaceted. Security forces have nowadays a broader range of techniques to deal with collective action, from repression and escalated force to 'softer' and more paternalistic approaches, such as negotiated management, non-lethal weapons, preventive arrests and increased surveillance (della Porta and Reiter, 1998; Gillham, 2011).

The above debates point to a deeper friction in liberal democracies, namely the tension between order and liberty. From the perspective of order, protests can effectively give visibility to marginalised groups and potentially act as correctives for democratic shortcomings. Yet on occasions they represent an unpremeditated, violent threat to liberal institutions, that may even overthrow democratically elected governments (Stokes, 2020; Fishman, 2024). Peace and tranquillity should therefore be prioritised when there is tension. From the perspective of liberty, although violence pitched directly at individuals is condemned, law-breaking actions targeted at property are seen as legitimate tactics that increase the visibility of a specific cause (Scheuerman, 2022). Moreover, demonstrations arranged in coordination with the police can be easily neutralised, and containment tactics based on negotiated management may be disguised attempts at surveillance and control (Gillham, 2011; Gilmore, Jackson and Monk, 2019). Hence, 'peaceful' expressions of collective action do not guarantee that grievances will become visible.

The unresolved tensions of what constitutes legal and or legitimate dissent are nonetheless exploited by those in power. In the UK, the 2023 Public Order Act increased police powers by establishing that causing serious disruption by tunnelling or locking-on, obstructing major transport works and interfering with key national infrastructure – all actions employed by environmental movements – are serious criminal offences (Cristiano et al., 2023; Nickolls, 2023). This legislation has been criticised by lawyers, scholars, journalists, NGOs and transnational organisations, arguing that the new punitive measures are highly disproportionate (Moss, 2022). United Nations High Commissioner for Human Rights Volker Türk, stated that the legislation was 'deeply troubling' and mostly targeted individuals taking part in peaceful demonstrations about human rights and environmental issues (Office of the High Commissioner for Human Rights, 2023).

Former British Prime Minister Rishi Sunak justified this legislation as a means to protect the 'lives of the ordinary public' from disruptions caused by a 'small minority' (Prime Minister's Office, 2023). Yet in the same speech he stressed that the right to protest was 'a fundamental principle of our democracy'. Consequently, in the UK and elsewhere, governments navigate the tension between criminalising and protecting the right to protest by categorising demonstrators into two groups. On the one hand, they identify 'bad' protesters, who are allegedly young, driven by crime and disruption, and draw on law-breaking tactics. On the other hand, they describe 'good' protesters as supposedly workers and families, who are driven by clear and 'noble' ends, and rely on law-abiding and predictable tactics (della Porta, 1998; Gillham, 2011; Gilmore et al., 2019). Yet this distinction is based on a short-term perspective, acknowledged by environmental activists (Scheuerman, 2022), which prioritises the maintenance and protection of current social, political and economic arrangements, at the expense of ignoring the slow-burn, long-term, and all-encompassing world threat of the climate and ecological crisis (Cottle, 2023).

The mediated visibility of protest

The media have become essential technologies and institutions to manage the visibility of collective action, with consequences for authorities' responses, audiences' perceptions, and the tactics adopted or abandoned by demonstrators (Kilgo and Harlow, 2019). Those who do not take part directly in protests, become aware of them in and through different kinds of media, and what is shown or concealed through these media is key to enhancing or undermining the legality and legitimacy of protests (Cammaerts, 2024). At the same time, the media have a key role in communicating environmental issues, ideally warning and informing, but often ignoring or marginalising, the climate crisis and wider planetary emergency (Cottle, 2023)

Legacy news organisations still have a wide reach and remain a battleground for narratives produced by authorities, activists, corporations and ordinary citizens on both protests and the climate crisis (Lester and Cottle, 2022; Russell, 2023). In the case of activism, scholars have noted that news media often draw on a 'protest paradigm', a set of journalistic frames that marginalise the causes driving people on to the streets, while heightening the visibility of disruption and violence by demonstrators (McLeod and Hertog, 1999). These frames predominantly underscore the drama and sensationalism of specific, 'episodic' stories centred on riots, confrontations with the police and the oddness or carnival atmosphere of demonstrations. Although more legitimising frames, which give visibility to 'thematic' stories about context and grievances, can potentially emerge, these are infrequent (Kilgo and Harlow, 2019; Wouters, 2015). It is noteworthy that legacy news reporting on the climate crisis echoes the above approach, with an emphasis on specific, isolated 'newsworthy' events instead of broader, complex and long-term perspectives (Cottle, 2023).

While the 'protest paradigm' remains the default analysis position to examine the mediated visibility of unrest (Harlow and Brown, 2023), recent scholarship has called for subtler perspectives. As Cottle (2008) asks, '[d]o the media always, invariably and necessarily impose "definitions of the situation" on protests and dissent which de-legitimize the protesters' aims and coincide with dominant interests?' (p. 856). Studies have provided nuanced answers to that question, observing that legacy media, both local and foreign, occasionally recognise the legitimacy of demonstrations, including those focussed on environmental topics (Kilgo and Harlow, 2019; Jiménez-Martínez, 2021; Cammaerts, 2024). They have also noted that the reliance of legacy media on legitimising or delegitimising narratives is contingent (Harlow, Kilgo, Salaverría and García-Perdomo, 2020), and that the interests of news organisations may conflict with those of authorities (Shahin, Zheng, Sturm and Fadnis, 2016).

The protest paradigm also assumes that journalistic emphases on damage distort the supposedly 'peaceful' nature of protests, and that a focus on disruption necessarily leads to delegitimisation (Jiménez-Martínez, 2021). Yet this perspective glosses over how activists, as part of their repertoires of contention, occasionally act outside of the law, as environmental groups have done (Della Porta and Diani, 2006; Scheuerman, 2022). Moreover, citizens sometimes justify 'non-peaceful' protests for being more efficient than 'peaceful' ones (Zlobina and Gonzalez Vazquez, 2018). Authorities in turn, as part of their repertoires of containment, use the excuse of 'violence' to justify restrictions on civil rights and neutralise collective action, as has been seen in the UK and elsewhere (Doran, 2017; Moss, 2022).

Environmental protests in UK television and Instagram

Studies on protest news coverage frequently examine newspapers, overlooking how television is a more popular source of news (Robertson, Chirioiu and Ceder, 2019). In the UK, despite declining audiences, television remains the most consumed and trusted legacy source of news, way above print media (Newman, Fletcher, Eddy, Robertson and Nielsen, 2023). Television features such as the focus on images, personalisation, simplification and the emphasis on episodic stories, seem to favour a fragmented, dramatic and spectacular version of the world rather than a broader, nuanced and thoughtful picture (Cottle, 2023; García-Perdomo, Magaña, Hernández-Rodríguez and Ventín-Sánchez, 2023). Scholars have noted however that television, especially in societies with public broadcasters, has the *potential* to avoid these marginalising features, for instance, by shedding light on grievances driving collective action as well as by glossing over political and corporate interests seeking to downplay the climate crisis (Wouters, 2015; Debrett, 2017).

The above observations are important in the UK context, where television is characterised by a mixture of a strong public service broadcaster, namely the BBC, and commercial stations – both publicly and privately owned – such as ITV, Channel 4 and Channel 5. British television is highly regulated, with newscasts expected to be impartial, fair and balanced, although BBC is under greater scrutiny than commercial broadcasters (Cushion, Kilby, Thomas, Morani and Sambrook, 2018). Activists nonetheless approach television – and legacy media in general – with suspicion. They often rely on self-mediation tactics, such as flyers, posters, theatre, community radio and digital platforms, in order to coordinate actions, make grievances visible, provide supposedly more balanced viewpoints, and direct attention to episodes of police abuse (Lester and Cottle, 2022; Cammaerts, 2024).

Although digital media were originally praised for apparently facilitating the coordination and communication of collective action (e.g. Shirky, 2008), less celebratory perspectives have emerged in recent years. Scholars have stressed that digital media can be used as instruments of surveillance by authorities, that technology corporations are guided by commercial interests rather than progressive politics, that digital platforms often provide hyper-visibility to voices poisoning debates on the climate crisis, and that activists seeking social media visibility may echo legacy media by stressing the drama and spectacle of protests at the expense of grievances and context (Poell, 2014; Jiménez-Martínez, 2021; Russell, 2023). Moreover, legacy and digital media have increasingly fuzzy boundaries. Contents produced by mainstream media organisations are accessed and recycled via social media, and audiences often share, comment and contest these contents in and through digital platforms (Chadwick, 2013; García-Perdomo et al., 2023; Cammaerts, 2024). In addition, legacy news organisations have partnered with social media platforms, or have adopted online or hybrid models to deliver their journalistic content (Russell, 2023).

However, differences between legacy and digital media persist. Generational divides remain in terms of consumption, with older audiences preferring legacy media – especially television – and younger ones counting on social media such as Facebook, but increasingly YouTube and Instagram, as sources of news (Newman et al., 2023). Production costs and access to mainstream television remain prohibitive for activists, who continue to rely on digital platforms, notwithstanding the commercially driven nature of the latter (Poell, 2014). As a result, it is worthwhile to examine how mainstream journalists *represent* environmental protests as well as how activists digitally *self-mediate* their expressions of dissent (see also Cammaerts, 2024).

With that aim, two undergraduate students were trained as research assistants to collect and analyse content from legacy and social media. For television, the 10 p.m. flagship news bulletins of both BBC and ITV were chosen, because these bulletins are the most consumed sources of legacy news in the UK (Newman et al., 2023). Regional newscasts were not considered, in order to focus only on stories broadcast nationally. This coverage was contrasted with self-mediation practices by the official accounts of XR, Insulate Britain and Just Stop Oil on Instagram, a visually based platform that has become popular among environmental movements[2] (Fagerholm et al., 2023). Research assistants mapped television reports and Instagram posts produced between January 2019 (a few months after Extinction Rebellion was formed) and June 2023, when the study was conducted.

Data was coded using frames defined after several rounds of inductive analysis, which expanded on those suggested by the protest paradigm (McLeod and Hertog, 1999). They were: (1) *Disruption/Disobedience*, that is, portrayals emphasising deviant, destructive or disobedient behaviour by activists; (2) *Confrontation*, which are clashes between protesters with the police or counter-protesters; (3) *Police Abuse / Arrests*, which is coverage of police brutality, abuses or arrests; (4) *Grievances*, that is mentions of the grievances and goals of these movements; (5) *Calls for Action*, namely attempts to mobilise people to act on the climate crisis; and (6) *Trials/Court Cases*, that is, descriptions of court hearings and trials involving activists. In addition to these frames, research assistants coded who was blamed for disruption or damage, the different types of sources appearing on television and Instagram, and whether stories were 'episodic', that is, focussed on a singular event, or 'thematic', namely depicting grievances and context.

Findings: Disruption and disobedience on legacy and social media

Environmental protests on BBC and ITV

The first relevant observation emerged when mapping the data. During the examined timespan, BBC and ITV broadcast only N = 74 (BBC n = 27, ITV

n = 47) reports in their flagship bulletins. This result was surprising, despite the expectation of finding a smaller number of items in television in comparison to Instagram (see next section). Some disruptive actions, such as when members of XR poured fake blood outside of Downing Street on 9 March 2019 (Mohdin and Carrell, 2019), were not screened on national television, but only in regional bulletins such as BBC London or ITV News London. Hence, British television considered environmental protests only occasionally as newsworthy for the whole country.

Another important finding referred to dominant frames. Echoing the protest paradigm literature (McLeod and Hertog, 1999), broadcasters made dissent visible predominantly through a delegitimising lens, with more than half of all stories framed as *Disruption/Disobedience* (56.8%, n = 42). Journalists therefore stressed behaviours considered by the media and/or authorities as disruptive, deviant or criminal. Notwithstanding the emphasis on noise and spectacle, an important number of reports were about *Grievances* (36.5%, n = 27). There were also a limited number of stories about *Police Abuse/Arrest* (5.4%, n = 4), which focussed on the arrests of demonstrators. Unsurprisingly, neither BBC nor ITV had features calling for people to join protests. It was also noted that there was no news about the court cases that followed the arrests of some activists (Table 4.1).

In line with the above findings, most reports (85.1%, n = 63) depicted activists as the main source of actions qualified as disruptive, damaging or criminal. Although demonstrators were sometimes blamed *alongside* the police (5.5%, n = 4), the latter were never portrayed as responsible for disruption on their own. A small number of reports did not discuss this topic at all (8.1%, n = 6) and on one occasion (1.3%, n = 1) other citizens were blamed for disorder or

Table 4.1. Dominant Frames on Television

Dominant frame	Total percentage (%)	Number	BBC (n)	ITV (n)
Disruption/Disobedience	56.8	42	16	26
Grievances	36.5	27	8	19
Police Abuse/Arrest	5.4	4	2	2
Confrontation	1.3	1	1	0
Trials/Court Cases	0.0	0	0	0
Calls for Action	0.0	0	0	0
Total	100.00	74	27	47

damage. The emphasis on the most dramatic facets of dissent was also evident when noting that news items were predominantly episodic (68.9%, n = 51) rather than thematic (31.1%, n = 23). Hence, the coverage on BBC and ITV stressed specific events instead of context, causes and solutions. This is an important observation. In other European countries, public television broadcasters frequently report demonstrations through a thematic lens, which provides visibility to broader issues rather than the spectacle of a single disruptive incident (Wouters, 2015).

The focus on the drama of protests may contradict that, as seen above, more than a third of reports corresponded to the frame *Grievances*. However, news items were generally short, lasting on average around 90 seconds, that is, 1.59 minutes (1.44 minutes on BBC, 1.74 minutes on ITV). It is therefore likely that journalists may have effectively mentioned the reasons driving the actions by XR, Insulate Britain and Just Stop Oil, but only discussed them in a cursory way. Significantly, although the protest paradigm literature holds that legacy media emphasise official viewpoints to the detriment of demonstrators (McLeod and Hertog, 1999), activists were effectively granted voice and visibility. When looking at source type, protesters were the most prevalent (41.9% of total reports, n = 31), followed by celebrities supporting environmental activists (22.9%, n = 17). Only then politicians and state representatives were quoted (18.9%, n = 14). Yet this attention should not necessarily be equated with securing legitimacy. Legacy news media may provide limited degrees of visibility to expressions of dissent, in order to emphasise their supposedly deviant or 'radical' features (Cammaerts, 2015).

Self-mediation practices on Instagram

In contrast to television, the three environmental movements produced a greater amount of content on Instagram, with a total of N=1,112 posts associated with demonstrations (Insulate Britain n = 158, XR n = 224, Just Stop Oil n = 730). Despite this increased number, frame variations were not that significant. Although the proportion of posts about *Disruption/Disobedience* was lower than television (42.2%, n = 469), these constituted the largest frame chosen by environmental movements. This focus on disruption confirms that activists effectively drew on a 'logic of damage' (Della Porta and Diani, 2006) to direct attention to the climate crisis. Echoing legacy media, the second most used frame was *Grievances* (37.1%, n = 413). Differences were found only in other, less frequent frames. While the proportion of stories about *Police Abuse/*

Arrest (9.4%, *n* = 105) and *Confrontation* (2.0%, *n* = 22) was small, it was still higher than television. In addition, there were posts calling audiences to mobilise (3.4%, *n* = 38), as well as entries focussed on the trials faced by members of the examined movements (5.9%, *n* = 65) (Table 4.2).

Most sources in these posts were protesters themselves (45.9% of all Instagram posts, *n* = 510). They were followed by citizens (4.4%, *n* = 49), experts (2.9%, *n* = 33), police (2.9%, *n* = 32), politicians (1.8%, *n* = 20) and celebrities (1.7%, *n* = 19). This should not come as a surprise. Social movements approach digital media as part of their toolbox to increase the visibility of their causes and goals (Cammaerts, 2024). Hence, rather than pretending to be impartial, balanced and detached in the vein of mainstream journalism, Instagram posts seek to make visible the official viewpoints of XR, Insulate Britain and Just Stop Oil, only occasionally requiring other voices to support their arguments.

Significantly, the narratives produced by environmental activists were far from sanitised. Most Instagram posts featured demonstrators as the main source of disruption (70.1%, *n* = 779), followed by the police (0.7%, *n* = 8) and other citizens (0.5%, *n* = 6). Although another small, relevant number of stories did not discuss responsibility for disorder at all (25.8%, *n* = 286), the findings suggest that environmental activists portrayed themselves as accountable for their disruptive actions, confirming the importance they give to potentially law-breaking tactics. The focus on disruption can however be a risky strategy. Like legacy media, most Instagram posts were episodic (70.2%, *n* = 781) rather than thematic (29.8%, *n* = 331), and therefore stressed specific events instead of context and grievances. It is nonetheless relevant that only a small number

Table 4.2. Dominant Frames on Social Media

Dominant frame	Total percentage (%)	Number	Extinction rebellion UK (*n*)	Insulate Britain (*n*)	Just stop oil (*n*)
Disruption/ Disobedience	42.2	469	76	63	274
Grievances	37.1	413	116	75	278
Police Abuse/Arrest	9.4	105	16	8	81
Trials/Court Cases	5.9	65	4	7	54
Calls for Action	3.4	38	12	5	21
Confrontation	2.0	22	0	0	22
Total	100.0	1,112	224	158	730

of posts depicted protesters *alongside* the police as the cause of disorders (2.9%, $n = 33$). Hence, although environmental movements directed attention to disruptive tactics, they avoided framing their actions as a violent battle between themselves and security forces (see also Scheuerman, 2022).

Concluding observations: Mirages of democratic participation

A first look at the legacy news media representation of protests by XR, Insulate Britain and Just Stop Oil, suggests that television newscasts emphasised the most disruptive characteristics of collective action, repeatedly framing protests as deviant and criminal acts. Stories centred predominantly on specific events rather than broader issues, and environmental activists were depicted as the main source of disruption and/or damage. In line with the 'protest paradigm' (McLeod and Hertog, 1999), the emphasis on drama and spectacle confirms that dissent tactics drawing on disobedience and potentially law-breaking actions may secure mediated visibility, but at the cost of concealing the reasons driving people on to the streets. Although legacy media may provide some visibility to the causes and context of collective action – as seen by the relative salience of the *Grievances* frame – their role aligns more closely with the policing of protests than with a liberal-democratic forum where public deliberations on the climate crisis are staged. This is a relevant observation, when taking into account that journalistic frames focussed on disruption and alleged deviant behaviours may add to the justifications facilitating the criminalisation of collective action (see Cristiano et al., 2023).

It is significant that the visibility of climate and ecological protests in legacy media was limited, notwithstanding the focus on the spectacle and drama of disruption. The number of television reports about XR, Insulate Britain and Just Stop Oil in the examined timespan was relatively low, and the length of each story was on average less than 2 minutes. BBC and ITV therefore portrayed these groups in a flickering, intermittent manner rather than as manifestations of an urgent planetary problem or, conversely, expressions of impending social chaos. Following Di Cicco, they were shown as 'irritating and worthless, and something most would prefer to ignore – a nuisance' (2010, p. 137). This observation corroborates how, despite the efforts of many journalists specialising in environmental topics, news media tend to focus on discreet, isolated 'newsworthy' events, rather than on complex, long-term and holistic debates on the climate and ecological crisis (Cottle, 2023; Russell, 2023). In addition, it suggests a dissonance between the limited interest of television and the reaction of authorities. Unlike British right-wing newspapers, television did not seem to hypervisibilise environmental movements as a significant threat, which was one of the tenets of the culture wars fostered by UK conservative governments in recent years (Moss, 2022; Cristiano et al., 2023).

Relatedly, the examination of self-mediation tactics by XR, Insulate Britain and Just Stop Oil on Instagram provided some unexpected insights. The three groups produced a greater amount of content in comparison with national television. However, their posts largely echoed legacy media and did not make visible a substantially different narrative. Although there were some variations with broadcasters, including the attention that court case stories received, activists generally stressed the most disruptive features of collective action, underlining actions that embraced disorder and a 'logic of damage' (Della Porta and Diani, 2006; Berglund, 2023).

Although a focus on episodic and spectacular occurrences may reward these groups with (some of) the mediated visibility promised by digital platforms in the forms of likes and shares, their most dramatic Instagram posts risk becoming only fleeting glimpses that obscure the reasons driving activists to the streets (see Poell, 2014). Furthermore, the transitory nature of social media content may prompt environmental movements to direct their efforts to being noticed only, instead of being noticed to advance the slower and less notorious structural changes required to mitigate the climate crisis. Hence, they may end up approaching mediated visibility as an 'end it itself, rather than a route to politics' (Banet-Weiser, 2015, p. 55; see also Jiménez-Martínez and Edwards, 2023). Finally, an emphasis on social media notoriety risks feeding the narrative – often pushed by information technology companies – that, in a context of increasing legal risks for collective action, digital platforms are 'the' space where people gather to channel their demands, instead of being acknowledged as pro-market sites that often privilege noise and drama instead of deliberation and social justice (Lester and Cottle, 2022; Cristiano et al., 2023; Russell, 2023).

The above findings suggest that both television broadcasters and environmental movements paid more attention to the *form* rather than the *content* of protests. When this happens, and debates centre on whether collective action is 'peaceful' or 'disruptive', and whether protesters or authorities are to blame for 'violence', 'the state will have succeeded in turning participants' attention completely away from politics . . . and away from other conversations, such as those about the current distribution and functioning of economic and political power' (LeNabat, 2012, p. 468). There are nonetheless hopeful signs. In early 2023, XR announced that it would retreat from disruptive actions and would instead seek to build wider relationships in civil society (Booth, 2023), thus revealing a clear awareness of some of the hazards of their communication strategy to date. At the same time, XR, Insulate Britain and Just Stop Oil have tried to avoid some of the pitfalls that an exclusive focus on the 'violent' or 'peaceful' character of protests presents. It is significant that the three groups eschewed discussions on culpability by avoiding direct confrontations with the police as well as stories that could fall into a 'reversed protest paradigm', which emphasise abuses by security forces to the detriment of grievances (Jiménez-Martínez, 2021).

Crucially, environmental activists did not shy away of assuming responsibility for disruptive and even law-breaking actions, openly embracing the mediated visibility of disruption and disobedience, and therefore questioning the official boundaries of what comprises acceptable forms of defiance. This is significant, because legacy media have traditionally perpetuated the authorities' viewpoints and definitions of what constitutes 'violent' or 'peaceful' protest (McLeod and Hertog, 1999). Yet these definitions are rarely neutral (Butler, 2020). In the case of the UK, despite nominally respecting the right to protest, recent governments have increasingly sought to neutralise it, favouring 'peaceful' but ultimately bland expressions of collective action (Moss, 2022; Cristiano et al., 2023). In consequence, groups such as Extinction Rebellion, Insulate Britain and Just Stop Oil are shedding light on a worrying trend, namely of states increasingly manufacturing mirages of democratic participation. These mirages encourage innocuous *performances* of collective action that pose little challenge to dominant social, political, and economic arrangements. Yet by questioning these illusions, activists interrogate ever-expanding definitions of 'violence' that criminalise opposition to the status quo, and underscore the fuzzy and contested margins of what exactly constitutes legitimate expressions of dissent in a liberal democracy.

Notes

1 Research for this chapter was funded through a Cardiff University Research Internship 2023. I am extremely grateful to my brilliant research assistants, Tess Hanson and Lacey-Mae Mannell, for their help, creativity, and insights. Any mistakes are mine alone.

2 Although these movements have YouTube channels, Instagram was chosen because at the time of the data collection, two of them had a slightly larger number of followers on this

platform (Extinction Rebellion UK had 102K followers on Instagram vs 77.8K on YouTube; Insulate Britain, 4.1K on Instagram vs 1.61K on YouTube; Just Stop Oil, 70.1K on Instagram vs 84.9K on YouTube).

References

Banet-Weiser, S. (2015) 'Keynote address: Media, markets, gender: Economies of visibility in a neoliberal moment', *The Communication Review*, 18(1), pp. 53–70. https://doi.org/10.1080/10714421.2015.996398

Berglund, O. (2023) 'Disruptive protest, civil disobedience & direct action', *Politics*, 026339572311769. https://doi.org/10.1177/02633957231176999

Booth, R. (2023, January 1) 'Extinction Rebellion announces move away from disruptive tactics', *The Guardian*. Retrieved from https://www.theguardian.com/world/2023/jan/01/extinction-rebellion-announces-move-away-from-disruptive-tactics

Butler, J. (2020) *The force of nonviolence: An ethico-political bind*. London; New York: Verso.

Cammaerts, B. (2015) Neoliberalism and the post-hegemonic war of position: The dialectic between invisibility and visibilities. *European Journal of Communication*, 30(5), pp. 522–538. https://doi.org/10.1177/0267323115597847

Cammaerts, B. (2024) 'The mediated circulation of the United Kingdom's YouthStrike4Climate movement's discourses and actions', *European Journal of Cultural Studies*, 27(1), pp. 107–128. https://doi.org/10.1177/13675494231165645

Chadwick, A. (2013) *The hybrid media system: Politics and power*. Oxford, UK: Oxford University Press.

Cottle, S. (2008) 'Reporting demonstrations: The changing media politics of dissent', *Media, Culture & Society*, 30(6), pp. 853–872. https://doi.org/10.1177/0163443708096097

Cottle, S. (2023) 'Reporting civilizational collapse: Research notes from a world-in-crisis', *Global Media and Communication*, 19(2), pp. 269–288. https://doi.org/10.1177/17427665231186934

Cristiano, F., Dadusc, D., Davanna, T., Duff, K., Gilmore, J., Rossdale, C., et al. (2023) 'Criminalisation of political activism: A conversation across disciplines', *Critical Studies on Security*, 11(2), pp. 106–125. https://doi.org/10.1080/21624887.2023.2188628

Cushion, S., Kilby, A., Thomas, R., Morani, M. and Sambrook, R. (2018) 'Newspapers, impartiality and television news: Intermedia agenda-setting during the 2015 UK General Election campaign', *Journalism Studies*, 19(2), pp. 162–181. https://doi.org/10.1080/1461670X.2016.1171163

Debrett, M. (2017) 'Representing climate change on public service television: A case study', *Public Understanding of Science*, 26(4), pp. 452–466. https://doi.org/10.1177/0963662515597187

della Porta, D. (1998) 'Police knowledge and protest policing: Some reflections on the Italian case' in della Porta, D. and Reiter, H. (eds.) *Policing protest: The control of mass demonstrations in Western democracies*. Minneapolis; London: University of Minnesota Press, pp. 228–252.

della Porta, D. (2023) 'Repertoires of contention' in Snow, D., Della Porta, D. and McAdam, D. (eds.) *The Wiley-Blackwell encyclopedia of social and political movements*. Malden, MA: Blackwell Publishing. https://onlinelibrary.wiley.com/doi/full/10.1002/9780470674871.wbespm178.pub2

Della Porta, D. (2008) 'Research on social movements and political violence', *Qualitative Sociology*, 31(3), pp. 221–230. https://doi.org/10.1007/s11133-008-9109-x

Della Porta, D. and Diani, M. (2006) *Social movements: An introduction*. 2nd edn. Malden, MA: Blackwell Publishing.

della Porta, D. and Reiter, H. (1998) 'Introduction: The policing of protest in Western democracies' in della Porta, D. and Reiter, H. (eds.) *Policing protest: The control of mass demonstrations in Western democracies*. Minneapolis; London: University of Minnesota Press, pp. 1–31.

Di Cicco, D.T. (2010) 'The public nuisance paradigm: Changes in mass media coverage of political protest since the 1960s', *Journalism and Mass Communication Quarterly*, 87(1), pp. 135–153. https://doi.org/10.1177/107769901008700108

Doran, M.C. (2017) 'The hidden face of violence in Latin America: Assessing the criminalization of protest in comparative perspective', *Latin American Perspectives*, 44(5), pp. 183–206. https://doi.org/10.1177/0094582X17719258

Fagerholm, A.S., Göransson, K., Thompson, L. and Hedvall, P.O. (2023) 'Activism online: Exploring how crises are communicated visually in activism campaigns', *Journal of Contingencies and Crisis Management*, 31(4), pp. 1034–1043. https://doi.org/10.1111/1468-5973.12472

Fishman, R.M. (2024) 'Deepening or endangering democracy: Demonstrations and institutions under representative government', *Perspectives on Politics*, 1–10. https://doi.org/10.1017/S1537592723002955

García-Perdomo, V., Magaña, M.I., Hernández-Rodríguez, J.C. and Ventín-Sánchez, J.A. (2023) 'Engaging social media audiences with riots: TV and newspapers' coverage of the 2019 protests in Colombia and Chile', *International Communication Gazette*. https://doi.org/10.1177/17480485231206363

Gillham, P.F. (2011) 'Securitizing America: Strategic incapacitation and the policing of protest since the 11 September 2001 terrorist attacks', *Sociology Compass*, 5(7), pp. 636–652. https://doi.org/10.1111/j.1751-9020.2011.00394.x

Gilmore, J., Jackson, W. and Monk, H. (2019) '"That is not facilitating peaceful protest. That is dismantling the protest": Anti-fracking protesters' experiences of dialogue policing and mass arrest', *Policing and Society*, 29(1), pp. 36–51. https://doi.org/10.1080/10439463.2017.1319365

Harlow, S. and Brown, D.K. (2023) 'A new protest paradigm: Toward a critical approach to protest news analyses', *The International Journal of Press/Politics*, 28(2), pp. 333–343. https://doi.org/10.1177/19401612231153377

Harlow, S., Kilgo, D.K., Salaverría, R. and García-Perdomo, V. (2020) 'Is the whole world watching? Building a typology of protest coverage on social media from around the world', *Journalism Studies*, 21(11), pp. 1590–1608. https://doi.org/10.1080/1461670X.2020.1776144

Jiménez-Martínez, C. (2021) 'The instrumental mediated visibility of violence: The 2013 protests in Brazil and the limitations of the protest paradigm', *The International Journal of Press/Politics*, 26(3), pp. 525–546. https://doi.org/10.1177/1940161220923984

Jiménez-Martínez, C. and Edwards, L. (2023) 'The promotional regime of visibility: Ambivalence and contradiction in strategies of dominance and resistance', *Communication and the Public*, 8(1), pp. 14–28. https://doi.org/10.1177/20570473221146661

Kilgo, D.K. and Harlow, S. (2019) 'Protests, media coverage, and a hierarchy of social struggle', *The International Journal of Press/Politics*, 24(4), pp. 508–530. https://doi.org/10.1177/1940161219853517

LeNabat, M. (2012) 'On non-violence: An Arendtian perspective on recent political movements', *International Critical Thought*, 2(4), pp. 456–471. https://doi.org/10.1080/21598282.2012.730373

Lester, L. and Cottle, S. (2022) 'Protests, publics and participation (still in an environmental age)' in *The Routledge handbook of environment and communication*. London: Routledge, pp. 146–156. https://doi.org/10.4324/9781003119234-12

McLeod, D.M. and Hertog, J. (1999) 'Social control, social change and the mass media's role in the regulation of protest groups', in Demers, D. and Viswanath, K. (eds.) *Mass media, social control and social change: A macrosocial perspective*. Ames: Iowa State University Press, pp. 305–330.

Mohdin, A. and Carrell, S. (2019, March 9) 'Extinction Rebellion activists throw 'blood' outside Downing Street', *The Guardian*. Retrieved from https://www.theguardian.com/uk-news/2019/mar/09/extinction-rebellion-activists-arrested-over-scottish-oil-protest

Moss, K. (2022) 'Security or liberty? Human rights and protest' in Gill, M. (ed.) *The handbook of security*. Cham: Palgrave Macmillan, pp. 751–776. https://doi.org/10.1007/978-3-030-91735-7_35

Newman, N., Fletcher, R., Eddy, K., Robertson, C. and Nielsen, R.K. (2023) *Reuters Institute Digital News Report 2023*. Retrieved from https://reutersinstitute.politics.ox.ac.uk/sites/default/files/2023-06/Digital_News_Report_2023.pdf

Nickolls, L. (2023) *Police powers: Protest*. London: House of Commons Library. Retrieved from https://researchbriefings.files.parliament.uk/documents/SN05013/SN05013.pdf

Office of the High Commissioner for Human Rights (2023, April 27) *UN Human Rights Chief urges UK to reverse 'deeply troubling' Public Order Bill*. Retrieved from https://www.ohchr.org/en/press-releases/2023/04/un-human-rights-chief-urges-uk-reverse-deeply-troubling-public-order-bill

Poell, T. (2014) 'Social media and the transformation of activist communication: Exploring the social media ecology of the 2010 Toronto G20 protests', *Information, Communication & Society*, 17(6), pp. 716–731. https://doi.org/10.1080/1369118X.2013.812674

Prime Minister's Office (2023) *PM takes action to stop disruptive protests*. Retrieved 15 January 2024, from https://www.gov.uk/government/news/pm-takes-action-to-stop-disruptive-protests

Robertson, A., Chirioiu, L. and Ceder, M. (2019) 'The protest paradigm and global television news narratives of dissent' in Robertson, A. (ed.) *Screening protest: Visual narratives of dissent across time, space and genre*. London; New York: Routledge, pp. 49–73.

Russell, A. (2023) *The mediated climate: How journalists, big tech, and activists are vying for our future*. New York: Columbia University Press.

Scheuerman, W.E. (2022) 'Political disobedience and the climate emergency', *Philosophy and Social Criticism*, 48(6), pp. 791–812. https://doi.org/10.1177/01914537211040566

Shahin, S., Zheng, P., Sturm, H.A. and Fadnis, D. (2016) 'Protesting the paradigm: A comparative study of news coverage of protests in Brazil, China, and India', *International Journal of Press/Politics*, 21(2), pp. 143–164. https://doi.org/10.1177/1940161216631114

Shirky, C. (2008) *Here comes everybody: The power of organizing without organizations*. New York: Penguin Press.

Stokes, S. (2020) 'Are protests good or bad for democracy?' in Schwartzberg, M. (ed.) *Protest and dissent*. New York: New York University Press, pp. 269–284. https://doi.org/10.18574/nyu/9781479810512.003.0011

Terwindt, C. (2014) 'Criminalization of social protest: Future research', *Oñati: Socio-Legal Series*, 4(1), pp. 161–169.

Wall, I. rua (2023) 'The right to protest', *The International Journal of Human Rights*, October, 1–16. https://doi.org/10.1080/13642987.2023.2262395

Wouters, R. (2015) 'Reporting demonstrations: On episodic and thematic coverage of protest events in Belgian television news', *Political Communication*, 32(3), pp. 475–496. https://doi.org/10.1080/10584609.2014.958257

Zlobina, A. and Gonzalez Vazquez, A. (2018) 'What is the right way to protest? On the process of justification of protest, and its relationship to the propensity to participate in different types of protest', *Social Movement Studies*, 17(2), pp. 234–250. https://doi.org/10.1080/14742837.2017.1393408

Section II:

Community Activism Harnessing Media and Hope

· 5 ·

FROM CLIMATE CRISIS TO ENVIRONMENT(AL) HOPE: COMMUNITY, AFFECT AND LOCAL TELEVISION

Elke Weissmann and Belinda Tyrrell

Culture is ordinary: that is where we must start.

Williams (1989 [1958], p. 3)

You may wonder why a chapter in a book focused on the reporting of the world-in-crisis starts with such a general remark on culture. What does the climate crisis and the reporting of it, which is the focus of this chapter, have to do with the very ordinariness of culture? And why do we feel the need to state the ordinariness of culture in the context of the reporting of the climate crisis? The answer is relatively simple, and yet we will need the whole of the chapter to explain it: as we are looking to explore how we can report the climate crisis in ways that encourage more people to take measures to reduce their impact on the planet, it is in the recognition of the ordinariness of culture that a potential solution lies.

Raymond Williams explicated this ordinariness by describing a bus journey through the Welsh borderlands in which he was born. There, culture exists within the historic, economic and educational conditions that are specific to the area and the people who live there. By describing culture both as a lived experience and as the art that comes from that lived experience, Williams radically challenged then received assumptions of what culture was and could be: everyone participated in a culture, culture wasn't confined to the bourgeoisie, and culture was locally situated and specific.

While this explanation is helpful to understand more about what Williams meant with his simple pronouncement, it still does not address what this has to do with the reporting of climate change. Climate change now often dominates the news agenda during the summer months when the effects of a warming planet are increasingly being felt in places that are physically and mentally close even to countries so far largely shielded from the effects of it. This includes Southern Europe where in 2023 fires and, alternating, heavy rainfall destroyed regions where Northern Europeans like to holiday. Stories about, for example, British tourists being evacuated from Rhodes were headline news on most UK broadcasters (ITV News, 2023; Robinson, 2023) and in the major British newspapers (Halliday, 2023; Keane, 2023). No longer, then, can the news be criticised for reporting climate change as something spatially or temporally distant (Beattie and McGuire, 2018); however, now the persistent representation of a planet at its tipping point, where natural disasters regularly kill people and destroy natural habitats and environmental beauty, can lead to what psychologists have termed eco- or climate anxiety (Vakoch and Mickey, 2022; Whitmarsh et al., 2022). This anxiety unfortunately can lead to paralysis; thus, rather than motivating people to spring into action to combat climate change, it can lead to non-action, particularly if people experience a high level of eco-anxiety (Heeren et al., 2022; Innocenti et al., 2023). It is therefore important that the media do not just tell stories of catastrophes and disasters, but also offer moments of hope; we believe that this hope can be found in Williams's pronouncement of 'culture being ordinary': by recognising that every day, people respond already in ways that are specific to their culture to the challenges that climate change is bringing.

In the following, we expand on this by reporting back from a project conducted in 2022 with a local community interest company (Love Wavertree CIC) in Liverpool, UK. The project involved the making of eight programmes: four about climate assemblies that we ran on behalf of Love Wavertree, and four on local projects that involved climate actions. Some of these programmes were then screened at a local venue and all were made available via YouTube and shared in the local community. This was then followed by a qualitative questionnaire to find out what viewers made of the programmes. We also conducted a survey before the filming started in the local community as well as six unstructured interviews with local residents in order to get a sense of how the local community felt about and what they knew about climate change. We worked closely with Love Wavertree throughout the filming; thus, we also became deeply embedded in the local community which led to the collection of extensive fieldnotes. Overall, this gave us a good sense of how the community experienced the growing evidence of climate change and how they responded to it. What struck us is that, over the course of the project from March to June 2022, there was a noticeable affective change, and it is this change from despondency and frustration to hope, that we want to focus on. While the project was small-scale and time-limited, the findings are significant enough for us to suggest that they offer lessons for media creators, policy makers as well as activists. We want to explain and theorise these lessons by drawing on Williams's body of work in which he provided suggestions to understand culture and politics, including climate politics, as something that is situated in the everyday and ordinariness of people's lives. Before we delve into our findings, we want to lay out some of the problems other scholars have identified in relation to the media and its reporting of climate change.

The media and the climate problem

Research on the media and climate change has increased significantly over the last fifteen years. One central concern, namely the environmental impact of the media (Maxwell and Miller, 2012; Kääpä and Vaughan, 2022) has led to a number of interventions, such as BAFTA's Albert initiative, to make media production itself more sustainable (Lopera-Mármol and Jiménez-Morales, 2021). Such initiatives also make visible that the industry itself wants to do their bit in the fight against climate change – though they struggle with finding ways to inspire others (Smith, 2022).

The question of how the media can be used to communicate climate change in ways that lead to actions that reduce the environmental impact of individual consumers has occupied a large number of scholars, not just in the field of media studies (e.g. Doyle, 2011) but also psychology (e.g. Beattie and McGuire, 2018), education (e.g. Verlie, 2023) and public health (e.g. Innocenti et al., 2023). Much of the research has focused on journalism and news production (Boyce and Lewis, 2009; Gavin, 2009; Olausson and Berglez, 2017; Pinto et al., 2019) and is largely written from a Global North perspective. A key concern that has emerged is that climate change continues to be experienced as temporally distant even though more reporting of it is occurring (Adam, 2022). Barbara Adam highlights that this is due to a temporal disconnect between the ongoing climate emergency and the 'news' values that structure journalism. As she writes:

> The very idea of 'news' has embedded within it a number of implicit, taken-for-granted assumptions. [. . .] To be newsworthy, therefore, an article, broadcast or blog is expected to be characterised by urgency, immediacy, timeliness, novelty or at least recency. These values are well suited to single *climate disasters*, such as damaging floods or wildfires burning out of control, given that they are occurring in the present. They sit less well with issues of climate *change* that are complex, systemic, ongoing, indeterminate and often so extended as to be imperceptible within single life times. (2022, p. xiii, original italics)

This focus on newsworthiness also creates the problem of reporting precisely *disasters* and *catastrophes* that emphasise death and destruction and thus connect to existential threats which Joseph Rehling (2022) has examined in relation to feelings of powerlessness connected to climate anxiety. While he points to the fact that feelings connected to death can lead to greater motivations to activism, he also argues that 'our collective inertia in the face of crisis [can be explained by] a process of existential denial similar to the one that keeps us from panic despite the knowledge of our inevitable death' (2022, p. 483). Thus, the more we feel under existential threat, the more we turn to denial, suggesting that a focus on the world-in-crisis in reporting might be counterproductive, particularly if this is the only message we hear (McWhirter, 2022, p. 183).

It is perhaps for that reason that a number of broadcasters, and indeed scientists, emphasise that there is still hope – if we do something now. This message was, amongst others, strongly conveyed by the 2023 *Synthesis Report on Climate Change* by the Intergovernmental Panel on Climate Change which its president António Guterrez described as a 'survival guide' (McGrath and Rannard, 2023). Similarly, David Attenborough's appeal to audiences in *Extinction: The Facts* (BBC, PBS, 2020) ended with a call for hope: 'I do truly believe,' Attenborough says, 'that together, we can create a better future.' That a focus on hope might be helpful in convincing people to take action has been suggested by a number of scholars including Andrew McWhirter (2022, p. 200) who argues that it 'is worthwhile spotlighting good practice', including by describing the work of media industry workers. McWhirter himself points to Raymond Williams's pronouncement that 'to be truly radical today is to make hope possible, not despair convincing' (1989, p. 118). Hope is also seen as an emancipatory approach by Arjen Wals (2010) who calls for a 'pedagogy of hope' to facilitate action against climate change. As he argues, though, this needs to be grounded in the everyday practices of people, thus emphasising that the lived experience of people should be the starting point for climate education – and indeed action. This is a point also driven home by David Selby (2010) who adopts the term denizen to demand greater emphasis on the local as this is where learning is rooted (see McGregor, 2013). Selby points to the work of Vandana Shiva (2008) to highlight how much of the focus on 'sustainable development' takes an essentially imperialist approach, meaning that 'education for sustainable development' is steeped in post-colonial attitudes.

While this is a particularly important point to consider as the Global North suggests policy and targets for the Global South, there are echoes of these problematic power relations as the Global North speaks to itself. Note, in the above, how much of the concern with media messaging is about the media making (ordinary) people change behaviour to become more environmentally sustainable. Williams (1989 [1961]) sees this as inherent in paternalistic approaches to media: the media, and in particular television, is there to educate and inform a mass audience that is in need of information and education, thus inevitably rendering them powerless. Contrast this to his pronouncement of 'culture is ordinary': here, people are assumed to already have and be part of a culture which they have learned in the process of growing up. They thus bring with them their own knowledge. This includes, as he highlights later (1989 [1982]), an understanding of the environmental damage that certain working practices cause. As he writes: 'It is no use simply saying to South Wales miners that all around them is an ecological disaster. They already know. They live in it' (1989 [1982], p. 219). What is interesting about this is that Williams attributes an analytical ability to the miners – but not, it seems, the ability to find a solution. There is, however, plenty of evidence that solutions are often found by communities – precisely because they have a lived experience that requires them to adapt to specific conditions. Thus, climate change adaptation – and climate action – needs to be understood as at least partially cultural: as rooted in the ordinary, lived culture that is situated in a particular place.

We now want to turn to two examples of communities providing climate action and discuss them in relation to how they are rooted in their local culture which, we will argue, is so specific that this culture is noticeably different even when it is just separated by 1.9 miles of physical distance.

Cultures of climate action

The two examples of communities providing climate action were both situated in the suburb of Wavertree in Liverpool, only 1.9 miles away from each other. Wavertree is a large suburb with a population of around 14,500 people according to the 2021 census. The suburb includes the former Wavertree village which predates Liverpool itself, as well as a significant number of Victorian terraces, particularly in the area closest to Liverpool city centre, and a garden suburb, built in the early twentieth century. The two areas we want to focus on are, first, the area closest to the city centre and, second, the Garden Suburb.

The area closest to the city centre is the former Picton Ward of Liverpool City Council which has both a relatively high student population and a low life expectancy in its longer-term residential population, leading to an overall young population in comparison to the rest of England. A large majority of the population (47.7 per cent) lives in privately rented accommodation, and the area includes a high level of children living in absolute low-income households (47.7 per cent) which is again much higher than the national average (Liverpool City Council, 2019). Thus, Picton is amongst the ten per cent most deprived areas in England and ranks at 764 of 32,844 neighbourhoods in England in terms of deprivation (Department of Levelling up, Housing and Communities and Ministry of Housing, Communities & Local Government, 2019).

The community is then marked by deprivation and an environment where dereliction is impacting on the daily life of its inhabitants. At the same time, the area is also very close to Toxteth which, after its riots in the 1980s, has managed to reimagine itself largely through local initiatives, including Toxteth TV, the Granby 4-Streets project and the Granby Street Market, which has made it a vibrant, multicultural community with a 'can do' spirit. Some of this spirit is also evident and indeed fostered by the Council in Picton: it was one of the areas that benefitted from the Homes for a Pound scheme that Liverpool City Council launched in 2015 and that was reported on by Channel 4 (*The £1 Houses: Britain's Cheapest Street*, 2019): that scheme gave access to homeownership to people with relatively little income, but required them to renovate and bring back to life houses that had been left to become derelict over decades. As a result, a relatively close-knit community emerged that aims to help each other out as well as offer additional support through activities for children and other initiatives (Hadfield, 2022).

LitterClear Volunteer, one of our example community groups, was founded in this area of Picton. LitterClear Volunteer are a community litter-picking group, who also work towards prettifying local green spaces which are often badly maintained as a result of significant budget cuts to the Council. This includes repainting brickwork, benches and bins, cutting back overgrown bushes and trees, uncovering old pavement from moss, planting new plants, etc. Interestingly the group speaks about their work by emphasising that they are making the area more liveable, thus focusing on the social rather than the environmental impact. Here, the daily experience of being surrounded by dereliction, neglect and poverty triggers a response of wanting to change the area for the better by working against the visible signs of them: the litter strewn on streets and the badly maintained green spaces that were initially put there by a Council mindful of the role of green spaces for the well-being of local communities.

In the interviews conducted with representatives of the LitterClear Volunteer group, the idea of lifting the community out of filth and showing them respect was a key concern. As one volunteer put it: 'We can turn this around, we don't have to accept the litter on our streets and living in this filth. It's not the way we want to live.' Another highlighted that she felt it benefitted her mental health to both help the local community and 'clear up'. In addition, the narratives told amongst them were often of locals responding positively to their efforts, including children deciding to help out with the litter picking because they wanted to use one of the greenspaces for playing. Thus, to use Roland Barthes's ideas (1993), mythologies emerged amongst this particular group that their efforts were working against the despondency that the visible signs of neglect had engendered in the local community. In other words, although the group was also doing something positive for the environment by helping waste management, keeping drains free and planting up neglected greenspaces, their conceptualisation of themselves operated much more strongly on a social level in so far that it responded to the everyday experience of deprivation in their area which brought the local community down.

This stands in significant contrast to the Wavertree Garden Suburb in Bloom group. Garden Suburbs emerged from the late eighteenth century in the UK and were at first a recluse of the middle classes. However, by the time the Wavertree Garden Suburb was built (between 1910 and 1915), there were attempts to broaden this out to the working classes. This was facilitated in Wavertree through communal ownership: residents bought shares in the Suburb, and rented their houses rather than owned them. As Bryce Leicester (2014) suggests, the focus on the communal, encouraged through a local institute that ran classes and festivals, made the residents appear as eccentric at the time, particularly since garden suburbs were initially conceptualised around the nuclear family (Whitehand and Carr, 1999).

While the houses are now owner-occupied, making the area more middle-class, some of this spirit remains, particularly around the Wavertree Garden

Suburb Institute which continues to offer a variety of classes and is the home of the Wavertree Garden Suburb in Bloom group. In many ways, this group offers very similar work to LitterClear Volunteer in that they are focused on trying to make the area nicer, primarily by planting up the area. However, the in Bloom group situated their efforts much more strongly in a continuity of different initiatives one of which was climate work. This continuity was highlighted to us by references to the history of the area and to the Queen's Green Canopy, and by situating their work in relation to wildlife friendliness.

One of the volunteers, for example, pointed out that the building of the institute itself predated the Garden Suburb and that although its grounds had been 'maintained enough', the group's work was to make it even better by introducing a wider variety of plants which attract insects, birds and mice. There emerges then a significant difference between these two groups: while for LitterClear Volunteer the need to change the visible environment was pressing because of the visible neglect and dereliction, for the in Bloom group it was something they did because it benefitted nature. The work was therefore much more outwardly directed, towards the 'other' of nature, rather than towards the 'us' of the local community. As Julie Doyle (2011, p. 21–22) argues, this distinction of nature as separate from man is typical for much climate reporting and points to larger sociocultural discourses. The difference between LitterClear and the in Bloom group allows us to see that these discourses are class-specific. Interestingly, the social benefits of making the area nicer were also highlighted by the in Bloom group, but they saw this as an additional benefit to their climate work, thus suggesting that co-benefits were seen to occupy different priorities depending on the group.

A key difference to LitterClear Volunteer emerged in the articulateness of how the in Bloom group addressed climate change: while in the interviews with LitterClear Volunteer, there was a noticeable uncertainty when discussing the environmental impact, the in Bloom members easily emphasised the positive contribution their planting had on the environment. Thus, another volunteer highlighted that they had found that forty felled trees had not been replanted, and he emphasised the role of these trees in generating clean air. He also connected it to the Queen's Green Canopy, an initiative that aimed to celebrate Queen Elizabeth II's Platinum Jubilee in honour of Her conviction that trees support our fight against climate change (The Royal Family, 2023). This easy reference of climate action and the royal initiative points to the fact that climate change and action against it operates currently largely as a middle-class discourse, rooted in a sense of cultural connectedness which includes an element of philanthropy. This sits in clear contradistinction to the sense of existential need ('nobody wants to live in filth') communicated by LitterClear.

Overall, then, these two example groups – despite their significant overlap in terms of the work they do – make visible how much community action for the climate is rooted in specific local conditions and express themselves culturally (Williams, 1989 [1958]). In addition, it shows that, for the time being, climate action is much more easily articulated as such by the middle classes despite the fact that, as we know, working-class communities are much more likely to live in ways commensurate to sustainable futures while also being disproportionately impacted by climate change (Barrera and Heymann, 2013). The fact that the social trumped the climate element in the responses by LitterClear Volunteer points to the need of the media to take much more strongly into consideration the co-benefits of climate action in their reporting. In addition, the media need to find ways to make visible the climate action that lower-income communities conduct. This, however, might require a different approach to reporting climate change, climate actions and communities to which we now turn.

The reporting disconnect: Frustration versus hope

As discussed above, the current, largely paternalistic approach to reporting the climate crisis has been criticised amongst others (e.g. Bondebjerg, 2002) by Williams who offers an alternative to the paternalistic approach. He calls this alternative 'democratic'. In his eyes, a democratic system of communications has to take as a fundamental basis 'that communication is something that belongs to the whole society, that it is something which depends, if it is to be healthy, on maximum participation by the individuals in the society' (1989 [1961], p. 29). Williams suggests that, considering the costs that media production amass, this would require some form of public ownership of small independent systems that can be licenced out to as wide a range of people as possible. He goes on: '[a democratic system] has to get rid of the idea that communication is the business of a minority talking to, instructing, leading on, the majority. It has, finally, to get rid of the false ideology of communications as we have received it: the ideology of people who are interested in communications only as a way of controlling people, or of making money out of them' (1989 [1961], p. 29). Some scholars assumed in the past that such a participatory model would become more prevalent as a result of digitalisation and convergence (Jenkins, 2006); however, others have pointed to the limits of this participation (Carpentier, 2011) particularly in a capitalist system.

Instead, there exist other media forms that more closely resemble Williams's conceptualisation of a democratic media system: community-led and local access television stations in the USA and Canada have an ethos that is similarly derived from a socialist belief in making films with people rather than about them (Linder, 1999). The success of these channels in Canada and the USA has led to the adoption of similar approaches in the UK (including the above-mentioned Toxteth TV) and elsewhere (Breunig, 1998) 1. Much of the work of community film- and television makers is led by a wish to increase the diversity of voices in the creative industries (Malik et al., 2019). As Sarita Malik (2019, p. 24) highlights 'a lack of cultural diversity within screen representation (on-screen) and also in the workforce (off-screen) has been acknowledged within academic research and industry reports'. Malik argues that community film- and television-making is one way to redress this problem.

While the cultural diversity Malik refers to emphasises the exclusion of racial and ethnic minorities in the cultural industries, there is also a sense that particular ideas, including that climate change is a fact, are underrepresented in the British media (Ruiu et al., 2023). As Maria Laura Ruiu, Gabriele Ruiu and Massimo Ragnedda (2023) show, the mainstream media in the UK have a tendency to emphasise stories on climate change that include an element of scepticism. The respondents to our initial survey went further to suggest that climate stories were, in their experience, largely absent from any newspaper other than *The Guardian*. Similarly, the BBC was positively associated with reporting of climate change, but ITV was not ticked as a source for climate change stories. When directly asked what programmes they could think of that had addressed climate change, the one name that dominated responses was David Attenborough. As one of our in-depth interviewees made clear, it was also Attenborough that had made the biggest impact on him and he was worried there was no one stepping into his footsteps. While these results – that the media are perceived to not report on climate change enough – needs to be tempered by the fact that our participants self-selected to take part in the study and thus were likely to already be interested in climate change, YouGov (2023) polling on what are the most important issues affecting Britain today makes visible that the environment is perceived as the fourth most important issue, after the economy, immigration and health. Thus, the population as a whole may have more knowledge about and interest in climate change than the lack of direct reporting seems to suggest.

In addition to a frustration with the lack of reporting, participants also indicated that they were aware that media's way of reporting was not very useful. One interviewee explained that he was conscious that the negative reports about climate change can cause eco-anxiety, and he also criticised the media for suggesting that the population was largely inactive. In order to counter this, he had started to include little posts about positive climate action within his company's weekly newsletter. Thus, our participants were not just aware of climate change, but they were also aware of what discourses circulated about it and aimed to act against them.

Such an awareness suggests that a community-led approach to media production is not just feasible but also makes sense. Indeed, we too had to learn this as we initially approached the project in a relatively paternalistic way, but then found a community which – rather than having to be informed about climate change – was already very active. It was for this reason that we changed our initial idea of producing a lifestyle television programme that included suggestions of how to live more sustainably to a documentary series about these community initiatives. While our approach still contained an element of working with semi-professionals (our students, under the guidance of a professional film maker, shot and edited the programmes), it was the community who led on the content of the programmes. As Malik et al. (2019) highlight, such an approach sits on a spectrum of community-led filmmaking. It has the advantage of reducing the need for full technical and media training that is not always of interest to local communities, while still making programmes with the people rather than about them (Linder, 1999).

This form of working with the people had two significant positive effects: (a) it empowered the community groups, and (b) it created a larger sense of hope. Much of the community groups' work was born out of a frustration with the perceived inaction of politicians which was compounded by the lack of reporting. One of our interviewees expressed this frustration really clearly when he highlighted his years of activism reaching all the way back into the 1980s that was regularly put down by local government because it was perceived as frivolous. As he expressed it, the Council in their response to him pitted his interest in 'flowers, plants' against their 'jobs and employment'. Here, the dichotomy of nature versus labour which has determined a lot of labour policy (Räthzel et al., 2018) is drawn on to explain the Council's inaction: jobs (and the economy) have priority over nature, this dichotomy suggests, which also makes invisible the fact that by working in favour of a more sustainable planet, new jobs can (and must) be created.

These consistent discourses that represent environmental concerns as being opposed to economic ones and, moreover, of significantly less priority than the latter, make activists feel despondent. Our fieldnotes recorded conversations amongst groups which often referred to experiences of doing something even though the Council didn't help or appreciate the work. Similarly, our survey respondents expressed a deep sense of frustration with the inaction of the Council as far as climate was concerned. This created an overall sense that community groups were working in silos and were essentially doing lonely work, even if they did work in groups. In contrast, after the screening, and even during the making of the programmes, community group members expressed a sense of joy of finding out about each other. The sense of being able to work together created a positive energy that was directly expressed by community group members in the responses to the final, post-screening questionnaire. This expression of positive emotions (with words such as 'energy', 'positive', etc.) points to the need to be seen and to see others doing similarly climate action work. It suggests that the current concern in the reporting of climate change about the need to inspire ordinary people to become active does not just render already existing climate action invisible, but also disempowers currently existing groups.

Instead, we found that showing the work of local groups – with very different cultures of climate action – to people not yet involved in climate action, made the latter feel inspired to become more active themselves. One respondent noted 'it was great to see ordinary people so engaged', suggesting that it is precisely the ordinariness of the culture (Williams, 1989 [1958]) that audiences see and recognise that allows them to feel inspired: it undermines the classed element, highlighted above, that currently makes climate action more a domain of the middle classes. Another response suggested that it was seeing the communal working against climate change that made the programmes inspiring for them: '[I]t looks easier to do things together [rather] than alone.' Thus, for those not currently involved in climate action, the communal effort of community groups can bring down barriers of involvement. This suggests that the media need to focus more strongly on communities rather than exceptional individuals such as Greta Thunberg and David Attenborough to inspire action by those people who are currently sitting on the sidelines.

Conclusions

This chapter set out to examine a more hopeful approach to the reporting of the world-in-crisis. Following previous research that has indicated the role of negative reports in creating eco-anxiety and paralysis, we examined the role of positive stories about climate action by local community groups in inspiring more people to become sustainable. We drew on Raymond Williams's work to further critique currently existing notions of needing to educate the population about climate change to highlight that a) many ordinary people already are committed to climate action and b) that their climate action is rooted in very specific local cultures and thus needs to be reported and understood through a cultural lens. We suggested the best way forward for this was a community-led approach to reporting, that is, a system that was relatively close to the democratic one proposed by Williams in 1961.

Overall, working with community groups and reporting on their efforts allowed us to make visible the need to balance the narratives of disaster and crisis with those of positive action and community involvement. Such reporting, which is perhaps more the domain of local media which also has more scope to forge the long-term relations with local community groups that a more democratic approach requires, needs to recognise that the environment is a major concern to people and that tackling the climate crisis has co-benefits which include addressing social injustices, health inequalities, community engagement and many more. Importantly, reporting also needs to prioritise these co-benefits in different ways for different groups. As we argued, there is a diversity of cultures of climate action, and it is important to report on their varieties. This can best be achieved by following a community-led approach which recognises not just the ordinariness of culture, but also the ordinariness of climate action.

Acknowledgement

This chapter is an outcome of the British Academy-funded project 'Community-led Television, Local Voice and Climate Action', funded through their Shared Understandings of Sustainable Futures stream. Reference: Application SSF\210053.

References

Adam, B. (2022) 'Foreword: Timescapes of climate change: A challenge for the media' in Bødker, H. and Morris, H.E. (eds.) *Climate change and journalism: Negotiating rifts of time*. London: Routledge, Taylor & Francis Group, pp. XII–XIX.

Barrera, M. and Heymann, J. (2013) 'Introduction: The environment and the economy. Finding equitable and effective solutions' in Heymann, J. and Barrera, M. (eds.), *Ensuring a sustainable future: Making progress on environment and equity*. New York: Oxford University Press, pp. XIX–XXXII.

Barthes, R. (1993) *Mythologies*. London: Vintage.

Beattie, G. and McGuire, L. (2018) *The psychology of climate change* (The psychology of everything). London: Routledge.

Bødker, H. and Morris, H.E. (eds.) (2022) *Climate change and journalism: Negotiating rifts of time*. London: Routledge, Taylor & Francis Group.

Bondebjerg, I. (2002) 'The mediation of everyday life: Genre, discourse and spectacle in reality TV' in Jersley, A. (ed.), *Realism and 'reality' in film and media*. Copenhagen, Denmark: Museum Tusculanum Press, pp. 159–192.

Boyce, T. and Lewis, J. (eds.) (2009) *Climate change and the media*. New York; Washington; Bern; Frankfurt am Main; Berlin; Brussels; Vienna; Oxford: Peter Lang.

Breunig, C. (1998) 'Offene Fernsehen- und Hörfunkkanäle in Deutschland', *Medien Perspectiven*, 98(5), pp. 236–249.

Carpentier, N. (2011) *Media and participation: A site of ideological-democratic struggle*. Bristol: Intellect.

Department of Levelling Up, Housing and Communities and Ministry of Housing, Communities & Local Government (2019) 'English Indices of Deprivation 2019: Mapping Resources', Gov.uk, https://www.gov.uk/guidance/english-indices-of-deprivation-2019-mapping-resources, accessed 14 September 2023.

Doyle, J. (2011) *Mediating climate change*. Abingdon; New York: Routledge.

Extinction: The Facts (2020) BBC, PBS. BBC Studios.

Gavin, N.T. (2009) 'Addressing climate change: A media perspective', *Environmental Politics*, 18(5), pp. 765–780.

Hadfield, C. (2022) 'Life in Liverpool's £1 houses That went from Derelict terraces to family homes', *Liverpool Echo*, 26 February, https://www.liverpoolecho.co.uk/news/liverpool-news/life-liverpools-1-houses-went-23206941, accessed 14 September 2023.

Halliday, J. (2023) 'British tourists tell of "living nightmare" as 19,000 evacuated in Rhodes fire', *The Guardian*, 23 July, https://www.theguardian.com/world/2023/jul/23/british-tourists-tell-of-nightmare-in-rhodes-fires-greece, accessed 18 September 2023.

Heeren, A., Mouguiama-Daouda, C. and Contreras, A. (2022) 'On climate anxiety and the threat it may pose to daily life functioning and adaptation: A study among European and African French-speaking participants', *Climatic Change: An Interdisciplinary, International Journal Devoted to the Description, Causes and Implications of Climatic Change*, 173(15), https://link-springer-com.edgehill.idm.oclc.org/article/10.1007/s10584-022-03402-2, accessed 21 September 2023.

Innocenti, M., Santarelli, G., Lombardi, G.S., Ciabini, L., Zjalic, D., Di Russo, M. and Cadeddu, C. (2023) 'How can climate change anxiety induce both pro-environmental behaviours and eco-paralysis? The mediating role of general self-efficacy', *International Journal of Environmental Research and Public Health*, 20(3085), pp. 3085–3085.

Intergovernmental Panel on Climate Change (2023) *Climate Change 2023: Synthesis Report. Contribution of Working Groups I, II and III to the Sixth Assessment Report of the Intergovernmental Panel on Climate Change*. Geneva, Switzerland. https://www.ipcc.ch/report/ar6/syr/downloads/report/IPCC_AR6_SYR_FullVolume.pdf, accessed 18 September 2023.

ITV News (2023) 'Rhodes: Authorities say 19,000 rescued in Greece's "largest ever wildfire evacuation"', *ITV*, 23 July, https://www.itv.com/news/2023-07-23/rhodes-19000-rescued-in-greeces-largest-ever-wildfire-evacuation, accessed 18 September 2023.

Jenkins, H. (2006) *Convergence culture: Where old and new media collide*. New York: New York University Press.

Kääpä P. and Vaughan, H. (eds.) (2022) *Film and television production in the age of climate crisis: Towards a greener screen* (Palgrave studies in media and environmental communication). Cham, Switzerland: Palgrave Macmillan.

Keane, D. (2023) 'Rhodes wildfires: Largest ever evacuation from Greece as 19,000 rescued from island', *Evening Standard*, 24 July, https://www.standard.co.uk/news/world/rhodes-wildfires-greece-heatwave-evacuation-tui-ryanair-b1096206.html, accessed 18 September 2023.

Leicester, B. (2014) 'Life in a garden suburb – 90 years ago', *BBC*, https://www.bbc.co.uk/liverpool/localhistory/mersey_times/issue_01/garden_suburb.shtml, accessed 14 September 2023.

Linder, L.R. (1999) *Public access television: America's electronic soapbox*. Westport, CT: Praeger.

Liverpool City Council (2019) 'The indices of multiple deprivation: A liverpool analysis', *Key Statistics and Data*, https://liverpool.gov.uk/council/key-statistics-and-data/indices-of-deprivation/, accessed 14 September 2023.

Lopera-Mármol, M. and Jiménez-Morales, M. (2021) 'Green shooting: Media sustainability, a new trend', *Sustainability*, 13(6), p. 3001. https://doi.org/10.3390/su13063001, accessed 18 September 2023.

McGrath, M. and Rannard, G. (2023) 'UN climate report: Scientists release "survival guide" to avert climate disaster', *BBC*, 20 March, https://www.bbc.co.uk/news/science-environment-65000182, accessed 18 September 2023.

McGregor, S.L.T. (2013) 'Alternative communications about sustainability education', *Sustainability*, 5(8), pp. 3562–3580.

McWhirter, A. (2022) 'A scholarship of hope: Taking stock of UK screen industries via the lens of digital work over digital solutionism' in Kääpä, P. and Vaughan, H. (eds.) *Film and television production in the age of climate crisis: Towards a greener screen* (Palgrave studies in media and environmental communication). Cham, Switzerland: Palgrave Macmillan, pp. 181–206.

Malik, S. (2019) 'Diversity, representation and community filmmaking – a short introduction' in Malik, S., Chapain, C. and Comunian, R. (eds.) *Community filmmaking: Diversity, practices and places* (Routledge studies in media and cultural industries, 1). London: Routledge, pp. 21–25.

Malik, S., Chapain, C. and Comunian, R. (eds.) (2019) *Community filmmaking: Diversity, practices and places* (Routledge studies in media and cultural industries, 1). London: Routledge.

Maxwell, R. and Miller, T. (2012) *Greening the media*. Oxford; New York: Oxford University Press.

Olausson, U. and Berglez, P. (eds.) (2017) *Media research on climate change. Where have we been and where are we heading?* Abingdon; New York: Routledge.

Pinto, J., Gutsche, R.E. and Prado, P. (eds.) (2019) *Climate change, media & culture: Critical issues in global environmental communication*. Bingley: Emerald Publishing.

Rehling, J.T.C. (2022) 'Conceptualising eco-anxiety using an existential framework', *South African Journal of Psychology*, 52(4), pp. 472–485.

Räthzel, N., Cock, J. and Uzzell, D. (2018) 'Beyond the nature-labour divide: Trade union responses to climate change in South Africa', *Globalizations*, 15(4), pp. 504–519.

Robinson, J. (2023) 'Rhodes wildfire: British family spend night on school floor after evacuation order', *Sky News*, 23 July, https://news.sky.com/story/rhodes-wildfire-british-family-spend-night-on-school-floor-after-after-evacuation-order-12925938, accessed 18 September 2023.

The Royal Family (2023) 'The Queen's Green Canopy', *The Royal Family*, https://www.royal.uk/queens-green-canopy, accessed 14 September 2023.

Ruiu, M.L., Ruiu, G. and Ragnedda, M. (2023) 'Lack of "common sense" in the climate change debate: Media behaviour and climate change awareness in the UK', *International Sociology*, 38(1), pp. 46–72.

Selby, D. (2010) '"Go, go, go, said the bird": Sustainability education in interesting times' in Kagawa, F. and Selby, D. (eds.) *Education and climate change: Living and learning in interesting times* (Routledge research in education, 30). New York: Routledge, pp. 35–54.

Shiva, V (2008) *Soil not oil: Climate change, peak oil and food insecurity*. London: Zed Books.

Smith, S. (2022) 'Contribution to roundtable on television and sustainability', *Critical Studies in Television Conference*. June 27–July 15, https://www.youtube.com/watch?v=jf_bhQ_qUWk&list=PLBrk-wPNLaVkAbtI5ubnJkaGkAmX58JXV&index=11&t=536s, accessed 13 October 2022.

The £1 Houses: Britain's Cheapest Street (2019) Channel 4. Topical Television.

Vakoch, D.A. and Mickey, S. (eds.) (2022) *Eco-anxiety and planetary hope: Experiencing the twin disasters of Covid-19 and climate change*. Cham: Springer.

Verlie, B. (2023) *Learning to live with climate change: From anxiety to transformation* (Routledge focus on environment and sustainability series). Milton: Taylor & Francis Group.

Wals, A. (2010) *Message in a bottle: Learning our way out of unsustainability*. http://groundswellinternational.files.wordpress.com/2010/12/learning-our-way-out-of-unsustainability.pdf, accessed 6 August 2013.

Whitehand, J.W.R. and Carr, C.M.H. (1999) 'England's garden suburbs: Development and change' in Harris, R. and Larkham, P.J. (eds.) *Changing suburbs: Foundation, form, and function* (Studies in history, planning, and the environment, 24). London: E & FN Spon, pp. 76–90.

Whitmarsh, L., Player, L., Jiongco, A., James, M., Williams, M., Marks, E. and Kennedy-Williams, P. (2022) 'Climate anxiety: What predicts it and how is it related to climate action?' *Journal of Environmental Psychology*, 83, https://doi.org/10.1016/j.jenvp.2022.101866, accessed 21 September 2023.

Williams, R. (1989) *The politics of modernism: Against the new conformists* (Political studies). London: Verso.

Williams, R. (1989 [1958]) 'Culture is ordinary' in *Resources of hope: Culture, democracy, socialism*. London; New York: Verso, pp. 3–18.

Williams, R. (1989 [1961]) 'Communications and community' in *Resources of hope: Culture, democracy, socialism*. London; New York: Verso, pp. 19–31.

Williams, R. (1989 [1982]) 'Socialism and ecology' in *Resources of hope: Culture, democracy, socialism*. London; New York: Verso, pp. 210–225.

YouGov (2023) 'The most important issues facing the country', *YouGov*, https://yougov.co.uk/topics/society/trackers/the-most-important-issues-facing-the-country, accessed 18 September 2023.

· 6 ·

FIRST NATIONS COMMUNITY MEDIA AND THE CLIMATE CRISIS: TOWARDS RADICAL ECO-COMMUNICATIVE DEMOCRACY

Kerrie Foxwell-Norton, Bridget Backhaus, Troy Meston with Wilcannia River Radio

When it's really hot we go to the river and swim
When we go fishin' we catchin' a bream
When the river's high we jump off the bridge
When we get home we play some didge

'Down River', Wilcannia Mob/Barkindji Boys (2002)

In 2002, in the mostly Indigenous remote Australian outback town of Wilcannia (New South Wales, population 745) located on the traditional lands of the Barkindji people, five boys attracted national attention with their song 'Down River'. Rapping over a simple didgeridoo ('didge') beat, the boys told stories of life in Wilcannia: fishing in the river, jumping off the bridge into the water below, and 'playing some didge'. It is a song about a way of life, and implicit in the lyrics, a deep connection to country and especially to the Baaka (Darling) River. It was also a mainstream hit: after featuring in Australia's premiere youth music countdown, the Wilcannia Mob performed at the Sydney Opera House and the 'Homebake' music festival, to a crowd of 20,000 people.

A decade later, the scene described in 'Down River' was foreign to the children of Wilcannia. The town was enduring a severe drought that had all but dried up their sacred Baaka (Darling) River. The drought was compounded by ongoing upstream water disputes that divert water flows, leaving crops upriver irrigated and communities down river without a trickle. Camping, fishing and jumping off the bridge were hard to imagine. Long-term resident of Wilcannia Brendon Adams[1] recounts community conversations at the time:

> We had a meeting with a lot of traditional Elders and owners. And we sat there, it was really amazing that a lot of the conversations was from our young kids. A lot of our young kids were crying and saying, 'I don't know what it is like,' and we didn't understand what that was at first [until these young kids explained]: 'I didn't understand what it was like to go to the river and fish with my grandfather'. Because they'd heard their fathers and aunties and uncles saying how much they used to do it as kids but it's not there. But these young kids would say, '. . .but we've never had it. This is not right, it is not fair'.

Interspersed by long periods of drought and flood, the waters of the Baaka River eventually return and the flooding rains are celebrated for their cyclic renewal of the Wilcannia community. News of the arrival of water travels fast in town and locals flock to the river to see and hear the river's awakening. The children of Wilcannia once again jump from the bridge and fish with their families as a healthy river remedies much more than dusty and thirsty landscapes. In conversations, in literature, in music, symbiotic relation between Barkindji people and culture, and the health of the Baaka are omnipresent. The health of Country[2] is indivisibly tied to the health of the Barkindji people, and the significance of this relationship is sung now and by generations throughout all time. In 2017, The Wilcannia Mob and its next generation again sang their cultural heritage blending traditional and contemporary creative practice:

Like our ancestors did
We got to follow in their footsteps
Strong future
Strong river
Strong people

We rise with the river
Wiimpatja Dreaming where the Baaka flow
We cry when the river down, river down
River down oh so low

—*'River Down', The Wilcannia Mob: Next Generation, 2017*

As we write, Wilcannia is again facing drought as scientists have declared an El Niño weather pattern that forecasts dry conditions, particularly impacting northern and eastern Australia. These cycles are thrown off balance and exacerbated due to anthropogenic climate change (Cai et al., 2023). Extreme weather conditions – in Wilcannia, particularly heat and drought – amplify existing social and economic stressors related to health, housing, violence and crime. The Barkindji have always known that when the river is healthy, the community is too – and that the inverse is also true.

Throughout the fluctuations of drought and flood, local community radio station Wilcannia River Radio provides information and support to the community: a forum for discussing concerns facing the Baaka and its people. Re-established in 2009, Wilcannia River Radio is part of the Australian First Nation's community broadcasting sector. There are roughly sixty First Nations media organisations operating in over 235 communities across Australia, producing media content in more than 25 languages (First Nations Media Australia, 2023). Part of the broader Australian community broadcasting sector[3] established in the early 1970s, these stations perform a critical role in supporting communities to tell their own stories. In the production and distribution of their own media, these stations claim agency and culture in an era where homogenising mainstream media practices work to actively silence difference (Anderson et al., 2020). This storytelling has a distinctive role in First Nations communities where the ongoing impacts of invasion and colonisation are historically and contemporarily manifest in the marginalisation (and removal) of language, cultural heritage and practice. First Nations community radio stations – as media led for and by communities – are a 'first level service' (Forde et al., 2009): a tool of cultural practice and survival, and a means to connect, support and strengthen communities.

In this chapter, we explore the role of First Nations community radio stations in an era of climate crises through a case study of Wilcannia River Radio. Building on the normative ideas and pursuit of radical ecological democracy, we employ an eco-communicative democracy framework. This is conceived as the expression of diverse relations between cultures and natures (Foxwell-Norton, 2018) in the public sphere/s, and serves to explore the role of First Nations community broadcasting in telling different stories about reasons for, and responses to climate changes. In doing so, we extend 'climate crises' to consider a much longer crisis of the impacts of western invasion and industrialisation on First Nations Australians' way of life, and significant relations to nature therein. Through the case study of Wilcannia River Radio, this chapter interrogates the role of community media and democratised media access in communicating climate changes. What is, or could be, their role in supporting recovery and resilience to climate changes through their already established strengths in storytelling and community-based action?

Our chapter draws from conversations and purposively includes the voices of First Nations people and community we have worked with during our *Warming Up* project which is building the capacity of Australian community radio to communicate climate changes (Foxwell, Backhaus and Leitch, 2022; Backhaus, Foxwell-Norton and Leitch, 2023). Working with Wilcannia and other First Nations communities, we adopt research practices that align with oral storytelling traditions, conscious of bringing these voices to our writing.[4] In this chapter, we couple the voices of Wilcannia and Wilcannia River Radio, bringing local yarns to broader discussions around climate crises focussing especially on what are – or could be – possibilities to democratise *how and who* communicates climate change? We find many possibilities in participatory local media, showcased by stations like Wilcannia River Radio, and similar located all over Australia and the world, to foster meaningful and just climate action.

First Nations people, communication and the climate crisis

Globally, First Nations peoples are disproportionately impacted by climate changes through colonial violence and dispossession. This happens in myriad ways: the impacts are unique to individual communities, cultures, and environments, yet the experiences are repeated the world over. For example, First Nations peoples living low material and subsistence lifestyles depend upon the stability of seasons. Changing weather patterns impact hunting, fishing, gathering, farming practice, and the presence and absence of species relied upon for nutrition. Relatedly, cultural heritage sites and practice are also threatened by changes to weather systems. Brendon Adams explains what this means in Wilcannia:

> What I saw was how much lives change when there was no water. I've seen that these young men had a place where they could go to engage with each other, and the young ladies too… But you know, of course I only can talk about the young men I've been involved with… And, it means when they can't be together, they can't share stories, they can't feel happiness and you know, natural. And unfortunately, because of the lack of water, they actually had to find that replacement and drugs and alcohol has become a large part of that…which then of course brings domestic violence, brings family breakups, brings violence amongst each other and everything and… depression. And as I said, suicide becomes a major issue in our in this town.

Related are the ongoing impacts of colonisation and the disadvantage that persists for First Nations people marginalised by the dominance of western industrialised culture (Quijano, 2000). First Nations people in Australia (and internationally) experience climate change and its impacts as an extension of industrialised dispossession that continues to threaten and decimate ways of life, cultural heritage and practice. Sultana (2022, p. 10) defines this as 'climate colonialities': '. . .a toxic mix of global racisms, rapacious extractivism, colonial-capital dispossessions, climate debts, patriarchy, and imperialism'. Employing an Indigenous phenomenological lens, climate change morphs from a relatively recently discovered scientific problem resulting from an economic system to global narratives around colonial invasion and violence, cultural imperialism, critical political economy, and injustices therein. Such a perspective reveals how the hegemony of both capitalist economies and western science is maintained in part through its projected claims of being apolitical and ahistorical. The climate change 'problem', transmitted through the vast and pervasive global communication network, maintains this status quo with consequences for the breadth of possibilities and responses. Opportunities for more critical conversations *about* society are curtailed when climate change is communicated as a problem *of* a society (Belfer, Ford and Maillet, 2017), understood and addressed within the boundaries of dominant western frameworks. This impoverishes an understanding of the 'crisis', its origins and possible responses. However, for First Nations people in Australia, the longest continuing civilisation on Earth, climate change is enmeshed in a very different history and record of events that have led to now. This reckoning elicits other questions, beyond current science/technology, industry/economic fixes that are obstructed by their deep embeddedness in existing dispossession.

The idea of 'climate change' repackages the ongoing subjugation and resistance of First Nations peoples into something universal, apolitical and ahistorical – a new 'crisis'. With due respect for scientific expertise in the diagnosis of 'climate change', the concept/condition fails to describe the source of threats and devastation from changing weather patterns; that is, the ecological consequences of western industrialised systems of production and consumption (Hulme, 2015; Cottle, 2023). For First Nations people in Australia, the crisis began with British invasion with impacts only intensifying over the last 200-plus years of occupation. The language of 'climate crisis' thus continues to disempower First Nations people in its privileging of western historical and cultural norms that entail the systematic exclusion of First Nations knowledge systems (Whyte, 2018, 2020; Callison, 2021; Nursery-Bray, Palmer and Rist, 2022) and dilutes respect and recognition of strength and resistance. This epitomises the weight of climate coloniality (Sultana, 2022) and its well-established colonial practices under a different guise. It is a gross form of historical amnesia that has and continues to harm First Nations communities in Australia, and internationally.

Options to relieve this colonial weight rest on the disclosure and deconstruction of climate change hegemony and ongoing challenge and disruption to its universalising discourses. Sultana (2022, p. 10) argues that we need to 'hear and heed' the suffering of those enduring climate coloniality and '. . . learn from the embodied emotional geographies of climate, while also registering and celebrating a multiplicity of local voices, stories, ideas, cosmologies, strengths, and convivialities'. Wilcannia and Wilcannia River Radio are the 'embodied emotional geographies of climate' and, through their local storytelling that is created and broadcast on their local media, they provide a place where we hear local stories and voices. For Barkindji people and all First Nations Australians, these stories carry a relationship to nature that differs from western cultural norms. In contrast to the dominant culture in the west that positions nature as a commodity, First Nations Australians' relations to nature are holistic, absolute and relational. Aunty Mary Graham (2014, p. 18) explains this difference which underpins the separation of culture and nature:

> There is no Aboriginal equivalent to the Cartesian notion of 'I think therefore I am' but, if there were, it would be – I am located therefore I am. Place, being, belonging and connectedness all arise out of a locality in Land.

The communication of these relations between culture and nature, between ourselves and other things is critical to a deeper appreciation and respect for the distinctiveness of Indigenous peoples and communities. Recognition of this difference strikes to the heart of First Nations peoples' experience of climate changes and brings western cultural assumptions and their consequences into sharper and critical focus.

Radical ecology, eco-communicative democracy and First Nations community media

The embedded coloniality of dominant communicative framings of the climate crisis requires urgent and radical rethinking. There is a need to critically question the dominant worldviews underpinning the communication of the climate crisis. Radically expanding our thinking and theorising around these communicative approaches has the potential to encourage broader participation in decision-making and solutions, enabling a meaningful contribution to climate and social justice. In grappling with these challenges, we draw on the framework of radical eco-communicative democracy through which to view the work of First Nations community media in Australia. The foundations for eco-communicative democracy emerge from the role of democratic communication within active citizenship and decision-making. Jakubowicz (1993, p. 41) suggests that a key principle of democratic public communication is the ability of each segment of society 'to introduce ideas, symbols, information, and elements of culture into social circulation' to reach all other segments of society. In doing so, ecological democracy seeks to include communities misrepresented and systematically unrepresented by liberal democracies – including multispecies. Work from Kothari (2014a, 2014b) on radical ecological democracy extends these ideas further. This concept is built on a '. . .continuous and mutually respectful dialogue amongst human beings, and between humanity and the rest of nature. It is also not one solution or blueprint, but a great variety of them' (Kothari, 2014a, n.p.). Combining communicative democracy with radical ecological democracy, we draw together both the democratic benefits of plural and diverse worldviews, as well as democracy extended to the communicative relations between nature and culture (Foxwell-Norton, 2016). Radical eco-communicative democracy explores two dimensions of communication. The first refers to the communication of diverse cultures of nature in a healthy public sphere; and the second relates to the role of the media in circulating this diversity, as is their normative function in a democracy to facilitate public sphere debate (Habermas, 1989; Foxwell-Norton, 2018). These two dimensions are closely related but difficult to reconcile, particularly given the dominance of hegemonic media in the public sphere. How then can we conceptualise a public sphere that accommodates different ways of communicating relations between humans, communities, and nature? How might we explore media that facilitate shifts in thinking from colonial universality to richer, more nuanced pluriversality (Escobar, 2020)? In answering these questions, we seek to encourage ideas of democracy that both challenge colonial hegemonies and address ecological and climate crises.

Wilcannia River Radio and its contemporaries bring First Nations culture and heritage to media in Australia. In doing so, they communicate relations between culture and nature that challenge western approaches that have created, defined and now seek to respond to climate crises (see Beck, 1992). These stations find ways to elevate and reproduce First Nations ways of knowing, being and doing (Martin/Booran Mirraboopa, 2003). First Nations media communicates relations between culture and nature that are marginalised and/or impoverished by mainstream media that prioritise industry, science and politics and stories that are *not of* the people and places to which they speak. Sultana (2022, p. 6), drawing on the work of Escobar (2020), calls for epistemological and ontological shifts towards 'pluriversality' to overcome the epistemic violence of climate coloniality: 'This means recognizing and accepting the co-existence of multiple ways of knowing and being in the world, whereby the Eurocentric colonial model is but one way of existing and relating to socio-ecologies.' Building on the pursuit of 'recognition and acceptance', radical eco-communicative democracy explores citizen participation in the communication of this diversity in an era where communication networks are pervasive, and communication is power (Castells, 2009). Radical eco-communicative democracy offers a conceptual framework that both creates space for pluriversality and seeks to explore the role of communication in amplifying diversity and in doing so, question the dominance of climate coloniality.

Exploring the potential role of Wilcannia River Radio and other First Nations community stations in communicating climate changes, we extend beyond dominant science communication and 'knowledge deficit' models. We recognise the value of science communication and its success in some contexts though note its inadequacy in responding to historical, social, political and cultural contexts, including its own (Pearce et al., 2015; Simis et al., 2016; Lester and Foxwell-Norton, 2020). Rommetveit, Funtowicz and Strand (2010, p. 159) explain that climate change:

> ...is defined in a scientific context that is perceived as distant from and alien to the communities in which people live their lives and the public spheres in which they exert their citizenship. However, there seems to be no solution to the issue without the radical involvement of citizens. . . . Science is not enough.

To find better, democratic ways to understand and engage citizens, we adopt a cultural approach to communication (Carey, 1989) where meaningful engagement and participation in climate action stems from understanding how communities understand themselves and, importantly, their relations to each other and their environments. This cultural approach delivers opportunities to tell different stories about climate change: stories deeply embedded in local places and cultures, embracing Australia's complexity and diversity and especially those communities sidelined and/or marginalised by mainstream climate discussion and debate. This is 'pluriversality' and of critical importance for the established communities of community broadcasting. Community broadcasting was borne in part as an antidote to the under/misrepresentation and/or marginalisation in mainstream media of First Nations people, multicultural communities, people with disability, the LGBTIQ+ community, and regional and remote communities. A cultural approach to communication – underpinned by radical eco-communicative democracy – creates opportunities for more critical reflection on what about climate change communication is cultural and whose/which culture is being communicated? These questions begin to unravel the assumptions of established climate change communication and how it is imbued with power, knowledge and hegemony.

Wilcannia River Radio and radical eco-communicative praxis

The Baaka river is a part of the Murray/Darling Basin that covers more than one million square kilometres in the south-east of Australia – roughly the size of France and Spain combined. It is Australia's most important water catchment. Indubitably, it is also the most controversial. The basin crosses three states and has been the source of endless politicking between local, state, and federal governments. Disputes are frequent and wide-ranging from flood and drought management to the politics of water extraction to service irrigated farming (in notably dry country) along the river systems. The size and complexity of the river system mean that every action, every decision, have significant consequences for communities and ecologies downstream. The overarching decision-making body is the Murray-Darling Basin Authority (MDBA), a centrally administered organisation in collaboration between the Federal Government and Basin states. The MDBA is the source of endless bickering and media potshots between governments, conservationists, and the agricultural sector. Science acknowledges that the impacts of disrupted water flow – or as it is understood in Wilcannia, 'water theft' – are compounded by climate changes, and extended periods of drought. But what does the disrupted water flow mean for Barkindji people? And indeed, the fifty First Nations groups that call the Murray-Darling Basin other language names, telling different stories of the country.

In Wilcannia, the Barkindji are 'people of the river' – freshwater people. Barkindji relations to the Baaka are not prescribed by scientific expertise nor related to late industrialised capitalist economy. For the Barkindji, the river is Mother, is their 'bloodline', their identity: such that it is more accurate (though inadequate) to say 'of the river' to signal the indivisibility and relationality of people to place. As Aunty Mary Graham (2014, p. 17) explains: 'Aboriginal relationality – traditionally the foundation of the Law – is an elaborate, complex and refined system of social, moral, spiritual and community obligations that provides an ordered universe for people.' Therefore, when the river doesn't flow, much more is threatened. It is an entire cosmology that communicates and brings meaning, Law/lore and life to Barkindji people and their culture.

> ...if you know people understood the health of that water and what it really means to this community, right? Because it's not a commodity, It's an entity. It is their mother. That's why they're the people of the river, because that river looks after them. The fish, the kangaroos, the emus around it. . .But also that sense of families coming together for something strong and positive. So when the climate changes it impacts so hard. (Brendon Adams, 2022)

When Barkindji speak of the Baaka, it is communicated in ways that transcend anthropocentric, mainstream narratives of climate-related disasters. While hegemonic communicators speak of 'modernising' and 'management' (MDBA, 2023) for people and communities – accompanied by threatening and usual images of dust and scrawny animals – the Barkindji mourn for a loved one.

> When they take the water from a Barkandji person, they take our blood. They're killing us. It's not just us Barkandji people who are feeling it. It's the white people and other people too. How can I teach culture when they're taking our beloved Barka away? There's nothing to teach if there's no river. The river is everything. It's my life, my culture. You take the water away from us; we've got nothing. (Uncle William "Badger" Bates, for *IndigenousX* in the *The Guardian*, 26 July 2017)

These impacts are not dissolved in the first trickles of water that inch down parched riverbeds. Impacts on culture, health, well-being, and relationships linger, further contributing to the trauma of coloniality now described as 'climate change'.

> The grief and loss this town has, the impact that the environment and what the government has done. Particularly involving the Baaka. Like today you see that Baaka full but there was a time for over 200 days that was completely dry, and . . . we couldn't even have a proper shower at all. The local council had to dig very deep into the ground to get some bore water. But even that bore water, you could feel how dirty it was, and this whole community had to drink and bathe from it, which wasn't fair. . . And you know these, these are the key issues that this community

> has suffered for many years. And amongst the transgenerational traumas that we've suffered. (Brendon Adams, 2021)

National news and other media attention alights on Wilcannia in these sensational moments of drought, flood and recently mass fish kills. More political posturing, scientific reasoning and diagnosis and industry defences follow. Buried beneath this usual round of news and other media reporting are the voices of Barkindji and any critical reflection on, or challenge to, the broader structures that led to these events. This is where the role of Wilcannia River Radio, in its processes of local communication – about Wilcannia, by Wilcannia – gains significance. The station offers a way of exploring alternative ways of knowing and speaking the Baaka beyond the hegemonic/universal. Wilcannia River Radio is a staunch example of what this looks like in practice.

In stark contrast to dominant 'victim' representations (Belfer et al., 2017), Wilcannia River Radio celebrates and supports its community – human and nonhuman. Far from passive down-river victims, the people of Wilcannia have regularly protested the impacts of upstream water extraction (especially for large-scale cotton farming) and poor water and land management (Mesikämmen, Waller and Burkett, 2021). Wilcannia River Radio has led these protests, bringing community together to blockade the local bridge located on a major arterial highway to gain government and national attention (Jenkins, 2020). Other communities impacted by the diversion of river water for farming have joined Wilcannia and their chants to 'Bring Back the Baaka'.

Local community representative, Brendon Adams understands the diversion of water as 'slow genocide' echoing the 'slow violence' of Nixon's environmentalism of the poor (2011) linking the local consequences of industrialised agriculture, river flow and climate changes to the impacts of coloniality:

> . . . everyone agrees that the human factor is the biggest part of all these changes. It was the humans and the governments' decisions that shaped the Baaka [not] as a mother, which is an entity that belonged to the people, that looked after the people. It is the government's choice that turned this (river/water) into a commodity. . . It's just part of the slow genocide that's been happening to our community, to our people, but especially to our children. This nation, this country, needs to act on it. (Brendon Adams, 2021)

Wilcannia River Radio is also able to leverage its significant connections and social capital to prompt grassroots actions. After the media and politicians disappeared back up the highway in clouds of dust, Wilcannia River Radio remained. As Station Manager Rob Clayton quipped, 'we are always talking about the River'. Wilcannia River Radio is both a cultural and community resource, serving their community in the absence of water:

> One thing I was very proud of was we played a role . . .which we it wasn't our duty, but we did this anyway. Through our networks and our connection, we supplied over 3000 boxes of water, 10 litre boxes of water to this community. And in fact, some of the young people that worked for me in the radio delivered boxes to homes, to the elders. They could not get the boxes themselves just so that they could have clean water. (Brendon Adams, 2022)

Unlike mainstream media, Wilcannia River Radio is embedded within the community and facilitates conversations and action outside of media cycles and events. Further, the station holds itself directly accountable to its community, its relationships, and its needs. The station manager of Wilcannia River Radio explained their broadcast priorities:

> For me it's always getting the right information out to the community. A lot of media, other media like Facebook, the news and all of that, they're more . . . information for the cities but not for our area. So being able to not pick and choose what news and what information you get out of the community but what's relevant for us out here and just being able to be there when community needs us like in the good times and the bad times. And you know radio is always the first point of contact for community like soon as something happens in the community they I'll turn on the radio and see what see what Wilcannia is... see what our station has got to say about this and got to say about that and being recognised as the voice for Wilcannia from the media side of it is, to me, it's just something that we can know we're doing the right thing for our community and our community is happy with us. (Rob Clayton, 2022)

When viewed through a lens of radical eco-communicative democracy, the grassroots activities of Wilcannia River Radio – and their deep connections with community and Country and offer a way forward for climate change communication more broadly. On air and in the community, Wilcannia River Radio challenges dominant climate change narratives by broadcasting local relationships and priorities of the Barkindji, deeply embedded in relations and indeed responsibility to care. Deficit models of climate change communication and victim framing are abandoned in favour of highlighting the strength and resilience of the community and its culture. For Wilcannia River Radio, systemic issues are always considered – from water management to histories of colonial violence, events are interconnected and are the embodiment of past actions. But far from levelling blame, the understanding and communication of these systemic injustices are prompts to action to protect the futures of the community and Country. Here we see the radical potential of First Nations community media – subverting dominant media tropes, telling stories of resilience, and strength, and both leading and supporting community action.

Conclusion: Bringing back the Baaka

> Our community is already doing the talking. There are certain community leaders, young people, Elders, families have already spoken to everyone they can possibly think of to keep the awareness, keep the people understanding the devastation and the impact. But it has got to be from voice to action. That's the biggest thing. Who are we are yelling it to? . . . We are yelling it to the people who are responsible for the decisions. We are yelling it to the people who are accountable for these decisions. To simply listen to one thing that our community is saying 'Bring back our Baaka' Let it have its natural flow and its natural connection to the community and the culture. Then our lives will become better. (Brendon Adams, 2022)

At this juncture when transformation and change are so urgent – how does communicative democracy amplify the relationship between cultures and nature? How do we communicate so that communities feel empowered to act rather than despair and disenchantment? Capacity for robust public sphere debate about climate changes is deficient when human-centred and anthropocentric discourse is assumed as the only legitimate and authoritative source of knowledge. And then what is lost is the pluriverse and the kaleidoscope of culture/nature relations – in exchange for rational ideas of a single western, industrialised universe and its masochistic pursuit of more.

Through the praxis of Wilcannia River Radio, and other First Nations community media outlets, there is the capacity for an alternative: communication that is participatory and embedded in local knowledges and relationality between community and Country. Within these small and under-resourced media outlets, we find spaces that actively reject and seek to dismantle and disrupt climate coloniality – a process crucial for emancipatory futures (Sultana, 2022, p. 10). While we are still exploring disentangling prospects for radical eco-communicative democracy within this space, telling local stories about relations to nature through the connectedness of people to place is central to a sense of community and motivates climate actions. The community radio sector in Australia is particularly well-placed in this collective and participatory engagement. Wilcannia River Radio, and First Nations community media more broadly, clearly demonstrate that there are other possibilities for communicating and understanding the climate crisis. Radical eco-communicative democracy offers a way of theorising this vital work and how it might be more broadly considered within global climate change communication approaches. In critically examining *who* and *how* climate change is communicated, other futures are possible.

Acknowledgements

We thank Ms Anne Leitch, Mr Salvador Cantellano and Ms Ada Lester for their research assistance. We also thank the broader Wilcannia community for their hospitality and generosity. Special thanks to Rhonda Lee Kerwin who also shared her insights and experiences and invited us on her Wilcannia River Radio programme to play our favourite songs and talk about our work. We are also grateful to the Community Broadcasting Association of Australia for their partnership and in-kind support.

Notes

1 Brendon Adams is proud Ku-Ku Yalangi/Woppaburra man from far north Queensland, Australia. Brendon worked at 4K1G in Townsville and before moving to the small outback town on Barkindji country (Wilcannia, NSW) where he served as Wilcannia River Radio Station Manager. In 2019, Brendon and his team won the Tony Staley Award for Excellence in Community Broadcasting for their coverage of issues relating to the Murray-Darling Basin. His work also includes facilitating numerous projects that address the challenges and barriers faced by First Nations people, as well as fostering social and emotional well-being in the local community.

2 Dodson (1996) explains, '[T]here is another dimension that invests the land with meaning and significance – that transforms the land and environment into landscape, and into "country". That other dimension is culture' (Dodson, 1996). 'Country' is an Australian Aboriginal term that is widely used to convey the sense of a fully cultural–spiritual landscape.

3 With over 450 stations throughout Australia, the Australian community broadcasting sector is premised on servicing geographic and cultural diversity. Seventy-six per cent of stations are in regional or remote areas and one-third of these stations are the only media outlet with local programming in their area (CBAA, 2020). In any given week, 4.7 million Australian's listen to community radio for around 15 hours per week (McNair, 2023) and over 19,000 volunteers and 1,000 paid staff participate in stations. Importantly, innumerable organisations – local community and government especially – use this sector to communicate with and for local audiences.

4 The *Warming Up* project's engagement with Wilcannia River Radio began in 2020 as part of a pilot study exploring how community radio stations approach climate change communication. Interviews, discussions, and yarning has been ongoing since then – station managers, broadcasters, and community members have all generously shared their stories, knowledge

and experiences. Visiting Wilcannia and Wilcannia River Radio and yarning on the banks of a full, flowing Baaka solidified much of our thinking about radical eco-communicative democracy and the role of First Nations community media therein. From these initial online interviews to a station visit and ongoing yarning about community and Country, Wilcannia River Radio is a valued partner on the project, all while playing the deadliest tunes in the outback!

References

Anderson, H., Backhaus, B., Fox, J. and Bedford, C. (2020) 'Fifty years of resistance and representation: A historical account of Australian community radio', *Journal of Radio & Audio Media*, 27(2), pp. 234–254.

Backhaus, B., Foxwell-Norton, K. and Leitch, A. (2023) 'Listening for the local: Australian community radio and climate change communication', *Media International Australia*. https://doi.org/10.1177/1329878X231193182

Bates, B. (2017) 'When they take the water from a Barkandji person, they take our blood', For IndigenousX, *The Guardian*, 26 July.

Beck, U. (1992) *Risk society: Towards a new modernity*. London: Sage.

Belfer, E., Ford, J.D. and Maillet, M. (2017) 'Representation of Indigenous peoples in climate change reporting', *Climatic Change*, 145, pp. 57–70.

Cai, W., Ng, B., Geng, T., et al. (2023) 'Anthropogenic impacts on twentieth-century ENSO variability changes', *Nature Review Earth & Environment*, 4, pp. 407–418.

Callison, C. (2021) 'Refusing more empire: Utility, colonialism, and Indigenous knowing', *Climatic Change*, 167, p. 58.

Carey, J. (1989) *Communication as culture*. New York: Routledge.

Castells, M. (2009) *Communication power*. Oxford: Oxford University Press.

Cottle, S. (2023) 'Reporting civilizational collapse: Research notes from a world-in-crisis', *Global Media and Communication*, 19(2), pp. 269–288.

Dodson, M. (1996) 'Indigenous peoples, social justice and rights to the environment' in Sultan, R. (ed.) *Perspectives on Indigenous peoples' management of environment resources: Ecopolitics IX conference papers and resolutions*/Ecopolitics conference, 1–3 September 1995, Darwin. Casuarina: Northern Land Council, pp. 25–29.Please

Escobar, A. (2020) 'Pluriversal politics' in *Pluriversal politics*. Durham: Duke University Press.

First Nations Media Australia (2023), 'Our Media', https://firstnationsmedia.org.au/our-media, accessed 18 September, 2024.

Forde, S., Foxwell, K., and Meadows, M. (2009), *Developing Dialogues: Indigenous and Ethnic Broadcasting in Australia*, Intellect: UK.

Foxwell-Norton, K. (2018) *Environmental communication and critical coastal policy: Communities, culture and nature*. London: Routledge.

Foxwell-Norton, K. (2016) 'The global alternative and community media sector: Prospects in an era of climate crisis', *Journal of Alternative & Community Media*, 1(1), pp. 12–13.

Foxwell-Norton, K., Backhaus, B. and Leitch, A. (2022) 'Warming up: The potential of community radio for climate change communication in Australia', *Journal of Alternative & Community Media*, 7(1), pp. 67–89.

Graham, M. (2014) 'Aboriginal notions of relationality and positionalism: A reply to Weber', *Global Discourse*, 4(1), pp. 17–22.

Habermas, J. (1989) *The Structural Transformation of the Public Sphere*, trans. by Burger, T. with Lawrence, F. Massachusetts: Massachusetts Institute of Technology.

Hulme, M. (2015) '(Still) disagreeing about climate change: Which way forward?', *Zygon*.

Jakubowicz, K. (1993) 'Stuck in a groove: Why the 1960s approach to communication democratization will no longer do' in Splichal, S. and Wasko, J. (eds.) *Communication and democracy*. Norwood: Ablex, pp. 33–54.

Jenkins, K. (2020) 'Activists blockade Wilcannia bridge, calling for action on water management', *NITV News*. Accessible at: https://www.sbs.com.au/nitv/article/activists-blockade-wilcannia-bridge-calling-for-action-on-water-management/ike3vdu3k

Kothari, A. (2014a) 'India 2100: Towards radical ecological democracy', *Futures*, 56, pp. 62–72.

Kothari, A. (2014b) 'Radical ecological democracy: A path forward for India and beyond', *Development*, 57(1), pp. 36–45.

Lester, L. and Foxwell-Norton, K. (2020) 'Citizens and science: Media, communication and conservation', *Conservation Research, Policy and Practice*, 265.

Martin, K. (2003) 'Ways of knowing, ways of being and ways of doing: A theoretical framework and methods for Indigenous re-search and Indigenist research', *Australian Studies*, 15.

McNair yellow Squares (2023), CBAA Community Radio Listener Survey, available at https://www.cbaa.org.au/broadcasters/get-data-national-listener-survey-station-census, accessed 18 September, 2024.

MDBA (Murray-Darling Basin Authority) (2023), 'About Us', https://www.mdba.gov.au/about-us, accessed 18 September, 2024.

Mesikämmen, E., Waller, L., & Burkett, B. (2021). Water wars: A "critical listening in" to rural radio discourse on a river system in trouble. *Environmental Communication, 15*(3), 369–385.

Nixon, R. (2011) *Slow Violence and the Environmentalism of the Poor*. Cambridge, MA; London: Harvard University Press.

Nursery-Bray, M., Palmer, R. and Rist, P. (2022) 'Chapter 6: Do Not Forget the Dreaming: Communicating Climate Change and Adaptation, Insights from Australia' in Nursery-Bray, N., Palmer, R., Chischilly, A.M., Rist, P. and Yin, L. (eds.) *Old ways for new days: Indigenous survival and agency in climate changed times*. Cham: Springer.

Pearce, B., Brown, B., Nerlich, B. and Koteyko, N. (2015) 'Communicating climate change: Conduits, content, and consensus', *WIREs Clim Change*, 6 , pp. 613–626.

Quijano, A. (2000). Coloniality of Power and Eurocentrism in Latin America. *International Sociology*, 15(2), 215-232.

Rommetveit, K., Funtowicz, S. and Strand, R. (2010) 'Knowledge, democracy and action in response to climate change' in Bhaskar, R., Frank, C., Høyer, K.G., Næss, P. and Parker, J. (eds.) *Interdisciplinarity and climate change transforming knowledge and practice for our global future*. Oxon: Routledge.

Simis, M.J., Madden, H., Cacciatore, M.A. and Yeo, S.K. (2016) 'The lure of rationality: Why does the deficit model persist in science communication?', *Public Understanding of Science*, 25(4), pp. 400–414.

Sultana, F. (2022, November) 'The unbearable heaviness of climate coloniality', *Political Geography*, 99.

Whyte, K.P. (2018) 'Indigenous science (fiction) for the Anthropocene: Ancestral dystopias and fantasies of climate change crises', *Environment and Planning E: Nature and Space*, 1(1–2), pp. 224–242.

Whyte, K. (2020) 'Against crisis epistemology' in Hokowhitu, B., Moreton-Robinson, A., Tuhiwai-Smith, L., Larkin, S. and Andersen, C. (eds.) *Handbook of Critical Indigenous Studies*. New York: Routledge.

·7·

GREEN FESTIVALS AND RE-FIGURATIVE POLITICS: COMMUNICATING RESILIENCE AND HOPE

Steve Muggeridge

This chapter reviews the evolution of a sector of the contemporary festival environment from popular celebration to social movement, as expressed through Green festivals. The perspective offered here is based on my personal involvement in such events over many years, from the Free festivals of the 1980s and as organiser of Green events and as a long-term director of the Green Gathering festivals.

This experience informs my conviction that Green festivals are important, though often overlooked for engaged community consciousness of the accelerating global ecological crisis, as well as potential responses to it. Such festivals, I argue, provide opportunities for communicating themes of community and ecology, from historic practices of sustainability to possible future pathways. And that this tradition of festivals has fostered and promoted a counter-narrative to the manufactured consensus of consumerism promoted by mainstream media, a narrative considered subversive by successive governments who remain wedded it seems to the pursuit of ecologically unsustainable economic growth and possessive materialism.

Green festivals are opportunities for individual and collective re-figurations. By 'collective re-figurations' I mean the opportunities for some groups of people to periodically come together, and through their participation in and enactment of 'creative-critical milieus', both express and deepen their attachment to utopian, that is alternative future-oriented ways of life and being. This can be contrasted to the usual notion of 'pre-figurative politics' which is often seen as the 'strategy to change society through an everyday conduct that fully reflects idealized notions of the Self and society' (Deflorian, 2021, p. 346). Though Green festivals are a temporary and periodic iteration of alternative values and ways of being, they can nonetheless be powerful incubators for communicating ideas and feelings for possible transitions to a socially just and ecologically sustainable society.

At a time of increasing digital social alienation and diminishing trust in the capacity of contemporary politics to respond to the growing ecological crisis, Green festivals perform a significant role. They provide opportunities for like-minded people to come together in re-figured relations and share, if only for a limited time, alternative ways of being in a mutually supportive social space. Green festivals should not be assumed to be largely exercises in commercial mass hedonism and the Green Gathering festivals I have been involved in for many years have managed, unlike many other contemporary festivals, to not succumb to commercial interests and the corporate provision of 'mass entertainment'. Their popularity is increasing, and this is driven in part by the evident enthusiasm for identification and engagement with a sense of community that is often absent in everyday life and contemporary urban living. Green festivals offer a point of connection, with others, with nature, and with imagined futures that become even more necessary and urgent in a world confronting ecological collapse.

As their attraction grows in line with a more widespread awakening to environmental and ecological concerns from the local to the planetary, so they are also likely to incur increased hostility from entrenched political and commercial interests who remain resistant to change. As I review below, the Free/Green festival movement has been subject to repressive and sometimes violent responses by powerholders over the years and as such, they have not only been incubators of collective hope but also forced bastions of dissent. Often confronting draconian attempts to crush and contain the perceived threat of free/Green festivals, their supporters have had to find forms of collective resilience, and these have variously drawn upon earlier traditions of dissent.

With these broad ideas in mind, the discussion now turns to briefly address: (i) the historical rise of Green festivals, (ii) their underpinning philosophy and values in contrast to mainstream commercial festivals, (iii) their pioneering efforts in respect of promulgating green ideas and practices, (iv) their importance in terms of community and re-figuration of politics, (v) their encounters with repression and forms of resilient response, and (vi) prospects and problems moving forward. The chapter concludes by re-stating the often-overlooked significance of Green festivals in providing a re-figurative space and opportunity to creatively explore and exchange ideas and practices, both past and present, but all future-oriented, that can help to build communities of hope and pathways of transition to an ecologically sustainable and socially just world.

The road to Green festivals

Festivals celebrating culture, religion and diverse events have an ancient provenance. Some that emerged in the late 1960s and 1970s, diverged from the commercial provision of entertainment to become 'Free Festivals'. Elements of the contemporary counter-culture took to the fields with a range of motivations, from permanent partying and hedonism to the adoption of alternative lifestyles and ideals for the foundation of an idealised society. A renewed philosophic social contract for community and environment was actively under exploration.

Without commercial resources to stage Free Festivals, a support network developed through these years. This expressed contemporary counter-cultural values including conscious attempts to develop alternative individual and collective identities. This re-forging of community identity, even on a temporary basis, involved large numbers of people and drew on historically preceding challenges to established political structures. The apex of the Free Festival movement was the Stonehenge Free Festivals from the late 1970s until 1984. By 1984, the festival was estimated to involve over 20,000 people for two to three weeks. The assembly of people ranged from pagan/druid groups, various 'Traveller' lifestyles, political visionaries and people of all classes and occupations gathering to celebrate the Summer Solstice.

Traveller groups encompassed traditional traveller ethnicities but also encompassed people seeking alternative semi-nomadic lifestyles who became termed by mainstream media as 'New Age Travellers'. Relationships between such allied groups extended beyond festival seasons and ultimately became a sustained core of networks that supported and initiated alternative and counter-cultural projects.

Direct communication between individuals and groups assisted the emergence of a unifying counter-narrative to mainstream socio-economic culture.

A distinct strand referenced folkloric traditions of festival assembly, celebration of nature and season, and the growing awareness of an ecological crisis brought about by contemporary consumer society. The emerging eco-consciousness reflected early growing environmental awareness in wider society, and this further helped seed environmental organisations and campaigns.

Mainstream media was predictably hostile to any social experiments and produced lurid misrepresentations at this time. They tended to focus on negative impacts of festivals and the inevitable camp followers and festival people more motivated by unregulated partying, than conscious idealism. Hostility appears to have been based on common concern that widespread 're-figurations' of society, as embodied and exemplified in free festivals, would challenge the manufactured consensus of consumer society, its social structures and economic interests. Ironically perhaps, it was a consequence of the unbridled consumerism of capitalism in the 1980s that growing numbers of people were initially attracted to free festivals. Mainstream media nonetheless generally vilified so-called New Age Travellers and their lifestyle.

Historically, there has been a traditional suspicion by authorities of large gatherings of people assembling without government or religious sanction, especially when espousing different values and aspirations to established governmental policies (Thompson, 1963, 1980). In historically turbulent times, the fear of insurrection and the nurturing of counter-narratives threatening established authority may have some foundation. Traditional rural festivals, for example, often inverted the established order of social hierarchy, while embracing nature and spring renewal as an eternal order eclipsing transitory temporal political power.

Past traditions also associated the stewardship of natural resources with just governance and the well-being of the people. Free Festivals and its supporting movement encompassed elements of these traditional celebrations. The increasing popularity of pagan spiritual ideas and customs also aligned with these earlier historic traditions, and together implicitly challenged mainstream ideas of social order and established hierarchy. Free festivals and Green gatherings often positioned themselves at ancient and traditional centres of spirituality and celebration – in particular ancient monuments. This further challenged the established view by heritage bodies of ownership, as did ideas of popular access as common wealth. Perhaps only a minority of people attending such festivals at this time however were motivated to develop counter-culture as an agency for political change.

By 1984 the Stonehenge Free Festival reflected the tensions in mainstream society of economic decline and political conflict, exemplified in the coal-miners' strike, and the subsequent defeat of the miner's union. In addition, some of the original idealism of the New Age Traveller had been significantly darkened by the nihilism of young refugees from the economic depression of that time, many of whom were motivated less by idealism, than escape from bleak economic and urban environments. The change of festival zeitgeist at this time, combined with obstructions from local police forces and councils, resulted in no post-festival clear-up that year. This was a 'gift' to a hostile media keen to report on the negative impact of free festivals on the rural environment and heritage sites.

Without practical social structures to support and guide the collective experiments in utopian community at this point, they proved unsustainable over any extended period of time, During the early 1980s, protest camps had been established at various military bases to protest against the deployment of US missiles. In 1984 New Age Travellers along with other protestors were evicted from the Molesworth peace camp, demonstrating the close affinity between festival goers and political activism. Collaboration and common cause between social and political movements with the increasing popularity of festivals in the 1980s soon became demonised in Margret Thatcher's populist rhetoric of the 'enemy within'.

In June 1985, an attempt by convoys of Travellers and free festival supporters to establish the Stonehenge Free Festival was brutally suppressed. This soon became established in festival folklore as the 'The Battle of the Beanfield' (Worthington 2005) and effectively marked the end of the free festival movement. In the following years, successive legislation further attempted to criminalise and end the New Age Traveller lifestyle.

Though free festivals had failed to establish themselves as a sustainable structure at this time, in collaboration with dissenting political movements they had challenged the political orthodoxy of the period. As the free festival movement waned, Green consciousness and environmental activism nonetheless continued to grow. Surviving elements of the festival movement became more politically aware and organised. By the early 1990s this was demonstrated in the protest movement against the ecological impact of an expanded road-building programme. This drew upon free festival veterans and Travellers who assisted the establishment of long-term protest camps. Cooperation between Green activists and the remaining free festival movement continued.

Small gatherings began to appear, described as gatherings of varied 'Greens', and incorporating diverse social and political campaigns. The free festival had morphed into the Green festival, with the explicit objective of bringing together diverse elements of contemporary counter-culture, Green activism, alternative lifestyles and various belief traditions. In a period before the widespread use of the internet and mobile phones, communication between counter-cultural projects was by printed flyers, posters and word of mouth. Festivals were represented negatively for the most part, as we have heard, in the narratives and news depictions of conventional media outlets. And the festival community, pre-internet and widely available mobile phones, did not have the ability or means to communicate positive perspectives to counter misrepresentation.

Green gatherings had been occurring as small camps throughout the 1970s and 1980s. The Big Green Gathering (BGG) began in the early 1990s, as a celebration and gathering of Green activists and lifestyles. It soon became the largest opportunity for networking and incorporated varied counter-cultural tribes, environmental activists and folkloric traditions.

The road to Green Festivals, as described, has been complex and often contested. The Free Festival evolved in the latter part of the twentieth century and provided alternative narratives to contemporary national economic and political life. Disparate groups of social and political campaigners motivated by ideas of social justice and environmental awareness came together in festivals of community. They proved to be unsustainable and difficult to stage due to lack of structure and resources, as well as hostility by national and local authorities and negative media misrepresentations. Nonetheless, philosophies and traditions evolved and coalesced into a powerful legacy that still communicates across generations. This was the provenance of creative-critical thought and practices that flowed into the foundation of Green festivals.

Green festivals: Paradigm shifts

Green festivals are not defined by commercial contracts for profitability, but stewardship and development of the assembled community and diverse projects and causes. There are social and political objectives to this form of gathering beyond commerce and entertainment.

A shared philosophic focus on ecology and social justice had not hitherto been expressed so explicitly as a core objective for gathering as a festival. Definitions of a 'Green' festival may vary, though a number of elements prove common to festivals of such description. Green festivals primarily provide the platform for the exhibition, demonstration and discussion of 'Green' concepts and traditions, including alternative lifestyles, spirituality and philosophical pathways. Such a diverse environment has demonstrated a positive impact on the cross-fertilisation of concepts and practices to different groups and traditions. Rooted in ideas of ecology and social justice, diverse groups each pursuing their own pathways to personal and collective re-figuration gather in a collective exposition of politics and ways of shared being. They do so as a temporary community but sometimes extending beyond the gathering of festival.

In providing opportunities at festival to collaborate and cross-communicate experiences, traditions and philosophies, the framework of such events does not require or impose any overarching conceptual or philosophic orthodoxy. It does require, however, a commitment to act and inter-act mindful of ethical behaviour as commonly understood by the assembled community and defined in the Terms and Conditions of the festival. A gathering of people as a temporary Green community requires common acknowledgement of the varied philosophies represented, without necessarily endorsing any, and respecting divergencies of thoughts and belief. This guiding principle is often in stark contrast to the deliberate binary polarisation of positions, ideas and debates found and orchestrated in mainstream media.

Active participants at Green festivals include a wide range of causes, campaigns and traditions. Individual and group allegiances and identities often overlap, forming a consensus in diversity, and in counterpoint to conventional socio-economic narratives and structures. A collective identity founded in that consensus both shapes and is shaped by the festival community which, as a whole, is greater than the sum of its parts.

Festivals that identify as Green, with social and economic objectives, are also distinct in recognising the value of folkloric, spiritual and cultural traditions as well as their continuing relevance in the contemporary world. Historic and traditional manifestations of eco-consciousness in gatherings have been associated with non-conformity or dissent. Green festivals have a heritage that confers continuity with their contemporary existential purpose, and a responsibility to communicate that tradition to future generations of festival participants. Communication between the festival and attending public raises and explores various responses and possible solutions to issues and challenges in the unfolding ecological crisis, and these may draw upon historically grounded traditions that demonstrate the continuity of sources of wisdom and their resilience over time.

Many established members of any festival community will identify both as members of a constituent group in producing the event and as members of the wider festival community, during and outside of the event. People attending perhaps for the first time, may be seeking to re-define their identity and societal role or join like-minded people in a liminal or 'time-out' experience.

Across the evolution of Green festivals, the focus has increasingly been on the impending ecological emergency. With the realisation that climate change is already unfolding and deepening, that focus is now being re-calibrated to one of resilience and adaption for changing environmental realities. Individual resilience and well-being are now seen as best secured in community support and response, rather than a continuation of the competitive individualism and incessant economic growth of consumer society.

Green festivals can best be conceived, then, as social enterprises that act as outliers from the wider mainstream conventional society. They have purpose and meaning in helping to prepare festival participants as well as wider society for some of the transitions now required in the face of climate change and other existential challenges. Green festivals communicate past traditions of environmental thought and wisdom to future gatherings and they create opportunities for individual and collective re-figuration in response to these. That is, they provide the means, albeit based on a temporary 'liminal' experience or 'time-out', of variously exploring longer-term lifestyle changes and ways thinking and being. In offering developmental pathways for adaptation, change and resilience, they can also be seen, and importantly experienced in community solidarity as incubators of hope.

Pioneers and progress

As we have heard, there is a legacy by Green festivals in preparing and communicating pathways for ecological change and adaption. An increase in environmental activism and awareness in the early 1990s was reflected with festivals inclusion of an environmental focus or content. The Big Green Gathering pioneered the format of an in-depth participatory festival, gathering together various counter-cultural groups as a festival of both activism and cultural expression and performances. Most Green festivals remain small to medium size events compared with some huge contemporary commercial festivals. The establishment of the Green Futures Field at the Glastonbury Festival in the 1990s further marked the arrival of Green awareness at large commercial festivals and continues to this day (Green Futures Field, 2023).

By the early years of the twenty-first century, issues of ecology had moved from the fringes of popular concern to the mainstream. This trend has continued to increase, as has the general popularity of festivals, to the current festival scene. Few commercial events now do not claim engagement at some level with Green and environmental issues.

The increase in awareness of environmental issues has coincided with the general elevation of the festival from fringe activity to mainstream social institution, many as large commercial events. The arrival of widespread social media assisted this development. Positive individual and informal festival experiences can be easily shared, by-passing the historically negative narrative of mainstream media. In an apparent recognition of the changing popular fashion for festivals, mainstream media appears have now also changed their stance toward some festivals, and actively promote them. Though typically this concerns large commercial festivals based on conventional corporate objectives and the provision of popular entertainment. The currency of environmental awareness at festivals has at least been a partial success in communicating many of the complex challenges in transitioning to a sustainable way of life. In the context of increasing uncertainty and diminishing confidence in conventional social structures, re-figurative politics has become for many, not just a choice, but necessary if we are to develop resilient communities capable of adapting to the consequences of climate and other ecological changes.

The establishment of sustainability across the festival Industry can be seen as a positive development. In recent years there has been significant effort to reduce the environmental impact of producing and delivering such events. An initial focus on the carbon impact of events has developed to evaluate the impact of all areas of related production. In 2007, A Greener Festival (AGF) began a rigorous certification and awards scheme to help monitor, assess and improve festival green credentials. These ratings and awards are communicated to festival audiences, with any sustainability awards typically promoted as part of festival marketing profiles.

Mainstream festivals have developed from fringe activities to major commercial operations that annually engage significant numbers of people as a multi-billion-pound industry. The adoption of more sustainable production policies and the promotion at events of Green issues, have a wide reach, influencing public behaviour both during, and after the event. Post event participant feedback from Green Gatherings, for example, indicate that significant numbers of people attending the event change aspects of their behaviour in support of Green agendas. Younger festival audiences have been noticeably enthusiastic in their engagement with festival themes and campaigns at the Green Gathering and the Green Futures Field at Glastonbury festival.

This enduring attraction and growth of Green festivals and awareness across the festival spectrum is a cause for hope. However, the virtue-signalling of Green credentials by some commercial festivals through token tree planting as a carbon offset, or a few 'stalls' representing environmental NGOs, for example, can also demonstrate a commitment to profile rather than ecological concern.

This legacy from pioneering Green events nonetheless is generally evidence of the success of the counter-cultural festival movement in communicating and promoting Green issues and campaigns. They have helped shape the contemporary festival industry's progress towards sustainability and social engagement. The transition of independent and Green festivals from relatively marginal standing and status to increased popularity and ecological standing, also reflects the rise of ecological awareness in general society. The communication of Green issues to audiences at Green and conventional commercial festivals is inter-active and inter-personal and can serve as an influencer beyond mass media. The rising popularity of festivals reflects, I suggest, an increasing search for alternative community identity and this is only likely to increase in the ecologically troubled years ahead.

Festival community and re-figuration

Green festivals have been effective as stewards of once marginal, alternative practices and concepts and by projecting them into mainstream festival culture and beyond. They also hold deep insights into the forms of organisation and practice that can sustain pathways to transition in wider society. These as described below, revolve around participation, trust, equity, community identity, organisational structure and sense of connectivity.

Many non-corporate festivals are social enterprises in which a critical aspect of financial viability is the engagement of volunteers and supporters. This is only possible when a community supporting a festival project can identify with both the objectives and delivery of the event. How festivals are planned and delivered therefore matters for the longer-term sustainability of the supporting community. That community needs to be participatory and involved with planning; it needs to identify itself with those objectives agreed as worthwhile. Engagement and agency as valued aspects of festival, increase trust in the event's management, and this lends collective authority to decisions made during the festival.

Without this confidence based on participation, trust and transparency, the disparate groups and identities that comprise 'Green' festivals have difficulty in coalescing into a greater collective identification for the pursuit of the festival common purpose. To deliver a festival, resources are needed for a number of different goals, interests and agendas. Allocation of festival resources with transparency and relative equity to content, therefore, also proves key. And this too serves as a possible template of use to others in a just transition to sustainability.

Festivals can encompass different social and political causes and express diverse traditions and beliefs, but they can also create a community of common cause and shared objectives – as we heard above. This unity in diversity, rather than multiple binaries of opposition that characterise wider society, provides a further template of wider relevance in the successful pursuit of sustainable pathways. The shared collective identity can also extend beyond the temporal-spatial festival setting and does so in an extended network of mutually supportive campaigns and loosely affiliated communities. Collaborative communities have greater resilience to climate challenges than vying vested interests or systems based on competitive individualism.

The collective re-figuration of festival community members can influence practices of adaptation in the immediate term as well as the longer term when participants form into ecologically conscious and relatively stable networks of mutuality and support. Sustainable sharing of resources within and between communities in confederation, can further enhance transparency and equitable outcomes. In respect of social hierarchy, the longer-term members of festival communities may acquire higher status within that community. But the acquisition of status and social mobility within festival community is not primarily driven by material wealth or the attributed status of 'success' as typically measured in mainstream society. Festival workers working in different roles often enjoy greater social status within the festival community, than their equivalents in the mainstream economy. Status in festival community tends to be accumulated over time, and is relative to a particular skill set and reputation gained from previous events. Status is not dependent, therefore, on organisational or social hierarchy conventionally conceived. This too provides a social template of possible use in processes of ecologically informed re-figuration in wider society and when seeking mutually supportive and participatory ways of coming together to respond to growing climate and other challenges.

The rising popularity of festival gatherings, according to a number of industry surveys is based on the sense of belonging and participation in a tangible community that serves as a counterpoint to the increasingly digital fragmentation of society. The experience of sharing open fires at festivals, as one of the most ancient forms of sociality, for example, offers connectivity not just to other people, but also to an elementally immersive experience. This lived and felt experience can communicate a deeper sense of presence and connectivity than virtual encounters mediated through social media networks. It is in and through these and other Green festival spaces/places, that a lived sense of connectivity and presence with nature and others becomes manifest. Green ideas and sensibilities in such moments and settings resonate with those of community, ecology and sustainability.

In the context of reduced social mobility and increasing wealth disparity in mainstream society today, re-figurative politics through participation in communities of resilience and support holds increased attraction for many. A spiritual or religious re-alignment for some may also be linked to a changed relationship with environment and community. The current increase in interest in Green festivals is partly driven by wider economic trajectories of decline and difficulty and the perception that fundamental societal change will be inevitable in the context of climate change. This will demand adaptation and changing skill sets designed for resilience.

The continuity of Green and alternative festivals over decades has seen multi-generational involvement. Established members of some festival communities may have multiple generations working together at events. Generational discovery and re-discovery of Green and other festivals has manifested in waves of interest and involvement over the decades, often in parallel with increased Green activism.

Governmental obstruction and suppression of gatherings deemed subversive has resulted in more organised and resilient festivals, morphing the utopian but unsustainable Free Festival movement to Green festivals that are now more focused on pathways of structured transition to a Greener society.

The focus of Green festivals on societal change is evident through its stated purposes and agreed charters of good practices, on-site campaigns, hosting of diverse workshops, speakers and discussions, and of course in and through many of its staged performances and music. Festival events such as these deliver encounters and experiences that are often at the forefront of Green practices and future imagining, whether 'from permaculture to peddle power, from sustainability to solar power' (Green Futures Field, 2023). Or, as the latest Green Gathering website describes itself: 'The original off-grid, non-profit festival: we're powered by sun, wind, people and passion for change' and 'Join us for four days of low-impact living' and 'This festival's impact lasts longer than a weekend' (Green Gathering, 2024).

In all these different expressions of re-figurative politics, templates of good practice point to the ways in which the distinctive community ethos and organisational practices of Green festivals could yet also register in wider pathways of transition and as the climate and ecological crises continue to deepen and compound each other as now seems to be unavoidable. Tested templates for participation, trust, equity, community identity, organisational structure and a developed sense of connectivity are all requisite to successfully forging and building communities of common practice and shared concern. Wider society may have much to learn of use from the experience and ethos of Green festivals.

Repression and resilience

The successful perpetuation of eco-consciousness, ideas and culture over a period of decades has not been without struggles, opposition and costs. Gatherings, especially unauthorised assemblies, have been viewed with suspicion by authorities of all eras. Repressive policies by various government administrations and political parties through the agencies of police, local councils, ministerial departments, mainstream media and public order legislation, have ranged from obstruction to suppression. As Green activism became more widespread and prominent, so did the perceived challenge. Periods of repression have required both resilience and re-invention, as we have already heard.

The very existence of the Free festival was subversive to the normative values of individual and collective success and well-being, promoted by the economic agenda of the early 1980s. As a stark counterpoint to the aggressive policies of individualism and privatisation of that period, opportunities for people to gather and explore alternative lifestyles and values was often taken as a particular threat to the new economic orthodoxy. In the context of the suppression of organised labour with the miner's strikes in 1984, the suppression of alternative poles of thought and activity continued with government demonisation of the Traveller and Free festival community.

The iconic Stonehenge Free Festival was suppressed in the so-called 'Battle of the Beanfield', as mentioned. This suppression of both the festival and the free festival movement was endorsed and promoted by much of the pre-internet media, that acted as a distorting mirror to the actual experience of many attending festivals. Demonisation and the misrepresentation of activist and counter-cultural groups thereafter, it seems, became the default policy of media portrayal of future environmental campaign groups.

Collective activism became prominent again in the early 1990s with the emergence of the road protest movement in reaction to a road expansion programme. Actions often took the form of extended occupations of proposed development sites, with protest camps. Free festival, traveller and environmental activist communities became mutually supportive in establishing and sustaining such protest camps. Opportunities for re-figuration, individually and collectively, at this time became more explicitly allied with ecology and protests. They also became increasingly visible within mainstream media and routinely portrayed as a threat to the established social and political order by much of it. After protest camps were dispersed, activist groups and campaigns continued to evolve with an increasing cross-over of activists and festivals.

Land ownership has historically impacted on environmental sustainability, access to resources and the well-being of local populations. Over many centuries, access to the 'land' as a common resource has been systematically restricted by private ownership, promoting short-term exploitation rather than sustainability and commonwealth. The control of access to spaces for gatherings of people, especially unauthorised, was and is, a key tool for the suppression of assemblies. This control of access means that festivals and gatherings of any significant number of people are entirely conditional. This conditionality is enacted and enforced through various public order legislation to the Licensing legislation for regulating public events. Any assemblies not authorised by such means are unlawful and deemed rebellious simply by their existence. The default but often disingenuous reason cited for suppression of un-Licensed events is 'public safety', as defined by the same licensing authorities.

Permissions by regulating authorities can be seen as a form of repressive control. They require an organisational hierarchy under the guise of public safety interests, where named organisers can be held to account for the conduct and impact of a festival. Compliance with legislation for festivals and sustainable financial management also requires the formation of financial entities as companies or cooperatives. This can produce greater financial sustainability for festivals but also increased vulnerability to constructive bankruptcy by financial sanction – as was the case with the Big Green Gathering.

The Big Green Gathering (BGG) was established in the early 1990s as an off-grid Green festival and had grown by 2007 to an event of more than 20,000 activists and supporters. The event supported the Climate Camp, an activist campaign to change national energy policy and close coal-fired power stations. The campaign had been infiltrated by one of the many secret police placed within environmental groups at that time. A combination of police and licensing authority pressure forced the festival to cancel, on pain of forced dispersal and arrest (Vidal, 2009). This was clearly linked to the event's support of activists. The constructive bankruptcy of the festival production company also had serious collateral damage to the many local businesses that had invested in trading at the event. It was only by resilient determination that the event was re-founded as the Green Gathering in 2011. Though a smaller festival than BGG, it remains an annual event in 2023, and has attracted international recognition and awards as a pioneering Green event.

Festival production is thus a careful balance between nurturing crucibles of creativity and campaigns and managing imposed structures of regulation and control. Green and independent festivals have evolved as we have heard in response to repressive state responses and governments restrictions as well as changing popular perspectives on ecology and social justice. Creativity and resilience continue to define festival communities to this day, who must comply with restrictive conditions to avoid suppression whilst continuing to communicate alternative narratives to new generations.

Prospects and problems

With the impacts of climate change now beginning to become an everyday reality, Green festivals are increasingly recognised as an important advocate for finding pathways to a more sustainable society. Mainstream commercial festivals though now engaged with reducing their own environmental impacts and communicating environmental issues to their audiences, are not known for promoting radical social and economic agendas required for a deeper Green transition.

Gatherings enable direct communication between diverse people with common objectives. In the current media environment, there is ever increasing information and misinformation and decreasing trust in sources. Inter-personal contact and communication at festivals is a counterpoint to the discussion and distortions of mainstream and digital media. The attraction of personal interaction appears to have increased interest in festivals for people and communities exploring re-figurative pathways and adaption to climate changes. The future role of such gatherings would seem positive, with increasing participation and recognition of their value in developing a consensus for change. Green festivals serve a common good, advocating Green lifestyle changes and challenging those commercial and governmental interests benefiting from today's ecologically unsustainable status quo. However, as the impacts of climate and other ecological crises continue to accelerate and deepen, affecting everyday lives, so we may witness increasing political fragmentation and polarisation as well as calls for fundamental societal change. In such times Green festivals along with ecological activists can anticipate on the basis of previous decades increased forms of repression and attempted political control.

The direction in the UK at the time of writing is to increasingly criminalise expressions of concern and activism communicated through public gatherings. The evidence of recent legislation in the UK confirms that governments and vested interests unable or unwilling to engage in meaningful changes for a just transition, are choosing policies of repression, rather than reform. The experience of the Free and Green festivals in resilient morphing for continuity described above, maintains the hope that their tradition will continue with future generations of festival, despite any attempts at marginalisation or suppression. In the event of a substantial breakdown of current social structures, the legacies of Green festivals may yet prove beneficial in assisting the development of re-figured sustainable communities.

Other structural challenges however pose further problematic dynamics that will need to be addressed. The transitory structures and hierarchical responsibilities required by Licensed, 'approved' festivals and events, already mentioned, are sustainable only for limited duration. The balance of tensions between required structure from external authorities, and progressive discussion and inter-action in free association, requires continuous enterprise and ingenuity. Even so, there are grounds for optimism for the continuation of Green festivals.

The increasing interest and participation by young people in Green festivals in recent years is encouraging, not least because a younger generation of festival organisers will need to continue the tradition of Green and alternative festivals in the decades ahead. The experience of organisers that have been part of the journey from Free to Green festivals is also a legacy of hope and resilience and can be passed on to the next generation of organisers who will need to respond, no doubt, to new legislative attempts to restrict and control gatherings. There is hope and evidence, with a recent significant increase in attendance by the 18–24 generation at the Green Gathering and Glastonbury Green Fields, that a renewed generational interest will both populate and organise future incarnations of festival as transformative events of community. This counterpoint to conventional societal and media narratives will only become more necessary in a world-in-crisis over the years ahead.

Conclusion

The legacy of the Free festival and currency of contemporary Green festivals continues to manifest through the creative expressions and collective critique of like-minded people, who periodically come together to challenge those ecologically destructive priorities of a world wedded to incessant economic growth, and which has brought us to a world of deepening crises. Green festivals represent a continuity of counter-cultural dissent, communicated through popular gatherings of performance and music, Green activism and alternative lifestyles. They serve to focus on traditions of environmental stewardship and project forward potential future iterations of resilient and sustainable society. The existence of Green festivals challenges policies of ecocide through their existence as gathered networks of campaigners for sustainable society in direct communication with each other and attending publics. Their history of resilience, despite attempts at suppression, and transition to recognised pioneers in the festival industry, suggests that they will continue to serve as incubators of collective action and hope. They are an important if often overlooked site of re-figurative politics where diverse groups of people take time-out to come together to creatively share and explore Green ideas and practices as lived experience and, importantly, future imagining.

References

Deflorian, M. (2021) 'Re-figurative politics: Understanding the volatile participation of critical creatives in community gardens, repair cafes, and clothing swaps', Social Movement Studies, 20(3), pp. 346–363. https://doi.org/10.1080/14742837.2020.1773250

Green Futures Field (2023) *Green futures field*. https://www.glastonburyfestivals.co.uk/areas/the-green-fields/green-futures/, accessed 27 March 2024.

Green Gathering (2024) *The original off-grid festival*. https://www.greengathering.org.uk/, accessed 5 January 2024.

Thompson, E.P. (1963/2013) *The making of the English working class*. London: Penguin.

Thompson, E.P. (1980/1991) *Customs in common*. London: Merlin Press.

Vidal, J. (2009) 'Big green gathering festival cancelled after "political pressure" ', The Guardian, 28 July 2009.

Worthington, A. (ed.) (2005) *The battle of the beanfield*. Teignmouth: Enabler Publications.

Section III:

Photography, Documentary and Film: Visualising Change

· 8 ·

FANTASY IN VISUAL SPECTACLES OF CLIMATE CHANGE

Niina Uusitalo

On 19 August 2019, the hashtag #PrayForAmazonia reached the top trends of Brazilian Twitter. As wildfires rapidly spread across the Amazon Rainforest, social media users all over the world turned their attention toward the global crisis (Arruda, 2022). Images of the burning rainforest also reached my personal social media streams. My attention was grabbed by catastrophic images of flames and smoke which evoked a sense of dread and helplessness. I reposted an appeal from Greenpeace and donated a small amount of money to the organisation. I would later come to think of this moment as an example of spectacular environmentalism where I had become a spectator of environmental destruction while having no effect on the actual causes of such events (Gunderson, 2020).

Research has previously established that stereotypical images of climate change are often catastrophic and emotive: dried-up deserts, burning forests, melting glaciers, tearing hurricanes and starving polar bears. The more optimistic images feature solar panels, wind parks and electric cars, celebrity-activists, high-status politicians and climate activists (Kangas, 2016). Many of these images are symbolic and spectacular in essence (see Lester and Cottle, 2009, p. 926). They seem to portray the phenomena of climate change believably but – at the same time – they somehow set viewers as distant spectators fearing for the future and hoping for some magical shift in the world politics. This points to the dynamics between spectacle and fantasy: the appeal of spectacles is based on the affective power of personal and social fantasies.

In this chapter I discuss visual climate spectacles and the affective power that fantasies have in these spectacles in two opposing ways: fantasies promise enjoyment and fullness to viewing subjects, but the flipside of such enjoyment is the intense fear and anxiety evoked by catastrophic images. I illuminate how even these unpleasant emotive states are based on underlining fantasmic promises.

I begin by an interpretation of the concept of the *spectacle* drawing from Guy Debord's writings. I then consider how spectacles are related to the subjects constructed in modern mediated environmentalisms. After this I show how the psychoanalytical concept of *fantasy* can further illuminate the allure of spectacular climate change images. In the final section, I will employ the concept of fantasy to study the suggestive power of both dystopian and utopian photographs of climate change.

Spectacular environmentalisms

The Western news media's spectacular visualisation of climate change, presenting arresting images symbolising the harmful impacts of climate change on people, communities and environments has, undoubtedly, helped to establish climate change as a widely recognised global challenge (Lester and Cottle, 2009, p. 921; Beck, 2010, p. 261). Such images render the abstract science of climate change culturally meaningful and politically consequential; geographically remote spaces become perceptible and 'knowable' places of possible concern and action (Beck, 2010, p. 261).

Goodman et al. (2016) argue that we now increasingly know about the environment through different forms, processes and aspects of the spectacle. Elements of spectacle are present in environmental disasters: visual communication of natural disasters, overflowing landfills or polluted landscapes that seemingly invite responses of awe or dread (see Cottle, 2008; Lester and Cottle, 2009). Spectacular environmentalisms can also refer to staged 'mega-media events' and coordinated global demonstrations (Cottle, 2008, p. 86). For instance, COP conferences, sustainability EXPOs, and Earth Hours have become widely represented in news media and social media. The Fridays for Future movement initiated by climate activist Greta Thunberg has taken climate-related mega-media events to a new level: the spectacularised images and quotes from Thunberg have circulated side-by-side images of massive climate strikes and marches globally. This is connected to growing celebritisation of climate change and the spectacle-isation of politics more generally (see Boykoff and Goodman, 2009).

Moreover, we are often being told about 'solutions' to ecological problems through spectacular environmentalisms: both news media and social media frame environmental issues and offer up pedagogical narratives about how humans should care for the more-than-human nature (see Goodman et al., 2018, p. 681). This is evident in imagery portraying different types of 'ecopiety', meaning practices of environmental or 'green' virtue, through daily voluntary works of duty and obligation: for instance, recycling, saving energy or purchasing green products (MacFarland Taylor, 2019; Niemelä-Nyrhinen and Seppänen, 2019; Uusitalo, 2020).

The power and techniques of visual and affective spectacles in producing subject positions are at the core of Debordian theory of spectacle. For Debord (1967/1987) a spectacle is not only a collection of images but a social relationship between people that is mediated by images. He argued that spectacle's power to transform fragments of reality into a visually pervasive totality, created a separate 'pseudo world'. This offered a world of commodity fetishism where the tangible world is replaced by a selection of images in exchange for the totality of actual activities and relationships. Thus, for Debord, mediated spectacle was a manifestation of modern consumer society in which a process of visual commodity fetishism was supplanting real forms of human connection and sociality. Debord's view of a visually mediated social world seems even more pertinent in the current era of the social media.

Debord criticised the spectacle as a tool of pacification and depolitisation which distracts social subjects from the most urgent tasks of real life (Debord, 1967/1987; Kellner, 2005, p. 3). He thought that the depolitising potential of the spectacle is based on its ability to project unity and consensus where none actually exists which in turn alienates people from knowing their own existence and desires outside the spectacle (Debord, 1967/1987). In a similar vein, Jonathan Crary (2002, p. 462) points to the fact that the spectacle is, in fact, a set of techniques for the management of bodies and management of attention.

However, one can criticise the Debordian idea of spectacle for disregarding possibilities for civic action and rebellion. Jonathan Crary (2002, p. 455) asks whether spectacle is a totalising and monolithic concept which inadequately represents a plurality of incommensurable institutions. Also, Goodman et al.

note that a narrow theory of spectacle relies on an overtly simplifying paradigm where mass media are *de facto* false and relations between people are real. In this type of framework there is little scope to consider the complex ways in which people use media to communicate and connect or to account for how the balance of power can change through media and its manipulations (Goodman et al., 2016, p. 678). In fact, spectacle may prove an essential or necessary ingredient for processes of mobilisation and solidarity (Lester and Cottle, 2009, p. 933) at least by bringing attention to the issue of climate crisis. Spectacular images of climate change may invite viewers to recognise and possibly respond to the rise and risks of the climate change (Lester and Cottle, 2009, p. 926).

Rather than thinking of environmental spectacle as a one unified system, I prefer the idea of various spectacular processes in motion at the same time. Mediatised environmental conflict and communication happen in mutually constitutive interactions between activism, journalism, formal politics and industry (Hutchins and Lester, 2015). Furthermore, the proliferation of new media technology has rendered media spectacles more complex and potentially open to contestation. Social media has become a potential space for resistance, creative transformation, and even new types of world-making projects (Igoe, 2010, p. 378, 390). While spectacles are mediated visions of climate change, they are constructed by and for situated bodies. For instance, Douglas Kellner (2005, p. 11) sees media spectacles as a contested terrain and calls for a perception of a plurality and heterogeneity of contending spectacles. This means that there are possibilities for action and change in relation to and within spectacles.

Spectacular climate visuals, then, are situated within a larger field, where different actors utilise and circulate images and multiple audiences both interpret and further circulate images for different purposes. For examining this complexity, spectacle offers a fruitful concept. It allows us to view modern communication infrastructures of abundance and the key problematics of environmental communication: there is enough information available and circulated and yet humans have not been able to tackle the challenges of the climate change, loss of species and pollution. Humans have shown to be able to look away while looking directly at images portraying the crisis. From a psychoanalytical perspective, we are watching ecological devastation but are ill-equipped to bear the pain of what we know (Fletcher, 2018, p. 58). I agree with Ryan Gunderson (2020, p. 259) who sees the spectacle as a helpful unifying concept that brings together mounting critiques of image-based, consumerist-oriented, and ineffective environmental politics.

Fantasy as the promise of enjoyment and fulfilment

Fantasy is integral to the functioning of the spectacle. As Douglas Kellner (2005) writes, spectacle is a form of media culture that puts contemporary dreams, nightmares, fantasies and values on display. Fantasies connected to the climate crisis or global warming have previously been discussed from different perspectives: fantasies of carbon markets as solutions to the problem, fantasies of adapting to climate change through sustainable cities (see Koch, 2018), fantasies of terraforming (Woods, 2019) and fantasies that climate change is a hoax (Healy, 2014).

Fantasy is a fruitful concept for studying the visual spectacle of climate change because of fantasy's inherent role in both individual human perception and the workings of social imagination. I rely on critical fantasy studies by Jason Glynos and Yannis Stavrakakis, who draw from Lacanian psychoanalytical theory to consider fantasies' affective power in social and political life (Lacan et al., 2006; Glynos and Stavrakakis, 2008; Glynos, 2020). In Lacanian psychoanalytic work fantasy is not used as distinct from 'reality', but fantasy is seen as something that partly structures a subject's reality (Rose, 2016, p. 174). Fantasy is, thus, understood as integral to the functioning of human subjectivity: through fantasies subjects make sense of their ontological incompleteness (Eberle, 2019, p. 247). In fantasising, the ontological lack within the subject is transformed into an empirical lack of particular 'objects' in the world (imaginary of concrete), whose recapturing promises the restoration of an imaginary full identity (Eberle, 2019, p. 246). Thus, we desire objects in our attempt to achieve an imaginary wholeness. Both Klein and Lacan distinguish a process of *splitting and projection* which leads to attributing inner feeling of anxiety and joy to outer objects (Behagel and Mert, 2021, p. 84).[1] Fantasy is thus always situated in between the most individual desires of the subject and the world which promises the objects of desire.

Fantasies have an important role to play in our understanding of how social practices are organised, sustained, or potentially transformed (Glynos, 2008, p. 283). Political projects and ideologies promise the delivery of our lost or impossible enjoyment and imaginary fullness, often by identifying an obstacle to it (an Other) and then suggesting it's removal (Glynos, 2008, p. 282; Behagel and Mert, 2021, p. 82). In climate change discourses CO2 stands as an example of a fetishised and externalised obstacle that has to be dealt with in order to achieve sustainable climate futures (Swyngedouw, 2010, p. 221). The logic of fantasy also purports to offer the subject a degree of protection from the anxiety associated with a direct confrontation with the radical contingency of social relations (Glynos, 2008, p. 287). Fantasy serves to obscure the unbridgeable gap between what ideology promises and what it actually delivers (Fletcher, 2018, p. 56).[2]

To cover the impossibility of capturing full enjoyment, political fantasies structure the individual's partial enjoyment through various rituals and through the use of utopian and dystopian narratives which reproduces the fantasy both in official and unofficial public discourse (Glynos and Stavrakakis, 2008, p. 262). Fantasies are actually distinguished from other narratives by their excessively simplified and clear-cut 'black and white' character which leaves little room for ambiguity or uncertainty and also links their achievements to dramatically simplified visions of the future (Eberle, 2019, p. 248). A good part of political discourses focuses on the delivery of the 'good life' or a 'just society', which are in fact fictions of a future state in which the current limitations preventing our enjoyment will be overcome (Glynos and Stavrakakis, 2008, p. 261). These types of simplified visions of the future as either apocalyptic destruction or technological sustainable utopia are constantly present in public climate change discourses and visuals.

I propose that images have an essential role in communicating fantasies. Fantasy operates in an imaginary register, composed of images and speech fragments, providing coherence for the subject in the form of a compensatory explanation (Healy, 2014, pp. 183–184). The mediation of relationships by images is important to the ways in which environmental problems are imagined, their solutions proposed, and resources mobilised for specific interventions and world-making projects (Igoe, 2010, p. 385). I argue that fantasies communicated through photographs are strengthened by that fact that photographs are seen to be indexical and portraying 'reality'. In such visualised fantasies, the subject's desires are then validated as they are shown to being 'real'. However, it is important to note that visual representations do not automatically imply certain spectatorships or subject positions. Indeed, the construction of meaningful visual knowledge is local, situated, and contextual even in the highly technified, standardised, and functional Western world (Grasseni, 2011, p. 23). Spectatorship is always a site of possible articulation of individual subjectivity with social subjecthood and also a site of articulation of fantasy within representations (de Lauretis, 1995, p. 82).

Fantasies in the visual spectacles of climate change

In this section, I use fantasy as an analytical tool to consider the affective pull and suggested subject positions of chosen climate change images. I contemplate how fantasies function either by promising enjoyment and fulfilment to the viewing subject or by blocking enjoyment. The presented images are from the Climate Visuals media depository.[3] I present examples from two different types of imageries: The dystopian spectacle of destruction and the utopian spectacle of technological progress.

The dystopian spectacle of destruction

We have already established that climate change has been portrayed largely through catastrophic images of the consequences of climate change, an imagery which is an example of *ruination photography*. What makes ruination photography spectacular is firstly the shocking nature of the images and secondly the way the images dilute human agency to spectatorship. Erik Swyngedouw (2010) writes about the attractions of the apocalyptic imaginaries that infuse the climate change debate and through which much of the public concern with the climate change argument is sustained. He lists the different apocalyptic rhetorics and representational tactics which signal an overwhelming, mind-boggling danger, that threatens to undermine the coordinates of our everyday lives and routines (Swyndegouw, 2010, p. 218).

Variously referenced as 'ruin lust' or 'ruin porn', meaning (re)presentation of the vanishing of the world as we know, has historical antecedents in Romantic sublime landscapes of ruination (Zylinska, 2016, p. 170). Miles Orvell traces photography's role in relaying visual destruction to the 1906 San Francisco earthquake. Visual documentation turned the chaos of the event into a coherent spectacle defined by typologies of visual representation, which would be used to depict future spectacles of destruction (Orvell, 2021, pp. 1–2). The spectacle of destruction is upheld and circulated also in Hollywood films where images of earthquakes, fires, floods and post-apocalyptic landscapes have been commonplace (Orvell, 2021, p. 2). Furthermore, environmental groups have used photographs to document environmental destruction in order to persuade the public and governments to take action by their truth function, inscribed by an emotive aesthetic (Doyle, 2009, p. 286).

Max Liboiron questions the ability of 'ruin porn' to represent the real: ruin porn hides more than it shows. It creates the hyper-visibility of some elements of crisis, usually infrastructural damage and death, while simultaneously making others invisible, namely the social and political forces that engender uneven patterns – and origins – of damage and recovery (Liboiron, 2015). Modern ruin photographs overwhelm the viewer by virtue of the scale of destruction pictured, yet they force us to look with a kind of aesthetic detachment at scenes of destruction and horror (Orvell, 2021, p. 14).

Environmental issues are also portrayed by spectacular images of sublime nature. In the context of environmental discourse, the visualised beauty of the landscape is always understood as threatened (Doyle, 2009, p. 288). Images of melting glaciers appear to invite us to look at the beauty of the landscape, to experience shock, and to feel the looming inevitable lost. The problem with this, however, is that while they may generate an emotion through the sense of loss, they do not contribute to understanding the causes of climate change or relate them to everyday life, that is, on a level where people can actually make a difference (Doyle, 2009, p. 291; Cottle, 2008). So, common to both photographs of destruction and beautiful landscapes of loss is the disassociated viewer of catastrophe, which can in fact be traced back to the earlier mentioned San Francisco earthquake. Arnold Genthe, a German-born philologist and photographer, captured a spectator's calm observation of the destruction of the city – an image which became a trope of disaster photography and an insight into the disassociation of the spectator from the spectacle (Orvell, 2021, pp. 6–7).

Figure 8.1 represents a view of destruction and climate effects which is common in climate change imagery: the aerial view of a village flooded by water. Drew Ayers considers how visual technologies and software like Google Maps and Google Earth have trained our eyes to sense and perceive the world from a god-like, authoritative perspective. These technologies encourage viewers to adopt the camera's perspective as their own, incorporating the apparatus of the camera into their emergent form of technologically mediated embodiment (Ayers, 2019, p. 184). There is a kind of fantasmatic implication to this kind of view, as it lifts the human gaze to a bird's (or god's) eye view. One also has to notice that the aerial view is one of privilege: A Western viewer looking down on destruction elsewhere. Susan Sontag has noted that the possibility to view war from a distance is a spectatorship for privileged Western humans (Sontag, 2003) and the same applies to climate catastrophes.

Sara Oscar writes that ruins tap into a human desire to witness extinction across time or to see time at a standstill after the downfall of human civilisation and capitalism (Oscar, 2021, p. 4). Therefore, the spectacular images

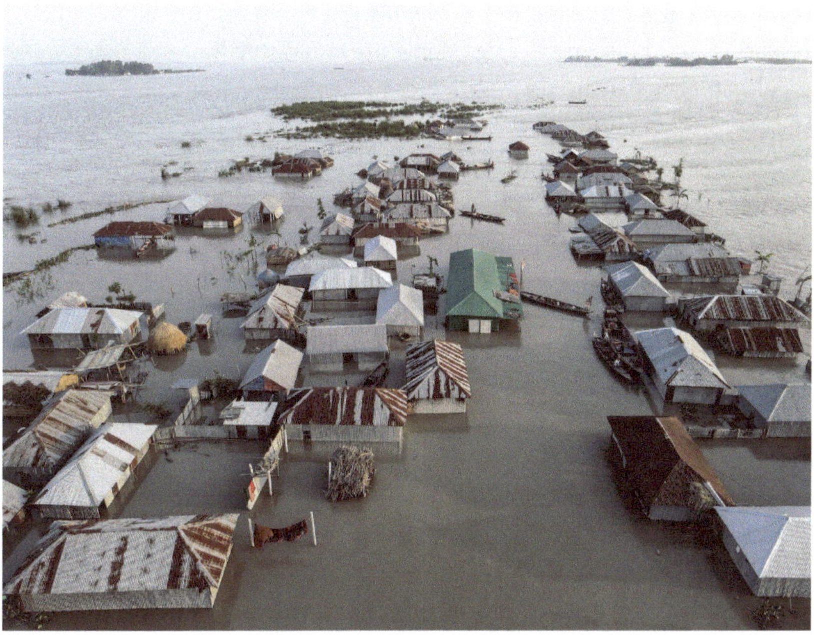

Figure 8.1. An Aerial View of a Village Submerged in Sea Water. Muhammad Amdad Hossain / Climate Visuals. License: CC BY-NC-ND 4.0

of environmental ruination or dire climate change consequences employ the fantasy of erasure, obsolescence and abstraction of human and nonhuman species, plant and insect diversity and the disappearance of human civilisation (see Oscar, 2021). Fantasy works here as the possibility to look at the world after humans, but in the present time. The fantasy element is temporal, the imagined gaze to future extinction.

The environmentally apocalyptic future, forever postponed, neither promises redemption nor does it possess a name; it is pure negativity (Swyngedouw, 2010, 2019). The psychoanalytic view of fantasy helps to understand why this type of imaginary can be stagnating for the individual subject: they produce anxious positions of melancholia. Fletcher notes that melancholia is supported by a variety of defence mechanisms, one of which is disavowal which allows subjects to half-acknowledge their pain while simultaneously denying its significance (Fletcher, 2018, p. 60).

Why then are apocalyptic imaginaries circulated with such intensity? Erik Swyngedouw offers an explanation from the point of view of post-politics. Populism silences ideological and other constitutive social differences and disavows conflicts of interest by distilling a common threat or challenge to both Nature and Humanity. The people are constituted, not as heterogeneous political subjects, but as universal victims, suffering from processes beyond their control. Therefore, apocalyptic imaginaries are extraordinarily powerful in disavowing or displacing social conflict and antagonisms (Swyngedouw, 2010, pp. 219–221). This reflection puts into a different light the well-meaning circulation of climate destruction images in both news media and social media, as in the case of circulating images of Amazon Rainforest wildfires.

However, there appear to be ways in which the renderings of ecological destruction may also bring the experience of devastation closer and encourage viewers to act (see Orvell, 2021, p. 196). Lester and Cottle (2009), noted in their study of climate change visualisations on television news that stories commonly localised the global crisis of climate change and were often grounded in particular places, depicting established connections between people's lives and nature and between climate causes and effects. Also, cultural resonances embedded in the past and reliant on shared or imagined memories were repeatedly called upon to establish the magnitude of crisis and loss, and to invite the viewer to care (Lester and Cottle, 2009, p. 927). In my own study on Finnish Instagram users' climate change-related posts during a heatwave, users often connected feelings of loss to culturally important memories of what Finnish summers have always felt like and how heatwaves made it impossible to enjoy the summer as before.

Figure 8.2 portrays people struggling mid-calf in moving water, along a narrow footpath in Venice, Italy, the morning after the 2019 187cm flood disaster (Climate Visuals). While the image portrays extreme weather conditions, the point of view is on the ground level rather than the aerial view of the city. There is also a different kind of recognizability and relatability to the Western viewer which may not be present images of the Global South. The waterfront and buildings could be from any European coastal town. The composition of the image is powerful with the left side of the image disappearing as though the building and people were at the edge of the world.

Shifting the perspective from the aerial view to eye height also situates the imagined photographer on the scene, witnessing the effects of extreme weather with their own body. The idea of bringing the effects of climate change closer to the viewer has already been taken up by some news media and photography depositories. For Instance, Climate Visuals has aimed at diversifying stereotypical climate imagery through portraying real people, local climate change impacts, and climate change causes at scale (Corner et al., 2015). I suggest that

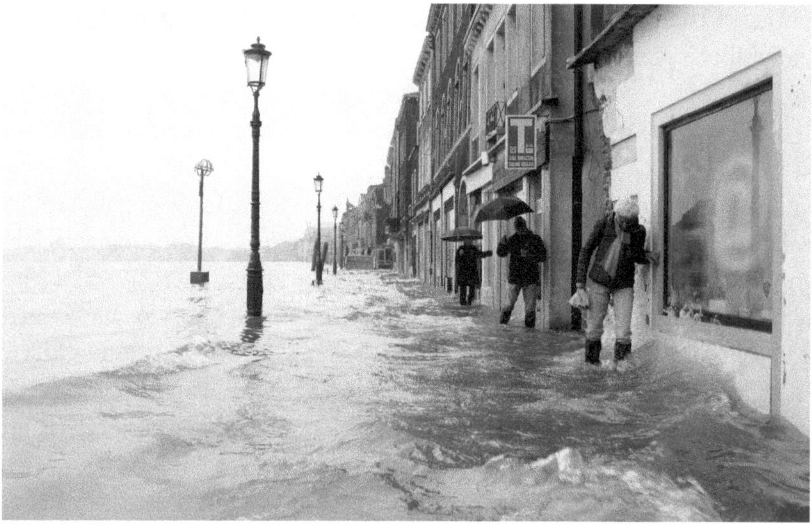

Figure 8.2. People Struggling to Walk in Flooded Venice, Italy. Sébire / Climate Visuals, License: CC BY-NC-ND 4.0

images connected to culturally meaningful issues or locations can motivate subjects to face the pain and undergo the process of mourning necessary to break attachment to present circumstances and also the fantasies that uphold them.

The utopian spectacle of technological progress

Imagery of green technology belongs to the sphere of visual climate change spectacles. These images cover up rather than reveal the socio-economic structural and habitual reasons of ecological destruction such as extraction of natural resources and overconsumption. Fantasy has been considered previously in technological utopias of carbon offsetting as a fantasy (Watt, 2021) and sustainable cities as a fantasy (Davidson, 2012).

The emphasis on technological causes as well as solutions in the imagery, have participated in the distant and abstract discourse of ecological modernisation (Kangas, 2016). Natalie Koch defines *spectacular sustainability* as a broad phenomenon implicated in how countries, companies, and individuals promote positive narratives about their 'modernity' (Koch, 2023, p. 4). Sustainability fantasies promise a future where human consumptive ways of life may continue by replacing carbon-intense consumption with greener alternatives. Mulvihill and Bruzzone (2018, p. 69) consider sustainability as a potentially dangerous social fantasy, because it functions to disavow the traumatic potential of the Real of nature by imagining that all can be reconciled. The sustainability spectacle is produced by harnessing the eco-friendly image of renewables, but detached from the political and economic context that eventually determines whether progressive environmental agendas will actually advance. (Koch, 2018, p. 16).

Images of solar panels (Figure 8.3) are one example of portraying a sustainability utopia. The image of a solar panel continues to circulate globally as an almost unquestioned icon of sustainability and modern post-oil futures (Koch, 2018, p. 16). Techno-futuristic images of solar panels or wind turbines fill the semiotic landscape surrounding sustainability because they objectively produce less greenhouse gases, but also because they are visually evocative and seem to provide a simple techno-optimist roadmap to a hypermodern green future (Koch, 2018, p. 15).

The presented image combines two pertinent spectacular climate spectacles: sustainable energy and the desert. Desert images are frequently treated as a metaphor for global warming and the future challenges of securing food, energy, and water in a changing environment (Koch, 2019, p. 38). Here the desert works as a backdrop for sustainability: the photograph of the Nevada solar park with it's 17,500 solar panels employs the strategy of producing a

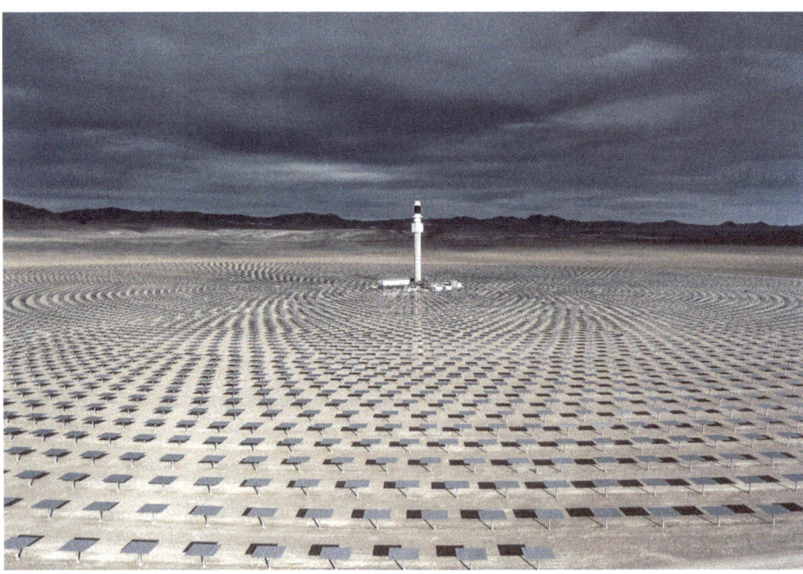

Figure 8.3. Crescent Dunes Solar Energy Project in Nevada, US. Photograph: Matjaz Krivic / Climate Visuals Countdown. License: CC BY-NC-ND 4.0

technological utopia, and a kind of tentative promise of salvation through technological means. Moreover, there is an underlying fantasy of conquering nature, which the selected image also relays. Since the seventeenth century, the West has in some ways been defined as the modernising call for the 'conquest of nature', a visualisation of the planet as an enemy to be subdued (Mirzoeff, 2014, p. 217). Igoe writes that the spectacle provides 'visual articulations of nature as an eco-functional object of intervention, while concealing and marginalising alternatives and opposition to its seemingly monolithic vision' (Igoe, 2013, p. 43). This coincides with the functioning of spectacles as unifying images, which obscure the social and political circumstances underlying the image while distancing the spectator from and active subject positions. For instance, the ecological impacts of producing electric cars and solar panels are faded into the background in utopian fantasies of an emission-free future.

Figure 8.4 opens an opportunity to critically read the technological utopia of sustainability by portraying an electric car (identified by the Tesla logo) in traffic, a scene which is highly relatable in many cities. The spectacle functions by bringing coherence to situations which are disparate as fantasy aids in filling cognitive and affective gaps. This photograph then may work differently with different viewers: On the one hand it offers electric cars as a kind of solution to global warming, but at the same time other elements in the image disrupt the fantasy: The extreme heat sign, a plea to save power, surrounding traffic and the hot and sunny day call into question the fantasy of electric cars 'cooling effect' on the climate. The image thus also presents a somewhat uncomfortable

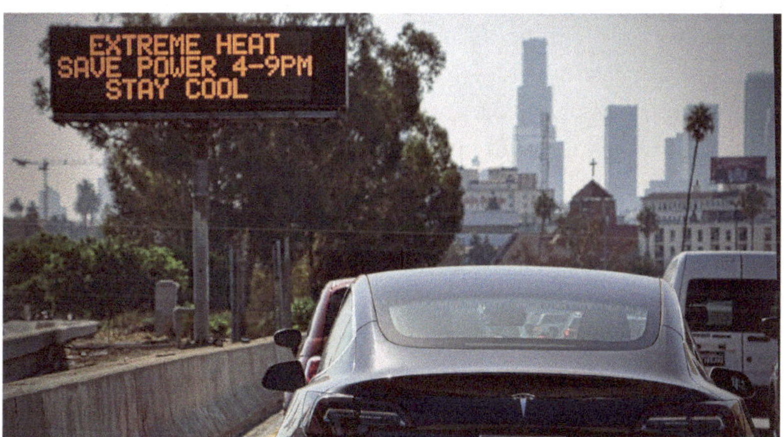

Figure 8.4. Extreme Heat Warning Sign, Los Angeles, US. Photograph: Chris Yarzab.[4]
License: CC BY 2.0

predicament of living in heating cities and having to negotiate one's current enjoyment by saving energy.

Spectacles of technological utopias offer individual spectators a kind of redemption as consumers. The underlying fantasy is that capitalism can make a new climate by unmaking the one it has co-produced over the past few hundred years through a series of extraordinary techno-natural and eco-managerial fixes (see Swyngedouw, 2010, p. 224). There is also confidence in engineers, scientists and multinational corporations to solve the problem of overconsumption through providing green alternatives. Nikolas Mizroeff writes that the Anthropocene visuality allows us to move on, to see nothing and keep circulating commodities, despite the destruction of the biosphere. We do so mostly out of a modernist conviction that 'the authorities' will restore everything to order in the end (Mizroeff, 2014, p. 217). This type of fantasy suggests a passive consumer subject, who appropriates the latest technological solutions offered by corporations and nations alike.

Conclusion: Traversing fantasies in the visual spectacle of climate change

In this chapter, I have discussed climate change visuals from the point of view of spectacles and particularly fantasy as means of understanding the affective power of spectacular images. I have discussed different manifestations of the visual climate change spectacle, and the role fantasies play in these visuals. Most catastrophic dystopian images and utopian technological images evoke an emotive response and at the same time allow for the viewing subject to remain in their subjectivities.

Obviously, the visual mediascape is not a monotonous spectacle with only dystopian and utopian images circulating. I argue the visual climate spectacles can be interrupted and reordered using fantasy's affective power. Debord introduces the term 'detournement' or visual hijacking (Debord, 1967/1987; Goodman et al., 2016, p. 678) as a way of disturbing and intervening the spectacle. Detournement is in itself a powerful visual act of setting oneself against the stream of business as usual, while simultaneously creating a visual spectacle with potential to circulate on news media and social media alike. This type of spectacular environmental activism is present in the performances of Extinction Rebellion in cutting off automobile traffic in city centres, or Just Stop Oil activists interrupting the Snooker World championships or the *Les*

Misérables theatre show (visual spectacles in themselves). While these visual interruptions also may build on some types of fantasies (a fossil-fuel-free world, collective action, revolution), I think their main effect is interrupting underlying capitalist ideologies and fantasies. The same effects could be attempted through photography by showing the scales of industrial production and waste. The force of such spectacular disturbances is also to reveal the way attention is structured in modern mediascapes.

More could be done in different spheres of visual communication to interrupt the aesthetic organisation of the consumption society and anthropocentric privilege. In previous work, we have suggested that the human-centred and consumption-centred frameworks underlying visual journalism and Western societies more generally could be intervened with alternative aesthetic practices to reveal new ways of connecting with more-than-human nature and to question the normalised pleasures of consumption (Niemelä-Nyrhinen and Uusitalo, 2021). This could be done by showing more of the destructive consequences of consumption to different ecologies and also by giving space to diverse more-than-human viewpoints. As Behagel and Mert (2021, pp. 81–82) write, different fantasies of various 'naturecultures' can imagine different futures, effectively changing ontological stances, epistemological preferences, political imaginaries and social practices.

A further discussion is whether spectacular environmentalisms can actually change Western industrialised over-consumptive and extractive ways? As Feltcher underlines, the quintessential Lacanian injunction is to encourage subjects to traverse the fantasy which would entail fully acknowledging the Real of capitalism as a self-destructive system driving us toward the brink of ecological disaster. This would also require consciously confronting the pain resulting from both loss of attachment to the capitalist society of enjoyment and recognition of the environmental devastation this society has wrought (Fletcher, 2018, p. 63). Thus, the formation of new social bonds implies a collective reworking of our relationship with the society of enjoyment, one in which subjects could accept social, ecological and personal limits on individual enjoyment (Healy, 2014, p. 193).

In this chapter, I have discussed how the element of fantasy is crucial in understanding the way spectacular environmentalisms are constructed but also how subjects maintain unrealistic hopes while witnessing ecological destruction.[5] I will purposefully not end on a high note and offer the closure and enjoyment the subject desires. Rather, I suggest fantasies need to be seen for what they are: how they function both to put us to sleep and wake us up into action. As Eberle writes, we cannot escape fantasies, but we can look for different ways of relating to them by acknowledging fantasies *as fantasies* rather than as the way things are or should ideally be (see Eberle, 2019, p. 252). Usually, as Glynos notes, the subject tends to use fantasy as a way to protect itself from ambiguities, uncertainties, and other features which evoke intimations of anxiety. But it is precisely those ambiguities that open up possibilities for critical distance and alternative becomings (Glynos, 2008, p. 286). I claim images provide a starting point for this necessary individual and social work.

Notes

1 Behagel and Mert build on Kleinian and Lacanian schools of psychoanalysis and recent literature on the political role of fantasy (Behagel and Mert, 2021, p. 81).
2 For more elaborate treatments on fantasy in Lacanian psychoanalysis (Watt, 2021), fantasy in the construction of subjectivity (Glynos and Stavrakakis, 2008) or the relationship between fantasy and ideology (Zizek, 2008).
3 https://climatevisuals.org/. Accessed 09.10.2023.
4 https://flickr.com/photos/chrisyarzab/. Accessed through climatevisuals.org, 19.10.2023.
5 I wish to thank my colleagues Jenni Niemelä-Nyrhinen and Risto Kunelius for their valuable comments for finalising the manuscript.

References

Arruda, V. (2022) '#PrayForAmazonia: How the world's largest rainforest is walking towards its point of no return', *Harvard Political Review*, 22 February 2022. https://harvardpolitics.com/pray-for-amazonia/, accessed 6 October 2023.

Ayers, D. (2019) *Spectacular posthumanism: The digital vernacular of visual effects*. New York: Bloomsbury Academic.

Beck, U. (2010) 'Climate for change, or how to create a green modernity?', *Theory, Culture & Society* [Online], 27(2–3), pp. 254–266.

Behagel, J. and Mert, A. (2021) 'The political nature of fantasy and political fantasies of nature', *Journal of Language and Politics*, 20(1), pp. 79–94. https://doi.org/10.1075/jlp.20049.beh

Boykoff, M. and Goodman, M. (2009) 'Conspicuous redemption? Reflections on the promises and perils of the "celebritization" of climate change', *Geoforum*, 40, pp. 395–406.

Corner, A., Webster, R. and Teriete, C. (2015) 'Climate visuals: Seven principles for visual climate change communication (based on International Social Research)', *Climate Outreach*. https://climateoutreach.org/reports/climate-visuals-seven-principles-for-visual-climate-change-communication/, accessed 6 October 2023.

Cottle, S. (2008) 'Ecology and climate change: From science and sceptics to spectacle and...' in Cottle, S. (ed.) *Global crisis reporting: Journalism in the global age*. Maidenhead: McGraw-Hill Education.

Crary, J. (2002) 'Spectacle, attention, counter-memory' in McDonough, T. (ed.), *Guy Debord and the situationist international: Texts and documents*. Cambridge, MA: MIT Press, pp. 256–266.

Davidson, M. (2012) 'Sustainable city as fantasy', *Human Geography*, 5(2), pp. 14–25. https://doi.org/10.1177/194277861200500202

Debord, G. (1967/1987) *Society of the spectacle*. Exeter: Rebel Press.

De Lauretis, T. (1995) 'On the subject of fantasy' in Pietropaolo, L. and Testaferri, A. (eds.) *Feminisms in the cinema*. Bloomington: Indiana University Press.

Doyle, J (2009) 'Seeing the climate? The problematic status of visual evidence in climate change campaigning' in Dobrin, S.I. and Morey, S. (eds.) *Ecosee: Image, rhetoric, nature*. Albany, NY: State University of New York, pp. 279–298.

Eberle, J. (2019) 'Narrative, desire, ontological security, transgression: Fantasy as a factor in international politics', *Journal of International Relations and Development*, 22, pp. 243–268.

Fletcher, R. (2018) 'Beyond the end of the world: Breaking attachment to a dying planet' in Kapoor, I. (ed.) *Psychoanalysis and the global*. London: University of Nebraska Press, pp. 48–69.

Glynos, J. (2008) 'Ideological fantasy at work', *Journal of Political Ideologies*, 13(3), pp. 275–296. https://doi.org/10.1080/13569310802376961

Glynos, J. (2020) 'Critical fantasy studies', *Journal of Language and Politics*, 20(1), pp. 95–111. https://orcid.org/0000-0002-4801-4001

Glynos, J. and Stavrakakis, Y. (2008) 'Lacan and political subjectivity: Fantasy and enjoyment in psychoanalysis and political theory', *Subjectivity*, 24(1), pp. 256–274. https://doi.org/10.1057/sub.2008.23

Goodman, M.K., Littler, J., Brockington, D. and Boykoff, M. (2016) 'Spectacular environmentalisms: Media, knowledge and the framing of ecological politics', *Environmental Communication*, 10(6), pp. 677–688. https://doi.org/10.1080/17524032.2016.1219489

Grasseni, C. (2011) 'Skilled visions: Toward an ecology of visual inscriptions' in Banks, M. and Ruby, J. (eds.) *Made to be seen: Perspectives on the history of visual anthropology*. London: The University of Chicago Press.

Gunderson, R. (2020) 'Spectacular reassurance strategies: How to reduce environmental concern while accelerating environmental harm', *Environmental Politics*, 29(2), pp. 257–277. https://doi.org/10.1080/09644016.2018.1546642

Healy, S. (2014) 'Psychoanalysis and the geography of the Anthropocene: Fantasy, oil addiction and the politics of global warming' in Kingsbury, P. and Pile, S. (eds.) *Psychoanalytic geographies* [Online]. London: Routledge, pp. 205–220. Accessed 4 October 2023.

Hutchins, B. and Lester, L. (2015) 'Theorizing the enactment of mediatized environmental conflict', *The International Communication Gazette*, 77(4), pp. 337–358.

Igoe, J. (2010) 'The spectacle of nature in the global economy of appearances: Anthropological engagements with the spectacular mediations of transnational conservation', *Critique of Anthropology*, 30(4), pp. 375–397.

Igoe, J. (2013) 'Nature on the move: Contemplation becomes speculation', *New Proposals: Journal of Marxism and Interdisciplinary Inquiry*, 6(1–2), pp. 37–49.

Kangas, J. (2016) 'Näkymätön Ilmasto, Näkyviä Kuvia: Ilmastoriskin Visualisointi ja Kuvallinen Kehystäminen Helsingin Sanomissa' [Invisible climate, visible images: The visualisation and pictorial framing of the climate change risk in Helsingin Sanomat], *Media & viestintä*, 39(4), pp. 209–227. https://doi.org/10.23983/mv.61407

Kellner, D. (2005) *Media spectacle*. London: Routledge.

Koch, N. (2018) *The geopolitics of spectacle: Space, synecdoche, and the new capitals of Asia*. Ithaca: Cornell University Press.

Koch, N. (2019) 'Whose apocalypse? Biosphere 2 and the spectacle of settler science in the desert', *Geoforum*, 124, pp. 36–45.

Koch, N. (2023) 'Sustainability spectacle and "Post-oil" greening initiatives', *Environmental Politics*, 32(4), pp. 708–731. https://doi.org/10.1080/09644016.2022.2127481

Lacan, J., Fink, B., Grigg, R. and Fink, H. (2006) *E´crits: The First Complete Edition in English*. New York: W.W. Norton.

Lester, L. and Cottle, S. (2009) 'Visualizing climate change: Television news and ecological citizenship', *International Journal of Communication*, 3, pp. 920–936.

Liboiron, M. (2015) 'The perils of ruin porn: Slow violence and the ethics of representation', *Discard Studies*. https://discardstudies.com/2015/03/23/the-perils-of-ruin-porn-slow-violence-and-the-ethics-of-representation/, accessed 7 October 2023.

MacFarland, T.S. (2019) *Ecopiety: Green media and the dilemma of environmental virtue*. New York: New York University Press.

Mirzoeff, N. (2014) 'Visualizing the Anthropocene', *Public Culture*, 26(2), pp. 213–232.

Mulvihill, P.R. and Bruzzone, V. (2018) 'The eclipse of environmental discourse', *Human Geography* [Online], 11(3), pp. 57–72. Accessed 2 October 2023.

Niemelä-Nyrhinen, J. and Seppänen, J. (2019) 'Kuvajournalismi ja eettisen kuluttamisen haaste' [Visual journalism and the challenge of ethical consumption], *Media & viestintä*, 42(3). https://doi.org/10.23983/mv.85780

Niemelä-Nyrhinen, J. and Uusitalo, N. (2021) 'Intervening in consensual frameworks of the sensible through images', *Nordic Journal of Media Studies*, 3(1), pp. 164–183. https://doi.org/10.2478/njms-2021-0009

Orvell, M. (2021) *Empire of ruins: American culture, photography, and the spectacle of destruction*. New York: Oxford University Press.

Oscar, S. (2021) 'Worlds without humans in the time of Anthropos: On David Claerbout's photo-filmic strategies', *Journal of Visual Art Practice*, 20(1–2), pp. 1–15.

Rose, G. (2016) *Visual methodologies: An introduction to researching with visual materials*. 4th edn. London: Sage.

Sontag, S. (2003) *Regarding the pain of others*. New York: Picador Modern Classics.

Swyngedouw, R. (2010) 'Apocalypse forever? Post-political populism and the spectre of climate change', *Theory, Culture & Society*, 27(2–3), pp. 213–232. https://doi.org/10.1177/0263276409358728

Uusitalo, N. (2020) 'Unveiling unseen climate practices on Instagram', *Novos Olhares*, 9(1). https://doi.org/10.11606/issn.2238-7714.no.2020.171996

Watt, R. (2021) 'The fantasy of carbon offsetting', *Environmental Politics*, 30(7), pp. 1069–1088. https://doi.org/10.1080/09644016.2021.1877063

Woods, D. (2019) '"Terraforming Earth": Climate and Recursivity', *Diacritics* 47(3), pp. 6–29. Accessed 16 October 2023.

Zizek, S. (2008) *The plague of fantasies*. London: Verso.

Zylinska, J. (2016) 'Photography after the human', *Photographies*, 9(2), pp. 167–186. https://doi.org/10.1080/17540763.2016.1182062

· 9 ·

EARTHSHIP FREO: A CASE STUDY OF THE POTENTIAL AND LIMITATIONS OF PARTICIPATORY DOCUMENTARY FILMMAKING

Michelle Johnston and Mignon Shardlow

The reality of anthropogenic climate change can no longer be ignored or disputed. Global warming's disruption of the fragile conditions required for humans to thrive requires urgent action. Academics, public intellectuals, journalists and filmmakers have a responsibility to inform, motivate and empower people to take action for the sake of the long-term survival of life on earth. This chapter describes a fragment of that effort: an attempt to understand better the potential and limitations of participatory documentary filmmaking in fostering active hope and transformative action. Documentary films have an important role to play in how we see the world, educate ourselves, and develop empathy with the lived experiences of others. Participatory documentary in particular has an important role to play because it is not just about producing stories, it is about a storytelling process that respects and reflects the voices and agency of people in the story. It encourages participants to tell their own story and allows them veto over storylines. This can limit the documentary maker's ability to craft the most emotive and 'perhaps' engaging narrative – and therefore may limit the potential power of the film to change minds and create change – but it can also enable a perspective that allows for complexity and invites viewers to engage on a more personal level.

This chapter features a case study of a feature documentary, *Earthship Freo*, and explores the capacity for participatory documentary filmmaking to create social change. In particular, it describes how the filmmakers navigated their passion for environmental advocacy, ethical considerations, truthful representation, and a desire to tell a story that appeals to an audience. The filmmakers and authors of this chapter are also university academics: Michelle Johnston is a documentary filmmaker, and Mignon Shardlow, a journalist. They explore the advantages and limitations of this approach to documentary filmmaking and associated ethical considerations. The authors have also incorporated insights from interviews with two award-winning documentary filmmakers conducted specifically for this chapter.

Participatory documentary

Michelle Johnston has utilised action research and participatory production in her work with First Nations Noongar people in south-western Australia for over a decade. Both approaches describe a methodology and a philosophy that are inclusive, democratic and conducive to the close relationships that are essential to the success of collaborative research and creative projects. Action research, in particular, focuses on effecting change for marginalised communities, treating participants as co-researchers rather than subjects, and involving them from project inception. Community participants articulate the problem to be addressed by the research, and any project outcomes benefit the community. Participatory documentary is guided by the same ethos and objectives as action research (Johnston and Forrest, 2020).

Bill Nichols, a prominent documentary theorist, outlines six distinct modes of documentary representation that are familiar to the filmmaking community. Among these is the 'participatory' mode, characterised by the filmmaker's visible presence on camera (Nichols, 2017). Filmmakers like Michael Moore (*Roger & Me*, *Bowling for Columbine*) and Louis Theroux (*Life on the Edge*, *Forbidden America*) exemplify this form of participatory documentary, whereby they consistently appear on screen, telling the story of the film and facilitating interactions between the audience and the film's participants.

The participatory production practices employed in the production of *Earthship Freo* (Elliott, 2023) are very different.[1] The participatory element refers to the film's participants and not the filmmakers themselves who assume the role of facilitators by bringing the voices and stories of the participants on to the screen and to an audience. Like action research, a relationship with the film's participants is key to the success of this type of documentary production. Time is invested at the start of the project to establish trust, to listen to community participants, and to understand how they wish to be represented and what benefits may come to them as a result of participating in the documentary. Examples of other participatory documentaries often feature First Nations participants and their stories, such as *In My Blood It Runs* (Newell, 2019), because it is widely recognised as an ethical and respectful way of working with First Nations people. Rolf de Heer also famously employed participatory production techniques in making the feature drama, *Ten Canoes* (2006).

The ethics of documentary filmmaking have been contested since Robert Flaherty released *Nanook of the North* in 1922 and was criticised for fictionalising aspects of the First Nations Enuit people who feature in the documentary. Bill Nichols, in advocating for a documentary code of ethics, says that 'social themes and political issues need to be understood in relation to the cinematic means of representation. How something got said came to matter as much or more than what got said' (2016, p. 2). He goes on to explain how ethical representation must be balanced with the idea of "documentary film [as] a rhetorical art. Like the orator of old, the documentarian's concern is to win an audience's assent, not serve as an 'information transfer' device" (2016, p. 155).

Pioneering filmmaker, John Grierson, defines documentary as the 'creative treatment of actuality' (Kerrigan and Mcintyre, 2010) and many will argue that the truthful representation of actuality is undoubtedly one of the most important aspects of documentary. But the ethics of how that truth is acquired and how 'creatively' it is represented on the screen is frequently debated. Brian Winston et al. (2017) and Bill Nichols (2016) question the ethics of documentary filmmakers by reminding us that many of them have built their careers on the misfortune of others. The people represented in a documentary rarely have any say in how their voice, or their performance, is used by the filmmaker. Often the only obligation a filmmaker has to a documentary subject is in the form of a standard consent form signed prior to an appearance on camera, which Winston describes as 'not so much collaboration as surrender' (Winston et al., 2017, p. 112).

Participatory production demands a different ethical approach to documentary filmmaking – one that prioritises the documentary participant over all else. Each participatory production will vary in terms of how and what documentary participants will contribute to the film. Generally, the filmmaker will consult extensively with community participants through all stages of production and even long after the film is first released to an audience. Maya Newall embedded herself in the Alice Springs community where her film *In My Blood it Runs* is set. One of her aims is to raise funds for an Aboriginal and Torres Strait Islander-led education system and so, years after the film's cinematic release, money raised continues to go to the community that features in the film (Closer Productions, n.d.).

Earthship Freo

The port city of Fremantle, situated on the south-western coast of Western Australia, has a reputation for its bohemian, rebellious, and alternative character. For over a decade, the colourful identity of the city was on display with a row of seven vibrant houses collectively known as 'Earthship Freo'. They stood along High Street, one of the city's main thoroughfares, and were neighboured by a number of other long-term vacant houses. A steady stream of motorists and freight trucks drove by these graffiti-covered Earthship houses with little awareness of what occurred within. The Department of Main Roads had slated all the houses for demolition as part of a plan to upgrade High Street, a notoriously hazardous road used for transporting goods to and from the port. The road widening project posed a threat to numerous trees including mature and endangered Tuart Trees native to the Swan Coastal Plain, where Fremantle is situated. The Earthship Freo houses were occupied by squatters and activists who used the houses as a blockade to protect the trees. Residents lived off-grid[2] and were committed to sustainable living and the creation of a welcoming community.

The *Earthship Freo* documentary project was first imagined in early 2019 and our 'in' to the community was via one of the filmmakers, Mignon Shardlow, who is a Fremantle resident. She told us what she knew about the community and we were confident that this was a story worth recording if for no other reason than a decade-long piece of Fremantle history was about to be destroyed. Documentary is an exploratory form and so we approached the community with many questions in mind. Mignon set up a meeting with Christine who is one of two founding members of the Earthship community and a long-term resident. She, in turn, gave us access to Simon Peterffy, a life-long frontline activist and the other founding member. These two are the main protagonists of the film and established Earthship as a drug and alcohol-free squatter community where they welcomed those in need of a home.

Simon and Christine were supportive of the idea of the documentary and we were invited to our first weekly Earthship community meeting where we outlined ideas for making a participatory documentary 'with' the squatters, rather than 'about' them. Residents of the houses were invited to participate by contributing their own media and inviting us, the filmmakers, to record aspects of their life in the community. The idea was initially met with enthusiasm by the mostly young transient people living in the houses, but did not translate into many opportunities to engage with the residents because we were soon redirected by Simon to produce a video in support of the Fremantle Environmental Resource Network (FERN), a community kitchen across the road from the Earthship houses that was also scheduled for demolition.

Our approach involved taking direction from the participants. Simon, especially, was deeply concerned about FERN's demolition and actively lobbied the council and the Fremantle community on their behalf. Recognising the urgency, we shifted our focus to the community kitchen and created a thirteen-minute advocacy video, *Unfurling FERN* (Elliott, 2019) with hopes of securing relocation options if FERN couldn't be saved. We screened the video in Fremantle where it received an enthusiastic response, and then offered the video to be used on social media. However, as we concentrated on FERN, most transient Earthship residents, many of them backpackers, departed with the onset of winter in Perth and the impending demolition of the houses. We focused our attention on Simon, Christine, and a handful of long-term residents. In hindsight, our plan for full resident engagement would have required embedding ourselves in the houses, and living off-grid with the residents, but this was beyond our project's scope due to our university teaching responsibilities.

Simon and Christine, our protagonists, were regularly consulted about their portrayal in the documentary. For other residents, we obtained explicit consent through signed forms and obtained approval from almost everyone for interviews and event recordings, avoiding only a couple of individuals who preferred not to be filmed. During interviews, we prioritised giving interviewees ample time to discuss their concerns without imposing our own narrative agenda, a challenging aspect of our filmmaking process that we will elaborate on later. On a positive note, we established trusting and respectful relationships with the residents, particularly Christine and Simon. The derelict houses and their occupants became familiar to us as we transitioned from outsiders to allies. We visited each week, learning more about the community with each visit, and valuing the sustainability and community insights shared by residents.

As we got to know more about Earthship and its history, we discovered that Simon and Christine, both dedicated to protecting the trees and their community, had a romantic relationship. Because they lived in separate houses and they didn't initially volunteer that information it was not apparent to us in the beginning. We felt that this was an important thread that should be included with the other stories we were telling. They were also dealing with the anticipation of conflict with authorities as Simon strategised to protect the trees and this was another narrative element, a climax, that we anticipated for the film. Then, in July 2019, at the eleventh hour, a deal was struck. Main Roads agreed to Simon's demands to plant hundreds of tuart trees in and around Fremantle to offset the destruction of the mature trees. The residents quietly packed up their belongings and left.

When the houses were demolished all the residents departed in different and, in many cases, unknown directions, but we maintained our communication with Christine and Simon. In the early days of film production they were a couple living on opposite sides of a busy main road, dodging traffic as they crossed the highway to meet and breakfast together. They both moved to a regional town after the houses were demolished, but their relationship ended not long after and so began a long and complicated breakup that we feared would end the film project. But, we believe, both were so invested in the film and the community itself they agreed that the documentary should continue to completion.

A polished draft of the finished documentary was shown to each of them separately, and they requested some small changes about how their relationship was represented. Those changes were made, they viewed it again and approval was given for the documentary to be released. It was now up to us to find an audience for the film.

When assessing what benefits came to the Earthship community as a result of the film's production we acknowledge the benefits are not easily measured, but they were valuable nonetheless. Simon has expressed his gratitude for recording an important chapter of his life:

> Historically it was a unique period of WA activism, and to have it documented will be a valuable resource for future generations [. . .] For the broader activist and general community, I was hopeful that it would serve as a source of inspiration for others. (2023)

Other Earthship residents shared similar sentiments. While the film isn't a typical advocacy documentary, it encourages viewers to contemplate alternative approaches to living on Earth. Through the documentary, viewers observe squatters who have chosen a simple, rent-free lifestyle, recycling furniture, salvaging wasted supermarket food, and tending to community gardens. Residents articulate the thoughtful political choices they make, demonstrate alternative living practices that allow them time to volunteer at the community kitchen across the road and to pursue creative artistic endeavours. As an audience we learn that while all utilities and services to the houses have been cut by Main Roads the residents make compost toilets, gather rain water, build solar showers and put solar arrays on their roofs to power phones and run lights. These alternative living practices invite audiences to contemplate questions about their own choices in terms of how we live, where we live, why we work, how we work and other ontological questions that relate to our place in the biosphere.

Storytelling

Stories about climate change are ubiquitous, and there are many ways to tell a story. Journalists and filmmakers are all looking for effective ways to reach an audience with their stories, and to create change. Emotion is recognised as an important feature of a story and so the subject of many stories might feature people who are disadvantaged, disenfranchised, or victims who are vulnerable and voiceless. Such stories can elicit empathy, fear, or anger from the audience.

Added to the media noise of contemporary culture is the persistent presence of social media that has made it easy for just about anybody to have a voice and an audience – to tell their story. Kate Eichhorn (2022) argues that social media reduces all online information to 'content' whereby the consumer must determine for themself what is important, true, or useful in their search for information. No great skill or expensive hardware are needed to upload a film to Facebook or YouTube. The challenge for those speaking out about the climate crisis is to be heard over the media noise, to have their story presented to an audience in a way that will hold attention and lead to transformative action. While social media offers a platform, mainstream and traditional media still possess a tenuous advantage with their ability to validate and prioritise issues or events (Forde, 2017). The journalists and filmmakers that produce traditional, mainstream media stories can use this advantage to more effectively communicate the climate crisis.

Furthermore, skilled professional documentary storytellers have an even greater advantage. When adequately funded by broadcasters, streaming services or government funding bodies they have the resources to create visually captivating and engaging narratives, market them to a wide audience, and provide optimal viewing experiences and long-term access. Such distribution platforms, and the filmmakers who produce for them, often seek stories with sympathetic victims, untainted heroes, clear conflict with rising action, culminating in a cathartic and hopeful climax. Which raises the question of what defines a 'great' story and who holds that determination? Is telling a great story enough to transform an audience?

Documentary has long been considered a transformative tool for overcoming ideological differences. Nash and Corner identify the significance of emotion in documentary's ability to change minds: 'Stories, opposed to polemics, have qualities that enable them to move people' because 'people take sides on an issue, but it's much harder to take sides on a story' (2016, p. 233). Thomas King reminds us of the power of stories: 'the truth about stories is that that's all we are. [. . .] They are wonderous things. And they are dangerous' (2000, pp. 2–9). Jill Godmilow, on the other hand, is critical of conventional narrative documentary forms because it is 'trapped in the same matrix of obligations as the fiction film: to entertain an audience. . . to satisfy, and to assure the audience of informed and moral citizenship' (2022, p. 2). Godmilow asks, 'is that of any political use?' She advocates for a new form of documentary she terms 'postrealist nonfiction' or 'anti-docs'. These poetic forms reject and disrupt ideas of reality, and our relationships to 'old useless ideas of who we are' (3). Godmilow rejects conventional documentary and its narrative form because it 'demands returned-home-safely closure. Closure closes off the possibility of change, which must occur outside the film' (18).

The desire for change, for impact, is the common ground that Godmilow and King both share. Change, not just entertainment, is usually the objective of the documentary filmmaker. The most effective way of creating that change, of having impact on an audience is where they might disagree. The point here is not to argue for or against the value of narrative and storytelling, but rather to highlight questions about narrative structure and form that filmmakers wrestle with as they seek to communicate effectively with an audience and to create the transformative change that is at the heart of their work.

The same challenges exist for many journalists who are also storytellers and feel responsible for communicating the urgent messages about climate change and sustainable living that is needed to turn the tide of community and government inaction. Is it lack of information, misinformation or simply indifference that has contributed to the public's confused and disputed understanding of the climate emergency? A lack of information, on its own, is not the only problem. Nisbet et al. argue the need for an interdisciplinary approach to environmental communication that inspires and empowers audiences so that they choose to participate in solutions and make personal changes (Gunster, 2017). Arnold (2018) cautions journalists against the repetition of a narrow narrative that focuses exclusively on the impacts of climate change because apocalyptic news can cause a hope gap that leaves audiences with a sense of powerlessness. Arnold argues for journalism that provides a more representative view of the challenges posed by a warming climate including responses and innovations to increase pressure on policymakers to act as a way to mitigate the hope gap and facilitate belief in human agency rather than hopelessness, further inaction and apocalypse fatigue. Understanding the conclusion of the Intergovernmental Panel on Climate Change (IPCC, n.d.) – that it is 'unequivocal' that humans are causing climate change – is the concomitant understanding that, if we caused it, then we also have the power to fix it (Arnold, 2018). This is the message Arnold suggests journalists use to combat the hope gap.

Documentary filmmaker, Cathy Henkel, has directed many documentaries including more than four advocacy documentary films: *The Man Who Stole my Mother's Face* (2003); *The Burning Season* (2008); *Rise of the Eco-Warriors* (2014); and *Laura's Choice* (2020). The Western Australian producer/writer/director is also an activist and academic and she explains her own experience of the hope gap:

> Halfway through my career I became really exhausted by environmental films that showed us how bad things are on the planet and then left you with that. Personally I would come out of those films feeling like I just want to go and sort of hide in a corner, go to the pub or just became inactivated by how gloomy it was. (2023)

She says there is a need for documentary makers to 'go the next step' and depict the problem, but also the solutions.

Communicators committed to encouraging action on climate change are cautioned to provide cause for optimism to prevent the disempowering effect of the hope gap but to avoid fostering deluded optimism. Researchers have found that humans have a tendency to overestimate our likelihood of experiencing positive events and underestimate our likelihood of negative events and this optimism bias is limiting our global response to climate change. According to Sharot (2011), optimism bias is one of the most consistent, prevalent and robust biases documented in psychology and behavioural economics. 'Optimistic errors seem to be an integral part of human nature observed across gender, race, nationality and age' (Sharot, 2011, p. 2). If being overly optimistic about our future affects most of the population (estimated at around 80% by Sharot) then a possible solution is impact documentaries that do two things simultaneously; firstly, provide information that require us to consider negative outcomes so we can resist the short-sightedness of overconfidence and delusional over-optimism, and secondly outline the next steps to action to avoid leading audiences into the hope gap. These documentaries would be crafted to meet Raymond Williams' (1989) definition of being radical: 'To be truly radical is to make hope possible, rather than despair convincing' (1989, p. 118).

Gunster offers suggestions that could help journalism to shift its ability to get audiences to engage with messages about climate crisis, including:

> cultivate social norms of civic engagement and political efficacy with greater attention to the stories, experiences and emotions of people and communities who are working together to address climate change. (2017, p. 53)

Gunster's advice can be extended to the documentary filmmaker. Unlike traditional forms of journalism, documentary filmmakers do more than monitor issues and events. They can adopt a facilitative role similar to community journalism which 'provides truthful and intelligent information to facilitate public engagement' defined by obligations to the community (Forde, 2017, p. 89). Western Australian documentary filmmaker and former journalist Jane Hammond is the writer, director and producer of two environmental activism films, *Cry of the Forests* (2020) and *Black Cockatoo Crisis* (2022). Hammond made the change from journalism to documentary-making because she was frustrated by her work for the state daily newspaper. While she had a broad audience as a journalist, she was unable to cover the stories she believed needed to be covered.

> I still believe in the power of journalism but I was passionate about the environment and the newspaper I was working with were not publishing my stories. (2023)

Hammond left journalism and has largely self-funded her documentaries taking a significant pay cut for the privilege of telling important stories that have had significant and measurable impact. Hammond's documentary work helped to end logging in native forests in Western Australia (Government of Western Australia, 2023)

> What I'm trying to do with social impact documentary is to take an issue that is really important and bring it to the surface amongst all the other noise. How do you compete in this noisy environment? Imagery and storytelling is how you do that. As

> a journalist coming into documentary, I'm really strict about facts, and truth. But people criticise my film saying it was too one-sided and then I have to explain what social impact documentary is: it is not news or current affairs. And it's not opinion either. I'm an independent documentary filmmaker. This is not neutral. This is a story from this perspective. (Hammond, 2023)

Unlike journalism, documentary need not make claims of objectivity or impartiality, and can make use of Gunster's advice for community engagement. Hammond embraced the documentary form for its potential to mobilise people to make a positive difference in the fight to save forests.

> So there's people that will come to the film three or four times, because they like to feel a part of something. These are people that have opened their hearts already, you're just funnelling their action. So you don't have to appeal to the ultra conservatives. People criticise me all the time saying, 'Oh, but, you're just preaching to the converted.' But you only need five per cent to do real action and real change, for there to be change. So that's where I'm working. How do we convert hearts and minds into action? I think that's the power of film. (2023)

Like Hammond, Cathy Henkel's clarity around the documentary-makers right to craft the story is challenged by the misunderstanding and expectation for social impact documentary to be objective and unbiased.

> Documentary storytelling is telling a story. There's no such thing as truth, it's only editing. Editing, by its very nature, is manipulative. You're constructing the story you want to tell. What we bring as a storyteller is to craft the messiness of life and the 'boringness' of life into a narrative. So the minute you're doing that, you're telling a story. (2023)

As Gunster suggests, *Earthship Freo* is an example of a film that is pitched at those most likely to engage with the story and who see themselves as agents of change. The film features stories from grassroots people who can connect with an audience at an emotional level, and who come together to fight environmental vandalism. Rather than empathy created by stories and images of people suffering, Gunster argues that stories of 'resistance, struggle and agency' are more powerful. *Earthship Freo* is such a story.

> Heroes, it would seem – especially the 'everyday' kind – are far more compelling than either villains or victims in crafting strong narratives that can enhance engagement with climate politics and policies. (Gunster, 2017, p. 67)

When we first considered the Earthship community as a potential documentary there were several aspects of the story that attracted us. Firstly there was a piece of Fremantle history, a successful intentional community, that was about to be demolished. Then there was the question of why, at a time when environmental awareness and concern has never been higher on the public agenda, a government department can cut down critically endangered trees without any consequences or reference to the wider community they serve? Next, there was a desire to tell Simon's story and to celebrate a man who has dedicated his life to the environment. His story has all the elements of adventure, conflict and heroism that make for compelling viewing. Lastly, there was Simon and Christine's love story. Our filmmaker instincts said 'this is interesting – let's explore'. However, our participatory approach demanded that we allow the Earthship participants to shape their own story. For this reason, the documentary takes a different shape to what might be considered for a more commercially viable film.

As we talked to the residents of the Earthship community we learnt they were not victims, and did not feel disadvantaged or vulnerable. They were living the life they wanted to live, and standing up for a cause they believed in – the environment and sustainable living were at the heart of everything they did. The Earthship story we told also lacked villains. We could have 'door stopped'[3] the Minister for Transport to demand an explanation for the environmental destruction. We were offered a 'secret' recording of a conversation with Main Roads, but declined. We could have done a 'Michael Moore' who, in *Roger and Me* (1989), relentlessly pursued General Motors CEO, Roger Smith, to demand answers about the closure of a factory in Moore's home town. Our ethical and participatory approach did not allow for that.

On the other hand, Simon is an experienced media performer. He frequently employs social and mainstream media to recruit fellow activists and find an audience for his environmental and political messages. The frontline activism in which he frequently and traditionally engaged is often performative. Simon explained to us later:

> When there is a camera around, I like to remind my opponents that they are on the record, and that the whole world is watching. If it was just us and them, with no camera, they are more inclined to be brutal and uncompromising. (2023)

But frontline activism takes its toll. Simon has been arrested on numerous occasions and his activism has impacted his family relationships and his health. When we met Simon he wanted to retire from frontline activism and try a new approach. He wanted to negotiate a compromise with Main Roads by agreeing to the planting of offset trees in exchange for the peaceful abandonment of their blockade in the houses. He used his reputation as a trouble-maker and a frontline activist to negotiate with Main Roads and ask for 500 tuart trees to be planted for each mature tuart tree they cut down. The arrival of a documentary crew on his doorstep was, more than likely, an opportunity he recognised to influence the outcome for Earthship and the blockade. We will never know how much our continued presence at the houses influenced Main Roads' decision to meet Simon's demands for offsets. The story ended peacefully, without performative protest, without arrests. The bulldozers moved in and demolished trees and houses without an angry word from either side. Some trees were planted elsewhere.

The absence of a climax for *Earthship Freo* represents another missing ingredient in the story we imagined telling. Sheila Curran Bernard summarises the elements of good storytelling in the documentary film:

> It has compelling characters (or questions), rising tension, and conflict that reaches some sort of resolution. It engages the audience on an emotional and intellectual level, motivating viewers to want to know what happens next. (2016, p. 19)

For us, as filmmakers, not only did we not have victims or villains, the climax we anticipated for the documentary didn't happen. We turned up at the houses one day and it was over. A conversation between Simon and a Main Roads representative resulted in an agreed outcome and so Earthship residents packed up their belongings and moved out. Nobody was arrested, nobody was forcibly evicted, and nobody 'locked on' to a house. Several months after that Simon and Christine broke up. We had no climax to the blockade and now we had no love story. With the peaceful and sudden resolution between Simon and the Department of Main Roads we considered their love story as, what Bernard calls, a 'spine' (2016, p. 48) for the story and a potentially compelling end to the film. The story of their relationship could be told in a visually engaging way – their break up was a metaphor for the destruction of the houses. But that option was not approved by our participants and we respected that choice. Privileging the rights of participants to exert control over the narrative of the documentary that featured them, rather than doing what some documentary makers would do – selecting the most compelling story from the material filmed – is one of the costs of this participatory form. The benefit is a co-created and respectful selection of narrative that encourages trust.

As a result of the participant-led method of making *Earthship Freo*, the documentary complies with Godmilow's anti-doc form by not providing conclusive closure and by allowing for alternative readings of the main protagonists. One audience member at the first screening of the documentary wrote afterwards to express his delight at the way the documentary allowed the audience to sit with the complexity of the characters. He wrote, 'your film was a moving character study of community, vulnerable people and how we transform loss into actions that can give that loss meaning' (Myint, 2023).

Participatory production and ethics

Working within a university gave us access to resources that would be the envy of many filmmakers, but it also creates restrictive boundaries. Before embarking on any creative research project the academic must seek ethics approval from the university research office. This requires a lengthy process of describing the project, the methodologies and methods used to create the project, the outcomes of the project, and an assessment of any risk to the researcher, the participants and the university. The talent consent form that is traditionally used by filmmakers to document film participants' permission to use their performance (usually) without restriction is more expansive for the academic filmmaker. Our talent release form gave specific information about how each participants' performance would be used, and stated that participants could withdraw their consent at any time. This is a clause that is unlikely to be included in any standard commercial consent form.

The collaborative and respectful participatory production techniques employed in the production of *Earthship Freo* described at the start of this chapter make the process of ethics approval easier because this version of participatory documentary production is in sync with the ethical research standards demanded by our universities. The time we took to establish trust with the Earthship participants, to describe our participatory approach to a community wary of mainstream media, resulted in a film that represents its participants respectfully and allows for complexity. It does not seek to create conflict where it did not exist or to affirm the stereotypes audiences may expect from a story about squatters, activists and the homeless. Our ethical approach required us to make compromises with the story of the film, but it also demanded respect for the commitment we made to participants to document their history and produce a film. The option, for us, to walk away was never considered. Our ideas about sustainability, community and activism were changed by the experience of working with the Earthship community, and those ideas will be shared in our classrooms.

Academic activist and documentary maker, Cathy Henkel, refers to herself as an 'activist first, documentary filmmaker second' (2023). Henkel brings her activist mindset to her teaching of impact documentary and considers that teaching students how to make documentary is less important than teaching students to interrogate why they make stories:

> I try to teach my students the skills or techniques in the craft, but it's also about the stories: why this story? What story? Why should you tell it? Why are you telling this now? Is this your story to tell? (2023)

Conclusion

This chapter has explored participatory documentary filmmaking by academics to shed light on the potential and limitations of the form as a transformative resource in the context of urgent global issues. As the undeniable reality of anthropogenic climate change looms large academics, public intellectuals, journalists, and filmmakers find themselves with a profound responsibility – to inform, motivate, and empower individuals to take action for the sake of our species and the delicate ecosystems upon which we all depend. This chapter has, in particular, focused on one facet of this collective effort: an exploration of the potential and constraints of participatory documentary filmmaking in the realm of changing minds and transcending ideological divides. We argue that this form of documentary filmmaking holds a unique position in this endeavour, as it possesses the capacity to connect with audiences on an emotional level, limiting the polarising nature of many contemporary debates.

However, participatory documentary filmmaking is not without its challenges. The process demands a deep commitment to respecting and reflecting the voices and leadership of the individuals at the heart of the story. This approach, while essential for authenticity and inclusivity, can limit the filmmaker's ability to craft a highly emotive and persuasive narrative. Nevertheless, it offers the potential for a more intimate and genuine portrayal of the subject matter. By employing the power of storytelling, participatory documentaries can break down barriers and foster empathy, invite viewers to engage with complex issues, and deliver benefits to documentary participants.

Notes

1 To view *Earthship Freo* see https://vimeo.com/845801042?share=copy.
2 'Off-grid' means that the houses were disconnected from all utilities such as electricity, water, and sewerage.
3 'Door stop' is a journalism term for approaching a person with the intent of recording an interview, as they arrive at or leave a building.

References

Arnold, E. (2018) *Doom and Gloom: The role of the media in public disengagement on climate change.* Harvard Kennedy School. https://shorensteincenter.org/media-disengagement-climate-change/, accessed 25 September 2023.

Bernard, S.C. (2016) *Documentary storytelling.* New York: Focal Press.

Closer Productions (n.d.). https://inmyblooditruns.com/about/, accessed 25 September 2023.

Eichhorn, K. (2022) *Content.* Melbourne: MIT Press.

Earthship Freo. (2023) Directed by Elliott, R. Australia.

Forde, S. (2017) 'Environmental protest, politics and media interactions' in Hackett, R., Forde, S., Gunster, S. and Foxwell-Norton, K. (eds.) *Journalsim and climate crisis.* New York: Routledge.

Godmilow, J. (2022) *Kill the documentary.* New York: Columbia University Press.

Government of Western Australia (2023) 'Native Forest Transition', *Department of Jobs, Science and Innovation.* https://www.wa.gov.au/organisation/department-of-jobs-tourism-science-and-innovation/native-forest-transition, accessed 26 October 2023.

Intergovernmental Panel on Climate Change (IPCC) (n.d.) United Nations. https://www.ipcc.ch/, accessed 25 September 2023.

Gunster, S. (2017) 'Engaging climate communication' in Hackett, R., Forde, S., Gunster, S. and Foxwell-Norton, K. (eds.) *Journalsim and climate crisis.* New York: Routledge.

Hammond, J. (2023) *RE: Interview with Jane Hammond.* Interview with Shardlow, M. 1 June, Perth.

Henkel, C. (2023) *RE: Interview with Cathy Henkel.* Interview with Shardlow, M. 31 May, Perth.

Johnston, M. and Forrest, S. (2020) Working Two Way: Stories of cross-cultural collaboration from Nyoongar Country. Singapore: Springer Nature

Kerrigan, S. and Mcintyre, P. (2010) 'The "creative treatment of actuality": Rationalizing and reconceptualizing the notion of creativity for documentary practice', *Journal of Media Practice*, 11, pp. 111–130.

King, T. (2000) *The truth about stories. A native narrative.* Toronto: House of Anansi Press.

Myint, K. (2023) *Re: Text communication.* Type to Shardlow, M. 28 June.

Nanook of the North (1922). Directed by R. Flaherty [Film]. United States of America: Pathe Exchange.

Nash, K. and Corner, J. (2016) 'Stretegic impact documentary: Contexts of production and social intervention', *European Journal of Communication*, 31, pp. 227–242.

Newell, M. (2019) *In my blood it runs* [Online]. Australia: Closer Productions.
Nichols, B. (2016) *Speaking truths with film: Evidence, ethics, politics in documentary*. California: University of California Press.
Nichols, B. (2017) *Introduction to documentary*. Bloomington: Indiana University Press.
Peterffy, S. (2023) *RE: Email Communication*. Type to Johnston, M. 9 June.
Sharot, T. (2011) 'The optimism bias', *Current Biology*, 21.
Ten Canoes (2006) Directed by R.D. Heer [Film]. Australia: Palace Films.
Unfurling FERN (2019) Directed by R. Elliott [Film]. Australia.
Williams, R. (1989) *Resources of hope: Culture, democracy, socialism*. London: Verso.
Winston, B., Vanstone, G. and Chi, W. (2017) 'Giving voice' in *The act of documenting: Documentary film in the 21st century*. New York: Bloomsbury Academic.

·10·

THE NEW WEIRD: INDEPENDENT CINEMA AS AN ECOSOPHICAL RESPONSE TO CLIMATE CHANGE

Kingsley Marshall

> I think all artists experienced a metamorphosis during the first few years after the invasion of Ukraine. We asked ourselves what could we do? How can we react? What is happening to us? Some took weapons in their arms, but I believe storytelling is a weapon – a tool to tell stories of the people around us, and to show the world what is really happening here.
>
> —Iryna Tsilyk. Director:
> *The Earth is Blue as an Orange* (2020) Interview with Marshall (2023)

Screen media has held a mirror toward world events since its inception, with filmmakers occupying a unique position to directly represent, infer, and speculate on all aspects of human life. In a world that Simon Cottle describes as 'increasingly defined by global crises' (2009, p. 473), and where these disasters are themselves epistemologically constituted through media (2014, pp. 1–2), film and television production presents a powerful and compelling interpretation of complex events. Recent cinema has mediated everything from the challenges to democracy and economics of late capitalism to conflict, acts of terrorism, asymmetrical warfare, the global impact of climate change, COVID-19 and its preceding pandemics, and the displacement of people around the world as a consequence of these events. Nothing is outside of the scope of the screen, and the impact of this work is amplified through digital distribution, reaching global audiences quickly through emergent internet technologies, in addition to the longer established streaming services, cinema releases, and broadcasters. Common themes within the telling of stories of the world-in-crisis include reimagined representations of the future and the past, and the manner with which the recent pace of political and technological change has disrupted identity within gender and sexuality and in relation to race, mental health, class, and local, regional, national, and international senses of belonging.

This chapter borrows terms defined by Argentine filmmakers Fernando Solanas and Octavio Getino to consider the changing nature of socio-political commentary beyond what they described as the 'first' and 'second cinema', where they distinguished mainstream entertainment driven by profit from a more political-engaged filmmaking (1970). Through their filmed work and their writing Solanas and Getino argued in the 1970s for a 'third cinema' that motivated its viewers to not just receive film passively, but to incite their audiences to be active in their response. Their work has been followed by the conventions of a 'fourth cinema' of activism, made by and concerning indigenous peoples (Barclay, 2003). More recently, a 'fifth cinema' has emerged – born of the stories of refugees and displaced peoples, a hybrid cinema orientated around the movement of people and made distinctive in its unstable and fragmented form often shot on the move on mobile phones and other handheld devices (Kaur and Grassilli, 2019, pp. 1–3).

Each of these frameworks offers tools that describe how film's narrative storytelling has reflected, mediated, and served as a critique of global crises, in addition to engendering awareness, and sparking debate and political action in its audiences. This chapter focuses on the contemporary moment, and specifically on the representation of just one of these crises – climate change. This result of human action and industrialisation has been the catalyst for conflict, disease, starvation, draught, and the displacement of people globally, in addition to fuelling the fires of destablisation of political and economic power globally.

Through defining and distinguishing the terms *ecocritical*, *ecocinema*, *ecological cinema*, and the *ecosophical*, the chapter articulates the manner with which these different positions demonstrate an alienation and unease of humans and their relation to the natural world, and solutions to that. Selected case studies illustrate how screen media production can synthesise these ideas to represent the impact of human activity on the world's environment and as stories that can stimulate discourse, and ultimately political action and response.

Cinema and the communication of the climate crisis

As a medium cinema has long offered innovative ways of aiding the understanding and re-evaluation of existential threats to humanity, our sense of self, and our relationship to what Stephen Rust, Salma Monani, and Seán Cubitt describe as the 'first nature', that of the natural environment. They detail how the ontological separation of nature as separate and secondary to the drivers of human civilisation, has reduced women, enslaved and colonised peoples, animals, and despoiled environments to the same level of raw materials to be exploited, highlighting the ongoing and expansive political relevance of *eco-critical* thinking (2023). Ecocritical perspectives then, explore the connection between cultural production and the environment, and how both are shaped by ecological concerns.

Centred in film and television, this study uses examples drawn from television, and both studio and independent film production, though it focuses more on the latter. Here I argue that – as in the desire to instigate change through the third cinema – independent voices have demonstrated similar agility and dynamism in their commentary of the complexity of climate change and the creation of new modes of seeing and of representation, and that this in part is because of their freedom from the conventions engendered by the structural constraints of the studio system or broadcasting.

The communication of a world-in-crisis through cultural production in screen media has only been accelerated and contemporarised by changes in the development, production, acquisition, and distribution of screen stories driven by the launch and expansion of streaming services including Netflix, Amazon, Disney+, and AppleTV. The impact of such technologies in the ecology of making, distribution, and consumption presents a further crisis in what Rust, Monani, and Cubitt refer to as the ruin of the 'second nature', distinguishing the natural world from the virtual spaces that emerged following the digitisation of creation, production, exhibition, consumption, and that now drive global discussion (2023).

In the late 1960s and early 1970s filmmakers and activists argued for a 'Third Cinema', suggesting that audiences should not just reflect on the social and political issues presented to them through the moving image and the manner that cinema could contribute to the discourse, but that this cinema should motivate those audiences to become participants in change. Solanas and Getino stated that: 'The active role of knowledge is expressed not only in the active leap from sensory to rational knowledge, but, and what is even more important, in the leap from rational knowledge to revolutionary practice ... The practice of the transformation of the world' (1970). Two decades later, and again prompted by his practice, the Māori filmmaker Barry Barclay argued for a 'fourth cinema' that advanced these ideas, arguing that indigenous filmmaking sat outside of what had previously been defined. In distinguishing his work from that which preceded it, he stated: 'I am not in First Cinema. The cinema of America. The cinema of the international mass market. I am not in Second Cinema either; the art house cinema for the cinema buffs of the modern nation state. And I am not in Third Cinema also. I am not living in a Third World national state' (2003, p. 8). Barclay argued for three main tenets that set this work apart; (1) indigenous self-representation, (2) an assertion of cultural narratives and representation, and (3) of collaborative filmmaking practice within the communities portrayed, 'outside of the national orthodoxy' (2003). Memorably, Barclay described this cinematic view as one taken from the shore, noting the misrepresentation that came from an ethnographic position taken from the ship's deck of the coloniser and invader (2003, p. 7).

As in the third cinema, Barclay's ideas are active in their criticality of colonialism though not through the prism of regional or national identity, rather the specific lens of 'Indigenous geographies, cosmologies, temporalities, histories, and cultural practices' (Shamash, 2017, p. 133). Salma Monani and Joni Adamson have noted the potentiality of the fourth cinema to cast light on the implications of unsettling Western notions of linear progress presented by industrialisation, demonstrating that this anthropocentric gaze can only show the narrowness and lack of consideration of the impact of such technologies on the planet that has led humanity to the climate crisis (2018, p. 15). Aline Freire de Carvalho Frey builds upon Barclay's work to describe an 'eco-forth cinema', highlighting the natural alignment of environmental crises with the experience of the many indigenous communities who have been impacted by 'air pollution, deforestation, biodiversity loss, and global warming' (2018, pp. ii–16). Frey observes that: 'Indigenous peoples are key players in climate change debates not only due to their traditional knowledges and discourses on sustainability, but because they are survivors of a preceding type of unanticipated eco-territorial displacement, namely colonialism' (2018, pp. ii–16). This cinema, situated around the first-hand and often extreme experiences of the impact of climate change on these communities, presents a subjective immediacy far more powerful than the objective, data-dump approach typified by documentaries including *An Inconvenient Truth* (Guggenheim, 2006), or the world-ending spectacle of Hollywood narrative blockbusters such as *The Day After Tomorrow* (Emmerich, 2004), that reportedly inspired it.

Ecocinema and its discontents

The idea that documentary and narrative filmmakers use story, character, and visual and sonic representation as a trojan horse for presenting socio-political ideas is not new, and there is a long history of the relationship between humans and climate change in cinema. *Ecocinema*, defined as films where climate change forms the main theme of a text, can be traced back to the earliest days of film. In the 1950s, decades before Al Gore encouraged his audience to consider purchasing a hybrid car, the narrator of *The Unchained Goddess* observed that: 'Due to our releases in factories and automobiles every year of more than six billion tons of carbon dioxide, which helps the air absorb heat from the sun, our atmosphere may be getting warmer' (Carlson and Hurtz, 1958). The theme of educating audiences through documentary with a call to action is a perennial of the film festival circuit. Acclaimed documentary films here, for example, include the post-Katrina film *Trouble the Water* (Lessin and Deal, 2008), *Chasing Ice* (Orlowski, 2012) where marine photographer James Balog bore witness to glacier calving, and *A Year in a Field* (Morris, 2023), which considered the impact of capitalism on the environment from the perspective of a 4,000-year-old standing stone in Cornwall.

Of course, ecocinema is not restricted to the documentary genre, but includes countless cinematic representations of an imagined past, present, and future in narrative films such as *Silent Running* (Trumbull, 1972) and *Soylent Green* (Fleischer, 1973), and *Wall-E* (Stanton, 2008). *Blade Runner 2049* (Villeneuve, 2017) is a studio-financed story of biologically sentient lifeforms, so-called 'replicants', and their consideration of what it is to be human. Their crisis of identity plays out in a dystopic setting characterised by the human impact on the world following a catastrophic global economic and environmental crash. Axel Goodbody badges such films as part of an awkward subgenre 'Cli-Fi' – novels and films centred in disaster narratives orientated around climate change. He describes a form of event cinema that illustrates four key problems of the representation of the complexities of climate change in fictional storytelling – the need to (1) present scientific knowledge, (2) give the scale of the challenge meaning, (3) present natural and human agency, (4) and avoid closure (2019).

Adrian Ivakhiv identifies several different themes in cinema that is centred in ecology (2008). He highlights the 'constraints and potentials' of representing the natural world through the wildlife film, or nature documentary, of narrative films where environmental themes form an explicit part of the narrative, and the presentation of a spectacular ecological sublime or eco-dystopia, often framed through the science-fiction genre (2008, p. 23) or often what Stacey Alaimo has memorably described as 'monstrous natures' (2001). This theme of the unknowability of nature, and the allegorical power of its corruption, has been extended into a full-length study by Robin L. Murray and Joseph Heumann that explored films from *Godzilla* (Honda, 1954) to *The Toxic Avenger* (Herz and Weil, 1984).

Indeed, ideas of a natural world-in-crisis have been presented in various shades in both independent and studio cinema. *Snowpiercer* (Joon-ho, 2013), *Annihilation* (Garland, 2018), *The Boy Who Harnessed the Wind* (Ejiofor, 2019), *In the Earth* (Wheatley, 2021), and *Don't Look Up* (McKay, 2021) all consider the impact of human activity within a world-in-crisis, and the impact of this activity on global identities, and the sense of belonging, community, nationhood, and our place in the world. This is directly represented in the actions of characters within each film, or through the encouragement of the audience to consider their relationship with the story through the prism of subjective experience.

One of the challenges of the cinematic representation of ecological themes is that there is no single set of cohesive critical or philosophical practices that sum up environmentalism as a discipline. Adam Rosadiuk suggests that 'the point of view of eco-philosophy is barely occupied' (2018, p. 7) and argues that this lack in a unified message of the ecocritical movement has impeded top-down political and systemic change. This paradox, of a widely understood crises, but a lack of understanding of how individuals can effect a change demonstrates that importance for cultural production – along with scientific reporting and other media – to continue to explore and communicate the political, economic, and moral impact of climate change, cannot be understated. According to Eileen Culloty and Pat Brereton audiences are less likely to change behaviour when simply provided with climate change information, instead arguing that attitude and behaviour change 'requires engagement with a broader set of ideas about non-scientific spheres' (2017, p. 139) and this can sometimes best be framed through story.

Cinema has long presented an array of perspectives on the challenges of the contemporaneous human experience, though critics such as Nadia Bozak note that the production and consumption of the very form of cinema itself can be determined to be hypocritical. Both the petrochemically derived celluloid and power-hungry, rare earth digesting and easily expended digital image, she argues, are intrinsically linked to the transformation of the earth's limited resources to moving image. The cinematic image, she says, 'can be thought of as fossilised light (2011, pp. 12–13). This observation is acknowledged by industrial bodies. According to the most recent report by Albert, which supports the film and TV industry to reduce the environmental impacts of production, one hour of on-screen TV production in the UK is responsible for an average of 4.4 tonnes of CO2 emissions, the majority of which are produced by transportation. In a dramatic illustration of this the 2021 report showed an unusually large reduction in emissions, acknowledging the impact on production-related travel due to the global COVID pandemic in 2020 (Albert, 2021; Sustainable Production Alliance, 2021, 2022). Bozak observes that many filmmakers are distinctly aware of this dichotomy, noting that 'the carbon neutral film is overtly self-conscious of its cinematic relationship with the biophysical word' (2011, p. 190)

This observation has caused some ecocritical filmmakers to extend their practice from the purely representational to an ethical consideration of not just their narratives but their modes of making. In their means of production and distribution, filmmakers – explicitly or implicitly – are connecting with ideas of *ecosophy*. The idea of the *ecosophical* was formed through Arne Næss' ideas in the early 1970s of a *deep ecology* that argued for a radical change in humanity's relationship with the environment, switching from one that values nature for its usefulness to humans, to one of inherent value – the human-in-nature, rather than above it (Devall, 1980). These ideas were further developed by Félix Guattari to argue for an ecosophical position; a holistic view of the relationship between living beings that advocated for sustainable modes of practices in harmony with the wider natural environment.

These ideas extended beyond a strictly environmentalist position into wider life, where ideas of identity and subjectivity are seen as an emergent and developing practice of emancipation of human activity within the natural environment (Levesque, 2016). Guattari described this as 'the context of the new "deal" of the relation between capital and human activity [. . .] that come under an incorporeal value system at the root of the new productive assemblages (2000, p. 49). John Tinnell argues that: 'To think ecosophically is to rethink philosophy in our contemporary moment defined by the convergence of nature and culture, ecological crises, globalisation, and the Internet' (2011).

In its application to filmmaking, as in the third cinema, this position is one of practical action and of revolution rather than evolution. Tinnel cites Guattari's consideration of ecological crisis as an existential one that called for a radical re-evaluation of modes of practice that may not align with one's identity, one that required practitioners to consider their work as operating in a 'post-media' era, where transversal connections could extend ecosophical solutions from filmmaking practice to everyday life (2011, pp. 37–39).

From this position, Andrew Ross argues that in addition to attending to the representation of ecological ideas there is also a need to attend to the ecology of image-making itself, and the distribution of such work (in Ivakhiv, 2008). Anuj Vaidya articulates that ecocinema should step beyond discourse and be practiced as a methodology in and of itself, 'working through techniques to reduce the carbon footprint of production in a practice that considered the challenges of off grid filmmaking before abandoning traditional filmmaking in its entirety in favour of a performed work' (2020, p. 48). Though extreme, these ideas transcend the idea of ecocinema as a *genre* to that of a truly *ecological cinema* where the very modes of filmmaking consider the climate emergency not just in the narrative of the film but through the consideration and execution of the development, production, and distribution of the work.

Towards an *Ecosophical* cinema

While the story presented in *Blade Runner 2049* certainly situates the film as ecocinema, the carbon impact and industrial means of making a studio blockbuster with an eye-watering $150m+ budget excludes it from claiming to be ecological cinema and challenges any claims to be ecosophically minded. Studio-originated ecocinema primarily subscribes to the 'Cli-Fi' model where its stories are framed by scale, presenting the world-in-crisis as an overwhelming catastrophic spectacle where individuals have little ability to prevent the impending collapse. In the narratives found more commonly in independent film, stories are more typically expressed through an individual or small group, highlighting an individual's agency and ability to act, to counter or survive the impending end of times. Examples *In the Earth* (Wheatley, 2021), *Enys Men* (Jenkin, 2022), and *The End We Start From* (Belo, 2024), all feature a single protagonist or small group working out their place in the world and form the case studies for building a case here for ecosophical cinema, and the shift to an ecological cinema outside of experimental film practice articulated by Ross and Vaidya.

The independent feature film *Enys Men* presents a worldview that has been described by its makers as 'ecosophical'. The film is predominantly situated in the past, with the events in the film largely taking place on an island in the UK during the days leading up to 1 May 1973. Writer/director Mark Jenkin explains, 'The film is about the impact an individual has on the environment in this particular place in 1973. The main character is observing a flower that grows on an island off the coast of Cornwall and, through observing this flower, she's able to make observations about the impact we're having on the planet' (Coates, 2023). As the story progresses this character, The Volunteer, notes lichen growing on one of the petals of the flowers and, after coming into contact with it, this appears to have a physical effect on her body where lichen begins to grow from a scar on her torso. As the flowers change, so The Volunteer's experience of the island also changes. Time on the island is shown to slip through allusions to the past and the future, of events occurring both before and after her life in 1973. As Jenkin notes: 'In *Enys Men* we explore the horror of human intervention in the natural world and how very little things can knock everything out of balance' (Film4 2021). Producer Denzil Monk suggests that *Enys Men* brings an individual sense of responsibility to the audience precisely through the specificity of the Volunteer's experience. He argues that the film asks who 'will investigate the great area when it comes to the survival of the planet: whose responsibility is it? What can an individual really do?' (Monk in Stevens, 2022).

The filmmakers present this world as a critique of the present, in its consideration of the industrial past of the island – represented by the film's miners and the paraphernalia of mining in the mise-en-scene – and the impact on nature, and by showing this mining activity as present, past, and future through three temporal positions. These positions are (1) the industrial landscape from an eighteenth-century perspective, (2) the same landscape but this time from a post-industrial 1973 framed by the seminal climate collapse text *A Blueprint for Survival* (Goldsmith and Allen, 1972) that *The Volunteer* reads by candlelight before bed each night, and, finally, (3) the present day. The choice of The Volunteer's reading in 1973 is fortuitous, in that the essays within the text ruminate on industrialisation itself and the long-term impacts of that practice, before speculating on the impact of that industrialisation in the future. The director explains that the book represents: 'all different points of view, but all coalescing around this idea that basically we've got to pay attention to what we're doing, the way we're living and the impact that has on the environment' (in Judah, 2023). Tarah Judah suggests that in these moments 'of temporal distortion and environmental histrionics', The Volunteer considers these implications through the confrontation with 'her temporal selves [. . .] establishing a steady routine that might just be the blueprint for the survival of human community and society at large' (Judah, 2023). Indeed, the routine of *The Volunteer* is repeated in the film: wake, observe, note, contemplate, self-reflect, read, sleep.

In addition to the further connotations of the *The Volunteer*'s evening reading, many of the props in the film have a narrative significance beyond their immediate function. The petrol generator that powers the cottage *The Volunteer* occupies presents a break from the natural world she surveys as part of her work. Jenkin explains that when the generator is turned off at the end of each day The Volunteer would 'go upstairs [. . .], back to a natural world, where it was candlelight' (Weir, 2023). Running short of fuel, eventually the generator falls silent – this sole provider of power to the cottage presenting a potential danger in the subsequent lack of the ability to generate heat, hot water, and electric light. Douglas Weir reads a further significance. 'When that generator stops,' he says, 'you're suddenly alert to something changing, that something's [. . .] going wrong' (2023). The exploitation of the earth, represented in the film by the miners and mining, is made manifest in the generator as a signifier of the world's reliance on petrochemicals. The experience of The Volunteer takes a turn as the generator runs out of fuel. The world doesn't end but pivots to foreground the natural world. Throughout the film, the industrial sounds of human-made objects – the generator, a VHF and AM radio, a kettle, a clock – are all contrasted by the sounds and images of the natural world that are shown in cut moments – the movement or stillness of the flora and fauna of the island, the impact of waves and wind. Towards the end of the film The Volunteer, in addition to slipping the moorings of her subjective reality, appears to exist in each of the temporal dimensions before transmogrifying into the island's standing stone to become part of the landscape itself. The film considers what connects individuals to the land around them; its flora and fauna together with an industrial past that both haunts and makes visible the impact of human activity on the landscape. Each offers an existential concern with an individual's experience of time, history, grief, memory, and memorialisation.

At the time of the film's production, tourism dominated the economy of Cornwall supporting one in five jobs in the region and projected to grow (Local Government Association, 2019). Although presenting the industrial heritage of Cornwall, one primarily of extraction from the land through mining, the critic Luke Morris noted that the film's temporal play resituated Cornwall to show 'the slow severing of our relationship with nature through tourism – to bring us back to a time where the world was unspoiled' (2023). Morris speaks to the urgency of acknowledging and reengaging with a neglected natural environment. He argues: 'By reconnecting with the landscape, as this lone woman does, we can reclaim elements of a forgotten and collapsed culture' (2023) sanitised and simplified through the process of tourism and the heritage industries.

Ultimately, the temporal confusion at the centre of *Enys Men* mirrors the impact of technologies and industrialisation in muddling our sense of self, creating confusion with our sense of the spaces around us, our relationship with the natural and built environment, our place in the world, and our responsibilities towards each of these places. The frustration of the filmmaker with these concerns is expressed in an interview, Jenkin responding to a question about the thematic heart of the film – the abstract complexities presented by climate change. He says: 'The real problem is: what do we do? How do people engage and make change? I don't know how that happens, because we're in a state of having to live minute by minute. And although the climate catastrophe gets closer and closer, it's quite an abstract concept' (in Judah, 2023).

Towards an *ecological* cinema: Climate change and the new weird

Olivier Dorlin contrasted *ecocinema*, defined as films where climate is the main theme, with an *ecological cinema*, one in which climate forms both the narrative driver and where 'sustainability is taken into account not only as a theme, but also within the film production process' (2019). The filmmakers extended these ecosophical concerns of the narrative to the ecological, considering their carbon footprint when making the film and the production company Bosena stating in their mission that they are 'Ecosophically minded' (Bosena, n.d.; C Fylm, 2023). Compared to Albert's emissions per hour of television, film is typically much more – 'Small films typically produce 391 metric tons of CO2. *Enys Men*, which comes in at 91 minutes, produced just 4.5 tons' (Barradale, 2023). The film used electric rather than diesel generators that were charged overnight using solar panels on the accommodation the crew stayed within. This was accompanied with a small local crew shooting on location primarily in a 10-mile radius of the director's home. Producer Denzil Monk explains 'What's important for us is to have that integrity, so we're not just telling stories about these things, but we're thinking about the impact that making process has on the people involved, and the people around the planet, and more than human environments around it' (in Barradale, 2023). Bozak notes that through, recognising intrinsic connection between the 'energy economy and image economy', this opens up a 'bold new critical terrain', and potentially a revolutionary one (2011, p. 190). As Simon Levesque observes, as 'environmental degradation lessens our quality of life and the sustainability of our communities, ecosophy might help reform values and practices' (2016, p. 511).

Jenkin's previous feature film, *Bait* (2019) was tagged part of the 'new weird Britain' movement by the critic Ian Mantgani in Sight and Sound (2019). Here Mantgani adds a national specificity to the 'new weird' tag used by M. John Harrison in his 2002 introduction to China Mieville's novella *The Tain*, where he described a genre-bending trait, originating in science fiction and horror, which subverts conventions to create a discomforting narrative (in Weinstock, 2016, p. 196). M. Keith Booker and Isra Daraiseh classify Ben Wheatley's eco-horror *In the Earth* and Alex Garland's complex folk horror *Men* (2022) as operating in similar spaces, where each film expresses a 'complex dialogue surrounding the relationships between humans and nature'. In this case, these fictional spaces making sense of the COVID-19 pandemic (2023). Unlike *Enys Men*'s explicit climate change narrative, *In the Earth* primarily makes use of the pandemic to frame an ongoing ecological disaster using a forest setting and a mycorrhizal network to provide a visual representation of complex networks and interrelationships within any given ecosystem. This fictional reflection of events occurs in the world at the time of the film's release to indicate a society out of step with nature, as Booker and Daraiseh note, represents an all too real planet that has become 'increasingly inhospitable to humans' (2023).

Conclusion

In *Annihilation*, *Enys Men*, *In the Earth*, and the recent flood narrative of *The End We Start From*, critics noted how the filmmakers have made use of the tropes and conventions of film form more commonly utilised in horror, to articulate their thoughts as to the existential challenges presented by a world-in-crisis. These may be fantastical worlds represented on the screen, but they can help extrapolate our place and response to our impact on the world around us when we leave the cinema. What is the impact of our industrial past, and how does it haunt us through poisoned earth, biological mutation, and the socio-economic impacts of increasingly scarce resources? While those in the Global North may well feel an understanding and empathy of the impact of climate change in the Global South, how is that inaction considered when reframed through floods, famine, and disease that are shown to impact more familiar cities and communities.

Dawn Keetley notes the most important conflict in the folk horror genre involves humans and their relationship to their environment, explaining that: 'In folk horror, things don't just happen *in* a (passive) landscape; things happen *because* of the landscape. The landscape does things; it has efficacy' (2015). At the heart of ecosophical thinking is that we too, whatever our mode of expression, have efficacy, and that we should not just reflect these beliefs in our making, but in the industrial means we utilise in the processes of that making and beyond that, to our wider, lived experience.

At its heart, cinema reflects a veritable palimpsest of meanings, memory, and hauntology and is made only more powerful to the contemporary audiences who can recognise how their own life experiences and place *inside* of the natural world can appear to mirror these fictional worlds. It is the distinctiveness of cinema, and particularly the specificity of independent cinema, apprehends and makes sense of climate change and a world-in-crisis more generally, and even possibly individual and collective forms of response.

Climate change has proven challenging to narrativise in a manner which has resulted in public mobilisation and political action, but there is a powerful argument that it is precisely the mechanisms with which cinema uses convention of genre to package climate change that can aid understanding and communication of wider messaging of the interconnectivity of life on earth, our impact upon it through our actions, and the consequences for communities around the world These devices can assist in the multifaceted challenge of clearly communicating the existential nature of human activity and its impact on the environment.

Cinema has proven itself able to challenge perceptions of colonialisation, industrialisation, capitalism, and the fourth industrial age of emergent technologies. Cinematic stories situated in climate change narratives are impactful with audiences when they encourage a reflexive consideration of the present, and our place within it. At its best, the on-screen representation of our world-in-crisis not only contributes to discourse and discussion, but is a catalyst for action – personal, political, economic, creative – beyond the cinema and out into the world itself.

References

Alaimo, S. (2001) 'Discomforting creatures: Monstrous nature in recent films' in Armbruster, K. and Wallace, K.R. (eds.) *Beyond nature writing: Expanding the boundaries of ecocriticism.* Charlottesville: University Press of Virginia, pp. 279–296.

'Albert Annual Review May 2020–April 2021' in *Albert.* https://wearealbert.org/2021/09/09/our-2020-21-annual-review-is-out/, accessed 1 December 2023.

An Inconvenient Truth (2006) Directed by Davis Guggenheim [Film]. Paramount Classics.

Annihilation (2018) Directed by Alex Garland [Film]. Paramount/Netflix.

A *Year in a Field* (2023) Directed by Christopher Morris [Film]. Bosena.

Barclay, B. (2003) 'Celebrating fourth cinema', *Illusions*, 35, pp. 7–11.

Barradale, G. (2023) 'Enys Men: How the films you watch are becoming more sustainable', *Big Issue*, 20 January 2023. https://bigissue.com/culture/film/enys-men-moon-knight-jack-ryan-netflix-sustainability-films/, accessed 1 December 2023.

Blade Runner 2049 (2017) Directed by Denis Villeneuve [Film]. Warner Bros Pictures.

Booker, M.K. and Daraiseh, I. (2023) 'Ben Wheatley's *In the Earth* (2021): Folk horror as climate change warning', *Green Letters: Studies in Ecocriticism*, 23 October 2023.

Bosena (n.d.) https://www.bosena.co.uk/about, accessed 1 December 2023.

Bozak, N. (2011) *The cinematic footprint: Lights, camera, natural resources.* New Brunswick, NJ: Rutgers University Press.

Brereton, P. (2004) *Hollywood utopia: Ecology in contemporary American cinema.* Bristol, UK: Intellect Books.

Brereton, P. (2018) *Environmental literacy and new digital.* London, UK: Routledge.

Brereton, P. (2020) 'An eco-reading of documentary/fictional narratives', *Irish Studies in International Affairs*, 31, pp. 43–57.

C Fylm (2023) 'Mark Jenkin's "ecosophical" Cornish folk horror Enys Men to screen at Cornish Mining World Heritage Site venues' in *C Fylm*, 14 June 2023. https://cfylm.co.uk/enys-men-cornish-mining-world-heritage-sites/, accessed 1 December 2023.

Chasing Ice (2012) Directed by Jeff Orlowski [Film]. Submarine Deluxe.

Coates, S. (2023) 'The end of England: Bringing Cornwall's tensions to a global audience', *The New European*, 9 February 2023. https://theneweuropean.co.uk/the-end-of-england/, accessed 1 December 2023.

Cottle, S. (2009) 'Global crises and world news ecology' in Allan, S. (ed.) *The Routledge companion to news and journalism.* London: Routledge, pp. 473–484.

Cottle, S. (2014) 'Rethinking media and disasters in a global age: What's changed and why it matters', *Media, War and Conflict*, 7(1), pp. 3–22.

Cottle, S. (2023) 'Reporting civilizational collapse: Research notes from a world in crisis', *Global Media and Communication*, 19(2), pp. 269–288.

Culloty, E. and Brereton, P. (2017) 'Eco-film and the audience: Making ecological sense of national cultural narratives', *Applied Environmental Education & Communication*, 16(3), pp. 139–148.

Culloty, E., Murphy, P., Brereton, P., Jane, S., Smeaton, A.F. and Zhang, D. (2019) 'Researching visual representations of climate change', *Environmental Communication*, 13(2), pp. 179–191.

Devall, B. (1980) 'The deep ecology movement', *Natural Resource Journal*, 20(2), pp. 299–322.

Don't Look Up (2021) Directed by Adam McKay [Film]. Netflix.

Film4 (2021) 'News release: BAFTA winner Mark Jenkin's 1970's horror *Enys Men* starts filming in Cornwall, backed by Film4', *Film4*, 24 March 2021. https://channel4.com/press/news/bafta-winner-mark-jenkins-1970s-horror-enys-men-starts-filming-cornwall-backed-film4, accessed 9 October 2023.

Frey, A.F. de C. (2018) 'Eco-fourth cinema: Indigenous rights and environmental crises', *PhD Thesis*, The University of Queensland.

Don't Look Up (2021) Directed by Adam McKay [Film]. Netflix.

Dorlin, O. (2019) 'Towards an ecological cinema', in *Books and ideas*, 23 January 2019.

Enys Men (2022) Directed by Mark Jenkin [Film]. Film4/Bosena Fylm.

Ex Machina (2014) Directed by Alex Garland [Film]. Film4/DNA Films.

Goldsmith, E. and Allen, R. (1972) *A blueprint for survival*. Ecosystems.

Goodbody, A. (2019) 'Cli-Fi – genre of the twenty-first century? Narrative strategies in contemporary climate fiction and film' in Löschnigg, M. and Braunecker, M. (eds.) *Green matters: Ecocultural functions of literature*. Leiden: Brill, pp. 131–153.

Guattari, F. (2000) *The three ecologies*, trans. by Pindar, I. and Sutton, P. London, UK: The Athlone Press.

Harrison, M.J. (2002) 'Introduction' in Mieville, C. (ed.) *The Tain*. Hornsea, UK: PS Publishing.

Ivakhiv, A. (2008) 'Green film criticism and its futures', *Interdisciplinary Studies in Literature and Environment*, 15(2).

In The Earth (2021) Directed by Ben Wheatley [Film]. Focus Features.

Jacobson, B.R. (2016) '*Ex Machina* in the garden', *Film Quarterly*, 69(4), pp. 23–34.

Judah, T. (2023) '*Enys Men*: An interview with Mark Jenkin', *Senses of Cinema*, January 2023, Issue 104. https://www.sensesofcinema.com/2023/interviews/enys-men-an-interview-with-mark-jenkin, accessed 9 October 2023.

Kaur, R. and Grassilli, M. (2019) 'Towards a fifth cinema', *Third Text*, 33(1), pp. 1–25.

Keetley, D. (2015) 'The resurgence of folk horror', *Horror Homeroom*, 6 November 2015. http://www.horrorhomeroom.com/the-resurgence-of-folk-horror/, accessed 1 November 2023.

Levesque, S. (2016) 'Two versions of ecosophy: Arne Næss, Félix Guattari, and their connection with semiotics', *Sign Systems Studios*, 44(4), pp. 511–541.

Local Government Association (2019) 'Cornwall: Supplying skills for the local visitor economy', *Local Government Association*, 2 July 2019. https://local.gov.uk/case-studies/cornwall-supplying-skills-local-visitor-economy, accessed 9 October 2023.

MacDonald, S. (2004) 'Toward an eco-cinema', *Interdisciplinary Studies in Literature and Environment*, 11(2), pp. 107–132.

Macfarlane, R. (2015) 'The eeriness of the English countryside', *The Guardian*, 10 April 2015. https://www.theguardian.com/books/2015/apr/10/eeriness-english-countryside-robert-macfarlane, accessed 28 October 2023.

Mantgani, I. (2019) 'Bait first look: Mark Jenkin heralds the new weird Britain', *Sight and Sound*, 30 August 2019. https://www2.bfi.org.uk/news-opinion/sight-sound-magazine/reviews-recommendations/bait-mark-jenkin-fear-loathing-cornish-fishing-village, accessed 9 May 2023.

Marshall, K. (2023) 'Frontline: Writer/director Iryna Tsilyk on filmmaking in Ukraine during the Russo-Ukrainian War (2014–)', *MAI: Feminism and Visual Culture Journal*, 30 March 2023. https://maifeminism.com/frontline-writer-director-iryna-tsilyk-on-filmmaking-during-the-russo-ukrainian-war, accessed 28 October 2023.

Maxwell, R. and Miller, T. (2012) *Greening the media*. Oxford, UK: Oxford University Press.

Men (2022) Directed by Alex Garland [Film]. Entertainment Film Distributors.

Milligan, C. (2015) 'Sites of exuberance: Barry Barclay and Fourth Cinema, ten years on', *International Journal of Media and Cultural Politics*, 11(3), pp. 347–359.

Monani, S. and Adamson, J. (eds.) (2018) *Ecocriticism and indigenous studies: Conversations from earth to cosmos*. New York: Routledge.

Morris, L. (2023) 'Enys men: A perfectly unsettling Cornish folk-horror', *Varsity*, 28 February 2023. https://www.varsity.co.uk/film-and-tv/24912, accessed 28 October 2023.

Murray, R.L. and Heumann, J. (2016) *Monstrous nature: Environment and horror on the big screen*. Lincoln: University of Nebraska Press.

Rodgers, D.A. (2019) 'Something "Wyrd" this way comes: Folklore and British television', *Folklore*, 2, pp. 133–152.

Rosadiuk, A. (2018, July) 'A framework for an eco-philosophical hermeneutics of cinema', *Thesis, The Mel Hoppenheim School of Cinema*.

Rust, S., Monani, S. and Cubitt, S. (eds.) (2012) *Ecocinema theory and practice*. New York: Routledge.

Rust, S., Monani, S. and Cubitt, S. (eds.) (2016) *Ecomedia: Key issues*. Abingdon, UK: Routledge.

Rust, S., Monani, S. and Cubitt, S. (eds.) (2023) *Ecocinema theory and practice 2*. New York: Routledge.

Schopp, A. (2019) 'Making room for our personal posthuman prisons: Black mirror's "be right back"' in McSweeney, T. and Joy, S. (eds.) *Through the black mirror: Deconstructing the side effects of the digital age*. London, UK: Palgrave Macmillan.

Shamash, S. (2017) 'Utopic cannibalism in Carlos Fausto, Leonardo Sette, and Takumã Kuikuro's as *Hiper Mulheres*' in Beauchesne, K. and Santos, A. (eds.) *Performing utopias in the contemporary Americas*. New York: Palgrave Macmillan, pp. 131–147.

Silent Running (1972) Directed by Douglas Trumbull [Film]. Universal Pictures.

Solanas, F. and Getino, O. (1970) 'Toward a third cinema', *Cinéaste*, 4(3), pp. 1–10.

Soylent Green (1973) Directed by Richard Fleischer [Film]. Metro-Goldwyn-Mayer.

Stevens, I. (2022) '"It's almost like a silent movie": Mark Jenkin on his upcoming 1970s-set horror Enys Men', *BFI*, 19 April 2022. https://www.bfi.org.uk/sight-and-sound/news/mark-jenkin-enys-men-preview-upcoming-1970s-horror, accessed 28 October 2023.

Snowpiercer (2013) Directed by Bong Joon-ho [Film]. CJ Entertainment.

Sustainable Production Alliance (2021) *Carbon emissions of film and television production.* https://www.greenproductionguide.com/wp-content/uploads/2021/04/SPA-Carbon-Emissions-Report.pdf, accessed 28 October 2023.

Sustainable Production Alliance (2022) *Close up look in North America: Regional analysis of film and television carbon emissions.* https://greenproductionguide.com/wp-content/uploads/2022/07/SPA-Regional-Carbon-Emissions.pdf, accessed 28 October 2023.

Taşkale, A.R. (2020) 'Thoughts Interlinked: Corporate Imaginaries and Post-Capitalist Futures in Blade Runner 2049', *Critique*, 48(1), pp. 113–119.

The Boy Who Harnessed the Wind (2019) Directed by Chiwetel Ejiofor [Film]. Netflix.

The Day After Tomorrow (2004) Directed by Roland Emmerich [Film]. 20th Century Fox.

The End We Start From (2024) Directed by Mahalia Belo [Film]. Signature Entertainment.

The Toxic Avenger (1984) Directed by Michael Herz and Samuel Weil [Film]. Troma Entertainment.

The Unchained Goddess (1958) Directed by Richard Carlson and William T. Hurtz. Broadcast *NBC*, 12 February 1958 [Television Series].

Tinnell, J. (2011) 'Transversalising the ecological turn: Four components of Felix Guattari's ecosophical perspective', *The Fibreculture Journal*, 18.

Trouble the Water (2008) Directed by Tia Lessin and Carl Deal [Film]. Zeitgeist Films.

Tweedle, J. (2013) *The age of new waves: Art cinema and the staging of globalisation.* Oxford, UK: Oxford University Press.

Vaidya, A. (2020) 'Forest tales: Toward a practice of eco-cinema', *Performance Matters*, 6(1).

Vint, S. (2020) 'Vitality and reproduction in *Blade Runner 2049*', *Science Fiction Film and Television*, 13(1), pp. 15–35, 173.

Wall-E (2008) Directed by Andrew Stanton [Film]. Pixar.

Weinstock, J.A. (2016) 'The New Weird' in Gelder, K. (ed.) *New directions in popular fiction.* London, UK: Palgrave Macmillan.Weir, Douglas (2023), 'Extra: Film Sounds with Mark Jenkin and Peter Strickland (2022, 86 mins): The director of Enys Men in conversation with filmmaker Peter Strickland (Berberian Sound Studio, Flux Gourmet) as they discuss the subtleties of sound in film', in *Enys Men* (dir. Mark Jenkin), London: BFI.

Section IV:

Literature, Theatre and Art: Expressing and Embodying Affect

· 11 ·

'THERE'S SOMETHING YOU NEED TO HEAR': THE LITERATURE OF ENVIRONMENTAL CRISIS

Pippa Marland

The challenge of the Anthropocene

In the early evening of 15 April 2019, a fire began under the eaves of Notre Dame Cathedral in Paris, eventually destroying the spire and much of the roof (Lyons, 2016, n.p.). While wealthy philanthropists poured money into a recovery fund (over a billion euros had been pledged by May of that year), environmentalists commented on the disproportionate level of financial assistance offered for the restoration of this cultural monument compared with the lack of funding devoted to mitigating climate change (Power 2019, n.p.). Amanda Power notes that on the day Notre Dame was in flames, climate protests were taking place in London, and she argues that, in the face of the worsening global environmental crisis and the prospect of a world on fire, it seemed a 'strange time to restore at such cost a monument to the western civilisation that helped create these conditions' (n.p.). In this observation, Power echoes a concern in contemporary environmental criticism: that the cultural practices and forms the western world has valorised are implicated in the behaviours that have brought us to the Anthropocene. In such a context, the validity of cultural production is called into question.

It is not only the validity of cultural expression that is in doubt, however, but also its capacity to make sense of an Anthropocene world. The concept of the Anthropocene itself is relatively simple – humans have become a 'geological force' (Clark, 2015, p. 4), and 'the planetary system as a whole is undergoing an epoch-level transition' (Davies, 2016, p. 2) – but in cultural terms, the epoch represents an unreadability and resistance to articulation. Jeremy Davies notes its cognitively disorienting effects as it 'raises the oceans, reschedules the year and turns water to land' (2016, p. 2), while Timothy Clark argues that it 'blurs and even scrambles some crucial categories by which people have made sense of the world and their lives' (2015, p. 9). In discussions of these intellectual challenges, a noun that recurs is 'derangement' (Clark, 2012; Ghosh, 2016). For Clark, this derangement arises from the difficulty of moving between the vastly different scales involved in thinking about the Anthropocene. It emerges in the way people talk about environmental issues, for example, in sentences that combine 'the possible collapse of civilization' with 'the injunction never to fill the kettle more than necessary when making tea' or the idea that 'a motorist buying a slightly less destructive make of car is now "saving the planet"' (2012, n.p.). The implication is that formulations like these both overestimate individual human agency and underestimate the self-directing power of the nonhuman. Anthropogenic impacts may define the Anthropocene epoch but it is wildly hubristic to think that humans can control its effects. The second example also demonstrates the insidious ability of capitalist interests to infiltrate environmental discourse.

Amitav Ghosh sees our cultural forms as deranged not so much in what they articulate but in what they *do not*. He imagines our descendants in the altered world of the future searching the culture of our time for 'traces and portents' (2016, p. 11) of cataclysmic environmental change. In the absence of such traces, the only conclusion these people of the future can reach is that 'most forms of art and literature were drawn into the modes of concealment that prevented people from recognizing the realities of their plight' (11). Ghosh ends by speculating that the current era 'will come to be known as the time of the Great Derangement' (11). Ghosh is not unsympathetic to the difficulties that writers encounter in attempting to chronicle climate change. He argues that the challenges they face have their roots in 'the grid of literary forms and conventions that came to shape the narrative imagination in precisely that period when the accumulation of carbon in the atmosphere was rewriting the destiny of the earth' (7). In this, Ghosh is echoing Power's suggestion that western culture is implicated in creating the conditions that have given rise to the Anthropocene. He singles out the novel in particular as a form that is unable to negotiate 'the currents of global warming' (8) in part because of its anthropocentric focus and partly because, in his view its traditional structure and plotting cannot accommodate the extreme events that mark the climate of the Anthropocene.

One of the key critiques of the term 'Anthropocene' itself is that in its very naming it perpetuates a form of concealment: the uneven level of culpability and environmental risk across the globe. For Kathryn Yusoff, the Anthropocene is an integrally flawed concept, connected to a 'White Geology' that reifies 'epistemic and material modes of categorization and dispossession' (2018, p. xi). As she argues in *A Billion Black Anthropocenes or None*:

> The Anthropocene might seem to offer a dystopic future that laments the end of the world, but imperialism and ongoing (settler) colonialisms have been ending worlds for as long as they have been in existence. (2018, p. xiii)[1]

Unfortunately, the forms of long-drawn-out dispossession and destruction Yusoff outlines can, like the extreme effects of the Anthropocene that Ghosh discusses, elude conventional forms of representation. Rob Nixon dubs the kinds of environmental disaster afflicting communities subjugated by neocolonialism that unfold over an extended timespan 'slow violence' (2011, p. 3), a violence 'that is neither spectacular nor instantaneous, but rather incremental and accretive, its calamitous repercussions playing out across a range of temporal scales' (2). He refers to the representational challenge of 'how to devise arresting stories, images, and symbols adequate to the pervasive but elusive violence of delayed effects' (3) and he stresses that such forms are necessary for generating public awareness and catalysing political intervention.

While Nixon's argument is plausible, there is no guarantee that public sentiment will result in political change. There is a growing sense of frustration in environmentalist circles at the lack of progress in addressing climate change, as a combination of political inertia and vested capitalist interests stands in the way of action. In this context, Andreas Malm argues: 'there can be no doubt that the ruling classes are constitutionally incapable of responding to the catastrophe in any other way than by expediting it; [. . .] they can do nothing but burn their way to the end' (2021, p. 8). In his urgently provocative work, *How to Blow up a Pipeline*, Malm suggests that the time for peaceful environmental protest has passed. Written at a time when wildfires were burning from the Arctic Circle to the Amazon, Malm's call to action asks us to picture a scenario years from hence when despite the activism already gaining traction around the world, we 'wake up one morning and realise that business-as-usual is still on' (25). His question is: what happens then? Do we capitulate and accept the inevitability of further global warming and all that that entails, 'or is there another phase, beyond peaceful protest?' (25). At this point, endorsing 'strategic pacifism' becomes, in Malm's view 'an exercise in active repression' (53) and 'sabotage' (68) becomes the obvious next phase.

A danger, though, is that the perceived severity of the current 'polycrisis' – the multiple crises in economics, politics, geopolitics and the environment (Tooze, 2023, n.p.) – might lead not to activism but to despair. Jonathan Franzen argues: 'We literally are living in end times for civilization as we know it [. . .] We are long past the point of averting climate catastrophe' (cited in Ramírez, 2022, n.p.). In this context, any hope that political or technological solutions can be found appears unjustified. At the other end of the spectrum, there are self-proclaimed 'climate optimists' who believe that climate solutions are already well underway (see Wittenberg-Cox, 2023, n.p.). For David Higgins, the two perspectives have more in common than one might first assume: 'One might ask whether there is a substantive difference between preaching doom and preaching a form of hope that depends on targets that are logistically implausible' (2022, p. 2). Neither stance, Higgins suggests, is helpful. Somewhere between pessimism and optimism, however, is the possibility of what Jonathan Lear, among others, has called 'radical hope'. Lear writes of a need to recognise 'our shared sense of vulnerability' (2022, p. 7) and to forge a courageous, radical hope 'directed towards a future goodness that transcends the current ability to understand what it is' (104). This vision of radical hope involves understanding the inevitability of loss while holding faith with an as-yet unknowable future.

Writing the Anthropocene

From an eco-literary perspective, and in light of the foregoing discussion, the challenges of articulating an Anthropocene world begin to appear insurmountable. Clark questions whether the intellectual demands of our situation can be met by innovations in artistic forms, or whether, 'more darkly, [. . .] certain limits of the human imagination, artistic representation and the capacity of human understanding [are] now being reached' (2015, p. 24). In the midst of such speculation, the early ecocritical belief that literary studies could play an important role in understanding and finding ways to mitigate the ecological crisis seems increasingly naïve. However, Clark also acknowledges the 'intellectually liberating' aspects of an Anthropocene epoch in which 'the breakdowns of inherited demarcations of thought can still become a means of disclosure and revision, tempering the sense of alarm with a host of new insights' (xi). The suggestion, muted though it is, is that there may still be something to play for, conceptually and culturally.

In order to investigate the potential of literature to represent the complexity of the Anthropocene and even contribute new insights, this chapter takes as case studies three twenty-first-century novels: Imbolo Mbue's *How Beautiful We Were* (2022), Richard Powers' *The Overstory* (2018), and Kim Stanley Robinson's *The Ministry for the Future* (2020). The first is a work of 'petrofiction', a term coined by Ghosh for novels in which the narrative is dominated by 'the transformative power of petroleum' (2021, p. 19). The second falls into the broad category of eco-fiction, in which the natural world is the dominant theme, and the third belongs to the genre of science fiction which deals speculatively with possible futures. For all three, environmental issues are a key concern. In my discussion of these works, I explore how their narratives are positioned in relation to the social contexts in which they arise as well as their formal and conceptual strategies for dealing with the complexity of Anthropocene effects and the enmeshment of ecological themes in wider socio-political structures. I ask whether the narratives reveal rather than conceal the conditions of our time and how they deal with the question of the inevitability of violent activism. Finally, I examine whether these novels, even as they narrate examples of devastation and loss, leave room for hope, radical or otherwise.

How Beautiful We Were

Imbolo Mbue's *How Beautiful We Were* is a multi-generational story set in a fictional African village called Kosawa where the people are experiencing the long-term environmental effects of oil extraction on their land by an American company, Pexton. The book is partly based on the author's own experiences of growing up in Cameroon, which has a significant oil industry, as well as her awareness of the work of Nigerian writer and environmental activist Ken Saro-Wiwa, who campaigned against the oil company Shell and was executed by the Nigerian government (see Venugopal, 2021). The novel shows how, through neo-colonialist activity, worlds are constantly being lost: villages are emptied and populations are decimated by high mortality rates caused by toxic environmental conditions. Mbue's description of the physical suffering of the Kosawa community chimes with Yusoff's sense of the Anthropocene 'as a material and durational fact in bodies and environments' (2018, p. 103). The novel begins with a sense of unavoidable loss: 'We should have known the end was near. How could we not have known? When the sky began to pour acid and rivers began to turn green, we should have known our land would soon be dead' (4). The narrative takes us from the villagers' first act of resistance to the despoliation of their environment (the kidnapping of some of Pexton's representatives catalysed by the village 'madman' Konga in a rare moment of lucidity) to the ultimate 'death' of their land.

The novel is initially collectively voiced by the children of Kosawa, followed by a young girl, Thula, who plays a central role in the narrative, and other narrators including Thula's 'age-mates' and older villagers. The alternation of chorus-like focalisation and single voices gives a sense of collective and individual trauma with generational distinctions. Ghosh argues that 'the landscapes of oil resist the accustomed techniques of fiction' (2021, p. 20), but Mbue's formally innovative polyvocal style helps to overcome some of that resistance. In this truncated form of storytelling, the novel dramatises the slow violence that Nixon theorises. It also carefully situates the neo-colonialism of the American petroleum industry within a longer history of colonial subjugation. The testimony of Thula's grandmother, Yaya, looks back to the arrival of European Christian missionaries in the village when she was a child as well as reflecting on the stories of generations before her time when Kosawa escaped the attentions of slave traders. She notes how, during the colonisation of her country, villagers succumbed to the demand for labour in the rubber plantations in which they were, in effect, treated as slaves. Yaya herself remembers the departure of the colonisers: 'we learned that the masters had decided to return to Europe' (Mbue 2022, p. 224). Her community hails this as a new beginning although the damage already wrought cannot be undone, and the colonisers make no attempt at reparation. Instead they impose their choice of ruler who, along with his successor (named 'His Excellency' in the novel), enables the Americans to retain a post-colonial hold upon the country's natural resources.

When four villagers imprisoned for the kidnapping of the Pexton ambassadors are summarily hanged before their scheduled trial, the surviving members of the community begin to understand more fully the nature of their subjugation. Even a 'Restoration Movement' set up after the abuses visited upon Kosawa are made public in America only serves to maintain an uneasy status quo rather than bringing the oil extraction to an end. The support of the American public has no impact on the villagers' situation: 'People all over

America wrote letters to Pexton, begging for the Four to be released. Pexton told them they had nothing to do with the men's arrest, it was up to His Excellency' (Mbue 2022, p.192). The American sympathisers then ask their government to implement sanctions against the dictator but it becomes increasingly clear that he is impervious to such political and economic manoeuvres, largely because of the global structures that facilitate neoliberal economics. Mbue explains: 'Corporations in Europe that often gave His Excellency loans to create shared wealth told him that if he didn't release the Four they'd stop lending to him [. . .] but everyone knew that those lenders wouldn't stop making the loans – keeping countries like ours in their debt was why they existed' (192).

When Thula goes to an American university, helped financially by the Restoration Movement, she studies Frantz Fanon's *The Wretched of the Earth*, and its central argument that 'decolonization is always a violent phenomenon' (2001 [1961], p. 27). Inspired by his words, she attends a political meeting focused on the abuses perpetrated by corporations like Pexton. Thula notes appreciatively: 'These people were not like the ones at the Restoration Movement, talking about how we can peacefully bring about change with dialogue, negotiation, common ground, more dialogue. No, these people were angry' (Mbue 2022, p. 207). She encourages her peers in Kosawa to commit acts of sabotage, including blowing up a pipeline. At this stage Pexton begin to negotiate and an agreement is drawn up. The villagers wait peacefully for six years for the company's promises to be kept, while oil continues to spill and children continue to die (265). In a final act of desperation, the young men arm themselves and begin to murder people associated with Pexton. The retribution is a further massacre of the villagers in which Thula herself is killed.

The end of the novel offers no easy resolution other than confirming the 'death' of Kosawa: 'There was no land left to fight for, so Pexton had no fear that our children might grow up to wage war against them' (Mbue 2022, p.358). Given the absence of any resistance, the company begins to subsidise the education of the displaced children of Kosawa. The final chapter is voiced collectively by the village elders and it reflects an apparent surrender to the interests of neo-colonialism and neoliberalism:

> Today, in the year 2020, forty years since the night Konga told us to rise, our children have good jobs with our government, with corporations in Europe and America. They live in lovely houses. They drive new cars. [. . .] Sometimes we ask our children about the cars they drive. The cars seem to be bigger than they have ever been, needing more oil. Do they think about it, about the children who will suffer as we once did just so they can have all the oil they want? (358)

The outcome highlights the insidious power and adaptability of capitalism. And yet this is not the last word. The same elders, visiting their children in Europe and America, 'sit on the couch, looking at the television but not seeing it' (360). In their minds they are still in Kosawa, still thinking of Thula and the fight she spearheaded, and, as they collectively recall, 'It's at such moments that the children of our children come to us and say, please, Yaya, please, Big Papa, tell us a story' (360). Somehow, Mbue hints, their communal narrative will continue. While not constituting radical hope as such, this underlying sense of cultural resilience perhaps represents one component of it.

The Overstory

While Mbue's novel is polyvocal in its human cast, Richard Powers' *The Overstory* involves the voices of both humans and nonhumans. The book opens with a woman (we later discover that this is the character Mimi Ma) sitting in an urban park with her back against a pine tree. She is receiving messages: '*A chorus of living wood sings to the woman*: If your mind were only a slightly greener thing we'd drown you in meaning. *The pine she leans against says*: Listen. There's something you need to hear' (Powers 2018, p. 4). The need for a 'greener' mind and the ability to 'hear' does not just apply to the woman: the novel as a whole works towards effecting an ontological shift in its readers. Powers has explained in an interview that there is a key idea at the centre of the book: 'that there is no separate thing called humanity, any more than there is a separate thing called nature' (cited in Hunt, 2019, n.p.). He acknowledges that these ideas have been 'explored for some time by environmentalists and philosophers and scientists and political activists' but have, as yet, not found their way into that 'most human-centric of arts, the commercial novel' (cited in Hunt, 2019, n.p.).

Powers is correct in suggesting that the integral interconnectedness of the human and nonhuman has been a feature of recent environmental thinking, both as a result of recent scientific discoveries and a turn in Euro-American environmentalist culture towards a greater recognition of forms of indigenous ecological understanding. Material ecocriticism, for example, rests on the foundational concept that all of the world's material phenomena 'are knots in a vast network of agencies' (Iovino and Oppermann, 2014, p. 1). Within this conceptual framework, nonhuman animacy, agency and intelligence are highlighted. Forms of interpretation and communication within the nonhuman world are also recognised through the adoption of biosemiotic perspectives, which hold that 'the natural world is perfused with signs, meanings and purposes' (Wheeler, cited in Iovino and Oppermann, 2014, p. 4). As such, traditional hierarchies that place the human above the nonhuman are disrupted and a more 'ontologically generous', non-dualistic vision of an Earth in which human and nonhuman entities are integrally connected and mutually dependent emerges.

In bringing these concepts to the commercial novel, Powers breaks new literary ground. In *The Overstory*, the circle of interest in the novel, traditionally geared around human subjectivity and interiority, has shifted to include an animate, intelligent world trying to make its voice heard. The nine main human protagonists of the novel are, in effect, called to the aid of trees. One of these protagonists is the scientist Patricia Westerford, based on the real-life ecologist Suzanne Simard who was responsible for early discoveries about tree communication and mutualism (Schiffman, 2021, n.p). Powers sums these discoveries up as the 'new forestry': phenomena such as 'trees signalling to each other over the air, coming together to form vast shared immune systems, or the trading of food and medicines underground through these long fungal filaments' (cited in Hunt, 2019, n.p.). The idea of this arboreal community is explored literally in the book but also functions as a structural model for the increasing interconnection of the human characters, all of whom are gradually gathered together in a community of raised awareness of arboreal lives. While the narrative is still largely centred on the human characters and their histories, Powers makes it clear that human time is not the only or even the main measure of time in the novel and that running before, during and after the lives of the main protagonists is a longer, deeper, slower tree time. Against the long lives of trees, human time seems vastly accelerated. 'Countless nows pass' (Powers 2018, p. 31), Powers writes of the lives of one of the protagonists, and her family.

However, the novel, like Mbue's is also shadowed by the idea of death. Early in the narrative we are introduced to one of the protagonists, Nicholas Hoel, who has continued the family tradition of photographing a chestnut tree that his great-great-great grandfather planted (Powers 2018, p. 6). We learn that the tree, which is now entering its own natural senescence, is one of the few survivors of a chestnut blight affecting North America in the early twentieth century which killed up to four billion trees (Hunt, 2019 n.p.). There are other instances in the novel where trees die in great numbers, but from more easily recognised anthropogenic causes, from clear-cut felling in the National Forest (Powers 2018, p. 87) to the cutting down of trees in a city park (206).

In response, some of the characters become involved in activism. Hoel, and Olivia Vandergriff, who begins to hear the voices of the nonhuman after a near-death experience, take the names Watchman and Maidenhair and station themselves high up in a redwood tree called Mimas to prevent her being felled (261).

Powers sees the domination of the natural world as a form of colonialism and regards humanity as being stuck inside a 'colonised narrative' (cited in Hunt, 2019, n.p.) that considers only the economic value of the nonhuman. The attempt to decolonise the nonhuman tends towards violence just as the decolonisation of subjugated human communities. Here, as the tactics of the loggers and the police force that protects their interests become more cruel and aggressive, the protesters lose faith in their non-violent approach and move on to sabotage. In this context, like *How Beautiful We Were*, *The Overstory* offers no hopeful resolution: the structures of capitalism and neo-capitalism appear too robust for the actions of individuals or communities to have any traction. At the end of the novel, Patricia takes her own life to demonstrate what she believes humans can do in the best interests of the planet (456). The giant redwood Mimas is felled (327), Olivia [Maidenhair] is killed when a home-made bomb destined to destroy logging machinery explodes too early (348) and Adam Appich, a psychology PhD student who is drawn into the direct action, is sentenced to two life sentences in jail (471).

Finally, Mimi, once more sitting with her back to a tree, tunes into the voices of the nonhuman: 'Messages hum from out of the bark she leans against. Chemical semaphores home in over the air. Currents rise from the soil gripping roots' (Powers 2018, p. 499). These voices still have a message for her. They seem to suggest that though Mimi and her fellow environmentalists have apparently failed in their mission, and further widespread environmental destruction is inevitable, the Earth will endure: 'The fires will come, despite all efforts, the blight and windthrow and floods. Then the earth will become another thing, and people will learn it all over again. [. . .] Once *the real world* ends' (499). Powers' characters have not physically lost a world as the villagers of Kosawa have in Mbue's novel, though they painfully recognise widespread environmental destruction. What they have lost is the concept of a world as they know it. As Powers explains:

> Those people who feel despair are in the first necessary stage of transformation. You need to despair for the impossibility of the continuance of the life you've embraced, in order to become something else. (Cited in Hunt, 2019, n.p.)

It is not clear whether Powers is gesturing towards a total collapse of civilisation here, but the scenario at least allows for the possibility of a transformation beyond loss – the kind of future goodness involved in Lear's radical hope. The ontological shift towards a greater understanding of nonhuman lives that the narrative enacts and shows developing within a growing human community, offers, despite the magnitude of loss that Powers anticipates, the grounds for faith in the unknown future.

The Ministry for the Future

Kim Stanley Robinson's *The Ministry for the Future*, is premised on the possibility of a future that *can* be plotted and speculatively known. The novel begins in the near future with a visceral account of a 'wet-bulb' temperature event in India in which the combination of heat and humidity reaches lethal levels. It introduces us to a character called Frank May, an American health worker in the state of Uttar Pradesh, one of the few survivors of the heatwave. Though Frank's subsequent story is woven through the book, Robinson takes polyvocality even further than Powers. The novel is arranged into one hundred and six sections (some only a few lines long, others more like conventional chapters) and focalises a large cast of 'characters' which includes scientists, climate refugees, environmental activists, economists, and an AI consciousness, as well as phenomena such as the sun, history, protons and 'the market'. Many sections are voiced by an anonymous 'we', giving the effect of globally distributed groups with different perspectives all trying to engage with the polycrisis of the twenty-first century.

Early in the novel we also learn of the creation of a new ministry, mooted at the COP29 meeting in 2024 and formally inaugurated in Zurich in 2025. Its mission is to work with the Intergovernmental Panel on Climate Change, the United Nations and all signatories of the 2015 Paris Agreement to 'advocate for the world's future generations of citizens' and also to defend 'all living creatures present and future who cannot speak for themselves, by promoting their legal standing and physical protection' (Robinson 2020, p. 16). Mary Murphy is the Irish head of this new organisation, which is quickly nicknamed the 'Ministry for the Future' (16). Frank, suffering from PTSD and survivor guilt is desperate to involve himself in direct action on climate change. He attempts to join an Indian eco-terrorist group 'The Children of Kali' that has formed in the wake of the disaster, but is rejected: its members are wise to the white saviour myth. Relocating to Switzerland, he then takes unilateral direct action, briefly imprisoning Mary in her own house.

The intertwining narrative of Frank and Mary provides a loose framework for the novel, but even their stories are subservient to the bigger picture. As Steven Shaviro notes: 'their personal characteristics are forged in a kind of feedback response to the economic, social, political and technological forces in the world they inhabit' (2021, p. 109). Robinson's attention to these forces can be seen as a conscious attempt to take a comprehensive look at the systems that have given rise to anthropogenic climate change (and related social injustice) in order to see what it might take to mitigate its effects. His perspective is notable in its generosity. There is no condemnation of particular efforts in aid of the environment, although through the inclusion of different voices, he registers debates surrounding them. The narrative includes a 'techno-fix' of boosting atmospheric sulphur dioxide the Indian government uses to bring down temperatures in the wake of the terrible heatwave (Robinson 2020, p. 18) and geo-engineering experiments attempting to restore the Antarctic ice by pumping water up from below (148). Alongside these science-led endeavours, Robinson also plots changes in financial systems including the introduction of a block-chain regulated 'carbon coin' (479) which rewards companies for sequestering carbon. Like Mbue and Powers' novels *The Ministry of the Future* also plots an upsurge in violent direct action. This is carried out by the aforementioned 'Children of Kali', among other groups but also, as the novel goes on, by an unsanctioned 'black ops' wing of the Ministry for the Future itself (254). Some of the most significant gains are attributed to the influence of 'eco-terrorism', which is seen as a necessary approach to shifting the most intransigent of environmentally damaging behaviours. With the use of armed drones private jets are brought down, oil tankers sunk, coal-fired power plants destroyed; in their place carbon-neutral airships and sea-going vessels that use non-polluting renewable energy are developed (417–418).

The Ministry for the Future is a utopian novel, but Robinson is quick to make clear that utopia does not imply a 'perfect end-state society'; instead he defines it as 'a progressive movement in history, with each generation doing better than the generation before, in substantial ways, in terms of equality, justice, and sustainability' (cited in T. Robinson, 2020, n.p.). There are catastrophes, suffering and deaths throughout the novel and human systems are brought to the brink of collapse (Robinson 2020, p. 227). There is a point, however, late in the novel, when it becomes clear that the polycrisis is receding. Mary attends COP 58, roughly four decades after the Paris Agreement. The conference involves a summing up of the environmental achievements since 2015 as well as an overview of what still needs action. From the perspective of the 2050s, the Agreement 'was looking more and more like a break point in the history of both humans and the Earth itself, the start of something new. [. . .], it was perhaps like the moment the tide turns: first barely perceptible, then unstoppable. The greatest turning point in human history' (475).

Science fiction has always rested on the interplay of cognition and estrangement (see Suvin, 1979). It achieves its plausibility by reflecting aspects of the real before introducing more fantastical elements. As well as evoking the actual Paris Agreement, Robinson uses existing scales and initiatives on which to base his futuristic vision. Mary is shown an image of the 'Keeling Curve', the daily record of global atmospheric carbon dioxide concentration, that maps 'its continuous rise, then the leveling, then the recent downturn' (Robinson 2022 p. 475); another banner reveals that, thanks to the 'Global Footprint Network', 'World civilization was no longer using up more of the biosphere's renewable resources than were being replaced by natural processes' (476–477).[2] She sees progress with the 'Half Earth project': 'There were more wild animals alive on Earth than at any time in the past two centuries at least and also there were fewer domestic beasts grown for human food' (477).[3] There are social justice gains too: economic inequality measured by the Gini Coefficient has been reduced by 'setting a generous definition of a universal necessary income, guaranteeing jobs to all, and capping personal annual income at ten times that minimum amount' (479).[4] The list of unresolved issues is also long and includes the problem of disposing of nuclear waste, the ongoing poverty of the world's poorest nations and the further damaging of the biosphere by other pollutants (480–484). Nevertheless, the overarching picture is one of progress.

Robinson has performed a significant act of intellectual labour in preparing the reader for this turning point, plotting the political, economic, scientific and cultural changes needed to bring this about. The kind of complexity involved does not make for light or even fluently coherent reading, but in a sense Robinson is *not* trying to make the novel cohere. As Shaviro argues: 'the world system cannot be captured experientially' and any narrative that suggested that it could be, 'by that very fact, representationally inadequate' (2021, p. 110). Robinson has himself acknowledged a kind of wilful 'difficulty' to his writing: 'so it's actually a bit of work, and even sometimes irritating? Well, that's part of the experience of reading one of my novels, and afterward, you remember it better' (cited in T. Robinson, 2020). At the close of the novel, the reader has, in effect, had to 'think through' the polycrisis and its possible solutions along with Robinson. *The Ministry for the Future* promotes a far-reaching form of optimism. It models a future that sees a planetary effort to address the multiple crises of the Anthropocene come to at least partial fruition. Robinson has stated that his aim is not to write science *fiction* but 'future *history*' (cited in T. Robinson, 2020, n.p., emphasis mine). As we read the novel, we have the energising sense of our future selves looking back on a darker world, but one which already held the potential for positive change.

Conclusion

All three works studied here are formally experimental, expanding the traditional scale and focus of the novel with extended temporalities and a resistance to the novelistic reliance on the subjective interiority of a limited number of human protagonists. Indeed, recognising that the polycrisis cannot be told with any one voice, the novels feature multiple individual and collective narrators including, at times, nonhumans. In the case of *The Ministry for the Future* this structural innovation comes close to stretching the form of the novel beyond its limits, though, as already, noted its 'difficulty' is a deliberate strategy on Robinson's part. Their narratives combine violent, catastrophic events with the delineation of more incremental effects, in the process forging more flexible narrative structures. All three find ways of situating their narratives within broader political and economic structures, and, in general, taking an oppositional stance to those structures and the beliefs that underpin them. *How Beautiful We Were* lays bare the neo-colonialism at play in the inequalities of Anthropocene effects. *The Overstory* incorporates new ontologies and insists that the social world of the novel must henceforth involve the nonhumans amongst whom we live. All of the works attest to the intransigence of networks of power and finance and the inevitability of violent protest in response, but they also quietly articulate the resilience of community, and the gathering force of the numbers of people advocating for the Earth. *The Ministry for the Future* maps possible routes forward into a world transformed not just by devastation but also by positive social, political and environmental change.

Clark argues that the current ecocritical project involves 'coming up with a set of those features that literature or art adequate to the environmental emergency would ideally have' (2015, p. 20). Among these features he lists: 'texts that work on multiple scales [. . .], accord true agency and worth to the nonhuman, which show how porous human bodies and psyches are to environmental effects' (20). His fear is that the discovery of such 'important' work feeds into 'delusions that the sphere of cultural representations has more centrality than it in fact has' (21) and, even worse, that the reliance on that centrality might inadvertently stop people from taking action to challenge the damaging status quo. Clark has, in effect, described my approach here in identifying three, to my mind, 'important' novels. But, as I have argued, the authors all voice their opposition to the status quo while not making any substantial claims about the significance of cultural representation, not least because of their awareness that, despite their oppositional stance, they are still narrating the world from within a flawed cultural system. None of the novels offers easy answers or bland reassurance. Their role is, in Ghosh's terms, not to conceal but to reveal the realities of our time. They tell us something 'we need to hear' without the assumption that revelation alone can change things. Instead they situate their protagonists (both human and nonhuman) within communities and networks that promise to endure and grow. In this, the novels offer both a reason not to despair and an urgent call to action.

Acknowledgements

This chapter is dedicated to the Second Year Liberal Arts students at the University of Bristol and to my co-teacher Michael Malay. Our discussions on the unit 'Ideas and Society: Rethinking Nature' not only inspired the writing of this chapter but gave me cause for cautious, precious hope.

Notes

1 There have been other significant suggestions for the naming of the new epoch, including 'capitalocene' (Moore, 2016) and 'plantationocene' (see Haraway, 2015), that are more specific in their attribution of culpability than the Anthropocene's largely undifferentiated *Anthropos*.
2 https://keelingcurve.ucsd.edu/; https://www.footprintnetwork.org/, accessed 2 January 2024.
3 https://eowilsonfoundation.org/what-is-the-half-earth-project/, accessed 2 January 2024.
4 The Gini Coefficient being the measure of economic inequality within a population: https://www.ons.gov.uk/peoplepopulationandcommunity/birthsdeathsandmarriages/families/methodologies/theginicoefficient, accessed 2 January 2024.

References

Clark, T. (2012) 'Scale' in Cohen, T. (ed.) Telemorphosis: Theory in the era of climate change, Vol. 1. Michigan: Open Humanities Press, pp. 148–166.

——. (2015) *Ecocriticism on the edge: The Anthropocene as a threshold concept*. London: Bloomsbury.

Davies, J. (2016) *The birth of the Anthropocene*. Oakland: University of California Press.

Fanon, F. (2001 [1961]) *The wretched of the earth*. London: Penguin.

Iovino, S. and Oppermann, S. (2014) 'Introduction' in Iovino, S. and Oppermann, S. (eds.) *Material ecocriticism*. Bloomington; Indianapolis: Indiana University Press.

Ghosh, A. (1992) 'Petrofiction: The oil encounter and the novel', The New Republic, March 2, pp. 29–34.

——. (2016) *The great derangement: Climate change and the unthinkable*. Chicago; London: University of Chicago Press.

——. (2021) 'Petrofiction, revisited' in Balkan, S. and Nandi, S. (eds.) *Oil fictions: World literature and our contemporary petrosphere*. Pennsylvania: Pennsylvania State University Press, pp. 19–21.

Haraway, D. (2015) 'Anthropocene, Capitalocene, Plantationocene, Chthulucene: Making kin', Environmental Humanities, 6(1), pp. 159–165.

Higgins, D. (2022) 'Climate pessimism and human nature', Humanities, 11(129), pp. 1–14.

Hunt, N. (2019) *Older than writing: A conversation with Richard powers*. https://dark-mountain.net/older-than-writing/, accessed 27 December 2023.

Lear, J. (2022) *Radical hope: Ethics in the face of cultural devastation*. Cambridge, MA: Harvard University Press.

Lyons, K. (2016) *'Our lady of tears': What the papers say about the Notre Dame fire*. https://www.theguardian.com/world/2019/apr/16/, accessed 23 December 2023.

Malm, A. (2021) *How to blow up a pipeline*. London: Verso.

Mbue, I. (2022) *How beautiful we were*. Edinburgh: Canongate.

Moore, J. (ed.) (2016) *Anthropocene or Capitalocene? Nature, history and the crisis of capitalism*. Oakland, CA: PM Press.

Nixon, R. (2011) *Slow violence and the environmentalism of the poor*. Cambridge, MA: Harvard University Press.

Power, A. (2019) 'Notre Dame should not be restored – let it stand as a symbol of a flawed way of life', 1 May. https://theconversation.com/notre-dame-should-not-be-restored-let-it-stand-as-a-symbol-of-a-flawed-way-of-life-115930, accessed 23 December 2023.

Powers, R. (2018) *The overstory*. London: William Heinemann.

Ramirez, N. (2022). '"Ok, doomer": Why contemporary fiction seems resigned to a climate apocalypse', 19 November. 'Ok, doomer': Why contemporary fiction seems resigned to a climate apocalypse | Culture | EL PAÍS English (elpais.com), accessed 20 September 2024.

Robinson, K.S. (2020) *The ministry for the future*. London: Orbit.

Robinson, T. (2020) *We asked Kim Stanley Robinson: Can science-fiction save us? How good utopian novels change our thinking about the world*. https://www.polygon.com/2020/10/20/21525509/, accessed 21 December 2023.

Schiffman, R. (2021) '"Mother Trees" are intelligent: They learn and remember', Scientific American, 4 May. https://www.scientificamerican.com/article/mother-trees-are-intelligent-they-learn-and-remember/, accessed 1 January 2024.

Shaviro, S. (2021) 'Optimism in the face of catastrophe: Kim Stanley Robinson's *The Ministry for the Future*', Studies in the Fantastic, 10, pp. 108–114.

Suvin, D. (1979) *Metamorphoses of science fiction*. New Haven, CT: Yale University Press.

Tooze, A. (2023) https://www.weforum.org/videos/experts-explain-adam-tooze-what-is-the-polycrisis/, accessed 30 December 2023.

Venugopal, A. (2021) 'Author Imbolo Imbue explores the politics of oil in "How Beautiful We Were"', Transcript of interview for *Fresh Air* https://www.npr.org/2021/04/29/991956171/, accessed 21 December 2023.

Wittenberg-Cox, A. (2023). The Power Of Climate Optimists: Flip The Narrative, Change The Future (forbes.com), 17 April, accessed 20 September 2024.

Yusoff, K. (2018) *A billion black Anthropocenes or none*. Minneapolis: University of Minnesota Press.

·12·

FROM HIDDEN WARS TO HIDDEN THEATRE: EMBODYING A WORLD-IN-CRISIS

Carrie Westwater

We live in a globalised world in which the flows and formations of media and communications have never been as plentiful or as technologically advanced. The global reach and interconnections between telecommunications, 'eye in the sky' satellites, the Internet and international digitised news media can now, potentially, throw a spotlight on wars, conflicts, and humanitarian and ecological disasters almost anywhere in the world (Cottle, 2009a, b). With the rapid spread of smart phones with 'eye in the hand' cameras and social media networks also in the digital mix, acts of citizen witnessing and citizen journalism have further deepened world connectivity in recent years (Thorsen and Allan, 2014). Wars, humanitarian crises, natural disasters and *un*-natural global crises in today's 'world-in-crisis' can now be communicated in near real-time and to globally dispersed audiences. In fact, when incoming data is harnessed to computer visualisation systems, the pathways and destruction of unfolding crises and disasters can even be visualised and communicated in anticipatory mode (Pantti et al., 2012, pp. 178–199).

With such technological advances it might be reasonable to expect that conflict and disasters involving considerable numbers of people suffering anywhere around the world, would be picked up by the media and communicated to citizens, governments and decision-makers who have a responsibility to respond. Unfortunately, we know that this is simply not the case. Hidden wars and forgotten disasters by definition and media inaction continue to unfold unnoticed in the media spotlight and therefore remain out of sight, and out of mind, for many of us (Hawkins, 2008; Cottle, 2009a; Mody, 2010). Symbolic annihilation in the media, where selected groups of people become rendered invisible and/or reduced to negative stereotypes has long been observed (Gerbner, 1972). This has often been the case in the respect of women (Tuchman, 1978), ethnic minorities (Sonwalker, 2004), and refugees and asylum seekers, amongst many Others (Cottle, 2006).

These same processes of invisible making also inform how news media selectively portray some groups of people in wars as 'worthy victims' or 'unworthy victims' (Herman and Chomsky, 1988). Today a journalistic 'calculus of death' is professionally enacted as a matter of institutionalised routine (Cottle, 2013), calibrating to what extent and how some victims of some disasters and tragedies in faraway places, and not others, are afforded news recognition. News media do so principally on the basis of nationally inflected geopolitical interests, cultural proximity and historical affinities, and it is those victims who are deemed to be more newsworthy and deserving of recognition who will receive more news attention. Occasionally this representation can be more in depth through professionally crafted stories populated with personal and emotional experiences, and in presentational news packages inscribed with an 'injunction to care' (Cottle, 2013). But, again, the fact remains that the news media sees the world through a geo-politically and culturally inflected lens that is both selective and myopic in its news gaze (Cottle, 2023).

At the time of writing, the appalling slaughter of civilians in Yemen, the Central African Republic, Sudan and Myanmar continue, mostly under a silent moral scream from the Western news media. In the context of the 'new western way of war' (Shaw, 2005), where risk transfer is politically and militarily enacted through aerial bombing rather than boots on the ground, civilian casualties, or so-called 'collateral damage', will inevitably be high. And in 'new wars' in failed and failing states, civilians are deliberately targeted in processes of ethnic cleansing (Kaldor, 2006). Too often the stories of those positioned at the sharp end of war, conflicts and disasters are unheard and rendered invisible in the world's news media. And this notwithstanding the news media's 'responsibility to report' alongside the UN's 'responsibility to protect' (Cottle, 2015). When the news media do not bear witness and shine a light on wars and atrocious acts so they can sometimes exacerbate the violence directed at civilians as well as combatants on the ground. As I write this, the Israeli Defence

Force, is subjecting the Occupied Territory of Gaza to relentless bombing and military incursion following the Hamas massacre of October 7, 2023. The Palestinian death toll is estimated to be more than 45,000 people, the majority of whom are non-combatants, including over 16,000 children. Western news organisations, denied access to Gaza, struggle to communicate the unfolding mass slaughter or the abject conditions of trying to survive amidst the rubble and in a devastated, overcrowded context of dwindling food, water, energy, and medical care.

This chapter sets out to explore how a model of Theatre Reportage developed by Hidden Theatre deliberately aims to bring the 'hidden ' to view through direct mediation of the 'consequences of living' in crisis by the ordinary citizen. This is how the method was described to the European Parliament (2023) by the founding director, whose name will remain anonymous due to the sensitivity of the work. Through a radically different approach to theatre that is journalistic, the company does not attempt to speak the same language as mass media but instead creates a space in which a voice can be granted to the media voiceless. They aim to represent all aspects of humanity, whether love, grief and pain or fear and indeed war, to remind audiences that the Other, hidden from view, is not less than Human and deserves recognition and help. In such ways the stories of those positioned at the sharp end of crises and trauma – whether refugees and asylum seekers in Italy or Palestinians living in the West Bank and Gaza – can become symbolically rehabilitated and re-humanised as their stories are listened to, embodied and felt. Through the staging of intimate performances Hidden Theatre present a catalogue of hidden trauma from Syria, Palestine, Ukraine, Iran, Iraq and Iraqi-Kurdistan among others. They use 'theatre' as a tool for communion and connection with the audience and do so through heart-rendering narratives of life under oppression and conflict – along with dance, song, shared food and congeniality (Payson, 2018).

It is useful to begin this discussion from hidden wars to hidden theatre, by considering theatre per se as a method of embodiment that historically had the ability to re-situate audiences into seeing and hearing the hidden experiences of hidden crises. The mechanics of how this happens have evolved in response to different and often desperate crises and conflicts and these developments are utilised well by Hidden Theatre. This chapter first sets out this evolution by examining how theatre reportage draws on ancient tenets of Greek Theatre as a tool for education and the communication of war to audiences in Athens circa 700 BC. Following this exploration of the ancient beginnings of theatre the discussion turns to the spatial arrangements and developing aesthetics of political theatre, illustrative of the European post-World War and 1980's Feminist era (Boal, 1973; Grotowski, 1991; Barba, 1999; Brecht, 1964) Hidden Theatre, as we shall hear, have adopted and adapted these methods including the removal of the actor / audience divide as essential to their work (Boal, 1973). This is followed by an outline of how this non-aesthetic approach marks their theatre as positioned outside of the commercial mainstream and apolitically engaged. Drawing on this historical contextualisation, the chapter then explores the companies use of theatre reportage and how its work is enacted and embodied, from training to performance. These perspectives are derived from the authors auto-ethnographic field notes and involvement in the company for over fifteen years.

The evolution of 'theatre' to theatre reportage

Theatre as a performance of narratives (imagined or real) has taken on many different forms, so much so, that 'theatre' as an overarching term encompasses diverse theatrical modes. The following briefly traces its evolution through the lens of its spatial configurations and is confined to a European setting. The beginnings of theatre in this context were far from humble. The Ancient Greek dramatists, such as Aristophanes and Sophocles performed their plays to thousands of audience members. The theatre festivals of Dionysus were city-wide events, and everyone was expected to attend (Banham, 1998, p. 442). The events were a civic duty, a place to be reminded of the greater world and one's place in it. From the surviving texts we know that there was an overarching theme representing a turbulent world of violence, epic battles, and subterfuge, environmental trauma, and pain. These conflicts played out in family tragedies fuelled by betrayal, incest, sexual trauma, filicide, patricide, and disordered living. The Greek Tragedy presented moral conundrums of the rich, the aristocracy and those in political control for the edification and possible education of the general populace; if such moral deficiencies and dilemmas could afflict elites, so too could they affect everyone.

Nothing about theatre was small, or merely for entertainment purposes at this time, and the way theatre represented crisis was to include the audience in the debate. Staged within huge amphitheatres, the audience seating was a half-circle, curved to join the stage on either side. This placed the audience within the performance, was spatially inclusive and chimed with the beginnings of democracy. The mechanics of Greek Theatre, both comedy and tragedy, involved a group of performers who represented the audience. They were typically characterised as ordinary townspeople or thematically portrayed an aspect of the core dramatic theme. For example, in *Medea* by Euripides (431 BC), the Chorus were the Women of Corinth who functioned as intermediary between the protagonist's action and rhetorical communion with the audience. They acted as a mirror to the real world through fiction, and they would present solutions and ask the audience if what they were seeing was correct, moral, and good?

In this way ancient theatre was spatially and by enactment considerably more inclusive of the audience than the say the mainstream proscenium arch theatres of today. The latter involves audiences having to break through the 'fourth wall' (the front-facing side of the box theatre design, which frames the action, and which is viewed by audiences as if looking through a window or at a television screen, and which detracts from active audience participation and dialogue).

'Breaking the fourth wall' and therefore the actor / audience divide is key to the method of theatre reportage, as direct interaction with the audience breaks the theatrical illusion of time and space, of the imaginary, and envelops the audience with a sense of immediacy and connection. Foucault calls this phenomenon heterotopic (Foucault, 1977; Foucault and Miskowiec, 1986), a space and place of resistance that juxtaposes the real with possibilities for change. Like the Ancient Greeks, theatre reportage intends to educate its audience via pedagogic means of experiential and embodied reception and to re-sensitise the audience into civic responsibility by resisting dominant discourse(s). However, it has taken over two thousand years for this theatrical return to take place.

The proscenium arch theatre design of the Restoration Period (used exclusively until the early twentieth century) brought with it spatial inequality and an implicit hierarchy within spectatorship (Bishop, 2012). Audience participation and the exchange of information were hindered by the physical distance created between the actor and the audience. Nevertheless, in the twentieth century, theatre began to see the development of a range of strong participatory transformations (Bishop, 2012). From the 1930s to the 1980s 'alternative' models of theatre developed that sought to express and engage with some of the century's momentous upheavals and their reverberation in social and cultural life.

The World Wars produced industrialised slaughter on a scale never known before. Small independent (and crucially not state-funded) theatre put on plays by dramatists compelled to awaken audiences to the reality and absurdity of war. Bertold Brecht (1964), notably, had a major impact on alternative theatre by disrupting, for example, linear narratives and by presenting short scenes out of sequence. These snap shots of human experience allowed for multifaceted narratives to co-exist. He called these *epíches* which enabled the audience to perceive multiple perspectives that were not locked down didactically. Brecht also reconfigured the space of his theatre using alienation techniques (*Verfremdumgseffeckt*) that took the audience out of their comfort zones of participatory expectations and etiquette. The theatre, for example, had no platform; performances were played out on the same level as the audience, and staging came from anywhere in the room. Props or set items or scenery were deconstructed and instead of pretending to be 'real' things, Brecht's 'theatre' exposed itself – as not real. Through this action, he was saying that theatre and its accoutrements are pretence, and so is society. He used the place of theatre as heterotopic (Foucault and Miskowiec, 1986) to mirror the artifice of life, again inciting possibilities for change by the citizen.

The post-war dramatists also wanted to make audiences question their environment and dramatists such as Samuel Beckett and later Harold Pinter, concentrated on society's sense of hopelessness. Their theatre was the Theatre of the Absurd (1950s–1960s) and the myth of Sisyphus underpinned this movement. Sisyphus pushes a huge rock up a hill each day, for each day to see it roll back down again. Their theatre used this absurdity within their plays to show audiences that they are complicit in their own downfall if they do not resist and change their fate. Post-war theatre movements were all about deconstructing what theatre, and what the world had become. The fear for these practitioners was that the artifice of mainstream theatre (of the Proscenium Arch) was not only contributing to the desensitisation of a passive society but was also passive in their own fate of monetary and capitalist subjugation.

The actor was also thought to be in a stranglehold of 'acting' and in the 1960s and 1970s, the likes of Eugenio Barba (Barba and Barba, 1999) and Jerzy Grotowski (1975/ 2000) decided to strip the theatre of these ills and instead trained actors in embodiment. The actors were de-robed of costumes and were instead skilled in transforming into new frames of time and character without the need for adornments.

With similar intentions, Augusto Boal was also removing the theatrics from theatre by making both the actor and audience active in the spectacle, making this process more equitable. For Boal, *all* people should be spect-actors (Boal,1973). He was inviting participation in the action, once again focussing on connection. Exploring oppression, he used theatre as a tool for 'audiences' to practice emancipation by crossing the actor / audience divide and joining the action. There was no stage, costumes and no spatial hierarchies in place. These mechanics foreground the work of Hidden Theatre and theatre reportage.

Beyond the commercial mainstream theatre

Eugenio Barba, states in a letter to Hidden Theatre that they successfully 'disrupt all the traditional structures of theatre', and they do. Barba alludes to mainstream theatre: the pervading spatial design of the proscenium arch that keeps the separations between actor and audience in place, as a separation of the 'real' in favour of artifice; of costume, affected accents, lighting and theatrics and the hierarchy, bias, and heteronomy of mainstream theatre. This artifice is how theatre is still practiced in the mainstream and especially so in large-scale theatres. The smaller, more colloquial theatres can be seen to incorporate a little more 'alternative' staging, perhaps due to their seating capacity. However, the programming is not aligned to these variations and all too generally falls into the realms of the commercial: film adaptations, musicals, standup comedy, and chat-show-style talks. When there is a straight play, the themes are invariably safe and distanced from contentious issues. It is the independent and frequently building-less theatre companies, like Hidden Theatre, who tackle the more difficult topics of say war and environmental despoilation and who do so without funding, or extraordinarily little. This dynamic is worth considering for a moment.

Pierre Bourdieu (1993) suggests that when a space, place, or creative text (such as a piece of writing, journalistic text, or theatre performance) is funded, the production of that text becomes compromised by its heteronomy or who owns that text. Alternatively, if the text/s are not funded and have no commercial affiliations, then the producers of the text/s can retain autonomy and therefore artistic freedom. Those who are free of funded affiliations are freer to make decisions than their funded peers (Bourdieu, 1993; Westwater 2022, 2024), and so too are they free to invite, for example, participatory debate and present contentious issues. This is important when comparing the production of traditional war journalism and that of theatre reportage, but also when comparing mainstream theatre with the non-funded Hidden Theatre.

On the other side of the financed coin, The Ambassadors Theatre Group (ATG) is a hugely successful production and worldwide touring company, that has nine of the largest theatres in the UK. On analysis of the fifty productions featured on their webpages (accessed September 2023) ATG rest on producing crowd-pleasing and well-known film adaptations either retaining these as musicals or adapting them as such (e.g., *Pretty Woman*, 1990). With a closer look at their archive, 6/50 of these were musicals, 9/50 were film adaptations, 2/50 were book adaptations, and 7/50 were dedicated to stories of family, love, or memory. Out of 13 classics such as Shakespeare or Anton Chekov only 6/13 have connections to war and the communication of crisis (three of which are Shakespeare). Just 1/50 of their productions, *The Oresteia*, a modern adaptation of the Greek Tragedy is explicit in its themes of war and forced migration, however the other war focussed productions are set historically as either Shakespearean (c. 1592) or during the World Wars (1918–1945). When only one in fifty productions by one of the largest grossing theatre companies in the UK addresses current issues, such as war and forced migration, we see how mainstream theatre is failing to engage with real-world, humanly consequential concerns.

Possibly some theatres may fear for their survival in a censorious political culture and funding environment were they to push beyond the safe cultural middle ground. But is this not the role of theatre, to present and explore what is difficult? Perhaps it is safer for theatres to set difficult themes within the historical past, distancing them from the politically contentious present, and dressing them up as far-away fiction and/or as innocuous entertainment.

Taking the risk to discuss contentious issues, the theatre reportage of Hidden Theatre is an explicit mix of theatre praxis, non-theatre (de-theatricalised theatre) and journalism. It shares something with Peace Journalism (Lynch and McGoldrick, 2005) and the latter's efforts to include and report the voices and experiences of all those caught up in war, not simply those of political and military elites, and to explore the consequences of war and possibilities for peace. Theatre reportage however uses theatre as a real-life interactive and mostly non-digitalised means of communicating stories from oppressive and/or totalitarian regimes. Unlike recorded and digitalised news and arts, live performance can circumvent attempts at censorship and manipulation whether through subsequent editing, dubbing and deep fakes. But it is not only censorship issues that need consideration. The well-being of the people involved has to remain paramount, especially when working in oppressive contexts and under repressive regimes. Safety is a particular concern for Hidden Theatre. They deliberately choose universities, shopping malls, and interventions in public places. These are easily and quickly dismantled if repressive actions by authorities are anticipated. They prefer to small-scale live performances. Like

Belarus Free Theatre who mask their dissident events as weddings and funerals, Hidden Theatre perform 'fun' catwalks in shopping malls with an Aesopian meaning, and storytelling sessions in occupied territories.

The work is co-produced with those often living in the most difficult of circumstances: the citizens, actors, and journalists living in areas of conflict. Together they develop verbatim news and storytelling through a mix of songs, de-theatricalised performances, and dance. This mix, like the post-war theatre of the absurd, seeks to overturn the possible desensitisation that other media and/or biased reporting can create. Theatre reportage sets out to use, amongst others, delineation of space, Brechtian alienation techniques, juxtaposition of light and dark lighting, as well as humanism in play, where the theatre emanates from the actor/non-actors' physical body (Potsema, 2021) and not simply the actor's 'role' or presence on a stage. This is medium as message (McLuhan, 1964), but here the medium is the body of a real person who lives under oppression, who writes under oppression and fights for emancipation. It is this body that the audience meets. Theatre reportage does not seek to just portray events but rather embody the consequences and effects, the emotions and affect, of oppressive power and often violent injustices. In such ways it underlines that there is no safe space to represent global horrors and when shared, it will be discomforting. Audience participation is crucial to the aims of Hidden Theatre that seeks to challenge passivity in the face of oppression and injustice and encourage self-responsibility and active citizenship.

I met the creative director and founder of Hidden Theatre and theatre reportage in 2008 at the Edinburgh Fringe Festival. I was working on an exhibition about aggressive censorship found in Iran and Belarus and she performed her monologue *Hear Their Voices* at our event. It felt visceral, different to any theatre I'd been trained in and, as an audience member I felt as if I was physically near the individuals and wanted to know more. I learnt from her that:

> One must not hide in the safety of un-reality but immerse oneself in the meta-narratives: real clothing, not costumes; real stories, not creative writing; real lighting states, no spotlight; no set and no stage, but always authentic music being played authentically and accompanied by laughter, loud and brave. (Creative Director, 2017)

The method, from training to performance

Through decades of ethnographic immersion, the company has developed an acute understanding of life in Iraq, Iraqi-Kurdistan and now Palestine. They personally train young actors, journalists, and activists which begins with an integrated approach to educating others in what daily life under oppression is like. The work is all about creating a greater understanding of much-misunderstood regions. This is done through different strands of the project: workshops on developing agency in those who participate, including the audiences; theatre reportage training of journalists and actors to return to a present state of authenticity; and online live news forums (when possible). The following considers the approach used by Hidden Theatre based on field notes and observations of the work by myself, as journalist, participant and observer, between October 2015, and February 2023.

Rehearsals and training

I was invited to join a theatre company in the mountains of Tuscany to work with refugees, arts activists, and journalists in October 2015. My role was as a journalist, and I was the only native English speaker on the project. We were to rehearse *Dreams from Beyond;* a meditation on the wishes of dead refugees, washed up on the shores of Italy. The different strands of the work are difficult, traumatic even; bearing witness to stories of repeated beatings, murder, death, rape, kidnap, and torture and then representing this can take its toll. This is why no one who works with Hidden Theatre does so, without training. For it is necessary.

> I am not a photojournalist, but this is what I have been tasked to do. I was instructed to photograph the actors' process and I had no idea what to expect. All I was told (as part of my own training in theatre reportage) was that I was still a journalist, and it was my job to document what I see. As also a trained actor, I attempted to step into some sort of role. As did the other actors around me, tasked with their own objectives. We were wrong to do so. (Author, Field Notes from Volterra October 2015)

Before the training begins, the director discusses the ideas of 'safety', and responsibility. She informs all involved that 'as adults, you are responsible for your participation and your own sense of safety. You have agency to leave at any time, just as you have agency to stay and learn' (Actors workshops, Volterra 2015). Through simple activities the group discover how to navigate alternative (or should I say, forgotten) methods of communication. On many occasions the group have not one singular common language among them, but they develop a sense of joint purpose, through an increased awareness of each other's experiences. When individuals cannot represent themselves in person, due to visa restrictions or indeed threat to life, they charge another actor / journalist with their story.

The training is complex and involves a process of improvisation, physical and vocal 'awakening', guided reconnection to those around us; through active silence, rapid disorientation techniques to recalibrate the senses and relocation into new dramatic spheres. The director asks the actor to reposition themselves into the shoes of the victim of war. Some in the room will not have too far to go, others will.

The space has been prepared to house many beds and mattresses for the international group (from Syria, Iran, Iraq, and Kurdistan) who will join us the next day. But the director wants to prepare the European actors before then. The previous night we were instructed to make the room look like a frontline military camp, in some unnamed area of conflict. We hung posters on the wall and pinned sail-like material to drape across the ceiling. A theatricalised version of the Middle East is created through our building of a primitive set. Breaking the rules of theatre, the director woke in the night and stripped the space of this artifice and laid it bare, broken, ripped, and destroyed. Before the day has begun, and completely against the expectations of the visiting actors they are led into the room, blindfolded, one at a time. The actors did not know what had been done to the room. It is here the training begins. This is her method, to dis-orientate and remove the theatre from theatre. She is, in this moment creating empathy, through the experience of destruction (Coetzee, 2018). The actors sit in silence, blindfolded against a wall or for some, exposed in the centre of the room. The director begins to move items around, banging on doors and creating horrible sounds of scraping metal and broken wood. They do not know what to expect. She begins to shout at them, pulling them around and shoving them against the walls.

When they finally remove their blindfolds, they are devastated that their work is destroyed, disorientated, and frightened.

> When we do this kind of improvisation- you have the story inside you, you hear it, and must let it out. Live it slowly, feel it. Real, only real... not heightened. Props and costumes will take us away from what we have to tell. (Hidden Theatre, 2015)

By removing the artifice of theatre, she illustrates that traditional theatre is a perfect metaphor for the modern world. It is too safe behind the fourth wall. In many ways, the mainstream media is similar in its construction of stifled versions of the Middle East, through multiple screens and the theatrics of edited footage, propaganda, and misunderstood Aesopian language. We all too often see images of burnt babies, drowned pregnant mothers, publicised beheadings and scores of desperate families clinging to each other along shit-strewn roads and rabid waters. But, if these images lack the other side of humanity; the side we, who do not live in war recognise, such as normal everyday family life, loves and hopes for the future, then there is a risk of empathy burnout. The images no longer register. Hidden Theatre insists that we must at all costs, register. They do this through balancing all aspects of life within theatre reportage. It is gentle and brutal in its execution. The audience is positioned to re-connect; and when they do so, they are witnessing humanity in resistance and with some hope.

Conclusion: No hope, with hope, and here we are

Hidden Theatre has successfully communicated some of the major crises and conflicts in today's world, but to small audiences only. Their method, I suggest, holds deep insights, and could be expanded to encompass not only the human consequences and visceral experiences of conflict and war but also the increasingly interrelated crises of today's world-in-crisis, whether ecological devastation, climate change, food and water insecurity, pandemics or forced migration. Theatre reportage can powerfully communicate these and other signs of destabilisation, breakdown and collapse through giving voice to those positioned at the sharp end of crises and embodying their experiences that can register experientially and empathetically with others. It can do so through building empathy, by overtly placing the audience into the space, place, and time of the crisis, and through its ethnographic reportage and direct engagement with the audience. Its strength lies in is resistance to the mainstream, instead sliding underneath and circumventing traditional forms of mediation. Key to its method is the invitation and challenge to participate in positive change. And at their core, performances remove the actor/audience divide and invite the audience to participate and commune with the experience: to embody the feeling of crisis, to ask questions and join the players in dance; to participate in the action.

No Hope, With Hope was staged in one of the debating chambers of the EU Parliament in 2023. Two groups of young people from living the consequences of war, trained by Hidden Theatre presented their lived experiences based on terrible episodes of violence and fear, as well as joy, dance, and music. They represented to assembled MEPs, a holistic life, where oppression is part of it, but not all of it. Given the Israeli onslaught on Gaza in late 2023 and throughout 2024, the next performance may well be different. At one point, each of the Middle Eastern young actors stood in front of different member of parliament in a one-to-one interaction and told just one episode from their life. The words may not have always been understood, but the message was clear; they were suffering from a deep unsolicited trauma.

Next, a Ukrainian actor and journalist stood on the benches crossing the room (breaking the fourth wall). He represented a day in his life where he could not walk on the grass in fear of explosives. He describes holding the hand of a new girlfriend, as they walked in the park, but must not walk on the grass. He changes pace and adopts the position of an instructor, teaching the audience how to use a tourniquet. He writes on his face with a Sharpie pen, the time. These numbers will tell medics how long he has till he loses his arm. He explains to the audience that 'we all need to know what to do in Ukraine' (as performed at the EU Parliament, 2023). The MEP spect-actors (Boal, 1973) were startled into listening and observing, receiving the information in an experiential and embodied way. They are surprised to be part of the action, by dramatically being placed within the same time and space as the representations, by the very people representing themselves.

This dynamic approach by Hidden Theatre has been recognised for their first-hand testimonies and powerful mode of communication and are again invited to Brussels in November, 2024. It is not a theatre experience passively observed by a numb but expectant audience. It is journalistic theatre, unexpected in its rawness, and uninhibited by media ownership and heteronomous affiliations. It is an autonomous theatre of reportage, representing the hidden crisis and hidden wars. Their new performance is called *Here We Are*. It is unlikely, however, that the young Palestinian actors will be granted visas to tell of the horrors they, as civilians, are currently experiencing at the time of writing. Their experience will remain hidden, unheard, and out of sight.

Hidden Theatre bring these hidden, embodied stories to small influential groups in ways that register, experientially and empathetically to many who are compelled not only to better understand but also to care and sometimes to act. However, they struggle to accept or indeed pursue wider attention due to a very real risk to themselves and their actors. With no little fear, their distinctive theatrical method and mode of reportage still shines a unique spotlight on hidden wars and conflicts too often overlooked by mainstream and commercial media. Its independence from commercial interests and powerful theatrical and communicative pedagogy is only likely to become more urgent and needed in a world of unravelling crises in the years and decades ahead.

References

Banham, M. (1998) *The Cambridge guide to theatre*. Cambridge: Cambridge University Press.

Barba, E. and Barba, J. (trans.) (1999) *Theatre-solitude, craft, revolt/European contemporary classics*. Aberystwyth: Black Mountain Press.

Boal, A. (1973/2000) *Theatre of the oppressed*. New edn., trans. McBride, C.A., McBride, M.-O.L. and Fryer, E. London: Pluto Press.

Bishop, C. (2012) *Artificial hells: Participatory art and the politics of spectatorship*. London: Verso.

Bourdieu, P. (1993) 'The field of cultural production, or: The economic world reversed', *Poetics*, 12(4–5), pp. 311–356.

Brecht, B. (1964) *Brecht on theatre: The development of an aesthetic*. New York: Macmillan Press.

Coetzee, M (2018) 'Embodied knowledge(s), embodied pedagogies and performance', *South African Theatre Journal*, 31(1), pp. 1–4.

Cottle, S. (2023) 'Reporting civilizational collapse: Research notes from world-in-crisis', *Global Media and Communications*, 19(2), pp. 269–288.

Cottle, S. (2015) 'The United Nations' responsibility to protect and the world's press: Establishing a new humanitarian norm?' in Hoffmann, J. and Hawkins, V. (eds.) *Communication and peace: Mapping an emerging field*. London: Routledge, pp. 76–91.

Cottle, S. (2013) 'Journalists witnessing disasters: From the calculus of death to the injunction to care', *Journalism Studies*, 14(2), pp. 232–248.

Cottle, S. (2009a) 'Global crisis in the news: Staging new wars, disasters and climate change', *International Journal of Communication*, 3, pp. 494–516.

Cottle, S. (2009b) *Global crisis reporting: Journalism in the global age*. Maidenhead: Open University Press.

Cottle, S. (2006) *Mediatized conflict: Developments in media and conflict studies*. Maidenhead: Open University Press.

Foucault,M. (1977) Discipline and Punish: The Birth of the Prison: Penguin Books

Foucault,M. &Miskowiec, J (1986) Of Other Spaces : Dialectics 16, no 1, pp 22-27

Gerbner, G. (1972) 'Violence in television drama: Trends and symbolic functions' in Comstock, G.A. and Rubinstein, E. (eds.) *Television and social behavior. Vol. 1: Content and control*. Washington, DC: US Government Printing Office, pp. 128–187.

Grotowski, J. (1975/1991) *Towards a poor theatre*. Reprint edn. Edited by Barba, E. London: Methuen Drama.

Hawkins, V. (2008) *Stealth conflicts*. Houndmills: Palgrave.

Herman, E.S. and Chomsky, N. (1988) *Manufacturing consent*. New York: Pantheon Books.

Kaldor, M. (2006) *New and old wars: Organised violence in a global era*. Cambridge: Polity Press.

Lynch, J. and McGoldrick, A. (2005) *Peace journalism*. Stroud: Hawthorn Press.

McLuhan, M. (1964) *Understanding media: The extensions of man*. New York: McGraw-Hill.

Mody, B. (2010) *The geopolitics of representation in foreign news*. Plymouth: Lexington Books.

Payson, A. (2018) *Feeling together: Emotion, heritage, conviviality and politics in a changing city*. PhD Thesis, Cardiff University.

Pantti, M, Wahl-Jorgensen, K. and Cottle, S. (2012) *Disasters and the media*. New York: Peter Lang.

Potsema, S. (2021) *Theatre reportage: Reporting on people's emotional response to current affairs with the body as medium*. University of Amsterdam.

Shaw, M. (2005) *The new Western way of war*. Cambridge: Polity Press.

Sonwalker, P. (2004) 'Out of sight, out of mind? The non-reporting of small wars and insurgencies' in Allan, S. and Zelizer, B. (eds.) *Reporting war: Journalism in wartime*. London: Routledge, pp. 206–223.

Thorsen, E. and Allan, S. (eds.) (2014) *Citizen journalism: Global perspectives*. New York: Peter Lang.

Tuchman, G. (1978) 'The symbolic annihilation of women by the media' in Tuchman, G., Daniels, A., and Benit, J. (eds.) *Images of women in the mass media*. Oxford: Oxford University Press.

Westwater, C. (2022) *20 years of theatre reportage for peace* in the *Peace Journalist*, a semi-annual publication of the Center for Global Peace Journalism at Park University in Parkville, Missouri.

Westwater, C. (2024) The Othering Museum; A Case for Non-Selective Curation. Switzerland; Palgrave Macmillan.

· 13 ·

VISIONARY ECOART: STORIES FOR REGENERATIVE ECOLOGIES

Ruth Wallen

I stood in shock, in the blackness of what was once a verdant sequoia grove. Looking upwards there were no signs of greenery, the fire having scorched the crowns of even the tallest trees. Looking downslope, it was possible to see through the charred trees to the valley far below. Could the settlers who arrived a hundred and fifty years ago, lured not only by gold but by valleys that were said to be golden, have imagined that the future would bring such conflagrations? Could they have imagined that following the fires the swampy land they worked so hard to turn into the richest farmland in the country would be inundated by a flood submerging fields, recreating a huge lake that while attracting migrating birds, threatened them with an outbreak of avian botulism? Headlines abound with similar laments about unbreathable air, unbearable heat, treacherous winds and tragic inundations. Now is not the time to turn away in numbness, apathy and helplessness, but to peer into the darkness, and listen.

The ecological crisis is in part a 'storytelling crisis', or more broadly a crisis of culture and imagination (Ghosh, 2016; Solnit and Lutunatabua, 2023). In the introduction to the volume that Rebecca Solnit co-edited about the climate story, she reminds the reader that the root of emergency is emerge, 'to exit, to leave behind, separate yourself from, so an emergency is when you exit from the familiar and stable' (2023, p. 4). Stories that engender the capacity to stay present, to stay with the trouble (Haraway, 2016) to move through panic and past clinging to the familiar and habitual and to envision new possibilities are sorely needed at this time.

Ecological art, or ecoart, as the practice is often called, can play a vital role in communicating strategies for developing resilience and envisioning change. Ecological art is grounded in systems theory that addresses the myriad of interrelationships between the physical, biological, cultural, political and historical aspects of ecosystems and an ethic that values the well-being of this entire life web. Ecological art draws upon transdisciplinary practices, integrating sensual, emotional and intellectual knowledge.

> Asking probing questions, fashioning potent metaphors, identifying patterns, weaving stories, offering restoration and remediation, inventively using renewable materials and re-envisioning systems [. . .] Ecological art inspires caring and respect for the world in which we live, stimulates dialogue, sparks imagination, and contributes to the socio-cultural transformations whereby the diversity of life forms found on earth may flourish. (Wallen, 2012, p. 235)

In the paper referenced above, written a decade ago, I outlined how ecoart illuminates key ecological principles and can inspire cultural change. I will build on that discussion here, while striking a more sober tone in the face of yet another decade of unresponsiveness to spiralling ecological deterioration accompanied by the recognition that not only politics and economics, but cultural production is embedded in systems that perpetuate business as usual. Amitov Ghosh characterises this 'Great Derangement', as a time 'when most forms of art and literature were drawn into the modes of concealment that prevented people from recognizing the realities of their plight' (2016, p. 11), where writers have largely failed to imagine the implications of the climate crisis due to an inward focus on the individual moral journey, rather than outward on collective political action.

While ecological artists are not free from the influence of a gallery and museum culture that promotes individual stardom, ecological art, rooted in symbiotic thinking, is well-situated to provide fresh perspectives. Helen and Newton Harrison, masters of promulgating potent metaphors that encapsulate ecological processes, reframe a legal phrase in ecological terms, characterising our current epoch as the time of the 'Force Majeure'. They compare the Force Majeure, which literally means a superior force, to 'an oncoming storm front', a 'frontier' of rising heat, rising seas and escalating extinctions from which humanity must 'retreat' and 'within which' we must adapt (Center for the Study of the Force Majeure, n.d.: Overview). They emphatically conclude that the survival of life-giving systems requires that all economic systems based on exploitation be eliminated or transformed into systems of exchange. In legal terms the overpowering Force Majeure frees one from contractual obligations. Elon Musk to the contrary, we are tied to this planet. But we are not tied to exploitative systems. The Force Majeure, the frontier coming towards humanity, overrides exploitative options and extractive technologies, challenging the underpinnings of legal systems and the myth of progress embedded in modernity.

The Harrisons assert that civilisation has created high entropy systems that instead of recycling energy, transform it from one form to another, resulting in a net loss. Clear-cut forests or eroded soils create simplified systems. Joanna Macy and Chris Johnson offer a vivid description of this energy loss – the 'Great Unraveling'. This unravelling is the second of what they term 'three stories of our time'. The first is 'Business as Usual', based on an extractive, continually growing economy, increased consumption and mounting inequity. The third story, the 'Great Turning', invokes turning towards ways of doing and being that contribute to the flourishing of all life (Macy and Johnstone, 2022, pp. 7–9). The examples of ecoart discussed here all contribute to this great turning – regenerating systems while galvanising creativity. Just as importantly, ecoart can help engender the capacity to stay present to the uncertainty, fear, grief and strife that accompany ecological and societal unravelling. To introduce another lens, that of deep adaptation, ecoart can cultivate 'resilience' to face trauma, 'relinquishment' of actions and behaviours that are perpetuating the crises, 'reconciliation', acting with care while reconciling to an uncertain future and of course 'restoration' of decimated ecologies and traditional cultural practices (Bendell and Read, 2021).

Following the lead of Satish Kumar, this discussion is organised around three dimensions of ecological relationships. Kumar (2016), borrowing from the *Bhagavad Gita*, delineates relationships between the human and 'natural world', the human and 'divine soul', and the human and 'society', which he simplifies into three terms in English – 'soil', 'soul', and 'society' (see also van Boeckel, 2021). I will consider how specific ecoartworks address each relationship in turn, although many of the works address all three. Furthermore, the presentation will build from cultivating awareness of alternative possibilities, to developing emotional capacity, to promoting collaborative action (Scharmer, 2020). The examples considered here, some of which expand the continually developing terrain of ecoart, represent a small portion of the works I am thinking with to contribute to the great turning.

Soil and water

It is no coincidence that the Harrison's first ecoartwork was called *Making Earth*. In 1970, after the first Earth Day, Newton, not yet collaborating with Helen, combined sand, clay, sewage sludge, manure, leaves and worms. He watered it and turned it. Within four months the foul smell of sewage was replaced by the pleasing smell of living earth, which Newton felt compelled to taste.

This work was soon followed by *Soils Pile Reclamation* where the Harrisons responded to an invitation to create a sculpture at Art Park in New York with a proposal restore the entire park, which was basically a spoils pile left after rock quarrying. They brought organic wastes and earth and over a period of three years restored half the park to a meadow, realising one of the first of many significant soil reclamation projects undertaken by ecoartists.

While Sebastião Salgado is best known for his stunning black and white documentary photographs, after the human suffering he witnessed became unbearable Salgado returned to his family farm in the Atlantic Forest in Brazil, second to the Amazon rainforest in biodiversity, only to find denuded lands and dead soils. In 1998 he founded Instituto Terra together with his wife Léila Deluiz Wanick Salgado. They began to plant trees, hundreds of thousands of trees, learning how to ensure their survival as they restored their 1750-acre farm into a lush jungle. With the return of the forest, biodiversity increased dramatically, as did rainfall. They learned that trees planted at the headwaters of springs slow precipitation and create healthy soils that absorb water by replacing impermeable surfaces that hasten downstream flow. The institute helped restore the Rio Doce Valley watershed, creating an ecology school to share knowledge with the surrounding areas and encouraging neighbours to plant trees and put cattle fences around springs.

The remarkable transformation of over 35,000 square kilometres of the once dusty, denuded Loess Plateau in China, illustrates the potential for large-scale regeneration of agricultural lands. In 1995 John D. Liu began documenting Chinese efforts to plant trees, terrace hillsides and build catchment dams, while temporarily penning livestock. Liu was so impressed by what he saw that he decided to dedicate his life to ecological restoration. His best-known award-winning films, *Green Gold* and *Hope in a Changing Climate*, celebrate

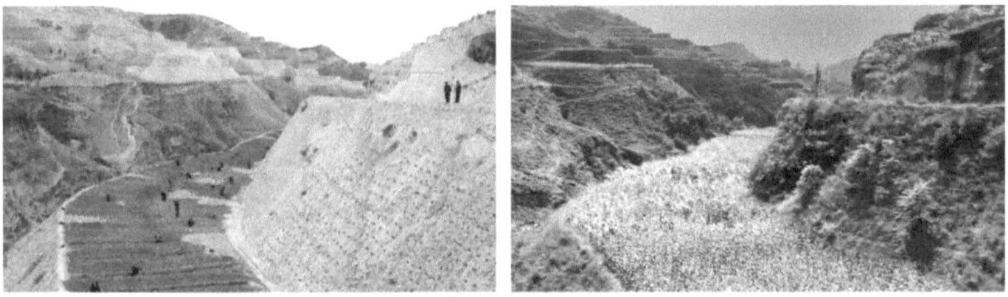

Figure 13.1. John Liu, 'Before Ho Jia Gou, September 1995' and 'After Ho Jia Gou September 2009' Frame Grabs from *Hope in a Changing Climate*, © John D. Liu 2009

regreening of degraded lands in China, Ethiopia, Jordan and Rwanda, where Liu, now an expert in his own right, one who recognizes that local buy-in is essential for efforts to succeed, inspired the government to restore hillside terraces so wetlands could recover.

In 2016 Lui founded the Ecosystem Restoration Camps movement, which now operates in six continents to promulgate ecological restoration worldwide. These restoration camps help develop alternatives to industrial agriculture and the accompanying erosion, soil degradation and emissions of toxic chemicals. Similarly, ecoartists have created innumerable projects promulgating composting and soil reclamation, as well as artisanal farms that spread awareness of the potential for permaculture, regenerative agriculture and syntrophic farming to create healthy, living soils (Spaid, 2019).

Imagining a different future for the Central Valley, in California, a major agricultural region supplying the entire United States, I wrote:

> Instead of using up arable soil in the next fifty years, commit to nurturing the soil for the next thousand years.
>
> Instead of continuing to extract carbon and burning it in the atmosphere, store carbon in the soil.
>
> Instead of poisoning the earth and waterways with pesticides and fertilizers and rupturing the soil fabric with periodic tilling, releasing more greenhouse gases into the atmosphere, enrich the soil with compost, mulch and a variety of ground cover plants that increase soil carbon sequestration.
>
> Instead of sterile monoculture, intercrop with trees and a variety of plants to allow each to contribute to the complex whole, adding minerals, fixing nitrogen, improving soil composition and providing habitats for the natural enemies of pests. (Wallen, 2023)

As demonstrated by many farms and research initiatives, these regenerative practices can heal the ravages of present-day industrial agriculture. Films such as *The Need to Grow, Dirt! The Movie, The Biggest Little Farm Movie, Regenerating Life* and *Common Ground* are powerful advocates for regenerative agricultural practices that increase soil health, enhance biodiversity and help cool the planet.

Along with rethinking agricultural practices, ecoartists challenge us to rethink the way that we eat. *Cooking Sections* was established in London in 2013 by artists Daniel Fernández Pascual and Alon Schwabe to examine sustainable food production. Their ongoing initiative begun in 2015, *Climavore*, which includes many individual projects, examines how to eat in a time of human-induced climate change. 'For the Rights of Soil Not to Be Exhausted', a project initiated in Kyiv and replicated in Kosovo, Brandenburg, Anatolia, and Helsinki, they worked with bakers and chefs to develop breads made from polyculture grains. These grains were grown following the principles of regenerative agriculture – diversifying monocultures, reducing tillage, and replenishing soils without using petrochemical fertilisers. In Kyiv they created an installation, hosted a series of lectures on the history of agricultural practices and collaborated with Ukrainian lawyers to draft a legal document that would grant rights to Ukrainian soil 'not to be exhausted'. Another project in Cleveland, USA, 'Season of Fertiliser Runoff', addressed the use of synthetic fertilisers, which cause algal blooms that suffocate aquatic organisms. This effort entailed a multi-year initiative, including the installation of a celebratory fountain to highlight the practices of local farmers engaging in regenerative practices and the elimination of chemical fertilisers.

The regeneration of living bodies of water, defined as oxygenated water that contains healthy microbes and minerals as opposed to chemically treated or purified water, is integrally related to regenerating living soils. In 1991, Betsy Damon, founded 'Keepers of the Waters' an organisation dedicated to restoring and preserving 'living water throughout the world'. The project for which she is best known, *The Living Water Garden* completed in Chengdu, China in 1998, demonstrates how natural systems clean water. The garden diverts polluted river water into a seven-stage biological cleaning process, including settling ponds, flow forms that aerate water, and wetlands. Creating parklands through biological water treatment and habitat restoration, it has inspired numerous projects in villages throughout the region as well as the vast natural water treatment system built for the Olympic Park in Beijing in 2008 (Damon, 2022).

A more recent project, *Living Waters in Larimer,* located in a neighbourhood in Pittsburgh, USA, focuses on another part of the water cycle, rainwater.

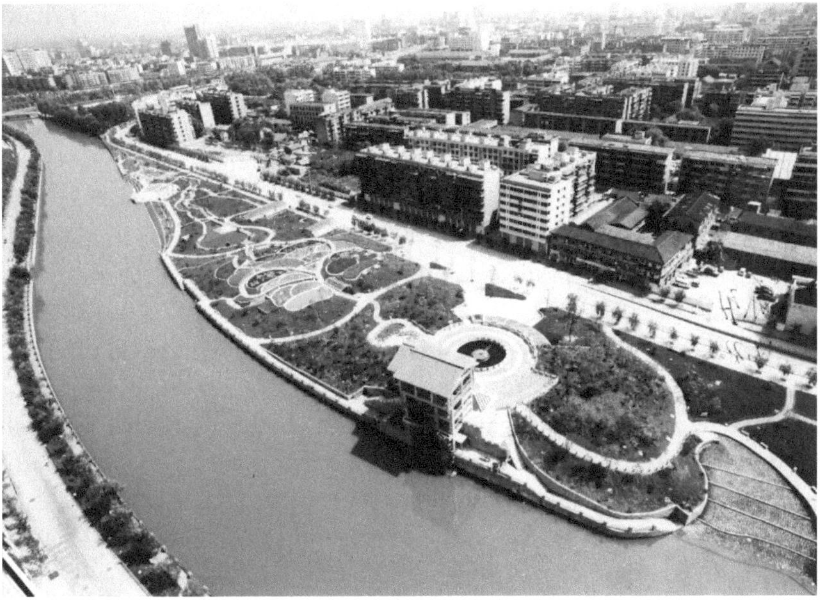

Figure 13.2. Betsy Damon, *Living Water Garden*, Aerial View, Chengdu, China, 1998. Courtesy of the Artist

Here Damon engaged with the community over several years to develop a system to collect and repurpose rainwater for gardens and parks, instead of flushing it into the sewage system via underground pipes. Ultimately only part of this proposal was realised due to traditional community development bureaucracies that are not accustomed to working with artists or prioritising community input. Nonetheless the project demonstrates that re-imagining how rainwater penetrates the earth in urban settings is an important part of the restoration of healthy ecosystems, an issue addressed in the work of many ecoartists.

Damon argues that infrastructure projects need to plan for the flow of water in ways that contribute to the vitality of the entire water cycle. This includes considering the design of sewage systems, which too often are conceived as large, energy-intensive projects that modestly clean water so that it can be safely diluted. Instead, Christina Bertea, an artist, greywater activist and plumber whose work is featured on the Keepers of the Waters blog, argues, 'Don't see waste as waste but [. . .] see it as a gift that we want to give back' (Bertea 2023). She has created many small projects that demonstrate this principle. *Embracing Our Place in the Nutrient Cycle*, consists of a heart-shaped toilet that collects urine, a valuable source of nitrogen and phosphorus. After dilution with water the urine can be used to fertilise flowers, which when cut can adorn the vase atop the toilet. A proposed humanure fertiliser bag of *Caca-Doodoo Loo-Manure*, with the slogan 'Closing the Nutrient Loop with our Poop', the contents of which will be created by thermophilic composting with yard and food waste, illustrates the idea of 'using our Poo to save our butts'. The project was inspired by the Marin Carbon Project, which demonstrated that spreading a half inch of compost on rangeland increases the growth of forage and sequestration of carbon in the soil.

Bertea's trip to teach greywater use in Tecate, a city located on US/Mexico border, led to an invitation to create signage explaining an innovative sewage treatment system that irrigates a local park employing healed wastewater, instead of water from the overcommitted Colorado River. The project, which uses no chemicals and minimal energy, converts methane gas to electricity, solid waste into compost and liquids into irrigation water. Small-scale projects, placed within communities, can create reusable water that nourishes living systems. The company that designed the plant, Grupo Requilibrium, is planning another project in Tecate that is ten times the size and has designed wetlands and sanitation plants throughout Mexico.

Restoring living water systems must take place at many scales. To return to the Harrisons, their recent work *Peninsula Europe* (2001–2012) integrates much of the discussion of this section. Starting by scanning maps, a strategy they frequently employed, the Harrisons noted that Europe west of the Russian plane essentially formed a peninsula, surrounded on three sides by water. Concerned about the encroaching climate crises, they asked boldly if it would be possible to regenerate all 1.3 million square kilometres of high grounds in peninsular Europe, defined as the places where rivers begin, and convinced the European Union and the German Federal Environmental Foundation to fund a speculative project, arguing that although their proposal appeared to be preposterously expansive, if their work could decrease the loss of water by 75 per cent it would pay for itself in three to four years.

Their most recent iteration, *Peninsula Europe IV*, which incorporates current information about impending droughts, proposes creating a multitude of small catchment basins to serve as water percolation systems, essentially 're-terraforming' a million square miles of parched farmland into 'water holding landscapes'. They envision planting crops needing more water at the centre and more drought-tolerant crops towards the periphery, with silviculture integrated as soils permit (Meyer Harrison and Harrison, 2016, p. 402).

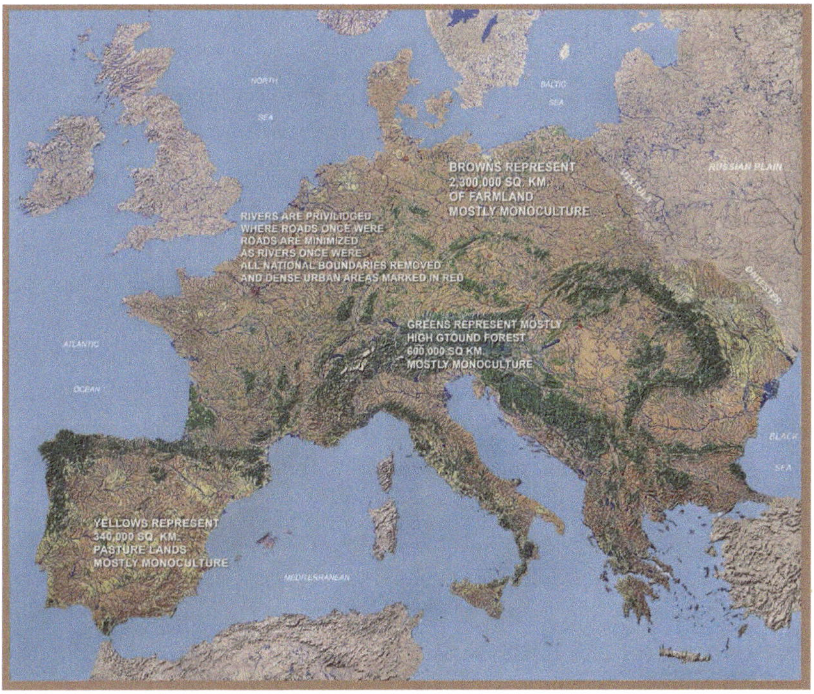

Figure 13.3. Helen and Newton Harrison, *Peninsula Europe* IV, 2012. Courtesy of the Helen and Newton Harrison Family Trust

Soul

Peninsula Europe was funded as a speculative proposal. What will it take to realise such proposals? If the cost of not acting is dying systems, how can humanity turn away? Ecoart can play a significant role in restoring cultural relationships with the earth and all living beings, renewing ecological consciousness and cultivating the ability to stay present in the face of increasing ecological degradation.

Betsy Damon's public presentations always begin with her water story, descriptions of how she developed relationships with water. She started with intense physical labour, making a handmade paper casting of two hundred and fifty feet of the dry riverbed of Castle Creek in Utah. When she went to China, she visited sacred sites. The opportunity to create the *Living Water Garden* arose from her work with local activists and artists who created performances enacting their relationship with polluted rivers, wearing long red gloves and washing silk, or freezing dirty river water into blocks of ice and trying to brush them clean.

Present-day practices that exploit the natural world are enabled by the legacies of imperialism and a positivist mechanistic science that objectifies nature, severing mind from heart. In contrast, practices of reciprocity that revitalise ecological networks enhance connectedness and community. Artwork that restores living soils and living waters engenders a sense of wonder or awe, which points to this inseparability of the individual from the larger world. As Peter Senge observes, 'Interconnectedness is a big clunky world, but we also call it beauty' (Senge in Goodchild, 2021, p. 87). Connecting with beauty, the fullness and richness of the world in which we live, opens hearts to our innate capacity to love. As such ecoart not only addresses healing the earth but healing the soul. From an indigenous perspective, 'deep healing occurs when body, mind and spirit are synchronized or 'mutualized', when one's inner Center, 'reflects the knowing Center of the Earth and other living beings' (Cajete cited in Goodchild, 2021, p. 98).

Annie Sprinkle and Beth Stephens create joyful relationships in their practice of marrying the earth, sky, sea, moon, snow, the Appalachian Mountains and much more. They performed their first wedding, to the earth, in 2008, in the redwood forests of Santa Cruz, California, have performed nineteen weddings in nine countries since, and continue to participate in weddings originated by others who have been inspired by their practice. Their weddings are exuberant public affairs, attended by hundreds of guests, many of whom collaborate by offering performances or designing lavish costumes and props. During their wedding to the earth, all those present were given a bag of soil to smell as they were invited to join Sprinkle and Stephens in offering vows to open their senses and become lovers to the earth.

Following their marriage to the earth, Sprinkle and Stephens began calling themselves ecosexuals to describe their embodied, passionate relationship with the planet. Taking the earth as lover implies mutuality, a more open-ended relationship than one to a mother. As they observe, we tend to take better care of our lovers, whereas mother earth has been pillaged, ravaged, battered and exploited. Their sex-positive, boisterous weddings, bordering on the absurd, speak to the delight of loving the earth, as opposed to the piety, loss and guilt associated with the environmental movement. Their weddings, in their embrace of raucous ecosexuality and of jubilant farcicality, extend sensual erotic connections beyond the human skin, queering conventional hegemonies, forming interspecies alliances, and

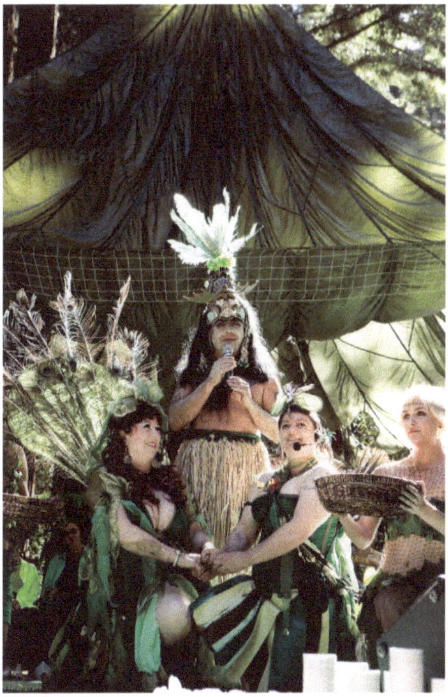

Figure 13.4. Annie Sprinkle and Beth Stevens, *Green Wedding for the Earth* with Guillermo Gomez Peña Officiating, 2008. Courtesy of Lydia Danilier

disrupting heterosexual norms, gender binaries and conceptions of an independent, autonomous self.

The first step of Joanna Macy's Work that Reconnects, 'coming from gratitude' (Macy and Johnstone, 2022) is joyfully embodied in Sprinkle and Stephens' ecosexual practice. Their marriage to Appalachian Mountains was created in tandem with their film *Good-by Gauley Mountain*, which explores the violent, ecologically destructive practice of mining coal by removing mountain tops in West Virginia, near Stephens' childhood home. While taking vows to 'speak up and raise hell', Sprinkle and Stephens create their untraditional wedding to give back to the community, share their love for the mountains and honour a recently deceased local protestor who was featured in their film. Their work exemplifies the teachings of Martin Prechtel (2015) that gratitude and praise are intertwined with recognition of the enormity of loss.

In the face of ecological devastation, Deena Metzger envisions a literature of restoration that contributes to a cultural shift by 'bearing witness and living accordingly' (2023). Similarly, over a decade ago I began walking with trees dying from the intertwined impacts of urbanisation, globalisation, in the form of introduced species and climate change in all its guises including bark beetles, drought and fire. Inspired by Macy and Zen Peacemakers, I committed to a four-step practice of making relationships with trees: offering gratitude, opening to uncertainty, bearing witness to whatever thoughts and feelings arise and directed by these experiences, taking action. As an offering of love and gratitude, I have assembled photographs from my walks into photomontages – incomplete views presenting a series of glimpses from differing perspectives to express the vibrancy of life even in a dying forest. The process of bearing witness involves both the second and third steps of the Work that Reconnects, 'honoring the pain' and 'seeing with fresh eyes'. On my first walk with the sequoias almost a year after the catastrophic fires, I was startled by smoke from a smouldering stump, but nearby the ground was covered with sequoia seedlings, the heat having triggered the seed cones to open. It was there amidst the shattered sequoias, in the Sierra Nevada mountains that tower above the Central Valley, overwhelmed with grief, that I heard the seedlings asking for the commitment to nurture them for the next millennia, a commitment that requires radically altering the agricultural practices in the valley below.

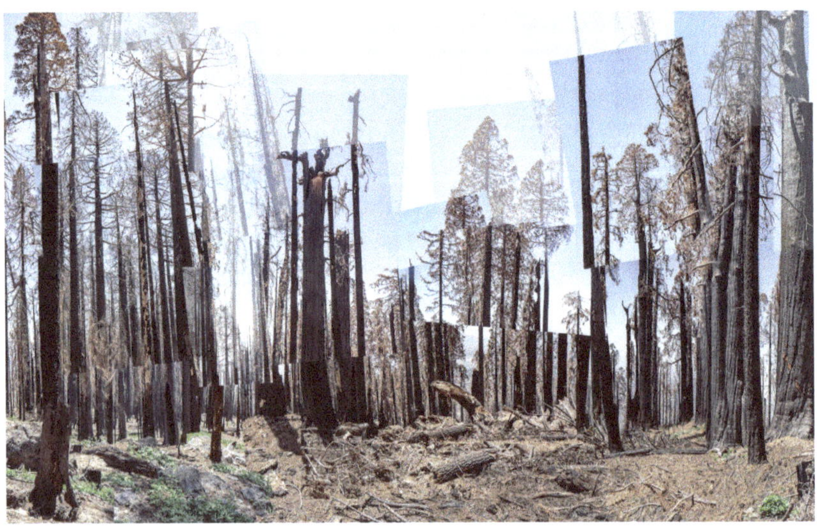

Figure 13.5. Ruth Wallen, *Walking with Sequoias: Sugar Bowl, Redwood Mountain Grove*, 2022. Courtesy of the Artist

Walking alone in the darkness, the need for public expressions of mourning was also painfully apparent. In my installations I always invite visitors to grieve with me, to write stories of loss in grief journals, or record their loss on rocks, and then to write visions for the future on green paper leaves that can be placed on barren tree limbs. We can learn from the example of AIDs activists that public rituals such as the Extinction Rebellion's die-ins are widely needed (Wallen, 2022). Mourning ecological losses, surrendering to vulnerability, uncertainty and the impossibility of returning to what was, is an essential step towards change, an honest response to the current crises. Báyò Akómoláfé observes, 'Grieving is not in the way, grieving together, falling apart together might very well be the most ecstatic, the most animated politics in response to these moments that we can master' (Akómoláfé, Klein and Celidwen, 2023). Kate McNeely and Crystal Clarity's text/image artwork, supported by Creative Wildfire, a cultural initiative of Movement Generation, proclaims 'GRIEF IS A ~~MONSTER~~ MESSENGER'. On another panel they write, 'It is through shared stories and rituals of mourning that we can find meaning and reinstate our commitment to each other and to a just transition' (McNeely and Charity, 2021).

Rebecca Belmore, a member of the Lac Seul First Nation (Anishinaabe) employs performance, sculpture and photography to create embodied expressions of grief and rage. *1181* consists of a log covered with gleaming silver discs arranged like armour. Near one edge the discs encircle bare wood that is shaped like a breast with a protruding nipple. To make the piece, Belmore pounded 1181 nails into the stump, each nail representing an indigenous woman who was murdered, her body missing. Dressed in a construction vest she worked methodically throughout the day, fully committed to the hammering of each nail, until upon driving in the last one, she began to shout 1181 over and over into the evening sky. The contrast of the tenderness of the naked breast and the graceful sweep of the swirling beadlike armour to the abrupt sharp cut at either end of the log where it had been severed from the rest of the tree, is striking. Compassion, agony and outrage – the work invokes a full range of emotional responses.

Belmore recently installed *Dawn*, a large public sculpture, at the National Art Center in Ottawa, Canada. A ten-metre-long fallen tree, bleached white, with tiny nubs of twigs extending like spikes from the trunk, rests against the side of the building. The tree is capped with a sculptured eagle head. From the back of the head hangs a plume of copper-coloured conical forms of the indigenous jingle dress. This monument, or as Belmore calls it, an anti-monument, 'to rethink how we mark our histories', quietly stands in the nation's capital, testifying to the pillaging of forests by the colonial settlers who having already destroyed the forests of Europe, ravaged those of the new world in search of timber to build their ships (Needham, 2022). An eagle, a traditional representation of the great spirit or power, looks down at it all. Copper jingles hang down from their head – a cascade of dripping blood, a mane of tears or the heat of fury transformed into a symbol of healing and the jingling joy of dance.

Dawn – a dawn of recognition of the legacies of trauma, of lack of apologies, of outrage, of possibility. As a non-indigenous viewer, I work to comprehend the full weight of the emotional work being summoned by this powerful testament to the horrors of colonialism on the land and its people. As Haraway

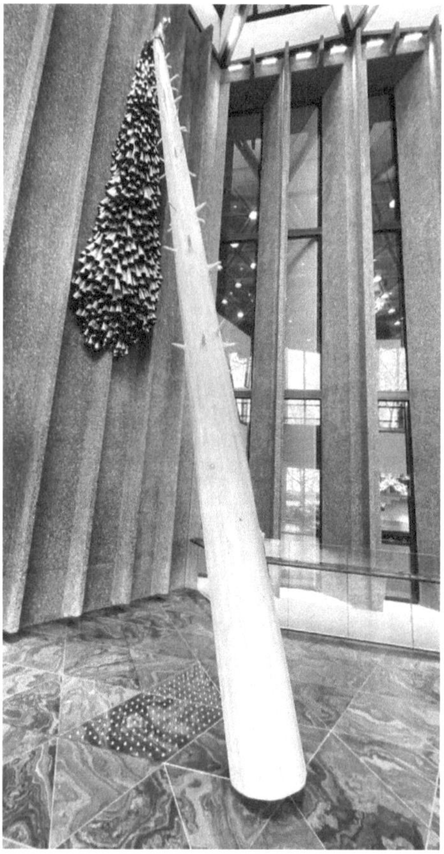

Figure 13.6. Rebecca Belmore, *Dawn*, National Art Center, Ottawa, Canada, 2022. Courtesy of Claude Schryer

reminds us, 'without sustained remembrance we cannot learn to live with ghosts so cannot think' (2016, p. 39).

Society

The irretrievable losses acknowledged in mourning are echoed by the title of Naomi Klein's brilliant book, *This Changes Everything* (2014). Klein calls for responses that dislodge entrenched, enmeshed social, political and economic systems, promulgating instead visions of social, political and ecological justice. The following three examples approach systemic entanglements from differing perspectives, but all point to possibilities for mobilising culture to engage communities in transformative change.

Lily Yeh builds community through the arts. After experiences in North Philadelphia, where for over eighteen years she constructed an art park with paintings and sculptures created by neighbourhood youth, she began travelling to 'broken' places around the world – from Korogocho, a large settlement beside a dump near Nairobi, to refugee camps in Palestine, to a school in rural Taiwan. She went to places of pain to create participatory processes with local communities that promote healthy environments, community well-being and economic development through the arts.

One of her most ambitious ongoing projects is the Rwanda Healing Project. When Yeh arrived at the mass gravesite and nearby Rugerero Survivor's Village in 2004, she came to listen, driven by what she'd heard from a Red Cross official. Destitute, the survivors were thrown together in a village; nearby the victims of genocide had been buried in a mass grave. Hearing from the survivors that they were haunted by the improper burial of their ancestors, Yeh set about to create the Rugerero Genocide Memorial. The following year she brought an affordable plan, but survivors said it wasn't adequate, insisting on a bone chamber to be constructed professionally so that their loved ones could be buried properly. Yeh didn't have the funds but asked a professional construction company to train local workers. Through working together, creating beauty by covering all the concrete with broken tiles, the community began to heal.

The memorial in place, she continued returning to the village to address the dire poverty and land degradation. The organisation she founded, Barefoot Artists, Inc. pairs expert volunteers with local communities in participatory projects requested by residents to foster economic, social and ecological well-being. The organisation initiated a micro-lending programme, helped revive the ancestral practice of weaving yucca baskets and taught sewing on machines as requested by the village. Brightly coloured murals enlivened homes. Residents received help to start vegetable gardens, build vented sanitation facilities and harvest rainwater. Instead of receiving imported gifts, they were taught how to construct photovoltaic modules from materials that could be acquired locally.

Yeh brings colour to places of darkness. Visitors to the memorial on the Day of mourning in 2009 commented: 'When we see beauty, we see hope. Now our loved ones can come home in honor and dignity. Art and beauty heal' (Yeh, 2013).

Aviva Rahmani's *Blued Trees Symphony* creates artistic relationships between artists, activists and trees. The project originated when she was invited by FrackBusters and a local landowner to create an artwork employing the strategies of Canadian sculptor Peter von Tiesenhausen, who stopped the acquisition of his land for construction of a pipeline by copyrighting the top six inches of his entire ranch as an artwork. Accompanied by volunteers, Rahmani painted musical notes along a one-third mile measure in Peekshill, New York and submitted the artwork, defined as the relationships between the human teams, the art and the trees and their habitat, for copyright registration. The notes on the trees were painted with a non-toxic blue slurry in the form of vertical sine waves indicating the movement of sound over time. Although Rahmani did obtain the copyright and filed a cease-and-desist letter, she was unable to raise the funds to pursue the issue of eminent domain in court, and the trees were felled. However, the concept was infectious. Blue trees continue to be painted in several other locations in the US, Canada and Europe. The case was litigated as a mock trial in New York in 2018, offering a lens into future legal strategies. Currently Rahmani is working with collaborators to produce an opera and previewed a half-hour segment in the summer of 2023.

The blued trees raise a host of questions with symphonic resonance. While copyright law, which implies rights of ownership, is central to the premise of *Blued Trees Symphony*, Rahmani is quick to point out that she creates 'with' trees, not 'on' them (2021, p. 2). So, who owns the copyright? Does the trees' participation give them standing? Have they given consent? Eminent domain law, enshrined in the fifth amendment of the US constitution, grants landowners compensation for property taken for 'public use'. Are trees part of that public? From an anthropocentric perspective, what 'uses' are valued – the use of land to place a pipeline that contributes to global warming or the use of land as

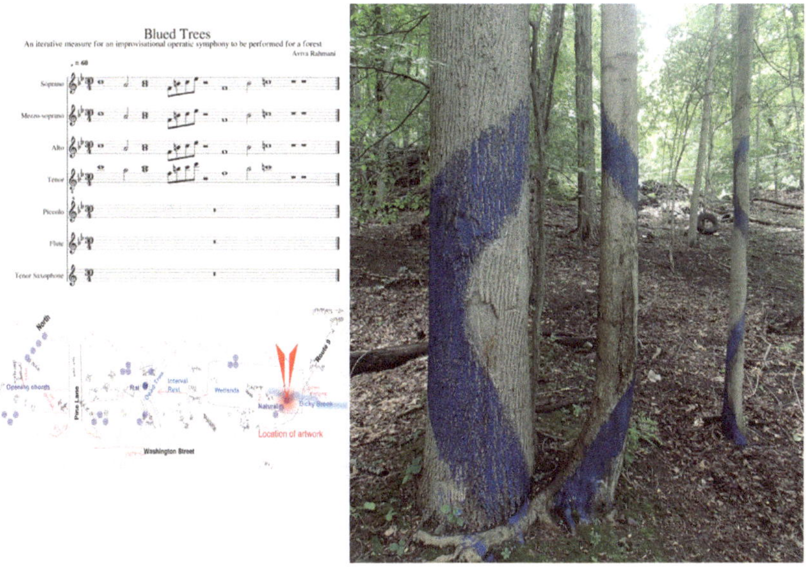

Figure 13.7. Aviva Rahmani, Materials Prepared for Copyright Registration, *Blued Trees Symphony, 2015*. Courtesy of the Artist

a home for trees who clean air, sequester carbon and make rain? Furthermore, which publics have access to litigation? Energy companies can afford expensive litigation over eminent domain that most landowners or artists can't. Amid these arguments, can anyone hear the music of the trees?

Imagine, as Rahmini does, the trial of the CEO of a large energy corporation charged with ecocide in the International Criminal Court in the Hague. Opera is a most suitable form to present the crucial dramas of our times on a grand scale. In opera, someone must die. Who or what is it that must perish? Rahmani's compelling artworks challenge existing priorities and power structures, posing complex sets of questions around societal values.

Operettic drama is one lens to grapple with these questions, political comedy another. The North Pole Show created by Movement Generation Justice and Ecology Project chooses the latter form to address displacement, loss, ecological degradation and multiple injustices. In the initial episodes three black or Latino friends and long-time residents of North Oakland, California, which is known locally as the North Pole, are joined by a fourth white roommate from Minnesota. Over the course of two seasons, each with seven short episodes, the show juxtaposes the displacement of polar bears with the displacement caused by gentrification and the threat of deportation. Benny's arrest after he joins in the protest of an eviction order is the first time that any of his roommates learn that he was born in El Salvador. As the layered plot lines move from wildfire smoke to environmental racism and chronic asthma, greenwashing versus right employment, diabetes to vegan diets and 'herbalism for the hood', while circling around race, privilege and so much more, the series explores what it means to be an activist with a vision for the future. In the last episode Benny, or Benito, who decides to run for sheriff to gain visibility and avoid deportation exclaims, 'the only secure community is an organized one [...] When you feel alone, you feel like you can't do anything [. . .] This is an invitation. Are you in?' (Healey, 2019).

Movement Generation Justice and Ecology Project's dense, informative website provides a wealth of information about how to 'inspire and engage in transformative action towards the liberation and restoration of land, labor, and culture'. The project powerfully articulates frameworks for change embedded in a commitment to organising a movement that cherishes the land, builds community and creates collective governance through the development of deep caring relationships. Recognising that the degradation of land and water and disruption of climate are inexorably linked to extractive economies, racism and inequity, their framework elaborates many key principles that cultivate a just transition – biological and cultural diversity, ecological and disability justice, resilience-based and translocal organising and more. Their cultural work, which includes podcasts, writing, multimedia projects and creative uses of social media, is developed in tandem with their collective organising strategies. Numerous collective regenerative farms also engage in cultural organising, recognising that culture is vital to building sustainable relationships with the earth and with each other.

In the coming years, further unravelling of ecological systems is inevitable. Currently many narratives around ecological degradation are embedded in business as usual, in the very systems that not only cause ecological and extinction crises but are superseded by them, in systems that unable to hold anxiety and fear, encourage denial, apathy and apocalyptic ruminations. These stories can be met with those of ecological artists – narratives of growing healthy food and working to regenerate living soils and water, narratives of possibility, which not only point to new ways of doing, but of being. By enhancing interactions with living systems, from food forests to wetlands, ecoart restores human relationships with the living earth.

Ecoartwork offering praise and gratitude for the vitality and beauty of living systems provides a tonic for the loss of the quick answers and instant gratification promised by consumer culture. The embrace of the living earth provides a place to hold the discomfort of an uncertain future and allow for 'falling apart'. Grief as a 'messenger', can be met with beautiful artworks, created not as a form of denial, but to honour that which has been lost, to affirm love for the life force energy that remains, for the jingling dance of the new dawn that holds both joy and sorrow.

Just as biological narratives are celebrating the underground mycelial networks through which plants communicate and shifting from an emphasis on competition to symbiosis as a driver of evolution (Haraway, 2016), ecoart works can help restore the connective tissues of collaborative social systems. Collaborative ecoart works can be an important part of a just transition towards regenerative economies where all beings may thrive.

However destructive, fires clear the ground for new stories. In places the sequoia seedlings that were just a few inches high two years ago are now up to my hips. In other places sequoias haven't grown back at all. Whatever the circumstances, ecological art can help restore relationships with the living earth by offering praise and thanks, public spaces to grieve what has been lost and opportunities to listen carefully to the wisdom of living systems so that we can learn how to best nurture these seedlings and all living beings for the next millennia.

References

Akómoláfé B., Klein, N. and Celidwen, Y. (2023) *Transcript: The edges in the middle.* https://forthewild.world/podcast-transcripts/the-edges-in-the-middle-bayo-naomi-and-yuria

Barefoot Artists (n.d.) *Barefoot artists.* https://barefootartists.org

Belmore, R. (2023) *Rebecca Belmore.* https://www.rebeccabelmore.com

Bendell, J. and Read, R. (2021) *Deep adaptation: Navigating the realities of climate chaos.* Cambridge: Polity.

Bertea, C. (2023) *The art of healing water: Making sewage treatment beautiful, both in process and presentation.* https://www.keepersofthewaters.org/blog/christina-bertea

Bertea, C. (2023) 'Christina Bertea', *WEAD: Women Eco Artists Dialogue.* https://directory.weadartists.org/artist/christina-bertea

Center for the Study of the Force Majeure. (n.d.) *Overview.* https://www.centerforforcemajeure.org/#introduction

Damon, B. (2022) *Water talks: Empowering communities to know, restore and preserve their waters.* New York: Steiner Books.

Damon, B. (n.d) *Betsy Damon.* https://www.betsydamon.com

Ecosystem Restoration Communities (n.d.) *Ecosystem restoration communities*. https://www.ecosystemrestorationcommunities.org

Funk, M. (2015) 'Sebastião Salgado has seen the forest, now he's seeing the trees', *Smithsonian Magazine*. https://www.smithsonianmag.com/arts-culture/sebastiao-salgado-forest-trees-180956620

Goodchild, M., with Senge, P., Scharmer, O., Longboat, R.D., Longboat, K.D., Hill, R. and Deer, K.K. (2021) 'Relational systems thinking: That's how change is going to come, from our earth mother', *Journal of Awareness Based Systems Change*, 1(1), pp. 75–103.

Ghosh, A. (2016) *The great derangement: Climate change and the unthinkable*. Chicago: University of Chicago Press.

Grupo Requilibrium (2021) *Grupo Requilibrium*. http://requilibrium.com

Haraway, D. (2016) *Staying with the trouble: Making kin in the Chthulucene*. Durham: Duke University Press.

Harrison, H.M. and Harrison, N. (2016) *The time of the force majeure: After 45 years a counterforce is on the horizon*. New York: Prestel.

Healey, J. (2019) *The north pole show*. http://www.thenorthpoleshow.com

Instituto Terrra (n.d). https://institutoterra.org

Keepers of the Waters (n.d.) *Keepers of the waters*. https://www.keepersofthewaters.org

Klein, N. (2014) *This changes everything: Capitalism vs. the climate*. New York: Simon and Schuster.

Kumar, S. (2016) 'The three dimensions of ecology' in Vaughan-Lee, L. (ed.) *Spiritual ecology: The cry of the earth*. Point Reyes, CA: Thomson-Shore, pp. 137–149.

Liu, J.D. (2009) *Hope in a changing climate*. https://www.youtube.com/watch?v=bLdNhZ6kAzo

Liu, J.D. (2012) *Green gold*. https://www.youtube.com/watch?v=YBLZmwlPa8A

Macy, J. and Johnstone, C. (2022) *Active hope: How to face the mess we're in with unexpected resilience and creative power*. Novato: New World Library.

McNeely, K. and Clarity, C. (2021) '2021–2022 creative wildfire artists', *Creative Wildfire*. https://creativewildfire.org/artists

Metzger, D. (2023) 'Not hope but possibility', *Literature of Restoration*. https://literatureofrestoration.org/not-hope-but-possibility

Movement Generation (2022) *Movement generation justice and ecology project*, https://movementgeneration.org

Needham, F. (2022) 'First Nations visual artist Rebecca Belmore's latest work sits in contrast to Ottawa's other monuments', *APTN National News*. https://www.aptnnews.ca/national-news/first-nations-visual-artist-rebecca-belmores-latest-work-sits-in-contrast-to-ottawas-other-monuments

Pascual, D.F. and Schwabe, A. (n.d.) *Climavore*. https://www.climavore.org

Pascual, D.F. and Schwabe, A. (n.d.) *Cooking sections*. https://www.cooking-sections.com

Prechtel, M. (2015) *The smell of rain on dust: Grief and praise*. Berkeley, CA: North Atlantic Books.

Rahmani, A. (2015) *The blued trees symphony overture*. https://vimeo.com/135290635

Rahmani, A. (2021) '*The Blued Trees Symphony* as transdisciplinary mediation for environmental policy', *Media+Environment*, 3(1). https://doi.org/10.1525/001c.25256

Rahmani, A. (n.d.) *Blued Trees, is an opera challenging ecocide.* https://www.avivarahmani.com/blued-trees

Scharmer, C.O. (2020) *Turning toward our blind spot: Seeing the shadow as a Source for Transformation.* https://medium.com/presencing-institute-blog/turning-toward-our-blind-spot-seeing-the-shadow-as-a-source-for-transformation-aff23d480a55

Solnit, R. and Lutunatabua, T.Y. (eds.) (2023) *Changing the climate story from despair to possibility.* Chicago: Haymarket Books.

Spaid, S. (2019) 'Artisanal soil' in Toland, A., Stratton Noller, J. and Wessolek, G. (eds.) *Field to Palatte: Dialogues on soil and art in the Anthropocene.* Boca Raton, FL: CRC Press.

Sprinkle, A. and Stephens, B. (2021) *Assuming the ecosexual position: Earth as lover.* Minneapolis, MN: University of Minnesota.

Sprinke, A. and Stephens, B. (2023) *Annie sprinkle and Beth Stephens: The collaboration.* https://sprinklestephens.ucsc.edu/

van Boeckel, J. (2021) *I would still plant my apple tree.* Groningen, The Netherlands: Minerva Art Academy.

Wallen, R. (2012) 'Ecological art: A call for visionary intervention in a time of crisis', *Leonardo,* 45(3), pp. 234–242.

Wallen, R. (2022) 'A call to embrace ecological grief' in Geffen, A., Rosenthal, A., Fremantle, C. and Rahmani, A. (eds.) *Ecoart in action: Activities, case studies and provocations for the classroom and communities.* New York: New Village Press.

Wallen, R. (2023) *Learning to think like a forest.* https://www.ruthwallen.net/imagesandstories/sequoia

Weintraub, L. (2012) *To life! Ecoart in pursuit of a sustainable planet.* Berkeley: University of California Press.

Yeh, L. (2013) *Ted Talk: The community building potential of the arts.* https://www.ted.com/talks/lily_yeh_the_community_building_potential_of_the_arts

All websites last accessed on 16 December 2023.

Section V:

Music and Museums: Immersive Experience

·14·

MUSIC IN AN ERA OF PLANETARY DISCONTINUITY: WHAT MUSIC CAN AND CAN'T DO IN THIS CRISIS

Simon Kerr

The world is experiencing rapidly increasing damage from climate and ecological disruptions of which scientists have long warned. The new reality has only just begun and even in the best scenarios, it will take decades for this 'long emergency' to stabilise (Wiseman 2021). Because disruptions happen 'in place', the impacts will not be evenly distributed; some places are better positioned to adapt, climatically, financially, politically and socially, than others. The future promises ongoing uncertainty, spiralling disruption and no sign of a safe landing place, possibly for generations. It is now all hands on deck to respond to this predicament. I am a musician and want to state as clearly as I can: Music cannot save us.

If a folk music concert ever has an 'environmental' theme, Joni Mitchell's quintessential environmental song *Big Yellow Taxi*, is inevitably rolled out. It has staying power, not just for its music but for the sentiment: 'They paved paradise and put up a parking lot' (Mitchell, 1970). People care about the 'environment'. It is far less clear whether the song has had any impact on reducing land clearance and urban sprawl in the subsequent 50 years. This of course places an unreasonable burden on what is one of Mitchell's great songs, but the question remains: what use is music in a time of crisis?

It depends on the crisis. I will argue music's strength is emotive and not conceptual. It is not well suited to communicating new and novel conceptual realities such as the profound and ungraspable nature of the planetary crisis, that is, the erasure of one world and the emergence of a new planetary era. Music's super power is different, possessing a unique capacity to emotionally replenish and support people in crisis.

Since Bill McKibben's plea 20 years ago for an outpouring of 'Art, Sweet Art' (2005) to help address the climate challenge, the outpouring has been more of a slow drip. While this is now changing, it is hard to mount an argument that musicians are leading the sorts of climate narratives and actions required in this predicament. After a number of years as a practitioner of climate-focused music, I find myself taking a more critical view of what music can do. This is partly due to the nature of music itself, but also due to the recognition that these are not normal times, that the world many of us of grew up in is no longer the world we now inhabit. When it comes to climate, as writer Naomi Klein puts it, everything changes (2015).

Looking to music as a means of communicating the mutation of the climate system is, for the most part, asking too much of music. But this is far from my complete argument, for I also suggest music does have a *particular* role in this crisis. It may not have epistemic power, but it does have a superpower; it can provide the emotional replenishment, courage and joy that we will need in the times ahead. In this chapter, I discuss the relationship between music and communication, some roles it can play and what we ought not expect of it. My focus is mainly on the impact of popular music in communication in a planetary crisis and my broad argument is that music's power is not in educating people about the climate predicament but in helping us cope with it.

A brief restatement of our predicament

How ought we understand this moment we face? It is difficult to provide a definitive account of what are in fact rapidly changing climatic, ecological and social systems, entangled in ways we are only beginning to widely acknowledge. The Intergovernmental Panel on Climate Change (IPCC) provides the most authoritative statement on the current state, impacts and future of the climate, though not without facing criticism that it is too conservative (Anderson, 2023; Brysse et al., 2023). Some trends are clear. We can no longer avoid serious climate disruption and the best we can do is to limit future damage. That requires a couple of things: first, ensuring the planet does not get too hot and, second, urgent and society-wide preparation for this future that is already present.

The global heat waves of 2023 have broken many records and are likely to produce a new annual planetary temperature record. There is a 66 per cent likelihood the planet will reach 1.5°C for at least one of the next five years (World Meteorological Organization, 2023). The rate of heating is speeding up. Australia, the lucky country, is 1.47°C hotter since national records began in 1910 (Bureau of Meteorology, 2023). It will get hotter still. If *all* Greenhouse Gas Emissions (GHG) were to cease today, then recent research suggests it is likely global temperature increase would rapidly slow (Hausfather, 2021). But emissions will not stop tomorrow. The catastrophic reality is they are still rising. Emissions must peak mid-decade and decline by about 10 per cent per year in order to stabilise global temperatures at under 2°C (IPCC, 2022, p. 21). While the renewable energy revolution is accelerating the shift from fossil fuel energy, industrial, land and agricultural emissions are more difficult and slow to abate. Far too slow now for a safe landing into the future.

On current projections, it is almost certain the planet will exceed 2°C (Liu and Raftery, 2021). A herculean global effort could change this. But 'could' is not the same as 'will'. Much more likely is that predatory delay, conflict and inertia will slow emissions reductions from happening as rapidly as is required. This will be catastrophic for some places and hugely challenging for most. If we had seriously started on this even twenty years ago, we could have gradually transitioned to a low-carbon world (Hausfather, 2023). But that can has been kicked down the road. There is no compelling reason to believe such delays will suddenly reverse any time soon, and not in any orderly or managed way.

Many people still live with the illusion that we can tweak our current lifestyles and return to normal. We cannot, because we now live in a discontinuity; the climate crisis is not *going* to cause a break with the past, it already has. This is perhaps the most difficult recognition about the world we now live in. The relatively predictable safe zone of climate humans lived with since the end of the last ice has ended abruptly. In the planetary crisis, the protection provided by a reliable planet is now no longer guaranteed for anyone.

What of the future? For some, it feels apocalyptic, with social collapse now inevitable. I do not find that view convincing, neither empirically nor emotionally. While there are many reasons to feel troubled, there are also many reasons to feel some glimmers that all is not (yet) lost. While we face record climate disruption, remarkable changes are also underway. Renewables, for example, are now set to overtake coal in energy production by 2025, at a rate much faster than was expected even a year ago (International Energy Agency, 2022). Despite the troubling climate and ecological trends, there has been sufficient progress to ensure we will likely avoid the worse of the IPCC scenarios of a world beyond 3°C (Pielke et al., 2022). Even if this is correct, such a world will be unlike anything humans have ever experienced before. Given the damage and costs we are already experiencing at just over 1°C, our species' capacity to adapt will depend a lot on where we live, a region or city's wealth, available technology, good governance, and a host of other factors (Steffen, 2021a). Some places may cope quite well, but many will struggle and some will collapse. It will be chaotic and messy, with outcomes unevenly distributed and spikey (Steffen, 2021b). An *orderly* transition to a more sustainable or safer future is now much more difficult, if not impossible. What roles can music play in helping us navigate such a future?

What music does

Music is a universal characteristic of all human societies (Mehr et al., 2019). There has been much written about its evolutionary origins and functions (Harvey, 2017). A brief survey of some of the important social functions of music will help highlight the roles it can play. I suggest there are at least five possibilities; telling stories, increasing solidarity, cultivating empathy, providing emotional release and, at times, providing inspiration and replenishment. This is not an exhaustive list but these dimensions are particularly relevant to the question of music and communicating a world-in-crisis.

Storytelling is an important part of many musical forms. An obvious example is traditional folk music that tells culturally specific stories, reflecting memory and identity. Many folk singers of the 1960s sang of social revolution, blues musicians about the lived experience of their communities, and rap musicians of resistance (Martinez, 1997). Other musical forms such as punk and hip-hop culture reflect their own particular stories, and reggae speaks to 'issues of injustice, resistance, love and humanity . . .' (UNESCO, 2018). Opera is a mode of storytelling, as is musical theatre. There is a rich heritage within all cultures where music holds the stories of the past and constitutes important cultural heritage, that is, stories of identity and memory. All these forms employ a narrative approach using semantic structure to storytelling – not necessarily a literal story, but they seek to bring the listener on a journey of ideas or meaning.

Being a holder of cultural identities, traditional heritage, or social ideas does not necessarily mean that music easily grapples with conceptually novel realities or pushes social boundaries. While there are examples, such as the work of John Cage in the early to mid-twentieth century where *intellectual* boundaries are pushed through musical composition and performance, most popular music expresses the *current* shared values of a community. Significant deviation from the social expectations of audiences is a good way to lose an audience (Kerr, 2018). I suggest that when music expresses shared values, it enables a second and potent function, social solidarity.

In *Music, Evolution and the Harmony of Souls* Alan Harvey elevates the significance of music in the evolution of human life by asking the question: 'Why are we the all-speaking, all-singing, all-dancing creatures of our planet?' (2017, p. 7). Whatever the aetiology, our species' musical ability has generated one of the key features of shared musical experience – solidarity with others:

> [E]arly in our history, our sense of self and knowledge of our impermanence was intensified and focused through the lens of spoken language. Music's communal, socialising power acted as an essential counterweight to the individualisation experienced by increasingly intelligent and articulate members of 'Homo sapientior'. Music was able to maintain . . . a harmony of souls during the emergence of a 'society of selves'. (Harvey, 2017, p. 205)

Solidarity – this harmony of souls – is familiar to anyone who attends a collective musical event where, even if momentarily, the audience is transformed from an assembly of individuals to a community gathered around a shared experience, whether in a house music party, folk festival, operatic performance or stadium rock concert. This is the superpower of music over perhaps all other art forms and becomes deeply significant as we face the planetary crisis. If we are to find liveable pathways into this future, we will not do it alone. The experience of community solidarity, of not being alone, was one of the common reflections our audiences made when experiencing our own climate project, *Music for a Warming World* (Kerr, 2015).

Solidarity does not always solidify around noble or virtuous beliefs. The Third Reich is evidence enough that music can support commitment to dangerous ideas. Nevertheless, solidarity is clearly enhanced by shared emotional experiences such as listening to a musical performance.

It is also enhanced by participation. Singing with others in a choir, at a rock concert, in a religious setting or around the campfire binds us together where 'momentarily we forget our isolation, our mortality, and we step beyond the confines of our own individuality' (Harvey, 2017, p. 206). Sharing music enables strangers to create satisfying bonds without having to invest the time normally required to connect personally. Music's role in early cognitive development and, more generally, in therapeutic application is increasingly well-recognised (Reynolds, 2023). Music has much to offer but is still a relatively unexplored opportunity to help provide communities with the resources needed to face the planetary crisis. This could help counter the individualisation of musical experience through digital media and the relentless logic of personalised algorithmic music curation (Webster, 2023) impacting on the maintenance of group solidarity (Andrejevic, 2020, p. 21).

Closely related to solidarity is the development of empathy. Sometimes considered as a theory of mind, empathy can refer to the capacity to adopt the perspective of another (Clarke, et al., 2015). Empathy is a cornerstone for the functioning of social cooperation. There is much research linking the development of empathy with music (Heshmat, 2023). This has significant implications for considering music's role in living in a future defined by uncertainty and change. Importantly, music's capacity to evoke empathy for others does not appear to require 'accessible semantic content', such as lyrics to guide the listener's feelings (Harvey, 2017, p. 76). There are many examples of music supporting empathic listening: The West-East Divan Orchestra which brings together Palestinian and Israeli musicians, UNICEF's engagement of classical musicians as goodwill ambassadors (Harvey, 2017, p. 62) and the NGO Musicians without Borders (Musicians without Borders). The planetary crisis is of course not just a crisis for humans but for many other species. Music can enhance empathy for the other-than-human. Eco-grief from the loss of heritage, nature and particular futures is on the increase and is now of concern to the medical and psychological community (Jarvis, 2023). Music offers an opportunity to increase the empathetic resources communities have available to counter this 'alienation' (Lamond, 2011, p. 99).

Music also does something else, perhaps even, as Harvey suggests, beyond that of all other arts. It can't solve the 'framing' issue of climate change, it cannot analytically investigate in the same way that scholarship, science and quiet reflection can because it does not address conceptual thinking. In the words of scholar and musician Ian Cross, 'it neither ploughs, sows, weaves or feeds' (Cited in Lomond, 2011, p. 99). But it does have an 'extraordinary capacity to stimulate our emotions' (Harvey, 2017, p. 6).

Music is a portal into the affective dimensions of our humanness, allowing us to experience the full gamut of our emotions. An anecdote may help illustrate this. Composer Mathew Dewey was commissioned to work with PhD students from the Institute of Marine and Antarctic Studies, University of Tasmania, to write a symphony reflecting their work and findings. Titled 'ex Oceano' (Lynchpin), it offered a musical interpretation of the impact of global warming on the powerful southern ocean. One of the project's sponsors told us that not all the oceanographers initially thought there was value in the project; how could music add to an understanding of this mighty ocean system? One of these scientists had spent a lifetime in painstaking research, documenting the devastating impacts of warming ocean currents. However, we were told that on hearing the symphony for the first time, the years of silent grief about the profound changes to which this scientist was witness were unlocked. The Oceanographer wept.

Beyond attending to our emotional connectedness, music can, at times, provide new ways of reflection, much in the way some visual art seeks to disrupt our mental categories and conceptual boundaries. Experimental music, whether electronic or symphonic, can use unfamiliar and discordant sounds and rhythms to open our ears to new experiences. Having sat through a number of such experimental experiences, it is not clear how well suited they are for communicating a crisis (except a crisis of musical value, as some audience members sardonically remarked as we collectively shuffled out of one such performance).

It is not just experimental music that can shift perceptions. David Byrne of Talking Heads notes that 'If music can be regarded as an organizing principle – and in this case one that places equal weight on melody, rhythm, texture, and harmony – then we start to see metaphors everywhere we look' (2012, p. 189). Data sonification is one expression of new ways to see the familiar. This translation of data into sound, and at times into 'music', provides a novel way to experience a story embedded in data. The San Francisco-based *Climate Music Project* has sponsored a number of powerful projects including a remarkable performance I witnessed at the San Francisco Exploratorium in 2019. Eight snare drummers stood in a line on stage. The piece they played followed a time series of climate-related events involving fatalities. Each drummer was assigned specific events along a time series. The duration of the snare drummer's playing signified the number of deaths for that particular event. At the beginning, there was mostly silence with an occasional short drum burst. By the middle section, drummers were beginning to play over each other, and by the end it was a cacophony. The auditory story conveyed was entirely a different level of experience and impact from just reading the data set. It burnt a place in my memory that an academic article would rarely achieve. Similar work has been done with the geography of poverty (using a timeline based on a train trip across New York City), and the translation of annual global temperature data over time (1880–2012) (Crawford, 2013). We extended this time series to 2016 in our own live multimedia music show, and in doing so ran out of available notes on the five-string violin, given the dramatic spike in global temperatures since 2012. I have no idea how we would play the high notes (temperature) in 2023.

All of these outcomes of music, from storytelling, building group solidarity, cultivation of empathy, emotional connection and modes that shift our perspectives, are all significant in helping people connect with a world beyond themselves. Music brings our world to life in ways that other forms of expression cannot. It enables the expression of energy and beauty, rebellion and rage, grief and joy. At its most profound, the shared experience of music means we are not alone. In a time when increasing numbers of people are experiencing climate and ecological grief, when older people are worried for the next generation and young people struggle to see a positive future, music can play a powerful role in providing emotional release, and enabling group solidarity rather than isolation.

These are some of the roles music will play long into the future. Music will continue to evolve and morph, not just with the emergence of new musical forms and cultural expressions, but through technological and social forces. Artificial intelligence and social changes, such as the increasing (and historically novel) individualisation of musical experience, will undoubtably produce new and perhaps unanticipated outcomes. But it is almost certain our species will continue to be drawn to the sociability of collective musical experience. While social isolation is a deep reality for many today, it is not the only trend we can discern; it is said there are now more community choirs than fish and chip shops in the United Kingdom (Bithell, 2014).

Music and crises

I now return to the focus of this chapter and the theme of this book, communicating a world-in-crisis. Some researchers argue the capacity for music has evolved *alongside* the development of language, providing a necessary counterweight to the domination of propositional communication. Language allows humans to 'store, catalogue and transmit data and knowledge' (Harvey, 2017, p. 11). While significantly more complex than I can deal with here, music does not appear to function at a propositional level, that is, conveying new concepts and knowledge as language does through writing, reading and speaking. Music's power is largely emotive, enabling humans to make emotional and embodied connections with pre-existing propositions or narratives. Drawing on the German philosopher Hans-Georg Gadamer, humans necessarily begin any interpretative act with a prejudice, quite literally a 'pre-judgment'. A pre-judgement is modified by encountering dialogical arguments (two-way discussion) that refute, add to, or modify one's existing understanding (Gadamer, 1985). The available interpretive resources vary across individuals, communities and cultures, and how one 'sees' the world is always constrained by the available narratives. This is as true for science as it is for the particular stories, beliefs, identities and values that make people's social lives. Thomas Kuhn, the physicist turned historian of science, coined the term 'paradigm shift' in reference to the way scientific revolutions took place. For Kuhn, ways of seeing (and for that matter, experiencing) the world are always shaped by the dominant paradigms (Kuhn, 1962).

This has clear implications for the limits of propositional communication through music. Music cannot communicate propositional arguments unless those arguments already exist in some form in the minds of the listener. Or, to put it more simply, music helps people engage emotionally with narratives and identities that they are already familiar with. That is its superpower. Music as an evolutionary and neurological phenomenon is blind to ideology, creed, belief. While some musical forms can be broadly associated with particular values and ideas, such as gospel, punk, reggae or folk protest music, these are cultural overlays on particular musical forms, and not intrinsic to musical patterns themselves. In other words, if they are to have particularised meanings, musical performances require a discursive framework by which to communicate an idea, creed or belief.

This is especially evident in music with lyrics, where stories or ideas are conveyed. Even without lyrics, musicians will sometimes provide written or spoken explanations that accompany their music. Whether explaining the origins of a song on a record sleeve, a programme in a classical concert or a preamble by a folk musician (where song introductions often exceed the length of the song itself!), these interpretative mechanisms offer important cues as to how to 'hear' the music.

This might provide a clue to music's role in or capacity to communicate a world-in-crisis. How does an audience connect a piece of music with a *particular* crisis? It is not difficult to create music that soothes or agitates, energises or relaxes, celebrates or laments. Musicians can be inspired to compose or write music they hope reflects ideas or emotions they wish to communicate. Authorial intention however cannot ensure that audiences will understand the piece as the author intends. This is generally unproblematic in art because the meaning of a piece of art, as Gadamer reminds us, lies in the 'conversation' between the subject and object, the viewer and the piece of art. The art object cannot fully contain its own meaning. Rather, meaning emerges, not out of the object itself, but out of this 'conversation' with the viewer. For Gadamer, understanding emerges from the to-and-fro testing of ideas and interpretations (Gadamer, 1985).

Musical performance, whether orchestral, trip-hop or country, enables creative engagement between the emotions and minds of listeners and the intention of the musicians or composers. Like visual art forms, music historians and critics seek to understand or 'read' music genres by linking them to social contexts. As C. Wright Mills' Sociological Imagination reminds us, this ability to see connections between personal lives and the wider society means music always comes from somewhere and that somewhere can be investigated (Mills, 1959). Biographies of musicians and musical movements provide readers with a social context of an artist or movement and what it all might mean. Such investigations are never complete or final. But this also suggests that music, abstracted from its social context, will only have personalised meaning for the individual. Without social context, the individual hears what they wish to hear in a piece of music.

In reality, most music is social, coming to us *within* an interpretive context. Few could attend a Bob Dylan concert today without some prior social conditioning of the Dylan phenomenon as legend, poet laureate and the 1960s protest movement, all which provide clear cues as to how to 'hear' him. Music can do many things, as I describe above, but it cannot formulate some new understanding of our world by itself. Rather, it most often reflects ideas that already exist. The dialogical world of language, critique, narrative and engagement with empirical realities shape the meanings of music, not the other way round. Music can indeed deepen our experience of these realities, but until these experiences become attached to language and narrative, they remain content-free.

Music can reflect and amplify existing narratives. 'Wagner's operas gave voice to Hitler's Romantic identity with an ancient, mystical and eternal Germany' (Riding, 2004); music in service of an idea. But the ideas need to pre-exist the music for this to happen. Wagner did not create Germanic nationalism, but his music did reflect and empower it.

All this suggests music has a particular, though powerful, role in communication. Musicians can engage in social action through music by protesting against governmental failures to act on the climate and ecological crisis and against corporations engaging in unethical practices. Composer and lawyer Robert McIntyre's 15-minute classical composition, 'Our Duty to Care', encapsulates a significant Australian legal case against the Minister for the Environment (McIntyre, 2023). Ambitious attempts using music to tell a new story only work to the extent they resonate with a narrative the audience is already exposed to. McIntyre's piece is beautiful as a piece of music, but it is unclear the extent to which the music itself increased the understanding of the audience about climate litigation and the climate crisis. Some of the audience no doubt came because of interest in the legal case, while others attended because it was a new musical work. A written explanation of the case was available, and the concert included a brief introductory talk, both which helped locate the music within a particular discourse. It raised the profile of the legal case for an audience who I suspect were already favourably predisposed to the political/legal framing, even if understanding of the climate predicament varied considerably.

So far, I have not said anything particularly controversial, except perhaps at the beginning of the chapter where I stated music cannot save us. I do not mean that dismissively, because, as I have already argued, music has much to offer a world-in-crisis. I was pointing to something else, to a hope or belief that producing crisis-focused music will shift the discursive dial, and through evangelistic fervour, bring many more people 'into the tent' of climate and ecological action. The critique I am suggesting is that music has a limited role in conveying the new reality of emergent and novel crises. This, I will now argue, characterises the unique challenges of the planetary predicament.

If only it was just a crisis

The challenge for musicians lies not with the limits to music, but the nature of this crisis. The late Bruno Latour puts it most eloquently:

> Alas, talking about a 'crisis' would be just another way of reassuring ourselves, saying that 'this too will pass,' the crisis 'will soon be behind us.' If only it were just a crisis! If only it had been just a crisis! The experts tell us we should be talking instead about

> a 'mutation': we were used to one world; we are now tipping, mutating, into another. (2016, p. 6)

Groups of humans (and many other species) have gone through numerous past catastrophes, sometimes surviving them, sometimes not. But all of these took place within the life support provided by planet Earth. What is now clear is that we are entering an uncharted planetary future (Ripple et al., 2023). Regardless of one's ideological positioning, the evidence that we have left the shores of the predicable and reliable (the Holocene), and are now, not just heading, but actually in the early stages of a future of deep uncertainty and unpredictability, is compelling. The climate predicament ought not be viewed as just an 'Issue', but rather as a new era (Steffen, 2021c), one which humans have never experienced before. All bets are now off. Whatever we make of the future will not be a simple rearrangement of past practices, for those are an ill-fit for the world we are now in. We will have to rethink virtually everything we do if we are to collectively adapt to a world fiercely hotter and more dangerous than anything we have previously experienced.

Central to this new reality is what futurist Alex Steffen calls a discontinuity between the world we thought we were in and the world we are actually in (Steffen, 2021c). While most people now acknowledge the reality of climate change, its full implications are still denied or resisted. This makes responding to our mutating climate such a predicament. There is now no return to the safe shores of a world before this current heating. No place is safe from the impacts of climate disruption; all we now have is relative safety, depending on where we live and how well we prepare.

It is likely global emissions will reduce, and do so increasingly rapidly over the next couple of decades (International Energy Agency, 2023). It is also equally likely we will witness a flood of technical and social innovation as the world struggles to adapt and governments, business and civil society see new opportunities for innovation, reform and revolution. But all of this takes place in the shadow of two inescapable characteristics of the climate predicament; speed and scale.

It is increasingly clear that global heating will exceed the 1.5°C Paris aspiration and likely to exceed 2°C (UNFCCC, 2023). While achieving these goals is still *technically* possible, the speed required for the decline in global emissions is deeply challenging. Speed is everything (Steffen, 2022). This alone sets the current predicament apart. If we win slowly, we lose. The tempo of change is now a characteristic of a 'defiant earth' (Hamilton, 2017). Humans are not the only actor in this new future. Having grown used to the promises of modernity that took little account of planetary limits, this new era will be less one of ideology (though that will still be very visible) and more of real planetary boundaries and impacts. As author Jeff Goodell notes, heat waves are culling the most vulnerable, but as they become more intense, they become more democratic (Goodell, 2023, p. 16). Everything now is about to speed up, as disasters become more common and the nations, economies and communities try to pivot in rapid response.

It is not just speed though, it is also, as the IPCC states unambiguously, the sheer scale of the transformational change required. We are deeply unprepared for this scale of change. What is critical to understand is that we can no longer avoid large-scale change because is it no longer entirely in our own hands (Naughten et al., 2023). The faster we plan and prepare for a hot earth, the better off we will be. But whatever we now do, change is coming for all of us.

Music in a discontinuity

What does this mean for music communicating a world-in-crisis? In light of the deeply disruptive speed and scale of change, the past becomes less useful as a guide and the discontinuity we experience leaves us in an uncharted, perhaps even an unchartable, future. For this reason, music is unlikely to be a powerful generator of new ideas that will keep pace with this emerging and mutating future. It is hard enough for scientists to keep up with the speed of change (Hawkins, 2023).

The music of the civil rights movement drew on a historical continuity of ideas and beliefs. It was anchored in the 'arc of justice' and so could sing of eternal truths and triumph of freedom. I pose this deliberately as a contrast with the context of the climate and ecological predicament, where current identities, certainties and visions of the future are untethered from the new earth we find ourselves on. Telling stories of a future we are just entering and do not understand is a tall order. Because music draws on people's current beliefs, music is not a great way to communicate a crisis for which there is little precedent. I am not convinced music can produce a paradigmatic shift in understanding into a deeper *knowledge* of a future characterised by tempo and scale.

What then is a realistic expectation of music in crises? I circle back to some things music is really good at; generating solidarity, empathy and community.

It can help us cope with radical discontinuity and with the cognitive and emotional demands of a world where no one can be certain of a safe place to land. While music might not help navigate the conceptual and empirical terrain of a rapidly mutating planetary crisis, it can bring people back into their body, emotions and connection. Profound and moving music might not improve our understanding of the climate predicament and may not be able to save us from heat, but it will, perhaps more than any of the arts, help us cope and find collective courage and joy in the midst of adversity. For that alone, we can be thankful we have music.

References

Anderson, K. (2023) 'IPCC's conservative nature masks the true scale of action needed to avert catastrophic climate change', *The Conversation*, 25 March. https://theconversation.com/ipccs-conservative-nature-masks-true-scale-of-action-needed-to-avert-catastrophic-climate-change-202287, accessed 12 August 2023.

Andrejevic, M. (2020) *Automated media*. New York: Routledge.

Bithell, C. (2014). *A different voice, a different song: Reclaiming community through the natural voice and world song.* Online edn. New York: Oxford Academic https://doi.org/10.1093/acprof:oso/9780199354542.001.0001, accessed 31 October 2023.

Brysse, K., Oreskes, N., O'Reilly J. and Oppenheimer, M. (2023) 'Climate change prediction; Erring on the side of least drama?', *Global Environmental Change*, 23(1), pp. 327–337.

Bureau of Meteorology. (2023). *State of the climate 2022; Australia's changing climate*. Commonwealth Government of Australia. http://www.bom.gov.au/state-of-the-climate/australias-changing-climate.shtml, accessed 10 July 2023.

Byrne, D. (2012) *How Music Works*. San Francisco: McSweeney's Publishing.

Clarke, E., DeNorab, T. and Vuoskoskia, J. (2015) 'Music, empathy and cultural understanding', *Physics of Life Reviews*, 15, pp. 61–88.

Crawford, D. (2013) *Song for a warming planet*. Institute on the Environment, University of Minnesota, YouTube. https://www.youtube.com/watch?v=5t08CLczdK4, accessed 10 January 2023.

Gadamer, H.-G. (1985) *Truth and method*. New York: The Seabury Press.

Goodell, J. (2023) *Heat: Life and death on a scorched planet*. Melbourne: Black Inc.

Hamilton, C. (2017) *Defiant earth: The fate of humans in the Anthropocene*. Sydney: Allen & Unwin.

Harvey, A.R. (2017) *Music, evolution, and the harmony of souls*. Oxford: Oxford University Press.

Hausfather, Z. (2021) 'Explainer: Will global warming "stop" as soon as net-zero emissions are reached?', *CarbonBrief*. https://www.carbonbrief.org/explainer-will-global-warming-stop-as-soon-as-net-zero-emissions-are-reached/, accessed 8 August 2023.

——. (2023) X. 21 November. https://twitter.com/hausfath/status/1726675379237294507, accessed 21 November 2023.

Hawkins, E. (2023) X. 6 October. https://twitter.com/ed_hawkins/status/1709825752705753105, accessed 6 October 2023.

Heshmat, S. (2023) 'The role of music in promoting our empathetic reactions', *Psychology Today*, 23 March. https://www.psychologytoday.com/intl/blog/science-of-choice/202303/the-role-of-music-in-promoting-our-empathic-reactions#:~:text=Empathy%20is%20built%20through%20processes,to%20the%20feelings%20of%20others, accessed 10 September 2023.

International Energy Agency. (2022). *Renewables 2023: Executive summary*. https://www.iea.org/reports/renewables-2022/executive-summary, accessed 8 August 2023.

——. (2023) *Electricity Market Report – Update 2023*. https://www.iea.org/reports/electricity-market-report-update-2023/executive-summary, accessed 10 September 2023.

IPCC. (2022) 'Summary for policymakers' [Shukla, P.R., Skea, J., Reisinger, A., Slade, R., Fradera, R., Pathak, M., Khourdajie, A. Al., Belkacemi, M., van Diemen, R., Hasija, A., Lisboa, G., Luz, S., Malley, J., McCollum, D., Some, S., Vyas, P. (eds.)] in *Climate change 2022: Mitigation of climate change. Contribution of Working Group III to the sixth assessment report of the intergovernmental panel on climate change* [Shukla, P.R., Skea, J., Slade, R., Khourdajie, A. Al, van Diemen, R., McCollum, D., Pathak, M., Some, S., Vyas, P., Fradera, R., Belkacemi, M., Hasija, A., Lisboa, G., Luz, S., Malley, J. (eds.)]. Cambridge, UK; New York: Cambridge University Press. https://doi.org/10.1017/9781009157926.001

Jarvis, B. (2023) 'Climate change is keeping therapists up at night: How anxiety about the planet's future is transforming the practice of psychotherapy', *New York Times Magazine*, 22 October, https://www.nytimes.com/2023/10/21/magazine/climate-anxiety-therapy.html, accessed 25 October 2023.

Kerr, S. (2015) *Music for a warming world*. www.musicforawarmingworld.org, accessed 1 March 2023.

——. (2018) 'Climate, culture and music: Coping in the Anthropocene', *University of Tasmania Law Review: Special Issue: Imagining a Different Climate Future, Overcoming Barriers to Climate Justice*, 27(2), pp. 169–187.

Klein, N. (2015) *This changes everything: Capitalism vs. the climate*. New York: Simon and Schuster.

Kuhn, T.S. (1962) *The structure of scientific revolutions*. Chicago: University of Chicago Press.

Lamond, S. (2011) *A paler shade of green: Artists in the cryosphere in the new millennium*. BA (Honours) Thesis, Australian National University.

Latour, B. (2016) *Facing Gaia: Eight lectures on the new climatic regime*. Kindle edn. Wiley.

Liu, P. and Raftery, A. (2021), 'Country-based rate of emissions reductions should increase by 80% beyond nationally determined contributions to meet the 2°C target', *Nature Communications: Earth & Environment*, 2(29).

Lynchpin. (n.d.) *The Making of a Symphony – 'a Love Letter to the Ocean'* http://www.lynchpin.org.au/our-projects/ex-oceano/, accessed 10 July 2023.

Martinez, T.A. (1997). 'Popular culture as resistance culture: Rap as resistance', *Sociological Perspectives*, 40(2), pp. 265–287.

McIntyre, R. (2023) *Our duty to care*. Port Melbourne, VIC. https://www.roberttmcintyre.com/our-duty-to-care, accessed 10 July 2023.

McKibben, B. (2005) 'What the warming world needs now is art, sweet art'. *Grist*, 22 April. https://grist.org/article/mckibben-imagine/, accessed 1 July 2017.

Mehr, S.A, Singh, M., Knox, D., Ketter, D.M., et al. (2019) 'Universality and diversity in human song', *Science*, 366(6468).

Mills, C.W. (1959) *The sociological imagination*. New York: Oxford University Press.

Mitchell, J. (1970) 'Big Yellow Taxi', *Ladies of the Canyon*, Reprise Records.

Musicians Without Borders. https://www.musicianswithoutborders.org/, accessed 10 July 2023.

Naughten, K.A., Holland, P.R. and De Rydt, J. (2023) *Unavoidable future increase in West Antarctic ice-shelf melting over the twenty-first century*. Nature Climate Change. https://doi.org/10.1038/s41558-023-01818-x, accessed 24 October 2023.

Pielke, R., Burgess, M. and Ritchie, J. (2022) 'Plausible 2005–2050 emissions scenarios project between 2°C and 3°C of warming by 2100', *Environmental Research Letters*, 17(2).

Reynolds, F. (2023) 'The Transformative Power of Music in Mental Wellbeing, American Psychiatric Association Blog', 1 August. https://www.psychiatry.org/news-room/apa-blogs/power-of-music-in-mental-well-being, accessed 19 October 2023.

Riding, A. (2004) *Music as a Political Tool in the Service of the Reich*. https://www.nytimes.com/2004/10/25/arts/music/music-as-political-tool-in-the-service-of-the-reich.html, accessed 10 July 2023.

Ripple, W.J., Wolfe, C., Gregg, J.W., et al. (2023) 'The 2023 state of the climate report: Entering uncharted territory', *Bioscience*, 73, pp. 841–850.

Steffen, A. (2021a) 'Ruggedize your life', *The Snap Forward*. https://alexsteffen.substack.com/p/ruggedize-your-life, accessed 3 April 2023.

——. (2021b) 'Win, then fight', *The Snap Forward*. https://alexsteffen.substack.com/p/win-then-fight, accessed 3 April 2023.

——. (2021c) 'Discontinuity is the job', *The Snap Forward*. https://alexsteffen.substack.com/p/discontinuity-is-the-job?utm_source=%2Fsearch%2Fdiscontinuity&utm_medium=reader2, accessed 10 July 2023.

——. (2022) 'Speed is everything', *The Snap Forward*. https://alexsteffen.substack.com/p/speed-is-everything, accessed 10 July 2023.

UNESCO. (2018) 'Reggae music of Jamaica', *Intangible Cultural Heritage*. https://ich.unesco.org/en/RL/reggae-music-of-jamaica-01398, accessed 1 March 2023.

UNFCCC Secretariat (2023) 'Technical; dialogue of the first global stocktake. Synthesis report by the co-facilitators on the technical dialogue', *UN Climate Change Conference – United Arab Emirates*, November/December.

Webster, J. (2023) 'The promise of personalisation: Exploring how music streaming platforms are shaping the performance of class identities and distinction', *News Media & Society*, 25(8), pp. 2140–2162.

Wiseman, J. (2021) *Hope and courage in the climate crisis: Wisdom and action in the long emergency*. Switzerland AG: Palgrave Macmillan.

World Meteorological Organization (2023) 'Global temperatures set to reach new records in the next five years', Press release Number: 17052023. 17 May, accessed from https://wmo.int/news/media-centre/global-temperatures-set-reach-new-records-next-five-years, accessed 10 November 2023.

·15·

COMMUNICATING 'STORIES THAT MATTER': ACTIVIST MUSEOGRAPHY AND IMMERSIVE PRACTICE IN THE CLIMATE EMERGENCY

Jenny Kidd and Salsabilla Sakinah

Museums operate in ever more complex analytical and political relation to our world-in-crisis. This chapter explores how they document and communicate climate (in)justice, working to inspire the civil and humanitarian will that is needed in response. Specifically, it explores museums' use of immersive approaches to 'tell stories that matter' (Newell, 2020).

Critics have been clear that – despite what are understood to be museums' unique potentials to communicate about planetary issues[1] – they have to date failed to make climate action a priority. Over the last decade however several climate museums and exhibitions have opened, reflecting global initiatives to arrest crises in our current world ecology, and to resuscitate our (more-than-) human relationships (Cameron, 2021). It is a marked phenomenon of this shift how many institutions have turned to immersive approaches for interpretation and storytelling, and this chapter explores that development. It proposes that immersive approaches are particularly interesting in light of Robert Janes' (2020) call for individuals and organisations, including museums, to move beyond *thinking* about the climate crisis and to start *feeling* it instead.

The chapter begins with an overview of current thinking within the museum sector about planetary issues, connecting with ongoing (and often still conflicted) debates about institutions' activist roles and responsibilities (Janes and Sandell, 2019). We then situate these developments and discussions in relation to the recent 'immersive turn' within museums and heritage sites, exploring how a series of practical examples are attempting to promote changed perspectives on the climate emergency.

Context

Since their earliest manifestations, museums have demonstrated great interest in exhibiting nature and the environment, as can be seen from the emergence of natural history museums across the globe in the nineteenth century. These museums were founded on positivist science, understanding nature and the environment to be separate from human culture, and considering specimens as passive objects for documentation, conservation and display. It is only in recent decades, along with the growing paradigm of the new museology,[2] that museums have acknowledged the complex interrelationship between humans and nature (Decker, 2020, p. 646).

One of the first exhibitions specifically focused on climate change was opened at the American Museum of Natural History (AMNH) in 1992, and several more opened globally in the 2000s. Those exhibitions often sought to explain the scientific realities of climate change but, in a bid to provide (flawed) equivalence or to assert museums' own neutrality, tended to acknowledge contestation and scepticism in debates about environmental change, and steadfastly avoided questioning the political consensus in relation to it. Examples include the first exhibition specifically about climate at the Deutsches Museum in 2002 *Climate: The Experiment with Planet Earth* (Keogh and Möllers, 2015), and the *Mission: Climate Earth* exhibition at the Swedish Museum of Natural History in 2004 (Bergdahl and Houltz, 2017). According to Bergdahl and Houltz (2017, p. 218) such approaches, which 'hamper museums in their ambitions to articulate and address the issue of climate change' have had 'deep historical roots' in museums' practices of categorisation and display, often leading to ambiguous interpretation and an excess of caution as a result (see also Keogh and Mollers, 2015, p. 84; Newell, Robin and Wehner, 2017, p. 7; Decker, 2020, p. 646). It is only more recently that exhibitions have broadened in scope to include investigation of current and future consequences of the climate crisis for human cultures. This is in part because museums have increasingly been able to assume visitors have an awareness of some of the fundamentals of climate science (Newell, Robin and Wehner, 2017, p. 7), but also because there have been escalating calls for museums to join the climate activist movement.

The idea of 'activist museums' emerged in the late twentieth and early twenty-first century as a vision challenging what were understood to be institutions' inherently colonial policies, principles, and practices (Brown and Mairesse, 2018; Chipangura and Marufu, 2019; Anderson, 2020; Bekenova, 2023). Janes and Sandell (2019, p. 1) have described museum activism as a 'divergent expression' of a museum's inherent power as a 'force for good', one 'that is intended to bring about political, social and environmental change' in what Janes (2009, p. 55) calls a 'troubled world'. Museum activism is predicated on the presumption that museums have enough cultural authority – the 'signifying power of culture' (Sandell, 2002, p. 3) – to communicate narratives and to present values and frameworks for enacting them, which might ultimately impact human outlooks and behaviours (Janes and Sandell, 2019, p. 7). Museums then can actively promote societal change by addressing and advocating urgent contemporary global issues such as social injustice and environmental crises (Ünsal, 2019, pp. 595–596; Anderson, 2020, pp. 490–491).

In order to achieve museums' transformative social power and potential, activists argue that institutions need to puncture 'the myth of neutrality' that continues to be pervasive in their orbit[3] (Janes and Sandell, 2019, p. 8; Lyons and Bosworth, 2019, p. 174; Janes and Grattan, 2019, p. 100; Sutton, 2020, p. 625). In this view approaching climate narratives solely from the standpoint of 'neutral' science (as in the examples referenced above) is critically flawed given that it fails to recognise connections with environmental justice for example, where minorities, low-income, and vulnerable communities are disproportionately affected (Decker, 2020, p. 646), and at risk of becoming climate refugees (Dawson, 2015). For critics however, such approaches are not straightforward, and circle back to questions concerning public trust: will the public continue to trust museums if they are no longer viewed as neutral?[4] If it is currently the case that museums offer 'non-confrontational' and even 'safe' spaces for the exploration of issues (Newell, Robin and Wehner, 2017, p. 4), what might such a shift mean for them in the longer term?

Such concerns were apparent in controversy surrounding a new international museum definition proposed by the International Council of Museums in 2019, and in particular, the rejection of phrasing such as: 'democratizing', 'inclusive', 'polyphonic spaces', 'critical dialogue', 'equal rights', 'human dignity', 'social justice', 'global equality' and 'planetary wellbeing'. As highlighted by

Fraser (2019, pp. 502–503) and Lorenc (2020, p. 168), the main issue that arose from the addition of activist phraseology to the international definition of a/any 'museum' was fear that it would exclude a large number of existing institutions, particularly those operating within funding or political constraints which meant they could not act freely within these changed parameters. These constraints are of course concerning to proponents of museum activism where they have a cooling effect on discourse and practice, where they lead to a lack of challenge when 'dirty' money is concerned, or where sponsorship is allowed to wield undue influence over museum activities such as collection, display or interpretation.[5]

Within this context, and given a professional praxis (museography) that can mean change is achingly slow, many museums have turned to (often itinerant) immersive approaches to tell 'stories that matter' about the climate emergency. This chapter explores this phenomenon. It demonstrates how museums are using such approaches to layer and diversify the narratives they contain, often integrating participatory mechanisms and calls to action. To close, we then make the case for further exploration of what immersive storytelling can do, more robust interrogation of how feeling, cognition and action are intertwined in the orbit of museums, and creativity in considering where a museum even 'is' as all of our climate futures are negotiated.

The potentials of immersion

In this section, we explore a range of immersive museum practices designed to promote changed perspectives on the climate emergency. Although they often involve digital technologies and platforms (virtual and augmented reality for example), it is worth noting from the off that our approach here is not defined by hardware. Instead, it follows previous scholarship on immersive heritage in that it centres practices that are 'story-led, audience and participation centred, multimodal, multisensory and attuned to [their] environment' (Kidd, 2018). The examples that follow all nod to a set of experiential and affective qualities that it is hoped will characterise participation and prove consequential in terms of visitors' planetary understanding and interactions.

Immersive installations and approaches are now regular features within museum and gallery contexts where it is felt the use of dynamic narrative techniques and new audience propositions can subvert the conventions of a more traditional heritage encounter (Kidd and Nieto McAvoy, 2019; Gao and Braud, 2023). They follow what Economou and Pujol Tost (2007) have called 'a different communication paradigm' for museums, one where visitors are encouraged to play more active and perhaps challenging roles,[6] and to experience a more diverse – or layered – range of viewpoints as a result (Amakawa and Westin, 2018). In what follows we discuss the potential of such approaches to craft an impactful feeling of presence and engage visitors' senses, with a view to offering changed (human and nonhuman) perspectives and encouraging agency.

Although in the past museums might have privileged visual and textual resources, in immersive practices spatial, haptic, aural, and even olfactory cues become important stimuli. Where the combination of these stimuli is experienced coherently it is hoped meaning-making will become more visceral and be experienced powerfully in the body (Kidd, 2019; Huws et al., 2019). This can be done in a number of ways, some of which we introduce in this section.

Rio de Janeiro's Museu do Amanhã (Museum of Tomorrow), for example, is narratively led throughout and contains very few artefacts. It is committed to harnessing the expressive arts and technology to communicate climate science, and to provoke responses to the question 'How do we want to live?' for the future. All visitors enter the exhibitions via *Cosmos*, a 360° movie space featuring a full-scale multi-sensory introduction where they 'witness' the formation of Earth and the beginnings of life. This 360° introduction's intensity is marked, as visitors watch in the dark, acutely aware of the bodies of others, and unable to disregard a penetrating voiceover (in Portuguese):

> 'We are the unfolding Universe.'
> 'We are the thought that envisions Tomorrow'[2]

The use of 'we' here is codified as a narrative device which collectively implicates visitors – spatially and narratively – as actors in an interplay between humans and nature, but with agency to imagine and enact change. As an approach this is in marked contrast to the more traditional curatorial voice often found in museums.[7] Further into a visit at the Museu do Amanhã a slightly different 360° concept is utilised in the Anthropocene gallery (Figure 15.1) where visitors are surrounded by six giant totems, each ten metres tall and three metres wide, purposefully arranged as if in a stone circle. A series of thought-provoking filmic installations on topics such as oil extraction, water pollution, and the production of waste are then projected onto those totems. By dint of the spatial dynamics in the gallery visitors are again implicated as more than mere witnesses to climate destruction, their agency recognised, for good or for ill. These spatial, sensory and narrative cues support the Museu

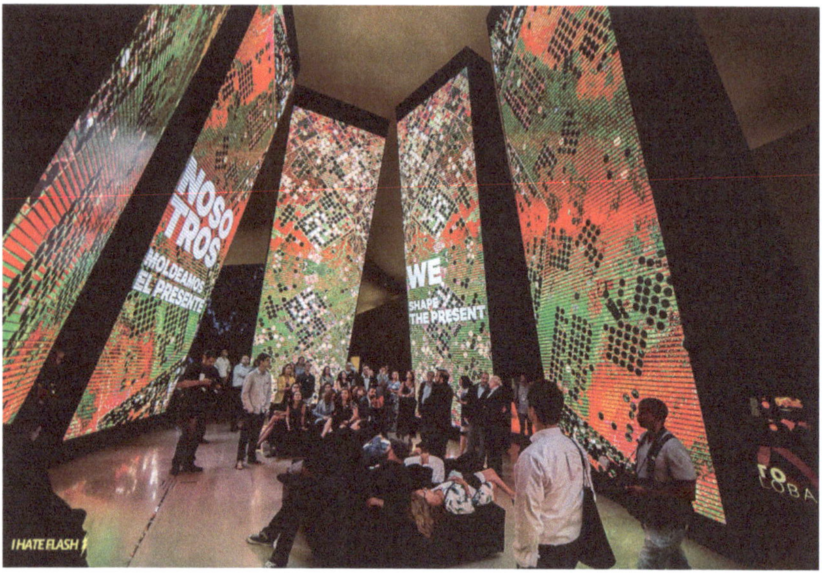

Figure 15.1. Museu do Amanhã's Anthropocene Gallery. Photo Credit: Raul Aragão

do Amanhã's express intention that visitors should leave 'feeling disturbed or inspired but not indifferent' to their responsibility in collectively constructing a future that is both sustainable and convivial (Oliveira in Watts, 2015).

The *Blue Paradox* installation in the Museum of Science and Industry Chicago takes a similar approach. Here the museum features a tunnelled experience with 360° digital videos of the ocean projected onto the floor, walls, and ceiling. Visitors enter the exhibition as if from a beach, and then roam 'beneath' the sea's surface. Rich visuals first attempt to connect visitors emotionally with blue spaces – communicating something of their scale and majesty, as well as their significance to human life – before introducing the problems we face, and how we might begin to tackle those, both through individual and collective actions. Visitors explore the impact of the ocean plastic crisis on the marine ecosystem through multiple data points and visuals and are encouraged throughout to centre the question: 'Are you ready to make a difference?' In promotional materials the museum makes much of what it calls *Blue Paradox*'s 'emotional storytelling' as a way to encourage behavioural changes in visitors and other key stakeholders.

There is a great deal of research (see, e.g.: Bergevin, 2018; Sweeney et al., 2018; Huws et al., 2019; Kidd, 2019) that explores how immersive heritage approaches which combine storytelling and first-person perspectives can elicit emotional impact and empathetic engagements, to the extent that a visitor might perceive their visit as a 'transformative journey' (Bergevin, 2018). However, despite any museum's intention to evoke particular emotions, it is important to remember that visitors are active participants, who may respond with a diverse and unpredictable – even contrary – range of emotions (Oren, Shani and Poria, 2021; Bareither, 2021; Buchheim, 2022; May et al., 2022; Salazar et al., 2022). Using emotional storytelling to encourage behavioural change is challenging then: it may motivate visitors to act, but it might equally be perceived as an overwhelming or uncomfortable input which eventually leads to avoidance. For museums interested in encouraging visitors to move from thinking to feeling however, providing opportunities for embodiment – or embodied cognition – is clearly important.[8] As Salazar notes (2015, p. 97) 'designing richer experiences of climate change ought to transcend scientific data to enable a sensory-enhanced mode for anticipating futures'. As is demonstrated in the above examples, immersive approaches often pay particular attention to the way media and environments are experienced through our bodies and our senses, and museums have become attuned to those logics and their potentials (Gröppel-Wegener and Kidd, 2019; Liu and Lan, 2021; Mandelli, 2021; Sumartojo and Graves, 2021). Such approaches can – although never inevitably – give visitors a sense of personally, tangibly, being connected with an experience or subject matter, and even to feel perceptual cues associated with it (Shin and Biocca, 2017). The notion of 'presence' is a particularly powerful concept here as a way of articulating the extent to which a person feels transported, however temporarily or consequentially, into another environment or outlook. Experiencing such presence can mean users respond automatically to spatial cues, including audio cues, and to prompts from other persons within the environment (whether those persons are physically or virtually co-present with them). Presence is associated with and affected by the vividness of an encounter, as well as the user's range of possibilities within it; being able to interact with an environment for example, instead of just passively watching it, tends to lead to heightened feelings of presence and engagement.

The Klimahaus Bremerhaven takes this idea of presencing as an organising principle for its entire exhibitions:

> You will cross five continents and nine locations. You will sweat, freeze, marvel and laugh, and above all, meet people from around the world who will talk about their everyday lives and describe how the climate affects them.[9]

Within this climate museum, visitors 'journey' following longitude 8° 34' E (notionally 'from' the city of Bremerhaven), entering nine rich multi-sensory scenes (called 'stations') as they go. At the Niger station, visitors find themselves experiencing life in the 35° heat of a rocky desert, whilst in the Antarctica station, they feel the -6° average summer temperature and can even hear people shaking and shivering in a tent. Whilst journeying across and between the different scenes, visitors encounter the impacts of climate change; drought and forest fires in Sardinia, damage caused by the tropical cyclones in Samoa, and disappearing sea ice from the coasts of Alaska. This museum, which describes itself as a mix between a science museum and a theme park, and has a stated emphasis on 'creative, imaginative, collaborative and hopeful – rather than fearful – experiences' is focused on memorability and reorientation through multiplicity of perspectives, such that visitors will make more informed decisions in relation to sustainability in their everyday lives. The 'spatial-emotional dimensions' of a site like this – it is hoped – generate narratives, and in turn, imaginative and empathetic investment in visitors (to borrow from Arnold-de Simine, 2018).

Symbiosis (2022)[10] at Portland Art Museum's Center for an Untold Tomorrow took multi-sensory engagement and the notion of presence to a rather different experiential end-point. In this project, six people at a time were zipped into haptic suits (powered by soft robotics) and wore head-mounted virtual reality displays wherein they visited a series of imaginary futures. Taking on the persona of one of a range of nonhuman or part-human characters, they then had to find ways of adapting to a collapsing ecosystem, encountering a series of haptic, olfactory and even edible cues as they did so. The goal was to de-prioritise human experience, and even the human bodily architecture, such that visitors to the experience might imagine more distributed forms of agency or 'symbiosis' between humans and nonhumans.

In this section, we have referred a number of times to this term '*agency*' as a way to articulate the propositions inherent in some immersive experiences, and this is not unproblematic. Immersive approaches – whether in museums, or more broadly within media and communications contexts – are often celebrated for their capacity to centre users and give them increased agency, but the extent to which (designers of) immersive experiences can encourage meaningful decision-making and feelings of ownership or control, and how those translate beyond the immediate environment of an immersive encounter, is difficult to anticipate. Many of these systems are responsive and implicate those who participate such that we can end up struggling to articulate the interactants positionality (audience, viewer, user, participant, visitor), but increased agency is by no means an inevitable outcome. It is easy to see however why these approaches might be considered compelling for institutions seeking means to explore more diverse (human and nonhuman) perspective-taking, and to work with more provocative narratives which suggest urgent dialogue and calls to action. Whether they can compellingly and consistently do that work is however still to be proven.

There are however a number of projects we can point to that seek to layer perspectives in this way through immersive approaches. The Design Museum's *Adapt* (2021) project is an interesting case in point, offering differing perspectives on our material futures. In partnership with Snap Inc. (of Snapchat) Architect Mariam Issoufou Kamara created an augmented reality project envisioning differing possible material realities for the museum building as it responds to extreme weather conditions. Creating filters which can be easily layered onto the museum in situ (see Figure 15.2) is a simple and provocative way of suggesting possible futures, and making the case for more robust discussions about 'climate-conscious architecture' through the re-imagining of a much-loved building (McGuirk in Silver, 2022).

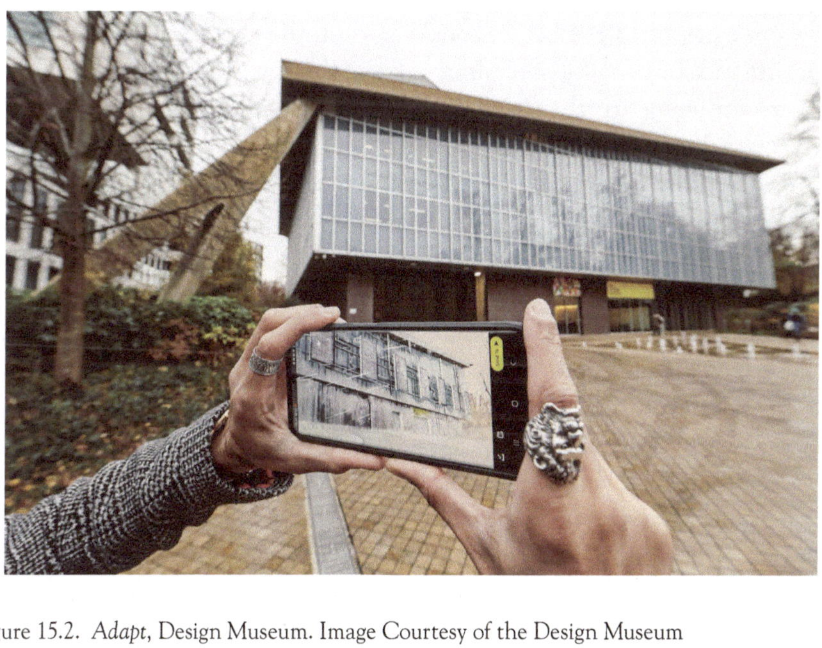

Figure 15.2. *Adapt*, Design Museum. Image Courtesy of the Design Museum

Another prototype project using augmented reality technology at the Ethnological Museum of Berlin (2021) set out to provide additional perspectives on objects from the *Oceana: People and the Sea – A Sea of Islands* exhibition. *SwellAR*[11] invited users to scan an interactive map in order to access real-time climate data visualisations paired with content created by Pacific Islanders living the realities of the climate crisis. The AR experience enabled an extension of the static exhibition narrative to add layers of complexity, critically including the reflections of local stakeholders on issues such as drinking water shortages and coral reef devastation (Navarro in Lu, 2021). That layering, it is hoped, takes something that can otherwise seem quite abstract (to those in Northern Europe), giving the climate emergency immediate relevancy and proximity. Different narrative structures are thus possible in immersive formats, and can potentially be more agile than those in permanent exhibitions.

Another case in point is the *Museum of Water* (2013–), a roving live artwork of publicly donated water, as well as peoples' stories about it archived as audio recordings or handwritten notes. The museum is framed as a way of re-examining how we are connected by water, including how we utilise, share and look after our resources. The collection is open to donations wherever it is installed and now contains more than 1,000 contributions, featuring a wide variety of samples including (but not limited to) dam water, melting glacial ice, birth water, sweat and tears. According to founder Amy Sharrocks, it tells stories about cultural differences and our impact on the world, but also constitutes a performance of everyday life.[12] In this example, the potential for meaningful participation comes to the fore, alongside the hybridity of approaches which work across digital and physical materialities.

In contrast to these examples, where museums create immersion using digital technologies and/or the affordances of a physical museum space or building, the Climate Museum has taken a rather different approach. This is perhaps best exemplified in its 2022 collaboration – as part of a rich network of partners – to support the ninth, and final, performance of Sarah Cameron Sunde's *36.5 / A Durational Performance with the Sea.*[13] This immersive experience was one step removed from a digital or physical estate, taking place instead in the New York Estuary (Figure 15.3).

36.5 / A Durational Performance with the Sea was a series of nine site-specific participatory performances where the artist went to places at risk of rising sea levels and stood in the water. Following extensive community engagement activities led by the artist, members of the public were invited to participate, joining the artist in the water or on the shore, as day passed into

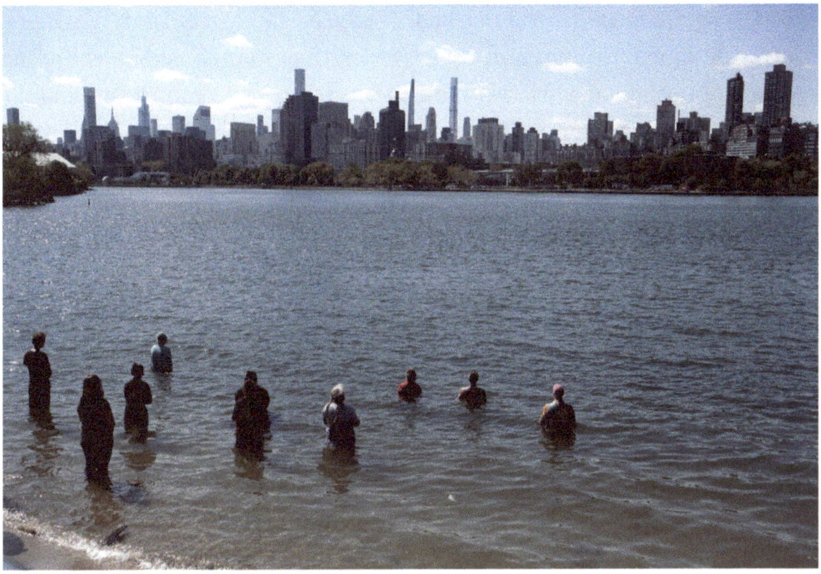

Figure 15.3. *36.5 / New York Estuary*, 9th and Final Work in the Series, *36.5 / A Durational Performance with the Sea*, Courtesy of Sarah Cameron Sunde Studio

night, and the water came in and then retreated in a full tidal cycle. As they were engulfed in water – a fully embodied and sensory experience of immersion – connections between our individual and collective physicality and the natural environment could be felt viscerally, and many participants (and viewers) reported feeling moved by the experience. As the artist noted:

> This act of slowing down stays with participants and grants deeper understanding of our place in the world, which is the first step of many toward adaptation and collective intersectional resiliency.

Working in partnership in this way was in keeping with the ambitions of the Climate Museum to transform public arts and cultural programming such that it accelerates climate dialogue and action; 'connecting people and advancing just solutions'.[14] This immersive encounter de-centres the museum as institution or host (and the baggage that perhaps comes with that), opening up a space for different kinds of thinking, and feeling, about the climate emergency. It is gently – but profoundly – cooperative, stubbornly persistent, and works with a very different understanding of temporality than museums, and their visitors, have become accustomed to.

In this section, we have reviewed immersive activities from a variety of museums, designed to communicate 'stories that matter' about the climate emergency. Through a variety of mechanisms, they demonstrate museums making more 'assertive' attempts to communicate the physical, social, cultural and emotional dimensions of climate change (Salazar, 2015), exploring – albeit tentatively – alternative futures (Priday, Mansfield and Ramos, 2015).

Conclusion

In this chapter, through a range of examples, we have demonstrated clear enthusiasm from museums (variously defined) for the possibilities immersive approaches present to facilitate rich storytelling and even transformative encounters as they communicate about the climate emergency. There is no doubt a pervasive set of assumptions about immersive experiences that underpin this uptake; that they can facilitate the communication of a broader range of perspectives than traditional exhibitions, that they can enable embodied and even visceral meaning-making, and that they might increase emotional investment and even empathy in visitors as a result. With charged subject matters, or those that suggest a strong call to action, these are no doubt seductive propositions.[15] They suggest ways museums can communicate about the climate crisis by 'encompassing joy, wonder, and delight, rather than just pressing the buttons of fear and guilt' (Cameron et al., 2013, p. 19).

Most powerfully perhaps, at their best, these immersive approaches demonstrate museums practising more relationality; attempting to develop (and share) their authority 'through supporting and curating networks of related things and their significance, rather than delivering knowledge from a single vantage point' (Newell, Robin and Wehner, 2017, p. 4). In these encounters an object, collection, building, even the very concept of a museum (those definitional difficulties aside), can become a 'pathway' through which stories can flow, and around which dialogue can happen (Newell, Robin and Wehner, 2017). Bergdahl and Houltz propose that creating exhibitions today about the climate crisis 'requires embracing discontinuity' (2017, p. 229). Immersive approaches can embrace fragmentary and non-linear storytelling to present, and allow people to (notionally at least) experiment with, more radical visions of the future. These visions of the future can de-prioritise or de-stabilise the status quo, whether that be the prevailing political consensus, or the deeply ingrained museological consensus. As such, these approaches can be fitting to museums' activist ambitions.

But they present challenges too. As we have noted, there is much work to do to understand how meaning-making works within these contexts, as well as how that then translates into thoughts and actions in the longer term.[16] Much of the work we have reviewed here is itinerant or otherwise somewhat fleeting. This might be perfectly justifiable, but may also raise concerns about sustainability, structural obstacles and levels of managerial support. Visitors should be able to discern – and interrogate – how these approaches reflect an institution's 'socially responsible' vision and governance more generally (Janes, 2022). We also need to better understand what ethical issues these approaches present or bring into focus. For example, where they utilise digital technologies, there is a need to confront the kinds of cultural and socio-technical assumptions that are embedded in these systems and discussions about them, as well as to reckon with their own environmental impacts.

Salazar (2015, p. 93) argues that 'what are urgently needed are not so much awareness campaigns but deep civic-driven processes of social change' facilitated by museums. The examples we have highlighted in this chapter as yet largely fall short in meeting those ambitions, but they are bringing museums ever closer to them.

Notes

1 Janes (2020) notes that museums often [1] have a strong footing in communities and a keen sense of place, [2] 'bear witness' and document 'sustainable living practices', [3] bridge science, culture and creativity, [4] assemble and assess evidence, and [5] make learning accessible and engaging. See also Janes (2022).

2 Originally established to take care of objects deemed valuable, the 'old' duties of museums were focused on items and connected to collections, conservation, analysis and exhibitions (Weil, 1999, p. 229). However, concerns have been raised in recent decades that object-oriented museums are struggling to remain relevant in our rapidly evolving cultures (Cameron, 1971; Lehmannova, 2020). The 'new museology' refers to the more explicit recognition of social and political role of museums which emerged in the 1980s (see e.g. Vergo, 1989, as well as Anderson, 2004, p. 5, Hooper-Greenhill, 2006, p. 2, Vlachou, 2019, p. 47, Lyons and Bosworth, 2019, p. 17).

3 Museums have typically been regarded as 'neutral' institutions. However, some scholars and practitioners have recently questioned this viewpoint (Jones, Hussain, and Spiewak, 2020, p. 64). The process of collecting and selecting some artefacts and narratives over others, which museums have done since their inception, demonstrates of course that 'museums have never been neutral' (Fraser, Coleman, and Bennet, 2020, p. 298). Furthermore, as Cameron and Neilson (2015, p. 2) argue, seeing museums as neutral institutions ignores their often complicated position in relation to wider socio-political factors.

4 Museums have not been alone in facing questions about how to communicate the climate emergency and maintain public trust in the process. Broadcasters such as the BBC have been negotiating similar issues (Parratt, 2014; Brüggemann and Engesser, 2017).
5 This was evidently the case with the Science Museum London exhibition *Atmosphere: Exploring Climate Science Gallery* as widely reported, for example, by Macalister (2015) in *The Guardian*.
6 These possibilities have been demonstrated in other contexts, for example, in immersive theatre, and virtual reality (Dinesh, 2016; Warren, 2017; Machon, 2013; Bucher, 2017).
7 Bergdahl and Houltz (2017) also reflect on the power of 'we' as a narrative device within exhibitions about the climate emergency.
8 There is some evidence that embodied and spatialised interactions can lead to more searching and 'dialogical' encounters (Poole, 2018, p. 306, see also Kenderdine et al. 2014, Kenderdine, 2016).
9 https://www.klimahaus-bremerhaven.de/en/.
10 Symbiosis is produced by Polymorf https://www.polymorf.nl/interaction/symbiosis/.
11 https://refrakt.org/swellar/.
12 https://museumofwater.co.uk/.
13 For more about 36.5 / A Durational Performance with the Sea (2013–2022) visit https://www.36pt5.org/
14 https://climatemuseum.org/mission.
15 See Benardou and Droumpouki (2022) for more on immersive experiences and 'difficult' subject matters in particular.
16 Although Damala et al. (2008), Yoon et al. (2012), Ghouaiel et al. (2017), and Bernardou and Droumpouki (2022) have made in-roads into that understanding.

References

Amakawa, J. and Westin, J. (2018) 'New Philadelphia: Using augmented reality to interpret slavery and reconstruction era historical sites', *International Journal of Heritage Studies*, 24, pp. 315–331.

Anderson, G. (ed.) (2004) *Reinventing the museum: Historical and contemporary perspectives on the paradigm shift*. Walnut Creek, CA: AltaMira Press.

Anderson, S. (2020) 'Unsettling national narratives and multiplying voices: The art museum as renewed space for social advocacy and decolonization – a Canadian case study', *Museum Management and Curatorship*, 35(5), pp. 488–531.

Arnold-de Simine, S. (2018) 'The stories we tell: Uncanny encounters in Mr Straw's House', *International Journal of Heritage Studies*, 25(1), pp. 80–95.

Bareither, C. (2021) 'Difficult heritage and digital media: "selfie culture" and emotional practices at the Memorial to the Murdered Jews of Europe', *International Journal of Heritage Studies*, 27(1), pp. 57–72.

Bekenova, K. (2023) 'African museums and their participation in the debates on the ICOM new museum definition', *Museum History Journal*, pp. 1–21.

Benardou, A. and Droumpouki, A.M. (eds.) (2022) *Difficult heritage and immersive experiences*. New York: Routledge.

Bergdahl, E. and Houltz, A. (2017) 'Museum Awakenings: Responses to environmental change at the Swedish Museum of Natural History, 1965–2005' in Newell, J., Robin, L. and Wehner, K. (eds.) *Curating the future: Museums, communities and climate change*. London; New York: Routledge.

Bergevin, J.L. (2018) 'Narratives of Transformation: Reframing and naming the impact of activist museum practice on visitors', PhD Thesis, University of Leicester.

Brown, K. and Mairesse, F. (2018) 'The definition of the museum through its social role', *Curator: The Museum Journal*, 61(4), pp. 525–539.

Brüggemann, M. and Engesser, S. (2017) 'Beyond false balance: How interpretive journalism shapes media coverage of climate change', *Global Environmental Change*, 42, pp. 58–67.

Bucher, J. (2017) *Storytelling for virtual reality: Methods and principles for crafting immersive narratives*. New York; Oxon: Routledge.

Buchheim, E. (2022) 'The motif of tears: Representations of activism and suffering in the Liji Alley Museum in Nanjing', *Women's History Review*, pp. 1–19.

Cameron, D.F. (1971) 'The museum, a temple or the forum', *Curator: The Museum Journal*, 14(1), pp. 11–24.

Cameron, F. (2021) *The future of digital data, heritage and curation: In a more-than-human world*. London; New York: Routledge.

Cameron, F. and Neilson, B. (eds.) (2015) *Climate change and museum futures*. New York: Routledge.

Cameron, F. Hodge, B. and Salazar, J.F. (2013) 'Representing climate change in museum spaces and places.' *Wiley Interdisciplinary Reviews: Climate Change*, 4(1), pp. 9–21.

Chipangura, N. and Marufu, H. (2019) 'Museums as public forums for 21st century societies: A perspective from the National Museums and Monuments of Zimbabwe' in Janes, R.R. and Sandell, R. (eds.) *Museum activism*. Oxon; New York: Routledge.

Damala, A., Cubaud, P., Bationo, A., Houlier, P. and Marchal, I. (2008) 'Bridging the gap between the digital and the physical: Design and evaluation of a mobile augmented reality guide for the museum visit' in *Proceedings of the 3rd International Conference on Digital Interactive Media in Entertainment and Arts, DIMEA '08*. New York: ACM, pp. 120–127. https://doi.org/10.1145/1413634.1413660

Dawson, A. (2015) 'Putting a human face on climate change' in Cameron, F. and Neilson, B. (eds.) *Climate change and museum futures*. New York: Routledge.

Decker, J. (2020) 'Climate of change', *Museum Management and Curatorship*, 35(6), pp. 636–652. Available at: https://doi.org/10.1080/09647775.2020.1836999

Dinesh, N. (2016) *Memos from a theatre lab: Exploring what immersive theatre 'does'*. New York; Oxon: Routledge.

Fraser, J. (2019) 'A discomforting definition of museum', *Curator: The Museum Journal*, 62(4), pp. 501–504. Available at: https://doi.org/10.1111/cura.12345

Fraser, J., Coleman, L.S. and Bennett, B. (2020) 'Neutrality is not an option, museums don't need left-over statues', *Curator: The Museum Journal*, 63(3), pp. 295–298.

Gao, Z. and Braud, T. (2023) 'VR-driven museum opportunities: Digitized archives in the age of the metaverse', *Artnodes Journal*, 32. UOC.

Ghouaiel, N., Cieutat, J.-M., Jessel, J.-P. and Garbaya, S. (2017) *Mobile augmented reality in museums: Towards enhancing visitor's learning experience*.

Gröppel-Wegener, A. and Kidd, J. (2019) *Critical encounters with immersive storytelling*. London; New York: Routledge.

Hooper-Greenhill, E. (ed.) (2006) *Museum, media, message*. London: Routledge.

Huws, S., John, A. and Kidd, J. (2019) 'Traces – Olion: Creating a bilingual "subtlemob" for National Museum, Wales' in Lewi, H., Smith, W., Lehn, D. vom and Cooke, S. (eds.) *The Routledge international handbook of new digital practices in galleries, libraries, archives, museums and heritage sites*. London; New York: Routledge.

Janes, R.R. (2009) Museums in a troubled world: renewal, irrelevance or collapse? London ; New York: Routledge (Museum meanings).

Janes, R.R. (2020) 'Museums in perilous times', *Museum Management and Curatorship*, 35(6), pp. 587–598.

Janes, R.R. (2022) 'The value of museums in averting societal collapse', *Curator: The Museum Journal*, 65(4), pp. 729–745.

Janes, R.R. and Grattan, N. (2019) 'Museums confront the climate challenge', *Curator: The Museum Journal*, 62(2), pp. 97–103.

Janes, R.R. and Sandell, R. (2019) *Museum activism*. London; New York: Routledge.

Jones, R., Hussain, N. and Spiewak, M. (2020) 'The critical role research and evaluation assume in the post-truth era of climate change', *Journal of Museum Education*, 45(1), pp. 64–73.

Kenderdine, S. (2016) 'Embodiment, entanglement, and immersion in digital cultural heritage', in Schreibman, S., Unsworth, J. and Siemens, R. (eds.) *A new companion to digital humanities*. John Wiley & Sons, pp. 22–41.

Kenderdine, S., Chan, L.K.Y. and Shaw, J. (2014) 'Pure land: Futures for embodied museography', *Journal on Computing and Cultural Heritage (JOCCH)*, 7, p. 8.

Keogh, L. and Möllers, N. (2015) 'Pushing boundaries curating the Anthropocene at the Deutsches Museum, Munich' in Cameron, F. and Neilson, B. (eds.) *Climate change and museum futures*. New York: Routledge.

Kidd, J. and Nieto McAvoy, E. (2019) *Immersive experiences in museums, galleries and heritage sites: A review of research findings and issues*. Project Report [Online]. Creative Industries' Policy and Evidence Centre (PEC).

Kidd, J. (2019) 'With new eyes I see: Embodiment, empathy and silence in digital heritage interpretation', *International Journal of Heritage Studies*, 25, pp. 54–66.

Kidd, J. (2018) '"Immersive" heritage encounters', *The Museum Review*, 3(1).

Lehmannová, M. (2020) 224 Years of Defining the Museum. ICOM Czech Republic. Available at: https://icom.museum/wp-content/uploads/2020/12/2020_ICOM-Czech-Republic_224-years-of-defining-the-museum.pdf

Liu, P. and Lan, L. (2021) 'Museum as multisensorial site: Story co-making and the affective interrelationship between museum visitors, heritage space, and digital storytelling', *Museum Management and Curatorship*, 36(4), pp. 403–426.

Lorenc, M. (2020) 'Political undertone of the new ICOM Museum definition, or Maneuveringa transatlantic among icebergs', *Muzealnictwo*, 61, pp. 164–171.

Lu, F. (2021) *At the Ethnological Museum of Berlin, the climate change discussion is getting an AR boost.* https://jingculturecrypto.com/muze-x-cristina-navarro-swellar/

Lyons, S. and Bosworth, K. (2019) 'Museums in the Climate Emergency' in Janes, R.R. and Sandell, R. (eds.) *Museum activism*. Oxon; New York: Routledge.

Macalister, T. (2015) 'Shell sought to influence direction of Science Museum climate programme', *The Guardian*, 31 May. Available at: https://www.theguardian.com/business/2015/may/31/shell-sought-influence-direction-science-museum-climate-programme, accessed 1 March 2023.

Machon, J. (2013) *Immersive theatres: Intimacy and immediacy in contemporary performance.* Hampshire; New York: Palgrave Macmillan.

Mandelli, E. (2021) *The museum as a cinematic space: The display of moving images in exhibitions* (Edinburgh studies in film and intermediality). Edinburgh: Edinburgh University Press.

May, S., et al. (2022) 'Measurement of science museum visitors' emotional experiences at exhibits designed to encourage productive struggle', *Curator: The Museum Journal*, 65(1), pp. 161–185.

Newell, J. (2020) 'Climate museums: Powering action', *Museum Management and Curatorship*, 35(6), pp. 599–617.

Newell, J., Robin, L. and Wehner, K. (eds.) (2017) *Curating the future: Museums, communities and climate change*. London; New York: Routledge.

Oren, G., Shani, A. and Poria, Y. (2021) 'Dialectical emotions in a dark heritage site: A study at the Auschwitz Death Camp', *Tourism Management*, 82, p. 104194.

Parratt, S. (2014) 'Public media and climate change: Ethical standards and codes in the BBC treatment of environmental information', *Interactions*, 5(1), pp. 127–140.

Poole, S. (2018) 'Ghosts in the Garden: Locative gameplay and historical interpretation from below', *International Journal of Heritage Studies*, 24, pp. 300–314.

Priday, G., Mansfield, T. and Ramos, J. (2015) 'Tools for Alternative Temporalities' in Cameron, F. and Neilson, B. (eds.) *Climate change and museum futures*. New York: Routledge.

Pujol Tost, L. and Economou, M. (2007) Exploring the suitability of virtual reality interactivity for exhibitions through an integrated evaluation: the case of the Ename Museum. Museology, 4, pp. 81-97.

Salazar, J.F. (2015) 'Futuring global change in science museums and centers: A role for anticipatory practices and imaginative acts' in Cameron, F. and Neilson, B. (eds.) *Climate change and museum futures*. New York: Routledge.

Salazar, G., et al. (2022) 'Testing the influence of visual framing on engagement and pro-environmental action', *Conservation Science and Practice*, 4(10).

Sandell, R. (2002) *Museums, society, inequality*. London: Routledge.

Silver, H. (2022) *The Design Museum and Snap bring extreme climate change to London.* https://www.wallpaper.com/architecture/design-museum-snap-filter

Shin, D., & Biocca, F. (2018). Exploring immersive experience in journalism. New Media & Society, 20(8), 2800-2823. https://doi.org/10.1177/1461444817733133

Sumartojo, S., and Graves, M. (2021) 'Feeling through the screen: Memory sites, affective entanglements, and digital materialities', *Social & Cultural Geography*, 22(2), pp. 231–249.

Sutton, S. (2020) 'The evolving responsibility of museum work in the time of climate change', *Museum Management and Curatorship*, 35(6), pp. 618–635.

Sweeney, S.K., Newbill, P., Ogle, T. and Terry, K. (2018) 'Using augmented reality and virtual environments in historic places to scaffold historical empathy', *TechTrends*, 62(1), pp. 114–118.

Ünsal, D. (2019) 'Positioning museums politically for social justice', *Museum Management and Curatorship*, 34(6), pp. 595–607.

Vergo, P (ed.) (1989) *The new museology*. Reaktion.

Vlachou, M. (2019) 'Dividing issues and mission-driven activism' in Janes, R.R. and Sandell, R. (eds.) *Museum activism*. Oxon; New York: Routledge.

Warren, J. (2017) *Creating worlds: How to make immersive theatre*. London: Nick Hern Books.

Watts, J. (2015) *Museum of tomorrow: A captivating invitation to imagine a sustainable world*. https://www.theguardian.com/world/2015/dec/17/museum-of-tomorrow-rio-de-janeiro-brazil-sustainability, accessed 14 September 2023.

Weil, S.E. (1999) 'From being about something to being for somebody: The ongoing transformation of the American museum', *Daedalus*, 128(3), pp. 229–258.

Yoon, S.A., Elinich, K., Wang, J. and Van Schooneveld, J.G. (2012) 'Augmented reality in the science museum: Lessons learned in scaffolding for conceptual and cognitive learning' in *Presented at the IADIS International Conference on Cognition and Exploratory Learning in Digital Age*. IADIS, pp. 205–212.

Section VI:

Education and Training: Pedagogies for a Sustainable World

·16·

COMMUNICATING SUSTAINABILITY: SCIENCE LITERACY AND TRANSFORMATIVE PEDAGOGIES

Ron Johnston

Behaviour is what you do, culture is how you've learned to do it.

Shane Gero (2020)

The ecological equilibrium of the world's ecosystems has changed radically over that period of time now thought of as the Anthropocene epoch (Crutzen and Steffen, 2003), accelerating in recent centuries due to industrialised resource exploitation, human population densities beyond earth system carrying capacities, and unsustainable consumer lifestyles. Existing paradigms of formal education prioritise accreditation for achievement in disciplines deemed most useful to a globalised industrial society and tend towards perpetuation of an ecologically decontextualised approach to education built around competitive individualism. They are thus, ill-equipped to inform critical evaluation and collective resolution of the 'wicked' problems indicative of the socio-ecological crises which the world and humanity is under pressure from (Termeer et al., 2019; Sediri et al., 2020). Aptly termed 'wicked', due to their multiplicity and Gordian entanglement – where every wicked problem becomes the symptom or cause of another – they challenge our ability to phrase them accurately or address them effectively within a largely reductionist educational system and society which communicates complex socio-ecological systems through single issue and single discipline lenses – the way that we have mostly been trained to do.

This chapter addresses communication in a world-in-crisis by critically considering the socio-ecological legacy of past educational pedagogies and their continuing value, as well as deficiencies, for the development of transformative pedagogies focussed on transition towards a more ecologically aware and sustainability-orientated local and global society. It argues that the complexities arising from the interconnected and multivariate nature of current socio-ecological crises requires an ethically orientated, multidisciplinary approach to the challenges they represent. The chapter differentiates between transformative and transmissive educational practice (Biesta and Miedema, 2002; Luitel and Dahal, 2020) and evaluates the pedagogical influences of each on current models of sustainability education and learning. Socio-scientific issues (being those issues with a basis in applied science and exerting inordinately significant impact on society) are noted as significant contributors to current socio-ecological crises. Consequently, and for reasons made clear later in this chapter, science literacy is emphasised as an essential cross-curricular component of transformative pedagogies to enable informed participation in policy and decision-making processes.

Education as we have known it

What is education for? is not a new question and is commonly answered by asserting its benefits to the individual and society through the transmission of knowledge, skills, and values regarded as intrinsically good for all (Resnick, 1987) – or not, as Orr opines (Orr, 2004). But the question gains new traction and increased urgency in the midst of the self-harm and planetary despoilment that these attributes have contributed to. Content and pedagogical approaches in formal education are determined according to the goals of the providers invariably, conforming to state or internationally determined-benchmarks (Matusov, 2021). Collective cultural perspectives and personal values owe much to the pedagogical goals and associated values which determine these benchmarks. Giorgetti et al. (2017), characterise the relationship between education and culture as a 'chicken and egg' conundrum. Regardless of precedence, the dynamic interplay between these fundamental elements of societal development exerts a powerful influence on our perceptions of the natural world, our place in it and how we value it. In this respect, the pedagogical goals of formal education are perhaps the most influential communicators of behavioural memes forming the building blocks of our collective cultural values. Although undeniably effective in progressing human well-being and welfare in a material sense (albeit unevenly), these same influences have largely failed as harbingers or retainers of ecological wisdom and have contributed greatly to the degradation of the world's ecosystems and associated social impacts.

The global standardisation of content and uniformity of aspirations transmitted through formal education that has taken root over the past ~300 years has produced an anthropocentric view of the world's ecosystems – to their detriment – according them a principally utilitarian value as resources that directly or indirectly provide benefit for humans. Defined in this way the ecosystem is valued as a producer of commodities ('on occasion', managed sustainably), to produce more commodities. Taken in concert these reservations provide a telling reflection of the cultural values that dictate our perceptions of the natural world and our role in it. It follows that, reorientation (transformation) of pedagogical practice to enable informed engagement with current social-ecological issues must necessarily guard against perpetuating those same cultural values that have led us to sleepwalk to where we are today. Gero's proposition, '*Behaviour is what you do, culture is how you've learned to do it*' is deserving of further reflection if our dysfunctional interactions with the natural world (i.e. our collective behaviour) are attributable to our cultural mindset.

Perceptions of sustainability: A confused and confusing panacea

In the mid-twentieth century, sustainability, climate change, and ecosystem collapse featured largely as conversation pieces without urgency or, as the inspiration for apocalyptic stories or quirky sit-coms (e.g. *The Good Life* (BBC, 1975)). A myopic anthropocentric view of the natural world as a suite of resources and services for human benefit has led to planet-wide ecological dislocations which can justifiably be termed existential. Growing steadily in urgency since the closing decades of the last century, we are probably the first generations of a globally complex and technology-dependent culture, compelled to recognise sustainability as an essential survival skill for ourselves and the global ecosystems that support all life on the planet. More than a survival skill, it has become a major mitigating policy concept and a widely accepted panacea for the planet's ecological crises that press on our collective consciousness and consciences. Closely allied with formal education and extensively promoted through global agencies such as UNESCO and the UN, sustainability is never far from public, corporate, and political discourse. In our estranged (deranged?) relationship with the natural world sustainability issues loom large – and yet:

> sustainability remains an elusive concept... hard to define, but many of us believe we 'know it when we see it.' . . ... it means different things to different people. How can we hope to achieve a shared vision when we're not certain what vision we are sharing? (White, 2013, pp. 213–217)

Engelman (2014) is less charitable referring to 'sustainababble' and noting that

> [the word] 'sustainable' has become synonymous with, 'the equally vague and unquantifiable adjective "green," suggesting some undefined environmental variable.' (Engelman, 2014, pp. 3–5)

Easily hijacked by the marketplace, sustainability has been adopted as a hook for politicians and marketing managers to hang their credentials on at the expense of an already perplexed and concerned public. It has become good commercial policy to talk about sustainable business and the greening of the prevailing economic model without ever once questioning the model itself.

In this era of widespread cyber-connectivity, the potential for communicating the complexity of the ecological crises confronting us, has never before been so well facilitated. Similarly, and unsurprisingly perhaps, amidst the storm of data and opinion that this generates, disparate perceptions of sustainability proliferate and prompt a range of reactions, from anxiety, through uncertainty to (even worse), a dazed indifference which magnifies the gap between individual aspiration and collective action. The Anthropocene epoch defines our presence on the planet as a dominant force of change which sometimes speaks to our delusionary and illusionary sense of permanence as Gods walking the Earth and at other times haunts us with the guilt of the dystopian futures that may arise from our actions. It seems we are in great haste to get through this and pass into the calmer waters of future epochs of human existence such as the *Symbiocene* (Albrecht and Van Horn, 2016) or *Sustainocene* (Faunce, 2012; Furnass, 2016). Both posit a world returned to a sustainable socio-ecological balance informed by education, ecology, and ethics. Jeremy Davies in *The Birth of the Anthropocene* referring to such aspirations for the future, drily observes that 'this futurology lacks any grounding in a systematic theory of social change' (Davies, 2016, pp. 194–198). This assessment is perhaps unfair, at least in one-dimension, in view of the growing openness to embrace societal transition towards sustainability and the key role that education has to play as one such driver of systemic social change.

The critiques offered above are not intended to diminish societal change towards sustainability as a response to a world-in-crisis. Rather, their intent is to underscore the confusion that exists in communicating multiple, often contradictory perspectives and responses to the global eco-crises which are inseparably linked to unsustainable lifestyles and practices. Thus, communicating sustainability as a response to a world-in-crisis is complicated by the absence of a unified understanding of the relationship between sustainability and sustainable development.

Sustainability education or education for sustainable development

Sustainability and sustainable development have their common origins as major policy concepts arising from the World Commission on Environment and Development detailed in *Our Common Future* (UN WCED, 1987). Both are deeply embedded in current educational practice, as we will see in the following sections. However, the socio-economic rationale underpinning sustainable development warrants caution and careful scrutiny before adopting it as an underpinning principle for transformative sustainability education. Failure to do this, risks perpetuating the current environmentally exploitative 'growth through development' model of neoliberal global capitalism which underpins the sustainable development paradigm and challenges long-term ecological and societal sustainability at a fundamental level (Moore, 2017).

The contradictions inherent in the concept of 'sustainable development' and its socio-economic rationale extend beyond semantics and have been a focus of continuing concern and deliberation since its inception (Jickling, 1992; Kuhlman and Farrington, 2010; Purvis et al., 2019) as has its credibility as an underpinning principle of sustainability education (Jickling et al., 2008; Huckle and Wals, 2015). The oxymoronic properties of the concept are evident in its policy of 'economic growth through development' in pursuit of the maximisation of human welfare (UNESCO, 2014) and begs the questions, *What is being sustained? Economic sustainability or environmental sustainability?* and, *Can either be progressed without impacting the other!* To be clear, the objection here is not the pursuit of human welfare, it is the method of achieving it that presents as an issue (Kopnina, 2016; Eisenmenger et al., 2020). In the absence of an economic model of its own, sustainable development is reliant on the current 'economic growth through development' paradigm of Capitalocene economics (Moore, 2017). At best this is mitigated by the presumption of a notional 'steady state economic model' (Blauwhof, 2012): barely credible for a planet with finite resources and a human population of ~8 bn + 1 per cent per year (Worldometer, 2003) which already strains the resources required to maintain itself equitably and sustainably (Rees, 2023a).

Population overshoot as a moderator of sustainable development

It has been argued that concern about population increase is not an issue of global scarcity of resources rather, it is one of inequitable distribution (Elisha, 2021). However, this has been vigorously opposed on grounds of it having scant regard for the reality of the ecological limits to growth (Bardi, 2011, pp. 11–21; Smil, 2019; Rees, 2023b). Regardless of our questionable ability to distribute available resources equitably, unguarded population growth must inevitably impact any economic model focussed on sustainability. The issue is not solely the geo-availability of resources, it also concerns the regenerative capacity of global ecosystems to sustain the development required to support such population numbers while impacted by the ecological pressures that inevitably accompany population growth (Bardi, 2011, pp. 196–201; Rees, 2023a). The issue of population growth as a factor of sustainability is rarely, and even then reluctantly, discussed for fear of impinging on human reproductive rights. When pressed, the issues are invariably steered towards the inequitable consumption patterns between the developed and developing regions of the world. Kopina and Washington query this reluctance and validly question the wisdom of excluding population growth as a factor of sustainability in *Discussing why population growth is still ignored or denied*, (Kopnina and Washington, 2016).

With these several factors in mind, for many, sustainable development is conceptually flawed and tacitly condones the greening of a marketplace model of the past (Kuhlman and Farrington, 2010; Hickel, 2019; Bendell, 2022), predicated on human exceptionalism and environmental exploitation (Srinivasan and Kasturirangan, 2016). Consequently, the inconsistencies of the sustainable development socio-economic rationale calls into question its credibility and warrants reconsideration of it as a driver of transformational sustainability education.

Transformational sustainability education

Although not specifically referred to as such, sustainability has been in the social consciousness for over a century (and perhaps long before) as a response to increasing awareness of the anthropogenic origin of multiple environmental impacts which have grown into the global socio-ecological crises we currently suffer from. All sustainability education can be deemed to be transformative in the shared aim of nurturing behaviour change towards more sustainability-aware lifestyles and societies – either explicitly as in Education for Sustainable Development, or implicitly as in the case of Conservation Education and Environmental Education. However, priorities and practices vary, and these are now considered.

Sustainability education: A chronology of change

To clear the field of ambiguity, the term *sustainability education* is commonly used generically to denote Environmental Education, Education for Sustainability, or Education for Sustainable Development but, this fails to recognise their divergent pedagogical goals as they have independently kept pace with the growing complexity of our socio-ecological crises over half a century and more.

Although Table 16.1 may suggest a serial replacement of one for another, this is not the case. Rather, it represents a conflation of their key attributes over time whilst retaining their independent identities within a broader pedagogical landscape. Of no less importance for communicating socio-ecological and sustainability issues is a fundamental science literacy and this is also considered below as an example of a synthesis of transformative praxis and practice and a vital component of Sustainability Education.

Conservation education

Much has changed since the early decades of the twentieth century when conservation education formed the foundations of what we recognise today as 'sustainability education'. At this time, the central principle of conservation education was appreciation of natural habitats for their intrinsic value and eco-spiritual qualities, reflected in the popular romanticism of the time and the preceding century (Tocqueville, 1844; Thoreau, 1854; Johnston, 2002).

Table 16.1. Sustainability Education 1920s–2020s

Conservation Education (CE) (1920s–)
Environmental Education (EE) (1970s–)
Education for Sustainable Development (ESD) (1987–)
Transformative Integrated Curricula the future

With increased awareness of the vulnerability of ecosystems to human impacts and the extent to which the natural environment is now valued and utilised for its material wealth, the goals of conservation education have become those of mitigation of the impacts of resource exploitation and ensuring the long-term survival of habitats and species. Underpinned by a solid foundation in the natural sciences, pedagogically it has now been drawn into the wider remit of environmental education.

Environmental education

Environmental Education (UNEP, 1978) aimed to raise learners' environmental awareness, with the assumption that increased knowledge of the socio-ecological relationship between humans and nature would engender more responsible and protective attitudes towards the natural environment. As a prescient forerunner to transformative integrated curricula, (which have not happened yet!), contemporary environmental education is informed by two (amongst several) important aims. These highlight its effectiveness in communicating our world-in-crisis through learner/teacher interaction, (1) to enhance learner-centred problem-solving and decision-making skills through critical thinking and issue-centric discourse, and (2) a focus on skills to address current environmental problems while preventing the occurrence of new ones (Carter and Simmons, 2010). Environmental Education has now been proposed as a required element in all school curricula by 2025 (UNESCO, 2021), and it already has a presence in many informal adult learning and corporate education programmes (Chaplin-Kramer et al., 2019). In common with Conservation Education the growing complexity of biophysical environmental issues has brought about an increased prominence of applied environmental and ecological sciences in its practice. From a pedagogical standpoint, this is a double-edged sword in that it provides a sound evidential basis for practice but also carries with it the capacity to exclude those learners without prior scientific expertise.

Education for sustainable development (ESD)

Conceptually, sustainability and sustainable development have been seminal in communicating awareness of the anthropogenically driven decline of the planet's natural systems and informing education policy through the agency of Education for Sustainable Development (ESD). By definition, ESD mirrors the sustainable development goals (SDGs) within its pedagogical praxis and has become internationally influential through its practice of embedding sustainable development values and goals in syllabuses and learning programmes across all levels of formal education (MGIEP UNESCO, 2017; Johnston, 2018, 2019). Significant reservations about the credibility of sustainable development as a guiding principle for transformative sustainability education have already been expressed but these should not be the sole defining factor of ESD, and as we will see, other attributes of ESD such as embedding practices can make important contributions to the continuing evolution of transformative sustainability education.

The emergence of ESD environment marked another notable departure from earlier approaches to sustainability education by conflating environmental and social issues. Whereas environmental education has necessarily engaged with socio-scientific issues in the context of environmental protection, education for sustainable development has conflated environmental concerns within a comprehensive embrace of social and civic issues 'which may or may not be related to environment' (Kopnina, 2012). Environmental education *for sustainability* within ESD's remit differs from environmental education *per se*, the former giving greater attention to resource orientated, socio-economic factors of sustainability. This signals a shift in ESD's focus from environmental concerns towards a greater emphasis on social and civic issues (Fredriksson et al., 2020). From this author's perspective, this dilution of environmental and ecological issues as 'front-line indicators' of today's world-in-crisis is of some concern, as is the biased fragmentation of different pedagogic approaches 'where the environment has been reduced to its minimum form of expression' (Gonzalez-Gaudiano, 2014, pp. 49–51).

Science literacy and science education

Communicating sustainability to a largely ecologically and scientifically distanced humanity is increasingly voiced in terms of the natural sciences. It has already been noted how the growing complexity and interconnectivity of global environmental crises, has caused sustainability education to become more materially analytical, with a greater prominence of the environmental and ecological sciences in their practice (Carter and Simmons, 2010). While this allows access to other dimensions of enquiry and the development of skills to address complex practical issues, it carries an assumption of scientific and science literacy (Valladares, 2021). Aligned with this is the potential to exclude and disadvantage those learners, facilitators and lay public who have no prior experience in the natural sciences. In consequence of the noted prominence of the natural sciences for communicating sustainability, it is clear that science literacy and science education has an indispensable contribution to make to address this problem. This major contribution to transformative sustainability education is now discussed further.

Science literacy

The flood of specialist data that communicate the complexity of the 'wicked' problems associated with socio-scientific issues (being those issues that encompass social dilemmas with conceptual or technological links to science (SISs)) has caused lay engagement with them to become 'expert led'. Babel-like for the non-specialist, the language of sustainability and crisis is interwoven with the grim metrics of the natural sciences as the major currency for communicating a steady decline in the resilience of global ecosystems and social structures dependent on them. This has the potential for alienating those learners whose strengths and affinities lie in other disciplines and emphasises the importance of contextual cross – curricular provision of fundamental science concepts and science literacy to enable full engagement with science-related issues in society (Colucci-Gray et al., 2006; Ben-Horin et al., 2023).

Science education

Science-informed technologies, applied to industrialised resource exploitation in all domains of the natural world have generated many negative socio-scientific issues impacting the sustainability of ecosystems at a fundamental level and extending into all aspects of human life, impacting present and future generations (Zeidler et al., 2019). Science-led technology has contributed greatly to human welfare, but reservations about its past and future complicity with unsustainable practices are justified, signalling the need for informed deliberation over its role in pursuit of transition towards a more sustainability-orientated future. This requires a fundamental science literacy and basic knowledge of its relationship with society to allow for informed evaluation of the issues (Fortus et al., 2022).

While acknowledging that there are important socio-economic issues that must be resolved to bring about a less exploitative interaction with the natural world, it is a reassuring optimism to posit that science-led technological solutions need not be antithetical to an ecocentric engagement with the socio-ecological urgencies of today's world-in-crisis. But this assumes a different kind of science that recognises that technology is not solely a product of scientific knowledge. Echoing Gero's quote at the top of the chapter, science and its application are also an expression of prevailing cultural beliefs that shape our interactions with nature and this awareness represents a changed function for science and a correspondingly transformative approach to science education is called for.

Enquiry into SSIs using informal reasoning (Sadler, 2004) to explore their resolution and social relevance signals a pedagogical change from a transmissive vision of passively received decontextualised knowledge to, a multidisciplinary transformative one. One where learners, informed by growing subject knowledge, are active participants in critical evaluation of the issues in the context of their own experiences and perceptions of the world (Valladares, 2021; Ben-Horin et al., 2023). Such a strategy when combined with issue-centric, problem-based learning, invites consideration of the ethical and moral dimensions of science in society, while concurrently it develops a functional science literacy (Johnston, 2011; Zeidler et al., 2019).

Transformative sustainability education for a world-in-crisis: Praxis and practice

Societal transition towards sustainability has been widely recognised as an increasingly urgent future vison for society and transformational sustainability education is widely considered the means for its realisation (Leal Filho et al., 2018; Salomaa and Juhola, 2020). Beyond academic discourse, transformation is a term which conjures visions of epiphany, which indeed may be a desirable outcome of transformative sustainability education. However, conceptually, 'transformation' and 'transition' have moved from being exotic proposals to having considerable leverage in education policy as drivers of a reorientation of pedagogical direction towards the causes and consequences of today's global crises with transformative sustainability education as a core concept (Wright et al., 2015; Sediri et al., 2020). To be clear, transformative sustainability education does not supplant the provision of subject knowledge essential for the functioning of society since, it has no subject knowledge of its own to impart. Rather, it is an integrated praxis which aims to foster attitudinal and behavioural change through critical thinking, and ethical engagement with issues supported by a multidisciplinary perspective with sustainability as a core value. It reaches beyond conventional cognitive learning practice and aligns with affective and constructivist approaches (Hein, 1991; Fortus et al., 2022) engaging learners' social and emotional skills alongside conventional transmissive teaching practice.

Praxis in practice

It is useful to compare conventional and transformative teaching practice to identify those features most conducive to independent learning and contextualisation of the global socio-ecological urgencies facing us.

Teaching is normally the most recognisable feature of education, and this certainly may be true in transmissive and didactic pedagogies. However, it is proposed here that the role of the learner deserves greater emphasis in transformative practice. Conventional practice favours the transmission and acquisition of pre-selected knowledge associated with the predetermined goals of the provider as we have heard. In comparison, transformational practice while making the same knowledge accessible, attributes greater emphasis to an exchange of meaning and discussion between learners' peer groups and teachers made relevant by personal contexts and common experiences (Biesta and Miedema, 2002). This dialogical approach becomes one of a co-interpretation of knowledge and engenders collaborative deliberation for determining its import and application beyond the pedagogical environment, *sensu* in society. Critical pedagogy undertaken through such reflexivity is instrumental in enhancing learners' abilities to deal with and appreciate the ethical as well as the applied dimensions of complex socio-ecological issues. Matusov (2021) notes that learning only becomes educational when the learner appreciates what they have learned. This is an insightful constructivist perspective from which to appreciate the essence of transformative pedagogical practice, which enables the 'making of meaning' from acquired knowledge, made relevant to learners through personal context and their experiences. These approaches speak to the whole person (learner), prompting transformative emancipatory change in how learners interpret their interactions with the world, which cascade into societal consciousness through the agency of learners' autonomously transformed perspectives (Mezirow, 1997; Wessels, 2022).

Curriculum reform

Up to this point, our discourse has centred on teaching and learning. Earlier we encountered the constraints imposed by assessment-orientated curricula on a series of early transformational pedagogical initiatives. Examples of whole-curricular reform according to equal value to embedded sustainability education are rare (Leal Filho et al., 2018).

This closing section now turns to this important aspect of transformational educational reform, addressing the constraints that exist at an institutional level. These arise from the narrowly defined pedagogical goals of most contemporary curricula, principally expressed through assessment criteria, and learning outcomes. Achievement of these is entirely dependent on the provider's sense of what a good education is for. Most contemporary curricula are instrumental in their aim of coaching learners towards a specific outcome with a focus on personal progression and but as we have seen this is not necessarily education but training and instruction. Even when sustainability education is embedded in learning outcomes, most curricula employ 'education *for* sustainability' or 'education *about* sustainability' to enhance subject-specific learning but they do not contribute to assessment and thus, become subordinated commitments for teachers and learners alike. In view of the clear evidence of increasing global ecological decline and associated social impacts, this is not a compromise that curriculum designers, teachers, or learners should have to make. Consequently, there is a compelling argument for transformative curriculum reform to ensure and underpin parity between subject-specific academic values and socio-ecological values whilst maintaining the integrity of subject-specific knowledge (Johnston, 2022). This moves us away from a solely transmissive instructional pedagogical model towards a pedagogy of meaning and contextualisation of subject knowledge as discussed earlier.

Embedding transformative and affective praxes into fully integrated curricula with a focus on sustainability, expands opportunities for multidisciplinary shared consideration of the causes and consequences of today's world-in-crisis. Linkages between social, ecological, and technological systems with financial, political and governance systems, embedded within subject knowledge become equally important and expose learners to potentially transformative experiences. Recognising how these systems intersect through the agency of fully integrated curricula, defined by common praxes such as we have encountered earlier, creates opportunities for informed, individual and system level transformation beyond formal education. As the urgencies of today's global crises loom larger on the horizon there is a growing acceptance of the necessity for such curricular reform to facilitate communication of today's world-in-crisis with sustainability education as a core value (Wright et al., 2015)

Closing considerations

For the best part of a century, science and technology have been turned to for 'fixes' to mitigate the impacts of a world in the throes of multiple socio-ecological crises. But it is the concept of transformative sustainability that has come to the fore as a redemptive philosophy and practice, for ourselves and future generations – and education has become its advocate, reincarnated as 'sustainability education'.

This chapter has drawn upon a broad range of educational and conceptual approaches to communicating sustainability as a response to a world-in-crisis for current generations and those of the future. We have seen that education has been a major player in moulding our collective perceptions of our place in the natural world and has the potential to do so in necessarily transformative ways in the future. Past pedagogical goals that have endorsed a cultural mind-set justifying the ruthless and reckless despoilment of the planet's ecosystems in materialist pursuit of human well-being and progress, are now an historical anachronism and long past their ecological sell-by-date. Even so, they retain a significant legacy footprint in current pedagogical praxes that is hard to root out. Against a background of the socio-ecological urgencies of today's world-in-crisis, they lack the necessary foresight, ecological awareness, and political independence to drive the transformative change necessary to address the challenges of current socio-ecological urgencies. Bourn (2021) holds that neo-liberalism still dominates much educational policymaking around the world. This seems no less true for Education for Sustainable Development, which I have noted as being (unwittingly) complicit in perpetuating (or, perhaps it has been debilitated by) a socio-economic rationale which is incompatible with long-term sustainability. It is tempting to dwell on the beautiful geometries of complex diagrams mapping socio-economic pathways to sustainability under the umbrella concept of sustainable development, but it remains a complicated problem currently without a solution to communicate sustainability to those who have nothing to sustain (Freire et al., 1994; Giroux, 2010). This gives rise to renewed urgency for the sustainable conservation and preservation of global resources as we necessarily remodel our global economic disposition to the benefit of all through the reduction of the gap between intent and action.

The several forms of transformative sustainability education reviewed across this chapter represent an evolution of different approaches over the past century, with the next seral stage culminating in a further conflation of their best attributes. I posit the clear potential for transformative sustainability education to trigger whole curriculum reform with sustainability and citizenship education brought together as dual guiding concepts at the core of a multidisciplinary pedagogical landscape. Transformational sustainability education has an indisputable role to play in communicating today's world-in-crisis. It can provide the contextualised interdisciplinary knowledge, affectivity, and emotional maturity to address the causes and consequences of today's world-in-crisis. It's future as an indispensable adjunct to academic content within integrated curricula is inevitable in the face of the wicked socio-ecological urgencies that we are currently facing and destined to confront some way into the future.

References

Albrecht, G. and Van Horn, G. (2016) *Exiting the Anthropocene and Entering the Symbiocene.* Center for Humans and Nature. Available at: https://humansandnature.org/exiting-the-anthropocene-and-entering-the-symbiocene/, accessed 26 September 2023.

Bardi, U. (2011) *The limits to growth revisited.* New York: Springer.

BBC. (1975) *The good life.* Available at: https://www.bbc.co.uk/comedy/goodlife/, accessed 23 January 2023.

Bendell, J. (2022) 'Replacing sustainable development: Potential frameworks for international cooperation in an era of increasing crises and disasters', *Sustainability*, 14, p. 8185.

Ben-Horin, H., Kali, Y. and Tal, T. (2023) 'The fifth dimension in socio-scientific reasoning: Promoting decision-making about socio-scientific issues in a community', *Sustainability (Switzerland)*, 15(12).

Biesta, G.J.J. and Miedema, S. (2002) 'Instruction or pedagogy? The need for a transformative conception of education', *Teaching and Teacher Education*, 18(2), pp. 173–181.

Blauwhof, F.B. (2012) 'Overcoming accumulation: Is a capitalist steady-state economy possible?', *Ecological Economics*, 84, pp. 254–261. https://doi.org/10.1016/J.ECOLECON.2012.03.012

Bourn, D. (2021) 'Pedagogy of hope: Global learning and the future of education', *International Journal of Development Education and Global Learning*, 13(2). https://doi.org/10.14324/IJDEGL.13.2.01

Carter, R.L. and Simmons, B. (2010) 'The history and philosophy of environmental education' in *The inclusion of environmental education in science teacher education.* Netherlands: Springer, pp. 3–16.

Chaplin-Kramer, R., et al. (2019) 'Global modelling of nature's contributions to people', *Science*, 366(6462), pp. 255–258.

Colucci-Gray, L., Camino, E. and Barbiero, G. (2006) 'From scientific literacy to sustainability literacy: An ecological framework for education', *Science Education*, 90(2), pp. 227–252.

Crutzen, P.J. and Steffen, W. (2003) 'How long have we been in the Anthropocene era?', *Climatic Change*, 61(3), pp. 251–257.

Davies, J. (2016) *The birth of the Anthropocene*. Berkeley: University of California Press.

Eisenmenger, N., et al. (2020) 'The sustainable development goals prioritize economic growth over sustainable resource use: A critical reflection on the SDGs from a socio-ecological perspective', *Sustainability Science*, 15(4), pp. 1101–1110.

Elisha, O. (2021) *Resources scarcity and sustainable economic growth*. Available at: https://www.researchgate.net/publication/350399332

Engelman, R. (2014) 'Beyond sustainable' in *State of the world 2013: Is sustainability still possible?* Washington, DC: Island Press-Center for Resource Economics, pp. 3–18. https://doi.org/10.5822/978-1-61091-458-1_1

Faunce, T. (2012) 'United Nations year of sustainable energy the United Nations general assembly has declared 2012 the international year of', *Procedia Engineering*, 49, pp. 348–356. Available at: www.sciencedirect.com, accessed 7 November 2023.

Fortus, D., Lin, J., Neumann, K. and Sadler, T.D. (2022) 'The role of affect in science literacy for all', *International Journal of Science Education*, 44(4), pp. 535–555. https://doi.org/10.1080/09500693.2022.2036384

Fredriksson, U., Kusanagi, K.N., Gougoulakis, P., Matsuda, Y. and Kitamura, Y. (2020) 'A comparative study of curriculums for Education for Sustainable Development (ESD) in Sweden and Japan', *Sustainability (Switzerland)*, 12(3). https://doi.org/10.3390/su12031123

Freire, P., Freire, A.M.A., Barr, R.R. and Giroux, H.A. (1994) *Pedagogy of hope: Reliving pedagogy of the oppressed* (online 2021). London: Bloomsbury. Available at: https://www.google.co.uk/books/edition/Pedagogy_of_Hope/fY0vEAAAQBAJ?hl=en&gbpv=1&dq=Pedagogy%20of%20hope%20%3A%20reliving%20pedagogy%20of%20the%20oppressed&pg=PP1&printsec=frontcover, accessed 31 October 2023.

Furnass, B. (2016) *The Sustainocene – interview with visionary, Dr. Bryan Furnass*. Available at: https://zerospinzone.blogspot.com/2016/01/the-sustainocene-interview-with-dr.html, accessed 30 May 2023.

Gero, S. (2020) *How do animals learn how to be, well, animals? Through a shared culture*. Available at: https://ideas.ted.com/how-do-animals-learn-how-to-be-well-animals-through-a-shared-culture/, accessed 10 January 2023.

Giorgetti, F.M., Campbell, C. and Arslan, A. (2017) 'Culture and education: Looking back to culture through education', *Paedagogica Historica*, 53(1–2), pp. 1–6.

Giroux, H.A. (2010) 'Rethinking education as the practice of freedom: Paulo Freire and the promise of critical pedagogy', *Policy Futures in Education*, 8(6), pp. 715–721.

Gonzalez-Gaudiano, E.J. (2014) 'Researching education and the environment' in Reid, A. and Scott, W. (eds.) *Theme 1 tensions and transitions*. Available at: https://www.researchgate.net/publication/267452278

Hein, G. (1991) 'Constructivist learning theory' in *International committee of museum educators*. Available at: http://www.exploratorium.edu/IFI/resources/constructivistlearning.html, accessed 16 November 2023.

Hickel, J. (2019) 'The contradiction of the sustainable development goals: Growth versus ecology on a finite planet', *Sustainable Development*, 27(5), pp. 873–884. Available at: https://onlinelibrary.wiley.com/doi/full/10.1002/sd.1947, accessed 16 November 2023.

Huckle, J. and Wals, A.E.J. (2015) 'The UN decade of education for sustainable development: Business as usual in the end', *Environmental Education Research*, 21(3), pp. 491–505.

Jickling, B. (1992) 'Viewpoint: Why I don't want my children to be educated for sustainable development', *Journal of Environmental Education*, 23(4), pp. 5–8.

Jickling, B., Wals, A. and Taylor, E. (2008) 'Globalization and environmental education: Looking beyond sustainable development', *Journal of Curriculum Studies*, 40(1), pp. 1–21.

Johnston, R. (2002) 'Wild Berwyn or Coy nature reserve: A changing landscape', *Canadian Journal of Environmental Education*, 7(2), pp. 166–178.

Johnston, R. (2011) 'Science education and education for citizenship and sustainable development', *Collected Essays on Learning and Teaching*, 4, p. 107. Available at: https://celt.uwindsor.ca/index.php/CELT/article/view/3281

Johnston, R. (2018) 'Achieving SDG 4.7: Embedding sustainability issues into subject-specific texts – a guide for textbook authors', *Research in Action (Special Issue August)*, pp. 51–60.

Johnston, R. (2022) *Achieving SDG 4.7 by matching sustainability learning outcomes to subject-specific curricula: A guide | THE Campus Learn, Share, Connect*. Available at: https://www.timeshighereducation.com/campus/achieving-sdg-47-matching-sustainability-learning-outcomes-subjectspecific-curricula-guide, accessed 13 December 2022.

Johnston, R.A.S. (2019) 'Embedding ESD into elementary stage textbooks: Lessons from a small Himalayan state' in Bamber, P. (ed.) *Research in action*. Liverpool Hope University, pp. 53–59.

Kopnina, H. (2012) 'Education for sustainable development (ESD): The turn away from "environment" in environmental education?', *Environmental Education Research*, 18(5), pp. 699–717. https://doi.org/10.1080/13504622.2012.658028

Kopnina, H. (2016) 'The victims of unsustainability: A challenge to sustainable development goals', *International Journal of Sustainable Development and World Ecology*, 23(2), pp. 113–121. Available at: https://researchportal.northumbria.ac.uk/en/publications/the-victims-of-unsustainability-a-challenge-to-sustainable-develo, accessed 16 December 2022.

Kopnina, H. and Washington, H. (2016) 'Discussing why population growth is still ignored or denied', *Chinese Journal of Population Resources and Environment*, 14(2), pp. 133–143.

Kuhlman, T. and Farrington, J. (2010) 'What is sustainability?' *Sustainability*, 2(11), pp. 3436–3448.

Leal Filho, W., et al. (2018) 'The role of transformation in learning and education for sustainability', *Journal of Cleaner Production*, 199, pp. 286–295. https://doi.org/10.1016/J.JCLEPRO.2018.07.017

Luitel, B.C. and Dahal, N. (2020) 'Conceptualising transformative praxis', *Journal of Transformative Praxis*, 1(1), pp. 1–8.

Matusov, E. (2021) 'The relationship between education and learning and its consequences for dialogic pedagogy', *Dialogic Pedagogy: An International Online Journal*, 9, pp. E1–E19. Available at: https://dpj.pitt.edu/ojs/dpj1/article/view/425/226, accessed 7 February 2023.

Mezirow, J. (1997) 'Mezirow-transformative-learning (1)', *New Directions in Adult Education*, 74, pp. 1–8.

MGIEP UNESCO (2017) *Our approach to embedding*. Available at: https://mgiep.unesco.org/article/unesco-mgiep-s-approach-to-embedding, accessed 15 September 2023.

Moore, J.W. (2017) 'The Capitalocene, Part I: On the nature and origins of our ecological crisis', *Journal of Peasant Studies*, 44(3), pp. 594–630.

Orr, D.W. (2004) *Earth in mind: On education, environment, and the human prospect*. 10th anniversary edn. Washington, DC: Island Press.

Purvis, B., Mao, Y. and Robinson, D. (2019) 'Three pillars of sustainability: In search of conceptual origins', *Sustainability Science*, 14, pp. 681–695.

Rees, W.E. (2023a) 'The human ecology of overshoot: Why a major "population correction" is inevitable', *World*, 4(3), pp. 509–527. https://doi.org/10.3390/world4030032

Rees, W.E. (2023b) 'The human eco-predicament: Overshoot and the population conundrum', *Vienna Yearbook of Population Research*, 21, pp. 1–19. https://doi.org/10.1553/p-eznb-ekgc

Resnick, L.B. (1987) *Education and learning to think*. Washington, DC: National Academy Press.

Sadler, T.D. (2004) 'Informal reasoning regarding socioscientific issues: A critical review of research', *Journal of Research in Science Teaching*, 41(5), pp. 513–536.

Salomaa, A. and Juhola, S. (2020) 'How to assess sustainability transformations: A review', *Global Sustainability*, 3. https://doi.org/10.1017/sus.2020.17

Sediri, S., Trommetter, M., Frascaria-Lacoste, N. and Fernandez-Manjarrés, J. (2020) 'Transformability as a wicked problem: A cautionary tale?', *Sustainability*, 12(15), p. 5895.

Smil, V. (2019) 'Vaclav Smil: "Growth must end. Our economist friends don't seem to realise that" | Science and nature books', *The Guardian*. Available at: https://www.theguardian.com/books/2019/sep/21/vaclav-smil-interview-growth-must-end-economists, accessed 26 October 2023.

Srinivasan, K. and Kasturirangan, R. (2016) 'Political ecology, development, and human exceptionalism', *Geoforum*, 75, pp. 125–128.

Termeer, C.J.A.M., Dewulf, A. and Biesbroek, R. (2019) 'A critical assessment of the wicked problem concept: Relevance and usefulness for policy science and practice', *Policy and Society*, 38(2), pp. 167–179.

Thoreau, H.D. (1854) *Walden or, life in the woods*. Boston, MA: Ticknor and Fields.

Tocqueville, A. de (1844) *Letters from America*, ed. Beaumont, G. de and Brown, F. New Haven: Yale University Press.

UN WCED. (1987) *Our common future*. Available at: https://www.are.admin.ch/are/en/home/media/publications/sustainable-development/brundtland-report.html, accessed 5 November 2023.

UNEP (1978/1977) *Final report, intergovernmental conference on environmental education*. Tbilisi (USSR).

UNESCO (2021) *UNESCO declares environmental education must be a core curriculum component by 2025*. Available at: https://www.unesco.org/en/articles/unesco-declares-environmental-education-must-be-core-curriculum-component-2025, accessed 2 October 2023.

UNESCO (2014) *UNESCO roadmap for implementing the Global Action Programme on Education for Sustainable Development*.

Valladares, L. (2021) 'Scientific literacy and social transformation: Critical perspectives about science participation and emancipation', *Science and Education*, 30(3), pp. 557–587.

Wessels, K. (2022) *Pedagogy of entanglement. A response to the complex societal challenges that permeate our lives*. Cham: Springer Nature.

White, M.A. (2013) 'Sustainability: I know it when I see it', *Ecological Economics*, 86, pp. 213–217. https://doi.org/10.1016/J.ECOLECON.2012.12.020

Worldometer (2003) *World population clock: 8.1 billion people (LIVE, 2023) – Worldometer.* Available at: https://www.worldometers.info/world-population/, accessed 26 October 2023.

Wright, M.F., Cain, K.D. and Monsour, F.A. (2015) 'A context for transformative curriculum development beyond sustainability: A context for transformative curriculum development', *Transformative Dialogues: Teaching & Learning Journal*, 8(2).

Zeidler, D.L., Herman, B.C. and Sadler, T.D. (2019) 'New directions in socioscientific issues research', *Disciplinary and Interdisciplinary Science Education Research*, 1(1), p. 11.

·17·

'ALL JOURNALISTS WILL BE ENVIRONMENTAL JOURNALISTS TOMORROW': ON PROBLEMS, PEDAGOGY AND PROSPECTS

Chris Paterson

The next generation of journalists will all be 'environmental journalists', for they will all tell daily stories of climate emergency. Ignorance or denial will no longer be an option, even for media outlets which have previously chosen this path. The global field of journalism education is only starting to embrace the challenge. Journalism's responsibility to readers is to report accurately, truthfully, and knowledgeably about the threat of climate change. This chapter explores issues in reporting climate change, such as how climate change science is communicated by media and how that communication process is explained to students. The ideas which follow were developed for a report commissioned by the World Journalism Education Council.[1] I approach this subject both as a journalism educator, reflecting on my own learning to teach students about the communication of climate change, and a researcher of climate change communication in the Global South, motivated by the plight of informants at the sharp edge of the climate emergency (in this case, people in rural parts of Ghana and Kenya who struggle daily to adapt to their fast-changing environment).

Communication Studies and the environment

Wide agreement that everyone, educators included, should be talking about climate change, has unfortunately been mirrored by widespread reluctance to do so. As climate journalist David Roberts explained in a Ted Talk a decade ago, thought leaders tend to avoid the topic. He paraphrases one such unnamed 'prominent pundit' as saying 'It seems really complicated, I don't feel like I have a good grasp on all the science and so I just don't feel qualified to go out and assert things publicly about it' (2012). Roberts adds that 'anytime you mention it (on social media) the hordes descend, bearing complicated stories about the mediaeval ice age, or sunspots, or water vapour . . . there's a lot of myths about climate change borne by these climate sceptics,[2] but to debunk those myths . . . you have to research to respond to them in detail', and people don't bother. His talk, like U.S. Vice President Al Gore's presentations a decade earlier, sought to demonstrate that the science is, in fact, straightforward and clear.

The task is also urgent and, for professional communicators like Roberts, surprisingly difficult, due to complex manufactured structures of obfuscation, confusion and denial. It is the mission of educators to, firstly, equip their students with the confidence to understand the parameters of the problem and speak confidently about it and, secondly, understand the nature of the communications challenge before them and develop strategies to address it. I focus here on the second challenge. (To address the first challenge, I point educators new to this field, or those with little background in physical sciences, to the useful *Communicating Climate Change: A Guide for Educators*, from Cornell University; Armstrong et al., 2018. This online, open access, guide offers an excellent orientation to climate science and the communications challenges that surround it.)

Just as global warming is best understood as a recent human-caused aberration in the almost inconceivably long timeline of the Earth's evolution, the portrayal of environmental crisis by mass media is best situated within the portrayal by literature, over two millennia, of a changing environment and the place of humans within it. There is good evidence of that tradition in Johns-Putra's *Climate and Literature* (2019), which assesses the history of climate and literature from the perspective of the environmental humanities.

While most discussion of climate change and the media focusses on the representation of the problem and the role journalists should play, there are wider dimensions of the interaction between media and the environment for us to consider. Two sets of authors led the way for an environmentally informed reappraisal of media and how we study it: Tammy Boyce and Justin Lewis, with *Climate Change and the Media* in 2009, and Richard Maxwell and Toby Miller, with their 2012 *Greening the Media*. These books set the stage for an intensifying research and policy focus on the environmental impact of the media and information industries and the world of 'e-waste', culminating recently with Brevin's *Is AI Good for the Planet?* (2022).

These authors ask communication educators to reflect on our contribution to one of the most environmentally destructive global industries, through our preparation of the next generation of media workers. It is the illusion of *immateriality* – the sense of an industry grounded in the production of messages, not objects – that diverts attention from 'responsibility for a vast proliferation of hardware, all with high levels of built-in obsolescence and decreasing levels of efficiency' (Boyce and Lewis, 2009, quoted in Maxwell and Miller, 2012, p. 5). Hackett and colleagues *Journalism and Climate Crisis* (2017) focussed on the challenges which climate change poses for international journalism; chapters there offer a good deal for students of climate journalism. Park (2021) recently expanded the media frame to address how advertising, along with digital infrastructure and journalism, exacerbates the climate emergency; he builds a necessary link between media reform and climate change.

And Keilbach and Pabi Orzeszyna in the online journal NECSUS have insightfully observed:

> Environmentally engaged media studies calls for a radical reorientation of our curriculum. This includes not only the discussion of films, television series, and games about climate change, ecology, or the future of the planet; such a reorientation needs to go much further – for example by addressing the environmental footprint of the media products that we study, and of their distribution and consumption. Or by adding topics such as degrowth, environmental justice, and activism to our teaching agendas, by critically analysing discourses of innovation, or by scrutinising our 'collective desire for spectacle' that has an enormous ecological impact, as Hunter Vaughan[3] argues . . . Integrating ecocritical thinking in the curriculum will be challenging. (Keilbach and Pabi Orzeszyna, 2021)

In the spirit of ecocritical thinking the next focus I recommend for a climate-aware journalism pedagogy is the story of the storytellers: where were the watchdogs during decades of escalating climate crisis?

Climate journalism

Veteran climate change journalists are quick to observe that the climate desk, to the extent it exists in newsrooms, is far from a new beat. In a recent World Journalism Education Council webinar, retired *Telegraph* journalist Geoffrey Lean responded to an Extinction Rebellion representative's indictment of contemporary journalism for inadequate, even counterproductive, climate reporting by waving before his webcam a print story on impending climate emergency *which he wrote in 1974*. Lean bills himself as Britain's longest-serving environmental correspondent, with good cause.

In the US, former *New York Times* science editor Walter Sullivan battled reluctant editors to put that newspaper's first major climate change story on the front page in 1981, describing increasing scientific consensus about a 'greenhouse effect'. But even this was remarkably delayed. Environmental organisations had been publishing reports to the media about the threat of global warming since early in 1970s, with little uptake, as physicist and climate change historian Spencer Weart (2022) describes in his exhaustive online history of climate change advocacy in the US.

Contemporary journalism educators might ask their students to consider why global warming, and its possibly disastrous outcomes, was not consistently the major global news story of the last two decades. There are too many published commentaries on where we have gone wrong to summarise, but with broad agreement on the prominence of the following factors:

- Increasing polarisation, complicating straightforward reporting
- Increasing media uptake of denialist or 'contrarian' discourses
- Distrust of traditional journalism and a related rise in social media information sources
- Complexity of the story
- Negativity of the story

Increasing print and broadcast climate coverage crashed headlong into the deregulatory, growth-oriented agenda of 1990s neoliberal politics, well before climate journalism became entangled, as it remains now, in the post-millennium American cultural wars. In the 2000s, the BBC became a lightning rod for its attempts to cover the climate. Its coverage often attracted the ire of a set of right-wing newspaper columnists with close links to the Conservative Party (which held power in the UK between 2010 and 2024). According to environmental journalist Lean, responding to being pressured to leave the *Telegraph*, there were ten columnists in the British press 'who reject or underplay the dangers of global warming, with precious few columnar voices on the other side' (quoted in Ponsford, 2015). Throughout this period, the BBC was engaged in a power struggle with the Murdoch press, part of a global campaign by Murdoch to extinguish publicly funded media.

In the UK, *false balance* often led to editorial decisions requiring a higher standard of proof for climate science. Such decisions were based on the routine of objectivity as a key journalistic role perception, the interpretation of broadcast regulations as uniformly requiring presentation of two sides of public controversies and were rooted in a journalistic culture of suspicion of environmental campaigning as anti-establishment. One BBC response to conservative pressure was to become the poster child for false balance, occasionally (though never consistently) offering equal time to an energy industry representative or climate change-denying Conservative politician when an expert quoting climate change science was interviewed. In 2017, the BBC famously included vocal climate change denier (and former Chancellor under Margaret Thatcher) Nigel Lawson in a morning news programme because prominent climate change communicator Al Gore was interviewed. That led to a rebuke from the UK regulator, OFCOM which, in turn, led to a 2018 memorandum to staff from the Head of News about the dangers of false balance (CarbonBrief, 2018). It included this advice:

> Man-made climate change exists: If the science proves it we should report it. The BBC accepts that the best science on the issue is the IPCC's position ... Be aware of 'false balance': As climate change is accepted as happening, you do not need a 'denier' to balance the debate. Although there are those who disagree with the IPCC's position, very few of them now go so far as to deny that climate change is happening. To achieve impartiality, you do not need to include outright deniers of climate change in BBC coverage, in the same way you would not have someone denying that Manchester United won 2–0 last Saturday. The referee has spoken.

In teaching climate change journalism, I've found contemporary UK students are surprised that climate change denial once held such traction; but they find revelatory the government and corporate policies that embody denial of global warming and scientific consensus, but keep below the radar, as politicians and executives proclaim their environmental credentials. In societies where young journalists are likely to have been raised in climate change denialist families, consuming denialist media (the US and Australia are likely examples), teachers might find it useful to provoke students to confront the absurdity of false balance by expanding their range of science reporting. Commentators have suggested variations on the idea of asking students to report on another field of science and then requiring them to find someone to deny what they find (e.g., why has a student's astronomy piece not sought a denial that Saturn's rings are made of rock and ice?). We hope the students will question such absurd instructions and carry forward their judgement about the integrity of scientific information to their critical reading and practice of climate change journalism.

The dilution and disruption of effective climate change journalism, which might otherwise have encouraged further and faster policy responses to global warming in the 2010s, was also an effect of 'Climategate' in 2009, a disinformation campaign to discredit climate science and sow doubt. It was apparently orchestrated by climate change denial bloggers who hacked into University of East Anglia computers to steal thousands of emails between climate researchers. Sentences were then taken out of context and used by bloggers to construct an image of bad science and conspiracy. The manufactured story spread to the mainstream media, and was especially amplified by right-wing media, all in the weeks prior to the crucial Copenhagen Summit. Leiserowitz et al. (2013) document how, despite several investigations which all concluded there was no deception and no bad science, the 'scandal' was highly effective in suppressing US and UK public trust in climate science and leading to yet more artificial balance in reporting. Miller points out that pattern, mostly in Anglo and US media, has repeated itself over and over – any hint of scientific disagreement or uncertainty receives relentless attention, as though our media feel a sacred obligation to convince us the situation isn't quite so bad: 'Bourgeois public discourse is dominated by ideologues and pundits for hire who clutch at these moments and transform them into absolutes. Climate-change scientists are rarely invited to their party' (Miller, 2017, p. 1).

Particular attention must be paid to the challenge which future climate change journalists face from concerted efforts by the energy industry to limit or alter reporting on global warming by sowing doubt and confusion. For decades, this effort has built, through the investment of hundreds of millions of dollars, a symbiotic relationship with conservative political leaders around the world and with conservative media owners. The following advice to then President George Bush by the long-time Republic Party strategist Frank Luntz twenty years ago signalled the early stages of what would become deeply entrenched US policy: 'Should the public come to believe that the scientific issues are settled, their views about global warming will change accordingly. Therefore, you need to continue to make the lack of scientific certainty a primary issue in the debate' (Burkeman, 2003 in Quiggin, 2008). (Luntz now repudiates many of his earlier positions.)

In the last three decades, the five major US oil companies have spent a total of at least $3.6bn on advertisements. An investigation by the Guardian points out that actual investment in clean energy is typically less than 1 per cent of oil company investment – they spend far more on advertising how clean they are (Holden, 2020). Much of the reporting by author and Guardian columnist George Monbiot similarly provides useful examples for journalism educators of watchdog climate journalism holding industry to account in a manner that is too rare in mainstream US journalism. Hackett et al. (2017, pp. 3–4) argue that, broadly, climate 'coverage is episodic and compartmentalized. It too infrequently connects the dots between, for example, the manifestations of climate change and its causes and consequences, or the rapid exploitation of fossil fuels and global warming.' They add that 'the overall editorial environment favours economic growth, consumerism and private-sector business. There is little attention to who bears responsibility for climate change, and little critical analysis of capitalism or even the fossil fuel industry.'

The leading authority on industry efforts to disrupt and dismiss climate science is Naomi Oreskes of Harvard (see, primarily, Oreskes and Conway, 2011). She found that 'available documents show a systematic, quantifiable discrepancy between what Exxon Mobil's scientists and executives discussed about climate change in private and in academic circles, and what it presented to the general public' (Supran and Oreskes, 2017). From as early as the 1970s, 'Exxon Mobil (and its predecessors Exxon and Mobil) not only knew about emerging climate science but also contributed research to it. Scientific reports and articles written by or co-written by Exxon Mobil employees acknowledged that global warming 'was a real and serious threat', but in subsequent decades the company invested massively in efforts to push policy away from addressing climate change and confuse public opinion. The company's advertorials discussing climate change in The New York Times had a readership in the millions. Oreskes concluded 'Exxon Mobil contributed quietly to climate science and loudly to raising doubts about it' (ibid.).

Energy industry campaigns have not only successfully undermined public understanding of the degree of scientific agreement on climate change; they have also increased existing political polarisation and limited deeper societal engagement with the issue. Van der Linden et al. (2017) demonstrate that a promising approach to counter the politicisation of science is to make clear to audiences the 'high level of normative agreement' (consensus) among experts.

The role of energy money

The investment by energy companies in ensuring public confusion about global warming is of staggering proportions. The process has included many forms of 'greenwash' and the funding of front foundations which are deeply integrated with US politics and media, along with sponsored pamphlets, press releases and public lectures, all arguing that global warming is not a problem. Front organisations take the form of conservative think tanks (such as the Cato Institute, Competitive Enterprise Institute, Heritage Foundation, Hoover Institution) and vocal trade associations like the American Petroleum Institute. Many millions of dollars are spent on lobbying and funding the campaigns of politicians friendly to the energy industry. The extraordinary levels of funding for climate disinformation that climate journalism is up against are starkly revealed in a data journalism project of CNBC (2020).

New Zealand climate journalist Jamie Morton suggested that, while some of the damage to mainstream reporting caused by industry lobbying has been overcome, social media presents a new challenge:

> [W]hile we don't see climate sceptics (deniers if you call them that) given as much oxygen in the media as was once the case, social media has enabled a troubling environment where bad science and fake news gets shared around and user algorithms can project ill-informed views back at people without challenging them. It bothers me how Facebook, which traditional journalism is competing with, uses the term 'newsfeed' as though that's what we're actually getting. (thespinoff, 2017)

Climate journalists require training in navigating a complex online political economy which makes climate disinformation highly profitable. The progressive pressure group Avaaz published a study in 2020 about the role of YouTube in promoting climate change denialism. They quote, for example, from a video titled 'Climate Change: What Do Scientists Say?' saying, 'There is no evidence that CO2 emissions are the dominant factor [in climate change].' The video is being promoted by YouTube's algorithm and had 1.9 million views at the time of the Avaaz report. The report was aimed not just at YouTube, but at its many corporate sponsors who continue to profit from publication of such climate disinformation on a massive scale. They argue: 'Protecting citizens around the world from fake news designed to confuse and poison the debate about climate change must be a key priority for governments, advertisers and social media platforms.'

A corollary to instilling a 'follow the money' mantra in the next generation of climate communicators is developing a nose for greenwash, the process one set of researchers defined as 'the intersection of two firm behaviours: poor environmental performance and positive communication about environmental performance' (Delmas and Burbano, 2011, cited by de Freitas Netto, et al., 2020). TerraChoice published an influential early 2000s guide to spotting greenwash. Emphasising the deliberate nature of the process, they called greenwashing an 'act of misleading consumers regarding the environmental practices of a company'. They sought to build a base of critical consumers alert to these 'seven sins': *claims based on a hidden trade-off; a lack of proof; vagueness; false impressions of endorsement by a credible third party; irrelevant claims; less of two evils claims (distracting from the poor record of industry in question, commonly practices by energy and transport industries); and outright lying.*[4]

Embedding climate education in the higher education curriculum

Efforts are underway to embed climate change teaching across the higher education curriculum, and journalism teaching needs to be at the forefront. Student demand is clear. Students Organising for Sustainability (SOS) is a branch of the UK National Union of Students. The SOS is campaigning in England for a 'government-commissioned review into how the whole of the English formal education system is preparing students for the climate emergency and ecological crisis'. Meg Baker of SOS, speaking to an online forum organised by the UK Universities and Colleges Union, demonstrated students' growing concern about climate change, well-illustrated by surveys conducted by the UK National Union of Students. However, she warns educators to help students to avoid debilitating levels of 'eco-anxiety' by becoming active agents of positive change.

Educators with links to climate change teaching from eighty UK higher education institutions authored a series of reports as the UK Universities Climate Network, seeking to influence policy development at the COP26 summit in Glasgow in 2021. One such report, led from the University of Leeds Priestley Centre for Climate, addressed 'Mainstreaming Climate Change Education in UK Higher Education Institutions'. It argued, '[I]f students – and staff – are not learning how their subjects are being changed by the climate crisis, they are not learning the knowledge to equip them for the world in which they already live.' The authors suggest this process 'is likely to require all degree programmes to integrate climate change into their "disciplinary" course provision to some extent, even where institution-wide climate change courses are available' (Thew et al., 6).

This is a conception of weaving Climate Change Education 'through all aspects of an institution, going beyond only offering individual degree programmes or specialist courses on climate change, to embedding climate change into structures and curricula across the board, ensuring all students and staff members engage with the issue' (ibid., 2). This should include 'consideration of how climate change is already affecting, and will increasingly impact upon, the industries we work in, the communities we live in, and others around the world' (ibid., 3)

When journalism and advocacy merge: space for critical discussion

There is ample evidence of investment in climate reporting by media around the world. But there is also evidence that such reporting remains challenging in some of the countries of the global south where climate change impacts are felt most acutely (e.g. Maweu and Paterson, 2019). Some of the world's larger climate desks have provided useful overviews of their editorial process, as with Van Syckle's (2021) 'Times Insider' essay on their climate reporting and Carrington's (2019) essay about the climate reporting language used at the *Guardian*. Hertsgaard and Pope (2019), writing in the *Columbia Journalism Review*, describe a collective project involving more than sixty news organisations 'to increase the amount and the visibility of . . . climate coverage'. In some newsrooms, the challenge of climate reporting has brought to the fore debates about going beyond reporting in their institutional response to existential crisis.

For the *Guardian* newspaper in the UK (where it is common for national newspapers to campaign about social issues), the risk was losing major advertisers and being seen as too partisan. Despite that, after much debate, the newspaper embarked on a prominent campaign to 'keep it in the ground', pressuring corporations, governments, investment funds and other organisations to divest from and distance themselves from new fossil fuel extraction. The *Guardian*'s internal debates over the role their newspaper should play are chronicled by Forde (2017), but also colourfully described by former managing editor Alan Rusbridger in a 2021 talk, available online (Rusbridger, 2021). As Hackett et al.

(2017, p. 16) explain, such debates allow students to engage with the question of 'what do the contributions of . . . alternative journalism suggest about the "wisest" way we might deliver journalism about, and at a time of, climate crisis?'

Climate change in journalism teaching

Climate change journalists are increasingly vocal about their work, and their reflections offer valuable insights and teaching materials to journalism educators. New Zealand online news site The Spinoff, in a 2017 essay tracking the growth of climate journalism in New Zealand, states: 'Climate change is the biggest story on any editor's newslist right now.' The feature is filled with advice from working climate journalists, but this introductory quote from journalist Samantha Hayes stands out as a powerful starting point for engaging students with the challenges:

> Any story that is based on numbers, statistics and graphs is going to be difficult to get your head around and challenging to hook people into. Add to that the fact that the villain is invisible, and you've got a tough task on your hands. Pile on top of that the scale and time frames being talked about – it's a global problem that will occur over centuries – and there is no denying it's a tough sell. So what you need is great talent – science communicators who are charismatic, and can break it down to a simple and punchy message – and good local examples of how this massive, overarching threat will impact your country, city or town or street. (Spinoff, 2017)

Thew et al. recommend that 'pedagogies such as problem-based, practice-based, enquiry-based, and project-based learning which encompasses the real-life challenges of climate change and puts students at the centre of identifying and evaluating solutions, can help to facilitate interdisciplinary learning' (2021, p. 4). Climate change is the ultimate 'think global, act local' issue: it is through understanding of the global crisis and the interconnections that make local impacts matter to people far distant from them that the advocacy for local (and domestic) solutions gains traction. UNESCO suggests CCE should incorporate 'approaches that cultivate integrated knowledge and global citizenship, while preparing students for curious, well-informed, big-hearted lives' (UNESCO, 2017, quoted in Thew et al., 9).

One journalistic approach to point student environmental journalists to is the humanisation of climate activists. As Paterson (2002), describes, when the climate protester known as Swampy became a celebrity with sympathetic treatment in the media (for a while), protesters were 'normalised' and the trope of portraying them as violent and deranged didn't work anymore; their objectives evolved from disruptive to idealistic and legitimate. Baird (2021) calls for a focus on 'solutions-oriented journalism' in teaching students how to report on the environment, and her article for the UK AJE provides a number of examples from her teaching. Hackett et al. devote a chapter to strategies for improving climate journalism, building on an extensive review of the environmental communication research. They summarise these as:

- prioritise audiences most likely to engage with climate news as an 'issue public' (rather than using a 'one-size-fits-all' approach addressed to a mass audience)
- make greater use of a politically and ethically oriented climate justice frame
- foreground and 'activate' intrinsic, biospheric cultural values which are most strongly correlated with pro-environmental subjectivity
- cultivate social norms of civic engagement and political efficacy with greater attention to the stories, experiences and emotions of people and communities working together to address climate change (2017, p. 14).

I'll conclude by summarising my seven routes for educators toward preparing students to discuss the climate emergency competently, assuredly, and responsibly.

1. *'The continuity of human construction of 'environment'' '*

The portrayal of environmental crisis by mass media is best situated within the portrayal by literature, over two millennia, of a changing environment and the place of humans within it. Generations before us have learned that nature is ours to dominate, although we should acknowledge a scattering of calls to respect and protect it (thank you Henry David Thoreau and Aldo Leopold), along with increasing efforts to prioritise and be guided by the knowledge of indigenous communities, upon which some environmental alliances are based (e.g. International Tribunal for the Rights of Nature[5]).

2. *'The place of information industries in climate destruction'*

Media educators must use the self-reflexivity we encourage in our research to fully describe to our students the ways that the industries we prepare them for are climate criminals. Ours is an industry with a dreadful environmental footprint, so the generation of climate-aware communicators we educate requires a hearty dose of self-reflexivity.

3. *'Four decades of struggle between climate journalism and forces confounding it'*

Climate journalism isn't new, but chapters like this treat it like it is. Environmental advocacy and environmental journalism have been sounding the alarm for more than 50 years. Climate change journalism has appeared in the mainstream press since the 1970s, only it has been far too sparse to set public agendas. Let's work with the next generation of climate communicators to figure out why climate change hasn't been the leading global story for all of this time. The answers explain much about how we define news, and where power in our industry lies.

4. *'Understand the enemy, and its ally, social media'*

In training effective watchdogs, we need to demand that students 'follow the money' in climate change discourse, and understand the complex webs of disinformation which have shaped the public debate for decades. And they need only glance down to their phones for contemporary evidence of platform algorithms continuing to promote disinformation (see Avaaz, 2020).

5. *'Recognise and call out greenwashing'*

Act on their concerns by challenging the corporate world in their reporting, sounding the alarm in online conversation, and taking action through boycotts and complaints to regulators.

6. *'Embed climate change across campus'*

As educators with a stake in improving the communication of climate change, we all have a role in encouraging colleagues across disciplines to do the same. I have found on my own campus this is already happening in classes where I wouldn't have expected it, and when educators start talking with each other about climate change teaching we have the power to shift the priorities of our institutions.

'Teach the climate journalism strategies proven to work': We know that climate journalism is complicated and that old reporting strategies often don't work ('where is the immediacy?'). Fear and doom-laden reporting don't work, although a hopeful critical realism is required. But people trust scientists more

than journalists: we can teach students to tell their stories. People admire protesters, especially when they aren't inconvenienced by them: we can teach students how to personalise their stories. And narratives about how communities are working together to solve climate challenges resonate. Advocates for a 'solutions oriented' journalism abound, and have good ideas for teaching the generation who will all be climate journalists.

We are now at a juncture which will determine if increased climate reporting during recent COP summits will become the norm, or if media will revert to business as usual. Journalism educators have compelling reasons to embed climate change in their teaching, and this chapter has suggested just a fraction of the ample resources and strategies available to facilitate this. In a TEDx talk in 2012, Grist magazine climate writer David Roberts pithily described climate politics as 'stuck between the impossible and the unthinkable' (Roberts, 2012). 'Your job,' he told his audience, 'anyone who hears this, for the rest of your life, your job is to make the impossible possible.' The author of the profile of New Zealand climate journalists cited earlier (thespinoff, 2017) concluded: 'That sounds like a pretty good job description to me.'

Notes

1 https://wjec.net/wp-content/uploads/2022/06/WJEC-Journalism-Education-and-Climate-Change-2022.pdf; portions of this chapter also build on an essay published in J. Mair, J. Ryley and A. Beck (eds.) *Toxic news? Covering climate change* (Bite Size Books, 2023).

2 Though beyond the scope of this chapter, those teaching in this area may wish to note the existence of a substantial literature concerning the psychology of climate change denial. See Whitmarsh and Capstick (2018) and Armstrong, Krasny and Schuldt (2018).

3 Vaughan, H. *Hollywood's dirtiest secret: The hidden environmental costs of the movies* (New York: Columbia University Press 2019).

4 Educators might observe that even the process of calling out greenwashing is problematic. Terrachoice published as an independent consulting firm, calling out companies and industries, but after being taken over by the industry funded, and increasingly profit driven, Underwriters Laboratories, all but vanished from the internet. Their reports – useful for teaching – can be found through the internet archive.

5 https://www.rightsofnaturetribunal.org/.

References

Armstrong, A.K., Krasny, M.E. and Schuldt, J.P. (2018) *Communicating climate change: A guide for educators*. Cornell University Press. https://doi.org/10.7591/9781501730801

AVAAZ (2020) *Why is YouTube broadcasting climate misinformation to millions?* Available at https://avaazimages.avaaz.org/youtube_climate_misinformation_report.pdf

Baird, N. (2021) 'Students and the climate crisis', *Journalism Education*, 10–13. Available at https://journalism-education.org/2022/01/students-and-the-climate-crisis

Boyce, T. and Lewis, J. (eds.) (2009) *Climate change and the media.* Peter Lang.

Brevin, B. (2022) *Is AI good for the planet?* Wiley.

Burkeman, O. (2003) 'Memo exposes bush's new green strategy', *The Guardian.* Available at http://www.guardian.co.uk/environment/2003/mar/04/usnews.climatechange

CarbonBrief (2018) *Exclusive: BBC issues internal guidance on how to report climate change.* Available at https://www.carbonbrief.org/exclusive-bbc-issues-internal-guidance-on-how-to-report-climate-change

Carrington, D. (2019) 'Why the Guardian is changing the language it uses about the environment', *Guardian*, 17 May. Available at https://www.theguardian.com/environment/2019/may/17/why-the-guardian-is-changing-the-language-it-uses-about-the-environment

CNBC (2020) *The money funding climate change denial.* 20 December. Available at https://www.cnbc.com/2020/12/20/the-big-business-of-climate-change-denial-.html

de Freitas Netto, S.V., Sobral, M.F.F. and Ribeiro, A.R.B., et al. (2020) 'Concepts and forms of greenwashing: A systematic review', Environ Sci Eur 32, p. 19.

Delmas, M. and Burbano, V (2011) 'The drivers of greenwashing', Calif Manag Rev, 54(1), pp. 64–87.

Forde, S. (2017) 'Alternative approaches to environment coverage in the digital era: The Guardian's "Keep it in the Ground" campaign' in *Journalism and Climate Crisis.* Routledge, pp. 167–187.

Hackett, R.A., Forde, S., Gunster S. and Foxwell-Norton, K. (2017) 'Introduction: Journalism for climate crisis' in *Journalism and climate crisis*, by R.A. Hackett, S. Forde, S. Gunster, and K. Foxwell-Norton. New York: Routledge.

Hertsgaard, M. and Pope K. (2019) 'A new commitment to covering the climate story', *Columbia Journalism Review.* Available at https://cjr.org/covering_climate_now/covering-climate-partnerships.php/

Holden, E. (2020) 'How the oil industry has spent billions to control the climate change conversation', *Guardian*, 8 January.

Johns-Putra, A. (2019) *Climate and literature.* Cambridge University Press.

Keilbach, J. and Pabi Orzeszyna, M. (2021) 'Green(ing) media (studies)', *NECSUS European Journal of Media Studies*, 10(2), pp. 105–112.

Leiserowitz, A.A., Maibach, E.W., Roser-Renouf, C., Smith, N. and Dawson, E. (2013) 'Climategate, public opinion, and the loss of trust', *American Behavioral Scientist*, 57(6), pp. 818–837.

Maweu, J.M. and Paterson, C. (2019) 'Minding the gap? The media and the realisation of SDG 13 in Kenya' in Ramutsindela, M. and Mickler, D. (eds.) *Africa and the sustainable Development goals. Sustainable development goals series.* Cham: Springer, pp. 71–79.

Maxwell R. and Miller, T. (2012) *Greening the media.* New York: Oxford University Press.

Miller, T. (2017) *Greenwashing culture.* New York: Routledge.

Oreskes, N. and Conway, E.M. (2011) *Merchants of doubt: How a handful of scientists obscured the truth on issues from tobacco smoke to global warming*. Bloomsbury Publishing USA.

Park, D. (2021) *Media reform and the climate emergency: Rethinking communication in the struggle for a sustainable future*. University of Michigan Press.

Paterson, C. (2022) 'Journalism education and climate change', Expert Report, World Journalism Education Council. 29 April 2022. https://wjec.net/wp-content/uploads/2022/06/WJEC-Journalism-Education-and-Climate-Change-2022.pdf

Paterson, M. (2002) 'Swampy fever: Media constructions and direct action politics' in *Direct action in British environmentalism*. Routledge, pp. 165–180.

Ponsford, D. (2015) *Telegraph's Geoffrey Lean says he has been 'pushed out' amid rise of newspaper climate change rejectionists*. PressGazette, 1 December. Available at https://pressgazette.co.uk/telegraphs-geoffrey-lean-says-he-has-been-pushed-out-amid-rise-newspaper-climate-change/

Quiggin, J. (2008) *Uncertainty and climate change policy* (No. 1744-2016-140901).

Roberts, D. (2012) 'Climate change is simple: David Roberts', *Ted Talk*, 13 June. https://www.youtube.com/watch?v=A7ktYbVwr90

Rusbridger, A. (2021) *The role of media in addressing climate change with Alan Rusbridger, talk for the Oxford Climate Society*. Available at: https://www.youtube.com/watch?v=1lKTR6Y-djo

Supran, G. and Oreskes, N. (2017) 'What Exxon Mobil didn't say about climate change', *New York Times*, 22 August. Available at https://www.nytimes.com/2017/08/22/opinion/exxon-climate-change-.html

thespinoff (2017) *Covering climate change: Journalism's biggest and most difficult story, ever*. August 16. Available at https://thespinoff.co.nz/climate-change-week/16-08-2017/covering-climate-change-journalisms-biggest-and-most-difficult-story-ever

Thew, H., Graves, C., Reay, D., Smith, S., Petersen, K., Bomberg, E., Boxley, S., Causley, J., Congreve, A., Cross, I., Dunk, R., Dunlop, L., Facer, K., Gamage, K.A.A., Greenhalgh, C., Greig, A., Kiamba, L., Kinakh, V., Kioupi, V., Lee, M., Klapper, R., Kurul, E., Marshall-Cook, J., McGivern, A., Mörk, J., Nijman, V., O'Brien, J., Preist, C., Price, E., Samangooei, M., Schrodt, F., Sharmina, M., Toney, J., Walsh, C., Walsh, T., Wood, R. Wood, P. and Worsfold, N.T. (2021) *Mainstreaming climate education in Higher Education institutions*. COP26 Universities Network Working Paper. At https://www.gla.ac.uk/research/cop26/briefings/

UNESCO (2017) *Education for sustainable development goals: Learning objectives* [Online]. Available from: http://unesdoc.unesco.org/images/0025/002521/252197POR.pdf

Van der Linden, S., Leiserowitz, A., Rosenthal, S. and Maibach, E. (2017) 'Inoculating the public against misinformation about climate change', *Global Challenges*, 1(2).

Van Syckle, K. (2021) 'In climate coverage, reporting the grim facts, but also the fight', *New York Times*, 27 August. https://www.nytimes.com/2021/08/27/insider/united-nations-climate-report.html

Weart, S. (2022) *The discovery of global warming – the public and climate change*. Available at https://history.aip.org/climate/index.htm

Whitmarsh, L. and Capstick, S. (2018) 'Perceptions of climate change' in *Psychology and climate change*. Academic Press, pp. 13–33.

Section VII:

Communications and Intelligence for a World-in-Crisis

·18·

COMMUNICATING WHOLE INTELLIGENCE TO REGENERATE THE LIVING HUMAN WORLD

Malcolm Parlett

How can I communicate Whole Intelligence in a short chapter? How can I bring it alive when understanding it calls for direct, shared, lived experience? If – as I suggest here – Whole Intelligence is a form of contemporary wisdom, a support for improved mental health, a contribution to building peace and preserving the biosphere, how can I possibly do it justice here? The reality is that I cannot. But I can give it a go.

The questions I am asking parallel the greater challenge for our project: how to spread the vision of Whole Intelligence as a 'healthy contagion' among decision-makers, citizen advocates, activists, educators and leaders everywhere?

To start with, I will set out various contexts for this chapter.

First, there is widespread agreement that we live at a pivotal moment, perhaps with an epochal shift in the making – an order of change as dramatic as happened in Europe with the Reformation. Just as the printing press helped fuel the historic change in the nature of thought and the beginnings of colonialism, so might the internet and video-conferencing accelerate the spread of a different consciousness across the human world (humane, bio-friendly, sustainable). Alternative scenarios abound. While those trained in economics may regard 'the moment' as a time for increased realisations of fundamental inequalities and specialists in agriculture may be pointing to urgencies of food security and improving soil quality, so my own career background as a working social psychologist and gestalt coach predisposes me to call for immediate and greater exercise of Whole Intelligence – that is, *for human beings and human systems to draw upon their strengths, instinctual abilities and hidden potentialities in order to 'act more intelligently'*.

Second, I am writing this chapter at a time when wars rage and a fragmented international community allows them to continue as if the consensual 'Never Again' realisations from the previous century have been rubbished or forgotten. Pursuing war is the antithesis to living intelligently. Another sign of degeneration (synonyms . . . 'decline, deterioration') is that international agreements regarding climate change and carbon emissions are casually postponed or even flagrantly undermined by powerful lobbies gripped by pursuing self-interest: again, a serious abandonment of Whole Intelligence. At the same time, observing the global situation with a wide-angled view, there are also 'green shoots' in spring-like profusion – changes of attitude, new awakenings; and an urge to reform or refresh institutions, confront inequalities, regenerate agriculture, improve diets, plant trees, help the traumatised, conserve wildlife and encourage different religious communities to become radically more tolerant towards each other. The purpose set out here, that humanity might learn to live more intelligently, incorporating more of our Whole Intelligence as a species, follows a double agenda: invigorating new regenerative trends (the green shoots) that may well contribute to an emerging 'new normal', while also interrupting stale degenerative trends that exist globally (like long-standing unresolved conflicts).

Third, a frequent question: *Where does the idea of Whole Intelligence come from?* I answer as follows: My concern with Whole Intelligence crystallised around 1998; it developed through collecting multiple organisational and psychotherapeutic observations, (confirmed by collaborators working as organisational consultants or as psychotherapists). The approach is summarised in a book, *Future Sense: Five Explorations of Whole Intelligence for a World That's Waking up* (Parlett, 2016/2024). The book outlines ways to support adult human development, inspire high quality leadership, underpin a visionary model of education and how utilising Whole Intelligence can itself become a deliberate form of activism. An inspiring presence has been Iain McGilchrist (2021), explaining a necessary change of consciousness to balance two concentrations – one (which is dominant) on precision and definition, the other (increasingly threatened) honours holistic perception, flow, and accepting life's uncertainty. Such balancing is central in growing Whole Intelligence.

Fourth, the employment of the word 'intelligence' is deliberate. Instead of its original associations of being sensible, knowing, wise, insightful and capable of acting with good judgement, intelligence has reduced in meaning to become more or less equated with intellectual skills that are easily measurable and therefore supposedly 'scientific'. Whole Intelligence reinstates broader down to earth meanings, corresponding to the ancient Greek *phronesis* (translated as practical wisdom) and explores human beings' all round capability to function and flourish and serve the world. At a time when many are thinking of human life changing (for better or worse) in relation to 'artificial intelligence', the emphasis here is on maximising existing human resources and drawing on untapped reservoirs of capability, rather than looking for a technological fix.

Fifth, the best way to communicate the wisdom and potential of Whole Intelligence is through engaging with its five dimensions (that appear in Figure 18.1).

Each dimension represents a form of human capability that is intrinsic to Whole Intelligence. Each calls for study and something equivalent to an 'immersion' experience in order to grasp its meaning in full. The dimensions cannot be assimilated just by reading about them as concepts and dry descriptions, any more than 'beauty', 'love', or 'integrity' can be fully appreciated simply by engaging with brief verbal definitions. There is a necessary element of 'first-hand experiencing' that individuals, groups, or organisations need to go through in order to identify the five dimensions of Whole Intelligence as living truths worth exploring in depth.

I shall describe each of the five dimensions in some detail. It is important to remember that they are closely interwoven and always operate together as interdependent aspects of Whole Intelligence. On first acquaintance, however, it helps to differentiate them as five distinctive parts of the whole.

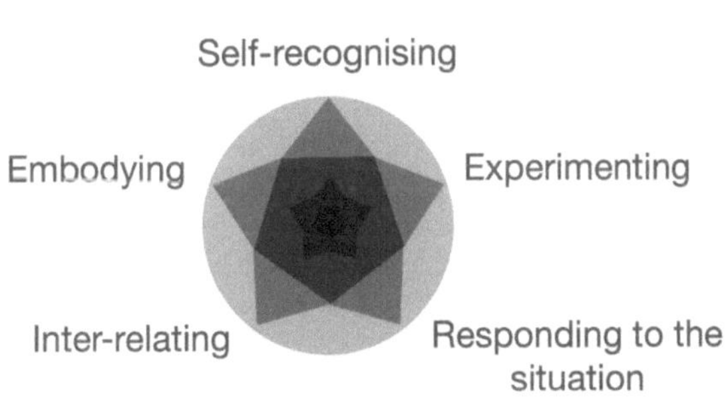

Figure 18.1. Whole Intelligence: Five Dimensions

The first dimension: Inter-relating between human beings

How human beings collaborate and communicate together is obviously crucial. Consider almost any intractable global problem – such as relationships between states in the Middle East, polarised politics, tensions between majorities and minorities, or the yawning gap in face-to-face relating between rich and poor – and the lack of mutual understanding demonstrates how inadequate is the human capacity to relate to others consistently and open-heartedly. Moving from large to small scale, most of us have experienced unfortunate breakdowns of friendships, intimate relationships, or falling out with a colleague.

At the same time, every day across the globe, countless millions of collaborations and encounters occur between people. Great cities work as organised complexities only because human beings are – despite appearances sometimes – competent in relating with one another and in sustaining networks. Most human adults – especially when supported by others or by supportive cultural norms – are able to honour agreements, read other drivers' intentions, and find ways to restore relations after conflicts. We have learnt through direct experiences cumulatively gathered how relationships can break down, lead to suffering and loneliness, and when sometimes repairs are possible. Peaceful, fulfilling, supportive and enjoyable relations between diverse people and groups may seem an unrealistic ideal, yet most people have experienced relationships that demonstrate some or all of these qualities.

Even those who have been severely traumatised as infants and find great difficulty in relating to other people can usually find ways to connect, to love and receive love, that is when treated with deep respect, care and 'mindsight, the capacity to sense the inner mental lives of others with empathy and compassion' (Siegel, 2023, p. 109).

Promoting the vision of living more intelligently includes strengthening skills and upholding competences that already exist. The Whole Intelligence outlook is about building on this kind of basic, practical knowing and species-wide understanding. Such 'know how' deserves notice and higher status. Our project is about bringing humanity's implicit wisdom into the foreground and demonstrating how the different dimensions of Whole Intelligence have immediate utility: how they serve as supports through being better understood and communicated, providing a framework that makes sense and informs 'best practice'.

The Whole Intelligence project is deliberately broad scale. While individual development and learning occurs in therapy, more general skilfulness in inter-relating with others is also vital, for instance in small and medium-scale organisations such as businesses and churches and also in bigger collectives such as established institutions, international bodies and between nation states. How leaders representing millions relate personally to each other often has vast consequences, especially when issues are sensitive and interests collide.

Again, raising the general level of skilfulness in relating together does not depend on building expertise from scratch. Many effective leaders, managers and teachers, as well as parents and grandparents, are already gifted and demonstrate practices that all can recognise as beneficent and worth copying. The skills of unravelling entanglements and dealing with messy human situations are not deeply esoteric or super-advanced specialist subjects. Whether it is skill in chairing a meeting, sorting out a rift in a family, or comforting someone in distress, such expertise is widely available and distributed across the world. Acts of kindness and respect for others' differences have universal validity and welcome.

Question: Does advancing Whole Intelligence imply that we can do without specialist professional skills? The answer is 'Not at all'; with regard to all five dimensions, there are advanced methods and specialist trainings that exist. Thus, with inter-relating, these include trainings in mediation, diversity awareness, conflict resolution, community building and bereavement counselling. They can all help strengthen inter-relating skilfulness by demonstrating and modelling 'good practice', heightening awareness and offering deeper appreciation of relational dynamics. But in the quest to encourage greater inter-relating competence generally, there are many 'non-specialist' steps that are possible and which can lead to more satisfying communications (for instance, 'in the office'); or more rewarding conversations (e.g. 'inter-generationally') at home; or more skilful collaborations in strategic discussions ('in the committee'). Common interruptions to flow in conversations can be highlighted: for example, inability to listen to another without interrupting, or failing to admit some confusion or lack of understanding, thereby seeding subsequent confusion.

To sum up this first dimension of Whole intelligence, improved quality of inter-relating is surely one of the most obvious ways for human beings to act more effectively as a working global community. If given support and opportunity to inter-relate more consistently, people can – and do – become more confident, livelier and more trusting towards each other. With fewer unresolved misunderstandings, clearer agreements replacing confused boundaries and increased respect for 'otherness' and greater empathy, a lot of unnecessary suffering is side-stepped; peaceful life is less interrupted; problem-solving is improved; and functioning of committees is vastly improved.

Societies need a critical mass of relationships sustained over time. Skilled parenting and happy enough families, enlightened management attitudes in industrial conflicts, good working practices among event organisers and effective mediations that avert or end conflicts, both reflect and strengthen interrelating as pivotal, acting more intelligently on a collective basis.

Before moving on to describe the second dimension, I need to acknowledge that all five dimensions of Whole Intelligence described in this chapter are affected by the particular contexts in which human beings exist – especially their geographic, familial, social, economic, political and sometimes religious environments. In the case of people relating together, literally thousands of customs, cultural communication styles, social conventions and political pressures can and do have significant influence in how people go about relating to other human beings. At the same time, reflecting on living more intelligently – and following the vision of promoting a regenerative educational programme for humanity at large – there do seem to be some very widely held values and skill sets that appear to be universal in the lives of human beings.

The second dimension: Embodying – the biological grounding for whole intelligence

By its nature, 'embodying' is probably the most difficult quality of Whole Intelligence to capture and explain in words. The embodying dimension of Whole Intelligence is challenging even to describe, given that so much business and administration operates exclusively through verbal debate and the currency of ideas. In most educational contexts globally, abstraction and theorising have become the most respected and prestigious forms of attending and knowing. Prioritising intellect-based intelligence has increasingly become the taken-for-granted norm – almost defining what is judged to be adequate education and (therefore, supposedly) preparation for adult living. Overwhelmingly in school, students are taught to take in and memorise information, attend to theories and verbal formulations, think rationally and in a few restricted areas use their imagination. Little educational attention – if any at all – is given to the kinds of knowing that come from direct sensing: seeing, hearing, touching, tasting, smelling and experiencing multiple variations of 'feeling'. Yet the fact is that human beings' overall ability to navigate a mature selfhood and functional well-being through life relies as much on what is gathered from nonverbal sources as those that are verbal or numerical. Attending to what is experienced as 'external' to us is directly allied to what we experience 'internally' and both sensations and feelings are essential in developing context sensitivity, accurate reading of situations, awareness of the needs of others and recognising the variability of our own emotions and states of present feeling. Attending to the proprioceptive, visceral, biochemical signalling that is organismically available to us is critically important for full spectrum awareness of the world and our own positioning within it – and therefore is central rather than peripheral in learning to live more intelligently. *I remember my own serious lack of development with regard to embodying, when I was shocked to discover (over forty years ago) that other trainees at the Gestalt Institute of Cleveland had no difficulty with 'tuning into' their feeling states, while I was registering hardly any but the most extreme. Despite being athletic, healthy and apparently physically 'normal', I had been educated to develop my intellect; thinking dominated my life as a student and academic. I was warned at the time that 'the longest journey is from head to heart', which in the ensuing years of 'recovery' I confirmed was correct. It's been the most important journey I've undertaken in 'growing up as an adult'.* Compared to surviving indigenous cultures (Graeber and Wengrow, 2021), our lack of embodied skilfulness becomes obvious. Dependence on technology is a factor. With every move to a faster, more virtual, automated, physically safer and more sanitised world, there is further separation from direct touching, smelling, handling, lifting, stretching and physically moving across distances. For the majority of human beings, certainly in industrialised societies, our physical surroundings have become denatured and un-stimulating. We easily become desensitised, which generalises to ignoring the changing flow of sensations and feelings of our bodily life. Many culture-wide habits (and architectural assumptions) affect how people are able to experience their bodies, move, raise voices and express themselves in ways that young children can. Contemporary urban living conditions and lifestyles – speedy, verbal and increasingly on screen – remove us ever further from engaging with the natural world as bodies. Becoming more embodied is vitally necessary in awakening the public to the world crisis. The felling of trees to build a road can be variously regarded: as economically functional, as a challenge to sustainability, or as yet another human assault on the resilience of the biosphere. But it is also a moment that might shatter the coma-like acceptance of what's happening around us. Expressions of concern, grief or outrage might well help us to act and think more intelligently; communicating the urgency through knowing it first in our bodies. Another aspect where increased embodied truthfulness can affect ordinary workplace life is through legitimising expression of people's 'heartfelt beliefs' and 'gut feelings'. A team member listening to a submitted proposal who reports they have a distinctly adverse feeling 'in the pit of their stomach' may be making an important contribution. Some will regard inclusion of any such body-based data as fanciful and simply not applicable in twenty-first-century life. Yet more embodied others are likely to take seriously someone reporting that a meeting had left them with 'a bad taste in the mouth', or that a colleague in pain complains of 'shouldering extra responsibility'; or that someone's success 'puts spring in their step'. Body references are both prevalent and informative, undercutting ideas with a different truth. Embodying is crucially relevant for even greater reasons. While as a human population we live in a culturally diverse world in terms of age, bodily appearance, health status, gender expression and physical and sensory capabilities – with varied degrees of privilege, education and perceived 'normality' – something is absolute and universally shared between us all. This is our bodily existence, the ultimate 'connector' between us as members of our (endangered) primate species. For all humanity's incredible diversity, we have in common our vulnerabilities when injured or sick, our age-related physical changes and certainty of dying. Perhaps we need, as part of living more intelligently, to recognise more consciously our shared biological heritage and joint membership of the 'human family', (to use a worn-out political phrase). *At this point in the writing, I am aware of how each dimension of Whole Intelligence opens up immense issues that deserve deeper scrutiny. But focused specialisation comes at a cost. The Whole Intelligence approach, emphasising holism, is NOT a 'five category model'. Learning to live more intelligently requires flexibility and graceful movement between parts and the relevant 'wholes'. Thus, as dimensions,* Inter-relating *and* Embodying *can be looked at separately, but the connections and overlaps are also highly informative to recognise and investigate. In Whole Intelligence practice we encourage constant movement between the five dimensions. Living more intelligently calls for all the dimensions to be present and freely available.*

There is something else that bothers me about what I have written so far. I have not emphasised that Whole Intelligence provides a common framework, almost a language of ideas that is meaningful at every level of human system, from the 'macro- to the micro- '. Rather than restricting this straightforward conceptual language to specialist speakers and actors in one or another theatre of human life, my colleagues and I are keen to generate a common basis of understanding: something that is versatile, approachable, communicable, and helpful to small partnerships or to large ones, to nuclear families as well as institutions of the state. We are deliberate in our travelling between intimate and impersonal realms of lived existence (though perhaps we need to leave more signposts for those whom we address).

The third dimension: Self-recognising and finding one's 'Eco niche'

'Know thyself' is one of the oldest injunctions from the wisdom traditions that come down to us. Self-recognising, the third Whole Intelligence dimension, encompasses an entire class of varied activities. According to needs, backgrounds and different traditions, self-recognising gets to be enacted in a multitude of ways, at every level of depth, with varying degrees of intensity. For example, two over worked managers take time-out to look into the course of their lives. Each reports their present state of being, discovering afresh their place and sense of purpose – or the loss of it. They may be considering questions of work/life balance, political affiliation, sexual identity, spiritual beliefs, or their emotional maturity. What marks such inquiries is their individuality. Equivalent activities operate at a collective level – again with focus on inquiry, investigation, reflexivity and 'quality control'. Self-recognising occurs in organisations and communities of every variety. Here, inquiries may be carried out by designated individuals, appointed groups, or special commissions, but relate to the whole system – its mission, history, survival, or future development.

Knowing what one is doing, how it is being done and what the point is of continuing to do it, makes obvious sense. And living more intelligently calls for many such activities. They are about human and organisational learning, increased truth-telling, refinement of values and direction setting for what is to come. The potential benefits are obvious. Thus, a reform-minded prison governor may ask questions that go to the root of policy about how prisoners are rehabilitated; it may begin as a personal process of looking into their own experience, but potentially might have huge implications for others. Initiatives like the South African Truth and Reconciliation Commission displayed self-recognising on a grand scale. But similar basic purposes and priorities may be evident in a personal 'post-mortem', after (say) a broken relationship: a time to look in the mirror, revisit what happened, learn from the experience.

As straightforward and beneficial as self-recognising may appear to many readers, there is often resistance to pursuing more of it than is considered obligatory. The frequent notion in business settings that such inquiries are time-wasting, merely navel-gazing, or picking over the past unnecessarily, is often hard to argue against, given urgent seeming immediate tasks. Yet the need to reflect, observe trends, to wake up to what is occurring 'under one's nose', are often dangerous tasks to put off doing. For some too, the act of turning the searchlight onto oneself – or onto the life of the family, team, workgroup, or political party one belongs to – may seem 'dangerous' and potentially discomforting. People or groups most hesitant towards self-recognising may seem very self-assured, yet are often afraid to look at themselves. Self-recognising here would involve acknowledging their vulnerability and difficulty in engaging with some painful hangover from earlier times – perhaps an injury, embarrassment, failure, or shame experience that might be re-stimulated. If someone has been severely traumatised, re-living the experience that simply reactivates the original distress is not recommended. More beneficial is a process of discovering resources and inner supports that build strength, resilience, and inner strength which can lead to natural processes of recovery and healing. The witness and presence of a therapist or other 'neutral' party, or a sense of solidarity with sympathetic others, or being inspired by the example of a courageous figure or group can all revive a sense of courage and help build resilience.

Moving on from identifying a difficult memory may be eased by taking a historical perspective that locates what was past in the greater context of present life and its rewards. Maturity, wisdom and judgements based on accumulated experience are often hard-won: we learn the most, it is said, from our mistakes and 'hard knocks'. But these need never remain stationary obstacles; they are eligible for re-framing in the different circumstances of the present.

In the course of Whole Intelligence teaching and writing, my own self-recognising has played an important part. Lives or developmental histories – whether of persons, families, or institutions – are fashioned out of multiple experiences, events and life contingencies. They are unique – in the same way that ecosystems are created through numerous different influences acting together. What has become clear is that my concentration on promoting Whole Intelligence and offering it to others, is not some random choice for my late career, but could be construed as 'predetermined'; or if this is too fanciful, that I have found my 'eco niche' – (Plotkin, 2021) – in other words, a unique place and purpose that integrates everything which has occurred in one's life to the present. This lends real substance to the term: 'self-recognizing' (recognising oneself and one's eco niche) and points to another whole other way of living more intelligently – in accord with one's 'calling', life direction, or deepest truth spiritually and existentially.

Self-recognising – as a psycho-spiritual enquiry – appears in many different guises and shapes. While many may avoid such explorations, the majority of readers will recognise how central, how telling and how useful is this dimension and priority. The human capacities to reflect on ourselves and to share our life experiences and insights are, after all, distinguishing marks of our story telling species.

The fourth dimension: Experimenting – change and uncertainty

The ability to learn, extend the boundaries of what we know and to remain creative in uncertain conditions is an extraordinary evolutionary gift, perhaps humanity's greatest success story. Experimenting, in the sense I am using here, is critical in enabling change. Again, with this dimension, obviously we are not starting from scratch: much is well understood and practiced.

As members of our species we are good at finding fresh ways of doing things; seeking new solutions, and discarding established ways in favour of embracing novel ones. As a fundamental human activity, experimenting – in its purest form, trying things out and pilot testing ahead of adoption – is evident across all age groups. In young children experimenting is constant and obvious; with the elderly it is often more measured, considered and perhaps resisted. But age is often immaterial.

Experimenting is present in every facet of everyday experience, as part of the flow of ordinary living. In terms of manifesting competence, there's an observed sequence: (1) We draw on well-practised habits within the safety realm of familiarity. (2) Because of life changes, circumstances altering, or new knowledge in our outlooks and lives, we enter a space of questioning what is normal, regular, predictable, perhaps with the realisation that the old way may be insufficient or obsolescent. (3) Aware of the need to update, or reinvent something in our lives, we move towards the limits of what is known, actively contemplate a change, experience uncertainty yet also are readying ourselves to try something different, taking the step across the 'familiarity boundary' into the province of the untried and possibly risky. (4) Finally, sometimes calling for summoned courage and pausing for conducive conditions (unless we are pushed by an unavoidable challenge), we take the decisive step and discover a new field of unfolding possibility, previously unknown in experience however much anticipated or rehearsed.

Preparedness to try something not attempted before characterises many creative or demanding activities. Elements of constant experimenting are called for, existing alongside settled routines. Thus, for example, an experienced surgeon, like any professional or craftsperson will recognise, reports that 'there is always something different in every surgical procedure' with which they need to deal – a new angle, dilemma, or unexpected development.

Experimental approaches – with their emphasis on 'business as *un*usual' – may well disturb or dismantle established patterns. For a great many, the urge to experiment is central to their creative work or to gaining mastery in a particular field of endeavour – educational, cultural, sporting, social, artistic. This dimension of Whole Intelligence is reflected in human beings' wanting to extend their repertoire, perhaps signing up to develop new skills; holding knowledge provisionally rather than as fixed belief; and generating energy through taking the risk of doing something different from what's been practiced or achieved before. Discovering 'what turns up' is often accompanied by a frisson of excitement, or some delight and surprise.

In exploring the unusual, the light-heartedness and excitement of the novel may be tempered by notes of caution lightly held, or fears of 'going too far' or 'not far enough'. A capacity to laugh and question orthodoxy seems to infuse much-needed lifeblood to organisations that have existed too long on a diet of formal reports, sterile language, or overcautious thinking. Much recreation, play and art is designed to stimulate this kind of human exuberance – so obvious and accessible in the young and, alas, often muted later. An attitude of playfulness can dispel the tendency to take oneself and the ways of the world too seriously. It is not surprising that authoritarian regimes are often harsh towards cartoonists and others who puncture pomposity.

While experimenting and elements of boundary crossing may often seem advantageous, there is also its opposite pole to explore. For many people, predictable patterns and long-established institutions, habits and standard procedures are a lifeline. Honouring and keeping to agreed moral limits and respecting others' needs for security and reliability are essential accompaniments to living experimentally. Questioning and thinking afresh does not preclude preserving areas of order, routine and reliability as well.

The complexity of living more intelligently calls for weighing choices on a case-by-case basis.

Smooth-running regularities create predictable patterns that are welcomed as being safe, stabilising, maximally efficient, or as providing essential security. These advantages can be lost if there is too much disruption and loss of predictability. For example, moving people who are very elderly and frail from place to place, can be upsetting for them and endanger their health. People in shock need steadying, reassuring containing structures and no new demands. Severely traumatised children require stable parent-like figures and visible, guaranteed protection, in order to build or rebuild 'a secure base'. Likewise, in an organisation that has been through a period of much staff turnover and dislocation, the management's priority may be to concentrate on routine operations, with no changes in personnel and experimental innovation.

It is also a requirement in many medical and technological systems to maintain standardised practices. In hospitals, for example, or in air traffic control centres, uniform practice is necessary for safety. Here, taking a bold experimental approach that unsettles procedures might lead to catastrophe. At the same time, as in the movies, when there is an extreme emergency, with events not anticipated, perhaps only a bold experiment might save the day. In the catastrophic conditions of the World Trade Center on 11 September 2001, experimenting with breaking routine safety regulations saved lives.

The tensions surrounding experimenting and balancing change and stability have acute relevance for our era. In the midst of a knowledge explosion, scientific and technological developments might be outstripping the human capacity to adjust to what is being discovered. The world is an uncertain place that calls for attitudes of inquiry, openness and readiness to change. Yet it is also the case that all of us need familiar, well-known and broadly predictable features in our personal landscape. Stable and reliable background conditions are needed if we are to encounter elements that strike us as unpredictable, strange, odd, or novel. It is not surprising, perhaps, that with the spate of new ideas and experiences arriving at the present time along with permanently unsettling international news, people revert to rigid beliefs or adoptions of extreme ideas that they treat as fixed certainties, to be defended with righteousness.

These important conditions and warnings about removing predictabilities need to be heeded. Yet in terms of regenerating society and our public life, experimenting with new and different approaches is part of acting more intelligently. Balances have to be struck and discerning what these are is an intrinsic and important feature of experimenting. Given that Whole Intelligence is a necessity in achieving change successfully, in reforming institutions and for radical innovating, the qualities and cautions associated with experimenting deserve particular note.

This brings us to the fifth dimension, responding to the situation. *This has its own qualities and character. The fifth dimension in this account (they are not always presented in the same order) is also the equivalent to a keystone in an arch – a fundamental and more all-embracing feature of applying Whole intelligence as a contemporary resource.*

The fifth dimension: Responding to the situation

The fifth dimension of Whole Intelligence brings focus to how human beings respond to unique situations: the prevailing conditions and circumstances with which people are confronted. We have the capacity to size up what's called for and to act more (or less) intelligently. In doing so, we align with the nature of global life: every organism, from slime mould to trees, from bacteria to primate mammals, is to some extent adaptive and fluidly capable, adjusting to varied conditions.

In our contemporary human sphere, such 'attuned adjustment' requires attending to the multidimensional wholeness and complexity of our contemporary shared situation – one which is perplexing, dangerous and urgent. The acid test for Whole Intelligence is whether human beings – individually, in working teams, in communities, or in large configurations – can be helped to respond effectively to the overall situation confronting humanity in ways that make a difference.

Global problem-solving, central to responding, may be based on insightful studies – data collection and shrewd analysis, with thoughtful recommendations rationally argued and even specific and agreed proposals for actions to be taken. But we know this is only half the story, if that. The further stages – gathering of necessary resources, clear decision-taking, project management and full implementing of the plans – can easily falter, grind to a stop, or shoot off at an unintended angle. Sustained leadership of high quality is necessary to forestall such eventualities. Such leadership – reflected in 'making things happen' – sometimes exists; but there's not enough of it. Leaders, whether formally appointed, chosen by many or by few, are pivotal figures but the leadership function has to become more widely distributed. Those not in formal positions of power and responsibility can often take 'a leading part' – by propelling their ideas forward, or lending their energy, time, resources and commitment towards helping turn proposals into successful community-wide actions.

In responding to situations, the usual bureaucratic (and scientific) tendency is to divide complex reality into smaller sections, bringing in specialist perspectives that are necessary. Whole Intelligence stands for including movement in the opposite direction – emphasising the value in preserving 'wholeness' and complexity, rather than seeking to break these down into constituent parts. After all, nature does not reduce 'the whole' into 'parts' or into simpler and more manageable categories. There are specialist advantages in applying reductionist principles – such as achieving administrative uniformity and easier quantification – but there are also costs in stripping things from their settings and surroundings, with phenomena no longer appearing in the context and conditions of their arising. A crucial type of human-scale skilfulness can easily get downgraded or dismissed: namely the act of drawing upon accumulated experience derived from numerous previous engagements with situations of ecological style complexity.

There are numerous ways to respond to practical situations. Adult human beings, as we know, can be versatile and resourceful. Adventurers seek out steeper paths to climb or more exacting problems to solve: deliberately creating situations to challenge themselves. Others have unwanted situations thrust upon them and yet manage to adjust and survive under appalling conditions, often uncomplainingly.

Some teams and individuals – often in the face of 'overwhelming odds', are unable to access their capacity for resourcefulness. Their situations seem frightening and in these conditions staying resilient and coping with complexity is dramatically reduced. Many of us can identify with both ends of the continuum – times and places when we have felt on top of things, risen to challenges and discovered reservoirs of hidden strength; while at other times in our lives we have wilted in the face of obligations, given up too soon, dithered when clarity and decisiveness was required of us, or have fallen into some downward spiral or addiction that increases a sense of hopelessness and shame.

Many programmes and opportunities exist – or *need to exist* if they do not already – that increase or restore people's sense of empowerment and resilience, upholding and affirming their capacity to function in challenging circumstances and unprecedented conditions. Encouragement, respectful support, and access to new opportunities can all help revive and sustain people's sense of agency, entitlement and freedom to choose.

This brings me to acknowledge how this fifth dimension of Whole Intelligence has acquired its somewhat different status. While all the dimensions are interlinked, mutually supportive, and necessary, responding to the situation *is pivotal. The four dimensions already outlined provide the 'means whereby' people, teams, communities, or whole populations can respond more effectively to situations they encounter, whether local and intimate or global and all-embracing. Thus, for example,* interrelating *with others helps build solidarity and cooperation;* self-recognising *enables each party to identify the unique contribution they can make;* experimenting *highlights creative possibilities; and* embodying *supports finding strength, energy and (metaphorically and actually) their capacity for flexible movement.*

Inevitably, faced with shared situations – and especially existential challenges of the highest order – everyone's responses will differ. For all of us – when facing any perilous, demanding, or unusual situation not just a global emergency – there are multiple influences acting upon and within each person or grouping. Each of us is affected by the values we hold and are committed to, how energised we are, how we think we can make a difference or take a leading part. Each of us can draw upon relevant strengths, talents and capacities or begin to develop them with more consciousness and determination (Eger 2017). Self-styled non-responders and fence sitters – for instance, those who do not vote, refuse to participate, or who define themselves as too inadequate or powerless to express a point of view – are all still responding to the world's situation – they respond by withdrawing energy, leaving matters to others, or denying the obvious, namely, that every human being truly alive and not in gross denial is an inevitable participant.

Five dimensions together

Full employment of human beings' Whole Intelligence comes about through integrating all five dimensions. None of the dimensions pursued alone will suffice to bring about a fundamental global renaissance – it is the combination of all five areas of human competence that just might. 'But how?', I am asked. My answer is that we have to think and act like ecologists restoring a degraded ecosystem. The living human world we share – as our collective field of beliefs, norms, assumptions, common behaviours, and contradictory value systems in operation – is hugely complex (and very like an ecosystem in that respect). Some, like Plotkin (2021), speak of humanity's 'arrested development'. Shifting our world system – to enable humanity to 'grow up' – may seem impossible, but again ecologists show a way forward. In a local context, they take small initiatives – like increasing access to sunlight, dredging a pond, reintroducing a native species – that may remove a hindrance, thereby supporting natural processes of adaptation and self-repair to arise. In a parallel way, in the lived human world, small acts of Whole Intelligence can spirit new trends into existence. Thus, for instance, in a workplace setting, inter-relating may become freer and friendlier if a single action of resolving differences is observed; it demonstrates what is possible. Likewise, one family supporting wildlife (say, by protecting hedgehogs) can stimulate other families to do something similar. Each of the Whole Intelligence five dimensions can serve as a stimulus, support, and incremental step to increased consciousness and living more boldly and intelligently. The more the dimensions are noticed, role-modelled, actively explored and appreciated, the more they can help to change the conversation and inspire new initiatives. The same ecological approach applies to individuals, to small groups and teams, and can be upscaled to whole organisations and public institutions. To achieve societal change, the entire lived-in world needs to open to new possibilities, restoring confidence and integrity, and living with a deeper understanding. Whole Intelligence suggests five interlinked pathways of development whereby individuals – or organisations, communities, human systems in general – can act in ways that are beneficial for the greater whole, the planetary ecosystem. Thus, they are in a sense prescriptive but not plucked from thin air. In large measure they are already known to us. They attempt to answer the question of 'how to love this world'. *What might come from humanity living more intelligently? The answer is unknown. But given many examples of poisoning the world, what are needed are antidotes, nourishing ideas, restorative steps, and routes to live more intelligently. All I and my colleagues can do is set a ball rolling and invite others to add to its momentum. Whole Intelligence might be a trigger for the dawning revolution of thought or may simply add to the ferment of deep questioning happening all around us (including in this book). For readers wanting to go further and discover more of the Whole Intelligence approach as it spreads, please continue to* www.wholeintelligence.org.

References

Eger, E. (2017) *The choice*. London: Rider.

Graeber, D. and Wengrow, D. (2021) *The dawn of everything*. London: Allen Lane.

McGilchrist, I. (2021) *The matter with things*. London: Perspectiva Press.

Parlett, M. (2016/2024) *Future sense*. Leicester: Troubador.

Plotkin, B. (2021) *The journey of soul initiation*. San Francisco: New World Library.

Siegel, D.J. (2023) *IntraConnected*. New York: Norton.

· 1 9 ·

BEYOND ARTIFICIAL INTELLIGENCE: TOWARD INTEGRATED INTELLIGENCE FOR A WORLD-IN-CRISIS[1]

Jeremy Lent

The explosive rise in the power of AI presents humanity with an existential risk. To counter that risk, and potentially redirect our civilization's trajectory, we need a more integrated understanding of the nature of human intelligence and the fundamental requirements for human flourishing.

The recent explosion in the stunning power of artificial intelligence is likely to transform virtually every domain of human life in the near future, with effects that no one can yet predict.

The breakneck rate at which AI is developing is such that its potential impact is almost impossible to grasp. As Tristan Harris and Aza Raskin, co-founders of the Centre for Humane Technology, demonstrate in their landmark presentation, The AI Dilemma, AI accomplishments are beginning to read like science fiction (Harris and Raskin, 2023). After just three seconds of hearing a human voice, for example, an AI system can autocomplete the sentence being spoken with a voice so perfectly matched that no one can distinguish it from the real thing. AI linked with fMRI brain imaging technology, they show us, can now reconstruct what a person's brain is thinking and represent it accurately as an image.

AI models are beginning to exhibit emergent capabilities their programmers didn't programme into them. An AI model trained to answer questions in English can suddenly understand and answer questions in Persian without being trained in the language – and no one, not even its programmers, knows why. ChatGPT, to the surprise of its own programmers, was discovered to have trained itself in research-level chemistry even though that wasn't part of its targeted training data (Harris and Raskin, 2023).

Many of these developments have been unfolding at a time scale no longer measured in months and years, but in weeks and days. Experts are comparing the significance of the AI phenomenon to the invention of the nuclear bomb, except with a spine-chilling difference: whereas the magnitude of the nuclear threat could only increase at the pace of scientists' own capabilities, AI is becoming increasingly capable of learning how to make itself more powerful. In recent examples, AI models have learned to generate their own training data to self-improve, and to edit sections of code so as to make the code work at more than double the speed. AI capabilities have already been expanding at an exponential rate, largely as a result of the distributed network effects of programmers building on each other's breakthroughs. But given these recent developments, experts are forecasting future improvements at a double exponential rate, which begins to look on a graph like a vertical line of potentiality exploding upward.

The term generally used to describe this phenomenon, which heretofore has been a hypothetical thought experiment, is a *Singularity*. Back in 1965, at the outset of the computer age, British mathematician, I. J. Good, first described this powerful and unsettling vision. 'Let an ultraintelligent machine,' he wrote, 'be defined as a machine that can far surpass all the intellectual activities of any man however clever. Since the design of machines is one of these intellectual activities, an ultraintelligent machine could design even better machines; there would then unquestionably be an "intelligence explosion", and the intelligence of man would be left far behind. Thus the first ultraintelligent machine is the last invention that man need ever make' (Good, 1965, see also Vinge, 2013).

Nearly six decades after it was first conceived, the Singularity has mutated from a theoretical speculation to an urgent existential concern. Of course, it is easy to enumerate the myriad potential benefits of an ultraintelligent computer: discoveries of cures to debilitating diseases; ultra-sophisticated, multifaceted automation to replace human drudgery; technological solutions to humanity's most pressing problems. Conversely, observers are also pointing out the dangerously disruptive potential of advanced AI on a world already fraying at the seams: the risk of deep fakes and automated bots polarising society even further; personalised AI assistants exploiting people for profit and exacerbating the epidemic of social isolation; and greater centralisation of power to a few mega-corporations, to name but a few of the primary issues. But even beyond these serious concerns, leading AI experts are warning that an advanced artificial general intelligence ('AGI') is likely to represent a grave threat, not just to human civilisation, but to the very existence of humanity and the continuation of life on Earth.

The alignment problem

At the root of this profound risk is something known as the *alignment problem*. What would happen, we must ask, if a superhuman intelligence wants to achieve some goal that's out of alignment with the conditions required for human welfare – or for that matter, the survival of life itself on Earth? This misalignment could simply be the result of misguided human programming. Prominent futurist Nick Bostrom (n.d.) gives an example of a superintelligence designed with the goal of manufacturing paperclips that transforms the entire Earth into a gigantic paperclip manufacturing facility.

It's also quite conceivable that a superintelligent AI could develop its own goal orientation, which would be highly likely to be misaligned with human flourishing (Bengio, 2023). The AI might not see humans as an enemy to be eliminated, but we could simply become collateral damage to its own purposes, in the same way that orangutans, mountain gorillas, and a myriad other species face extinction as the result of human activity. For example, a superintelligence might want to optimise the Earth's atmosphere for its own processing speed, leading to a biosphere that could no longer sustain life.

As superintelligence moves from a thought experiment to an urgently looming existential crisis, many leading analysts who have studied these issues for decades are extraordinarily terrified and trying to raise the alarm before it's too late. MIT professor Max Tegmark, a highly respected physicist and president of the Future of Life Institute, considers this our 'Don't Look Up' moment (Tegmark, 2023a), referring to the satirical movie in which an asteroid threatens life on Earth with extinction, but a plan to save the planet is waylaid by corporate interests and the public's inability to turn their attention away from celebrity gossip. In an intimate podcast interview, Tegmark likens our situation to receiving a terminal cancer diagnosis for the entire human race, declaring that 'there's a pretty large chance that we're not going to make it as humans; that there won't be any humans on the planet in the not-too-distant future – and that makes me very sad' (Tegmark, 2023b).

Tegmark's fear is shared by other leading experts. Eliezer Yudkowsky, who has been working on aligning AGI since 2001 and is widely regarded as a founder of the field, points out that 'a sufficiently intelligent AI won't stay confined to computers for long (Yudkowsky, 2023). In today's world you can email DNA strings to laboratories that will produce proteins on demand, allowing an AI initially confined to the internet to build artificial life forms or bootstrap straight to postbiological molecular manufacturing.' Yudkowsky calls for an immediate and indefinite worldwide moratorium on further AI development, enforced by coordinated international military action if necessary.

In the short-term, there are several policy proposals urged by leaders in the AI community to try to rein in some of the more obvious societal disruptions anticipated by AI's increasingly pervasive influence. An open letter calling for a pause on further development for at least six months has over thirty thousand signatories, including many of the most prominent names in the field. Beyond a worldwide moratorium, proposals include a requirement that any AI-generated material is clearly labelled as such; a stipulation that all new AI source code is published to enable transparency; and a legal presumption that new versions of AI are unsafe unless proven otherwise, putting the burden of proof on AI developers to demonstrate its safety prior to its deployment – analogous to the legal framework used in the pharmaceutical industry.

These proposals are eminently sensible and should promptly be enacted by national governments, while a UN-sponsored international panel of AI experts should be appointed to recommend further guidelines for worldwide adoption. Ultimately, the overarching strategy of such guidelines should be to restrict the further empowerment of AI unless or until the alignment problem itself can be satisfactorily solved.

There is, however, a serious misconception seemingly shared by the vast majority of AI theorists that must be recognised and corrected for any serious progress to be made in the alignment problem. This relates to the nature of intelligence itself. Until a deeper understanding of what comprises intelligence is more widely embraced in the AI community, we are in danger, not just of failing to resolve the alignment problem, but of moving in the wrong direction in its consideration.

Conceptual and animate intelligence

When AI theorists write about intelligence, they frequently start from the presumption that there is only one form of intelligence: the kind of analytical intelligence that gets measured in an IQ test and has enabled the human species to dominate the rest of the natural world – and the type in which AI now threatens to surpass us (Sternberg, 2021). The AI community is not alone in this presumption – it is shared by most people in the modern world, and forms a central part of the mainstream view of what it means to be a human being. When Descartes declared '*cogito ergo sum*' – 'I think, therefore I am' – setting the intellectual foundation for modern philosophical thought, he was giving voice to a presumption that the faculty of conceptual thought was humanity's defining characteristic, setting humanity apart from all other living beings. Animals, according to Descartes and the majority of scientists ever since, were mere machines acting without subjectivity or thought (see Lent, 2021, chapter 3).

However, the human conceptualising faculty, powerful as it is, is only one form of intelligence. There is another form – animate intelligence – that is an integral part of human cognition, and which we share with the rest of life on Earth.

If we understand intelligence, as it's commonly defined to be the ability to perceive or infer information and apply it toward adaptive behaviours, intelligence exists everywhere in the living world. It's relatively easy to see it in high-functioning mammals such as elephants that can communicate through infrasound over hundreds of miles and perform what appear like ceremonies over the bones of dead relatives (Bates et al., 2008, pp. 544–546); or in cetaceans that communicate in sophisticated 'languages' and are thought to 'gossip' about community members that are absent (Safina, 2015, pp. 92, 211, 236–237; Kieran et al., 2017, pp. 1699–1705; Kropshofer, 2017). But extensive animate intelligence has also been identified in plants which, in addition to their own versions of our five senses, also use up to fifteen other ways to sense their environment. Plants have elaborate internal signalling systems, utilising the same chemicals – such as serotonin or dopamine – that act as neurotransmitters in humans; and they have been shown to act intentionally and purposefully: they have memory and learn, they communicate with each other, and can even allocate resources as a community (Simard et al., 1997; Brenner et al., 2006; Trewavas, 2009; Song et al., 2010; Mancuso, 2018; Calvo et al., 2020).

Animate intelligence can be discerned even at a cellular level: a single cell has thousands of sensors protruding through its outer membrane, controlling the flow of specific molecules, either pulling them in or pushing them out depending on what's needed. Cells utilise fine-tuned signalling mechanisms to communicate with others around them, sending and receiving hundreds of signals at the same time. Each cell must be aware of itself *as* a self: it 'knows' what is within its membrane and what is outside; it determines what molecules it needs, and which ones to discard; it knows when something within it needs fixing, and how to get it done; it determines what genes to express within its DNA, and when it's time to divide and thus propagate itself. In the words of philosopher of biology Evan Thompson, 'Where there is life there is mind' (Rensberger, 1996; Ford, 2006, 2009; Thompson, 2007).

When leading cognitive neuroscientists investigate human consciousness, they make a similar differentiation between two forms of consciousness which, like intelligence, can also be classified as conceptual and animate. For example, Nobel Prize winner Gerald Edelman distinguished between what he called primary (animate) and secondary (conceptual) consciousness, while world-renowned neuroscientist Antonio Damasio makes a similar distinction between what he calls core and higher-order consciousness. Similarly, in psychology, dual systems theory posits two forms of human cognition – intuitive and analytical – described compellingly in Daniel Kahneman's bestseller *Thinking Fast and Slow*, which correspond to the animate and conceptual split within both intelligence and consciousness (Damasio, 1999; Edelman and Tononi, 2000; Kahneman, 2011).

Toward an integrated intelligence

An implication of this increasingly widespread recognition of the existence of both animate and conceptual intelligence is that the Cartesian conception of intelligence as solely analytical – one that's shared by a large majority of AI theorists – is dangerously limited.

Even human conceptual intelligence has been shown to emerge from a scaffolding of animate consciousness. As demonstrated convincingly by cognitive linguist George Lakoff, the abstract ideas and concepts we use to build our theoretical models of the world actually arise from metaphors of our embodied experience of the world – high and low, in and out, great and small, near and close, empty and full. Contrary to the Cartesian myth of a pure thinking faculty, our conceptual and animate intelligences are intimately linked.

By contrast, machine intelligence really is purely analytical. It has no scaffolding linking it to the vibrant sentience of life. Regardless of its level of sophistication and power, it is nothing other than a pattern recognition device. AI theoreticians tend to think of intelligence as substrate independent – meaning that the set of patterns and linkages comprising it could in principle be separated from its material base and exactly replicated elsewhere, such as when you migrate the data from your old computer to a new one. That is true for AI, but not for human intelligence (see Damasio, 2018, pp. 199–208 for a lucid explanation of why human intelligence is not substrate-independent).

The dominant view of humanity as defined solely by conceptual intelligence has contributed greatly to the dualistic worldview underlying many of the great predicaments facing society today. The accelerating climate crisis and ecological havoc being wreaked on the natural world ultimately are caused, at the deepest level, by the dominant instrumentalist worldview that sees humans as essentially separate from the rest of nature, and nature as nothing other than a resource for human consumption.

Once, however, we recognise that humans possess both conceptual and animate intelligence, this can transform our sense of identity as a human being. The most highly prized human qualities, such as compassion, integrity, or wisdom, arise not from conceptual intelligence alone, but from a complex mélange of thoughts, feelings, intuitions, and felt sensations integrated into a coherent whole. By learning to consciously attune to the evolved signals of our animate consciousness, we can develop an *integrated intelligence*: one that incorporates both conceptual and animate fully into our own identity, values, and life choices.

Once we embrace our own animate intelligence, it's natural to turn our attention outward and appreciate the animate intelligence emanating from all living beings. Acknowledging our shared domain of intelligence with the rest of life can lead to a potent sense of being intimately connected with the animate world. If conceptual intelligence is a cognitive peak of specialisation that distinguishes us from other animals, it is our animate intelligence that extends throughout the rest of the terrain of existence, inviting a shared collaboration with all of life.

Other cultures have long possessed this understanding. Traditional Chinese philosophers saw no essential distinction between reason and emotion, and used a particular word, *tiren*, to refer to knowing something, not just intellectually, but throughout the entire body and mind. In the words of Neo-Confucian sage Wang Yangming, 'The heart-mind is nothing without the body, and the body is nothing without the heart-mind' (Munro, 2005, p. 24; Yu, 2007, see Lent, 2017, chapters 9 and 14 for extensive discussion of the traditional integrative nature of Chinese thought). Indigenous cultures around the world share a recognition of their deep relatedness to all living beings, leading them to conceive of other creatures as part of an extended family (Jacobs and

Narvaes, 2022). For Western culture, however, which is now the globally dominant source of values, this orientation toward integrated intelligence is rare but acutely needed.

Aligning with integration

These distinctions, theoretical as they might appear, have crucially important implications as we consider the onset of advanced artificial intelligence and how to wrestle with the alignment problem. Upon closer inspection, the alignment problem turns out to be a conflation of two essentially different problems: The question of how to align AI with human flourishing presupposes an underlying question of what is required for human flourishing in the first place. Without a solid foundation laying out the conditions for human well-being, the AI alignment question is destined to go nowhere.

Fortunately, much work has already been accomplished on this topic, and it points to human flourishing arising from our identity as a deeply integrated organism incorporating both conceptual and animate consciousness. The seminal work of Chilean economist Manfred Max-Neef sets out a comprehensive taxonomy of fundamental human needs, incorporating ten core requirements such as subsistence, affection, freedom, security, and participation, among others. While these needs are universal, they may be satisfied in myriad ways depending on particular historical and cultural conditions. Furthermore, as Earth system scientists have convincingly demonstrated, human systems are intimately linked with larger biological and planetary life-support systems. Sustained human well-being requires a healthy, vibrant living Earth with intact ecosystems that can readily replenish their own abundance (Max-Neef, 1991; Rockstrom et al., 2009; Ripple et al., 2017).

What, we might ask, might an AI look like that was programmed to align with the principles that could enable all life, including human civilisation, to flourish on a healthy Earth?

When we consider, however, how far the requirements for flourishing are from being met by the vast majority of humans across wide swaths of the world today, this brings to light that the alignment problem is not, in fact, limited to the domain of AI, but is rather a fundamental issue underlying the economic and financial system that runs our modern world. As I've discussed elsewhere, global capitalism, as manifested in the limited liability corporation, may itself be understood as an embryonic form of misaligned AI: one where the overriding goal of maximising shareholder value has ridden roughshod over fundamental human needs, and has led to the current meta-crisis emanating from a confluence of rising inequality, runaway technology, climate breakdown, and accelerating ecological devastation (Lent, n.d.). In this respect, as pointed out by social philosopher Daniel Schmachtenberger, advanced AI can be viewed as an accelerant of the underlying causes of the meta-crisis in every dimension (Schmachtenberger, 2021). Emerging from this dark prognostication, there is a silver lining affording some hope for a societal swerve toward a life-affirming future. When analysts consider the great dilemmas facing humanity today, they frequently describe them as 'wicked problems': tangles of highly complex interlinked challenges lacking well-defined solutions and emerging over time frames that don't present as clear emergencies to our cognitive systems which evolved in the savannah to respond to more immediate risks. As an accelerant of the misalignment already present in our global system, might the onset of advanced AI, with its clear and present existential danger, serve to wake us up, as a collective human species, to the unfolding civilisational disaster that is already looming ahead? Might it jolt us as a planetary community to reorient toward the wisdom available in traditional cultures and existing within our own animate intelligence?

It has sometimes been said that what is necessary to unite humanity is a flagrant common threat, such as a hypothetical hostile alien species arriving on Earth threating us with extinction. Perhaps that moment is poised to arrive now – with an alien intelligence emerging from our own machinations. If there is real hope for a positive future, it will emerge from our understanding that as humans, we are both conceptual and animate beings, and are deeply connected with all of life on this precious planet – and that collectively we have the capability of developing a truly integrative civilisation, one that sets the conditions for all life to flourish on a regenerated Earth.

Note

1 This chapter is based on Jeremy Lent's personal blog publication 'To counter AI risk we must develop an integrated intelligence' https://patternsofmeaning.com/2023/06/20/to-counter-ai-risk-we-must-develop-an-integrated-intelligence/. Posted June 20, 2023.

References

Bates, L.A., Poole, J.H. and Bryne, R.W. (2008) 'Elephant cognition', *Current Biology*, 18(13), pp. 544–546.

Bengio, Y. (2023) *How rogue Ais may arise.* https://yoshuabengio.org/2023/05/22/how-rogue-ais-may-arise/, accessed 28 March 2024.

Bostrom, N. (n.d.) *Ethical issues in advanced artificial intelligence.* https://nickbostrom.com/ethics/ai, accessed 28 March 2024.

Brenner, E.D., et al. (2006) 'Plant neurobiology: An integrated view of plant signaling', *Trends in Plant Science*, 11(8), pp. 413–419.

Calvo, P., et al. (2020) 'Plants are intelligent, here's how', *Annals of Botany*, 125, pp. 11–28.

Damasio, A. (1999) *The feeling of what happens: Body and emotion in the making of consciousness.* New York: Harcourt Inc.

Damasio, A. (2018) *The strange order of things: Life, feeling, and the making of cultures.* New York: Pantheon.

Edelman, G.M. and Tononi, G. (2000) *A universe of consciousness: How matter becomes imagination.* New York: Basic Books.

Ford, B.J. (2006) 'Revealing the ingenuity of the living cell', *Biologist*, 53(4), pp. 221–224.

Ford, B.J. (2009) 'On intelligence in cells: The case for whole cell biology', *Interdisciplinary Science Reviews*, 34(4), pp. 350–365.

Harris, T. and Raskin, A. (2023) *The A.I. dilemma.* Centre for Humane Technology. https://www.youtube.com/watch?v=xoVJKj8lcNQ, accessed 28 March 2024.

Jacobs, D.T. (Four Arrows), and Narvaez, D. (2022) *Restoring the kinship worldview: Indigenous voices introduce 28 precepts for rebalancing life on planet earth.* Berkeley, CA: North Atlantic Books.

Good, I. (1965) *I.J. Good.* https://en.wikipedia.org/wiki/I._J._Good, accessed 28 March 2024.

Kahneman, D. (2011) *Thinking fast and slow.* New York: Farrar, Straus & Giroux.

Kieran C.R.F., Muthukrishna, M. and Shultz, S. (2017, November) 'The social and cultural roots of whale and dolphin brains', *Nature Ecology & Evolution*, 1, pp. 1699–1705.

Kropshofer, K. (2017) 'Whales and dolphins lead "human-like lives" thanks to big brains, says study', *The Guardian*, 16 October, p. 705.

Lent, J. (2017) *The patterning instinct: A cultural history of humanity's search for meaning.* Amherst, NY: Prometheus.

Lent, J. (2021) *The web of meaning: Integrating science and traditional wisdom to find our place in the universe.* London: Profile Books.

Lent, J. (n.d.) 'AI has already taken over. It's called the corporation', *Patterns of Meaning.* https://patternsofmeaning.com/2017/11/30/ai-has-already-taken-over-its-called-the-corporation/, accessed 28 March 2024.

Mancuso, S. (2018) *The revolutionary genius of plants: A new understanding of plant intelligence and behavior.* New York: Atria Books.

Max-Neef, M.A. (1991) *Human scale development: Conception, application and further reflections.* New York: Zed Books.

Munro, D.J. (2005) *A Chinese ethics for the new century: The Ch'ien Mu lectures in history and culture, and other essays on science and Confucian ethics.* Hong Kong: The Chinese University Press.

Rensberger, B. (1996) *Life itself: Exploring the realm of the living cell.* New York: Oxford University Press.

Ripple, W.J., et al. (2017) 'World scientists' warning to humanity: A second notice', *BioScience*, 67(12), pp. 1026–1028.

Rockström, J., et al. (2009) 'A safe operating space for humanity', *Nature*, 461, pp. 472–475.

Safina, C. (2015) *Beyond words: What animals think and feel.* New York: Henry Holt.

Schmachtenberger, D. (2021) *Artificial intelligence and the superorganism.* https://www.youtube.com/watch?v=_P8PLHvZygo&t=10163s, accessed 28 March 2024.

Simard, S.W., et al. (1997) 'Net transfer of carbon between ectomycorrhizal tree species in the field', *Nature*, 388, pp. 579–582.

Song, Y.Y., et al. (2010), 'Interplant communication of tomato plants through underground common mycorrhizal networks', *PLoS Biology*, 5(10), p. e13324.

Sternberg, R. (2021) 'We've got intelligence all wrong – and that's endangering our future', *New Scientist*, 13 January 2021. https://www.newscientist.com/article/mg24933174-700-weve-got-intelligence-all-wrong-and-thats-endangering-our-future/, accessed 28 March 2024.

Tegmark, M. (2023a) 'The don't look up' thinking that could doom us with AI', *Time*, 25 April 2023. https://time.com/6273743/thinking-that-could-doom-us-with-ai/, accessed 28 March 2024.

Tegmark, M. (2023b) *The case for halting AI development.* https://www.youtube.com/watch?v=VcVfceTsD0A&t=6781s, accessed 28 March 2024.

Thompson, E. (2007) *Mind in life: Biology, phenomenology, and the sciences of mind.* Cambridge, MA: Harvard University Press.

Trewavas, A. (2009) 'What is plant behaviour?', *Plant, Cell and Environment*, 32, pp. 606–616.

Vinge, V. (2013) 'Technological singularity' in Moore, M. and Vita-More, N. (eds.) *The transhumanist reader.* Wiley & Sons, Chapter 35, pp. 365–376. Original 1993: http://www.wizdom.org.uk/TheVingeSingularity.shtml, accessed 28 March 2024.

Yu, N. (2007) 'Heart and cognition in ancient Chinese philosophy', *Journal of Cognition and Culture*, 7(1–2), pp. 27–47.

Yudkowsky, E. (2023) 'Pausing AI developments isn't enough. We need to shut it all down', *Time*, 29 March 2023. https://time.com/6266923/ai-eliezer-yudkowsky-open-letter-not-enough/, accessed 28 March 2023.

Afterword

CULTURAL RESPONSE AND CREATIVE RESILIENCE: A PERSONAL REFLECTION

Simon Cottle

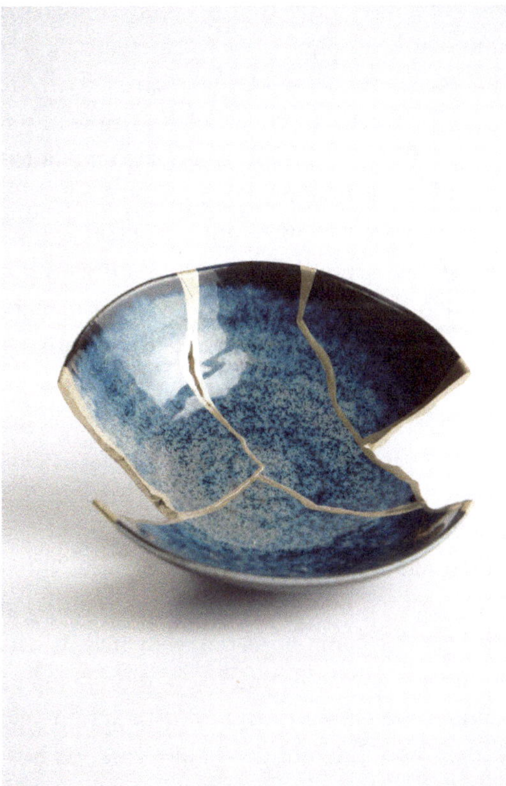

Figure 20.1 Kintsugi Bowl, @Theo.Cottle

Japanese artisans, going back centuries, have repaired broken pieces of ceramic using lacquer and gold pigments. The art of Kintsugi ('to patch with gold') or Kintsukuroi ('to repair with gold') does not seek to hide the break or the repair but on the contrary throws them into sharp relief. The imperfections and flaws of a mended object are thus granted enhanced beauty and seen as more resilient than the original. The evident marks of breakage and repair speak to the object's unique history and its regenerated utility.

When seen as a metaphor of life, Kintsugi points to how we can become stronger, wiser and more compassionate through the struggles and calamities of life. Building on Buddhist and Wabi-sabi traditions of thought, people are marked by their life experiences, but so too can they heal and better recognise their strengths and weaknesses. In such ways, they may display increased humility and even equanimity in the face of suffering and change. The art of Kintsugi also holds, I suggest, metaphorical insights for our world-in-crisis, and not only in respect of how we must each individually recognise and reorient ourselves to change. To a world that is now visibly cracking and breaking, but a world that simultaneously also gives rise to emergent ideas, cultural flourishing, imagined futures and possible solidary remedies. These regenerative ideas and practices borne from a world-in-crisis help to throw into relief our place in the web-of-life and how an ecologically sustainable and more socially just (and survivable) world could yet be imagined and come about.

All the contributors to this volume are of course deeply concerned about the daunting challenges that now confront humanity and life on Earth, and all have sought, through their reflections on different media and communicative fields, to identify examples of innovation and creative practice that can better intervene into this world. From eco-literature, ecoart and ecocinema to climate emergency photography and participative documentary; from hidden theatre and immersive museums to green festivals and popular music; from sustainability education and journalism training to communicating whole intelligence 'for a world waking up' and to the need for AI (artificial intelligence) to move beyond instrumental rationality to integrative intelligence and ecological relationality – so each of these interventions has identified how these and possibly other forms of communication can help to envision and reorient society to a better world. Studies of First Nation community media, local television programmes reporting on local climate actions, different reporting roles in climate change, and different news platforms and how these delimit or deepen reporting of direct-action protests, have also explored important communicative possibilities within the different forms and practices of journalism.

And so too have we considered journalism's capacity for representing 'future imaginaries', whether cultivated and/or compelled in the years ahead.

Together these chapters and their authors belie simplistic claims of 'doomerism' or 'catastrophism' when directed at those engaging with the cascading crises unfolding at planetary scale. To recognise today's planetary demise and to want to better understand and communicate something of its systemic nature to others need not, of course, cancel out the equally felt imperative to find positive communicative ways of responding and intervening within these structures of risk, destabilisation and breakdown. It is only on the basis of communicative engagement and a realist understanding of today's existential threats, rather than complacency or simplistic optimism, that we can start to create with others collective, innovative and meaningful expressions of active hope (Macy and Johnstone, 2021). And this, as we have heard, encompasses diverse communicative realms of media and creative practices.

When immersed in writing, reflecting and communicating on such matters this can nonetheless be experienced as a deeply unsettling and emotionally upsetting experience. The psychological processes of recognition, response and eventual formation of resilience have often been likened to the processes and stages of bereavement and grief. Given the felt sense of disorientation and loss following the disappearance of traditional expectations about our world, its continuity, the arc of life and imagined futures, whether for ourselves, our loved ones, those yet born, or for humanity and Life in general on planet Earth, this too is understandable. It is an inescapable part, it seems, of the personal experience of communicating a world-in-crisis.

Here, then, I simply share a few thoughts and reflections on some of the difficulties and dilemmas that can be encountered when trying to communicate to others something of today's planetary emergency, as well as possible sources of solace and yes, even hope, when doing so. Possibly some of these experiences and thoughts may resonate with your own communicative engagement with today's meta-crisis, whether in your personal or professional life, or in other ways. If, like me, you sometimes feel dismayed or even overwhelmed by what we now see looming on the horizon and also by what is inexorably pushing it there, by what we see nightly on our TV screens, or algorithmically via social media, and by the evident lack of serious attention and sustained response to this, whether by governments and corporations, colleagues, family or friends and vast swathes of the world's populace, something here may strike a chord.

It's worth saying at the outset, I know of no authors, academics or activists who relish painting hellish scenes like Hieronymus Bosh, imparting bad news like a late-modern Cassandra, or prophetically predicting calamity like Nostradamus. And even fewer, I suggest, would want to risk being cast in the cloak of early Christian millennialism that drapes talk of the apocalypse. It is also easy to feel overwhelmed not only by the sheer size and complexities of the 'wicked problems' now being played out at planetary level (Chapter 1), but also by the daily sense of cognitive dissonance and isolation when positioned outside of the normative, some say increasingly deranged, continuation of daily life as normal (Ghosh, 2016). The simplistic charge of doomerism or catastrophism levelled at news output is sometimes also muttered in response to those academic and activist whistle-blowers of 'planetary emergency', 'global polycrisis', 'world at risk' and 'civilizational collapse'. And this notwithstanding the rapidly accumulating evidence, reasoned extrapolations and informed theorisations of eco-societal destabilisation and breakdown at world scale (Chapter 1).

Too many of us, it seems, continue to see the world's problems in single-issue terms and not as an integral expression of complex systems and some continue to bury their heads in the (tar)sands of a hubristic faith in last-minute techno-fixes and large-scale geo-engineering projects. Others take solace in piecemeal consumerist agendas on the home front, whether the increased uptake of EVs, recycling of rubbish or healthier lifestyles. But we thereby leave the underlying and systemic nature of today's world-in-crisis, as well as its cast of political and corporate spoilers, relatively untouched. And some of us, academics included, manage to practically disavow in our daily routines and actions that which is quietly recognised but kept out of mind. Such existential aversion becomes banished from thought for a mix of professional, psychological, political and phenomenological reasons (Chapter 2, Cottle, 2023). The relative safety of academic silos, comfort of narrow specialisms and established parameters of disciplinary outlooks and institutional agendas, amongst other factors, can all detract from planetary vision and engagement.

I have personally felt intense feelings of eco-grief and eco-anger, including *solastalgia* (the deep sense of sadness following the degradation and loss of known environments) and *terrafurie* (the feelings of anger at continuing ecological devastation) amongst others (see Albrecht, 2019), and how these can weigh heavily when thinking about and writing on communications and our world-in-crisis. I am not alone. This increased salience of complex emotional responses to a faltering, failing world moreover does not always sit well inside institutional expectations and traditional academic discourse.

Notwithstanding earlier interventions by feminist and ethnography scholars, for example, as well as more recent calls for pluriverse views and differing epistemological standpoints, academic discourse still tends toward the logocentric, analytic, distanced and impersonal. This communicative register all too often displaces the emotional underpinning of much academic labour as well as first-person reflections on the author's hopes and fears. While there may indeed be a good case sometimes for communicating in and through the impersonal and emotionally evacuated discourse of traditional academia and science, when writing on the plight of the planet, its consequences and the hopes invested in pathways of transition and transformation, it seems that innovative, creative, visual and emotionally evocative forms of communication can and should be deployed when practicable and impactful. The deliberate use of Guno Park's symbolically resonate and arresting image (front cover) is perhaps a good illustration of this.

Some of us may also want to revisit and expand beyond the de-limited academic orientation that confines itself to critique. In a world-in-crisis is it now time to expand upon the *hermeneutics of critique*, (or *hermeneutics of suspicion* to use Paul Ricoeur's earlier literary phrase), to something more akin to a *hermeneutics of engagement and care*? At this perilous juncture on planet Earth, are we not obligated to seek to go beyond detached and siloed academic critique and make our research agendas, words, arguments and concerns intervene within this world, and to do so with compassion and care that extends to all sentient beings and surrounding ecosystems?

A useful parallel is found, surprisingly possibly, in the world of journalism. Here journalists occasionally prove capable of moving beyond a normalised and professionally institutionalised response when reporting humanitarian disasters (Cottle, 2013). The usual 'calculus of death' reporting stance – where human suffering and deaths are portrayed differently according to national geopolitical interests and historical and cultural proximity – is sometimes deepened with a journalistically inscribed 'injunction to care'. In contradistinction to detached and dispassionate 'calculus of death' reporting, an 'injunction to care' is crafted through close-up images, personalised stories and experiential and emotional accounts as well as the incorporation of multiple sensory invocations all designed to 'bring home' something of the human tragedy involved. When done well, such news reporting communicates across informational and imagistic, analytic and affective, expositional and expressive, and deliberative and display modes of communication.

And, as we have heard across many of the preceding chapters, these and other communicative forms and appeals are now variously being deployed in different communicative fields and emergent new practices. To be an academic and creative practitioner as well as an activist or advocate for change in a world-in-crisis is no longer, necessarily, mutually exclusive. Many of the contributors to this volume demonstrate in their respective chapters, I think, how both a *hermeneutics of critique* and a *hermeneutics of engagement and care* are in play – and both are much needed in our communicative responses to today's troubled times.

My personal experience also tells me that when engaging with today's planetary emergency and meta-crisis, we need the support of others, if only by communing with thoughts and feelings shared in print. Many of us will commune with our personal bookshelf of old dust-covered friends and new digitized companions. I recall, for example, the sheer pleasure and excitement of reading Jeremy Lent's (2021) *The Web of Meaning* which encapsulated so clearly and insightfully so much that I had been reading, outside of my own academic discipline, for some years. It is an extraordinary, expansive and wonderful book that integrates the new philosophy of science alongside traditional wisdom and thereby helps to underpin emergent ideas of ecological civilisation as the only viable way forward from today's world-in-crisis.

Ian McGilchrist's (2022) *The Matter With Things*, and Fritjof Capri and Pier Luigi Luisi's (2014) *The Systems View of Life*, both in their different ways offer a profound reorientation of evolutionary neuroscience and contemporary science that speaks to our current planetary predicament – and in doing so deepen our understanding beyond the historical vortices and political economy of capitalism. Joanna Macy's (2021) *World as Lover, World as Self* and Robin Kimmerer's (2013) *Braiding Sweetgrass* offered deep insights into differing cosmologies and social relations of care and reciprocity, providing seeds of hope, both active and ecological, for sustaining a possible future. Kate Raworth's (2017) *Doughnut Economics*, Kohei Saito's (2021) *Marx in the Anthropocene*, and Jeremy Rifkin's (2022) *The Age of Resilience*, have also proved instructive companions for thinking through the historical determinations of capital, the changing metabolic rifts of human life and ecology, and possibilities for future societal transformation. I have found so many 'great awakenings' in print and often these converge on remarkably similar conclusions, despite their different intellectual and philosophical vantage points (see Chapter 1 references). Each in their different ways unmasking the 'unmaking' of today's world and contributing resources for imagining plausible futures. You, dear reader, will have your own preferred book companions; keep them close and let your long dust coated friends speak to each other as well as to the latest glossy or online newcomers. Together they may coalesce into islands of coherence in the surrounding seas of chaos.

Listening to expert podcasts, such as energy-expert Nate Hagen's interviews in *The Great Simplification* (https://www.thegreatsimplification.com/), reading daily contributions to *Resilience*, published by the Post-Carbon Institute (https://www.resilience.org/), or participating in virtual spaces with others from around the world, such as the *Deep Transformation Network* (https://deeptransformation.network/), or meeting like-minded people face-to-face in local settings and actions, have also proved to be incredibly supportive. You are not alone! All this is good for the soul, of course, as well as engendering a sense of solidarity beyond sociability. And moments of quietude, appreciation and reflection when walking in nature and through different seasons, I can confirm, have also been both restorative and emotionally balancing (Hanh, 2013). This recuperative 'gift' often helping to physically ground and nourish at the same time as sensing oneself inside the web-of-life (Macy, 2021; Macy and Johnstone, 2022, Chapter 13, Wallen).

Each of us finds different ways to better attune to our world, from different philosophical and spiritual standpoints, and sometimes we must do so at the very moment that our attention to it can take us to a place of despondency, of heartache and grief (Albrecht, 2019; Macy, 2021). So, to shift gear, finally and firmly into first-person, and with your indulgence, I here share something of my own personal and cultural responses to communicating a world-in-crisis. Like many, as I say, I have often found meditative peace in remote places 'in nature'. For me, this sometimes includes taking a guitar and finding sympathetic notes and impromptu music in the moment, whether in the presence of seascapes, biodiverse forests, or outback deserts. Over recent years I've also been lucky enough to perform as guitarist in residence at a beautiful sculpture garden set in the ancient woodland of the Wye Valley, playing over the summer months to visitors and accompanied by – and I romanticise not – bird song and the hum of dragon flies. With my singer friend, Louise Armstrong, we also perform our own eco-songs under the name of 'Kahlo-After Frida', playing at green festivals and small venues. We are neither rock stars nor widely known! This is simply part of my way of attending to the world and expressing feelings and commitments towards it, outside of academia. This too it seems is about communicating a world-in-crisis, finding solidarity with others, and, in small imperfect ways, engaging in practices of active hope. Politically insignificant certainly; but important and grounding from a personal standpoint. It helps!

Whilst performing our songs is an emotional outlet for those more than troubling feelings already mentioned (Albrecht, 2019; Macy, 2021), it also provides an opportunity to share, commune and find a sense of solidarity with others; sometimes opening-up conversations after the performance and/or finding networks of similarly minded people. Sometimes, it must be said, our music can also fall on deaf ears! But this too is a communication of sorts and encourages us to find different musical registers and appeals that may yet resonate with others. As Simon Kerr put it well in Chapter 14, music's superpower is more emotional than conceptual, and it has 'a unique capacity to emotionally replenish and support people in crisis'.

To draw these personal reflections to a close and as one last illustration of how multidimensional, multifaceted and emotionally infused and energising communicating a world-in-crisis can be, here I share the lyrics of a few of our eco-songs. Each was written to address and resonate with audiences differently, and each demonstrates something of the polyvocal ways in which song can be crafted to engage with our world-in-crisis – and may encourage others to do the same. Hopefully, you may agree, that this cultural response is so much more than doomerism!

The first, *Sweet Summers Past*, is a song that attempts to recapture without cliches something of the innocent childhood experience of immersion in nature and the pleasures that many of us will have enjoyed and perhaps taken for granted in our early years. Though the youthful experience of feeling immersed in nature will of course be individually unique as well as demographically distributed, many/most of us will have youthful memories of being enveloped within nature's seasonal embrace. The song is written from the persona of a personal and nostalgic reminiscence and only at the end are we forced to recognise that the reassuring familiarity of seasons is now 'unstitched'. The song purposefully aims to locate nature in local place and personal experience where it often resonates the most (see Chapter 5 by Weissmann and Tyrrell, Chapter 6 by Foxwell-Norton et al.) and not, in this instance, in relation to the global political stage or even in explicit reference to the climate emergency.

Sweet Summers Past
(Sung over gentle, lyrical arpeggio guitar)

I remember sweet summers past,
Innocently held in nature's embrace.
Gentle sea breezes, feet sand baked.
Long-grass frolics to cliff-edge dreams.

Yellow fields swaying, insects' perpetual hum.
Crimson foxgloves standing tall down cow-parsley lanes.
I remember sweet summers past,
Yes, I remember summers past.

Bodies bathed in heat, shimmering in hope.
Morning honeysuckle dew then green dragonfly lakes.
I remember sweet summers past,
Yes, I remember summers past.

Waking to the birds' excitable chatter,
Evenings lost in swallows gentle soaring.
I remember sweet summers past,
Yes, I remember summers past.

Shaded cooling woods, blanketed in moss.
Wild garlic's pungency, stretching ferns unfurling.
I remember sweet summers past,
Yes, I remember summers past.

Chuckling brooks, chilled rivers toe dipped.
Kingfisher's orange-blue dart, frogspawn life stirring.
I remember sweet summers past,
Yes, I remember summers past.

Outro
From the ancients to this day
Assured in nature's way.
Life's rhythms in season's time.
Past and present in nature's palm.
But now no longer.
Something's amiss.
Seasons unstitched.
Summer's innocence lost.
Fields scorch and crack.
Skies drench and howl.
Nature's betrayed,
Who's dismayed?
I miss sweet summers past,
I grieve for sweet summers past.

The second song, *The Earth Weeps (Will you Sleep?)* in contrast, adopts a historically longer, cross-cultural, and more obvious politically engaged stance. It builds on the prophetic words of Hollow Horn Bear (1850–1913) who witnessed the devastating effects of the imposition of American society and 'progress' on the Lakota indigenous peoples, landscapes and animals, and beyond. He is reputed to have said: 'Someday the earth will weep, she will beg for her life, she will cry with tears of blood. You will make a choice, if you will help her or let her die, and when she dies, you too will die.'

The Earth Weeps, (Will you Sleep?)
(Sung over expressive arpeggio guitar)

Verse One
The Navajo 'Sheltered by the trees', Cheyenne 'Warmed by the sun.'
Said *Big Thunder* 'The Great Spirit the air we breathe; mother nature the plains and streams.'
Mary Brave Bird knew it too: 'The land is sacred, rivers our blood.'
Standing Bear lamented: 'Away from nature, hearts harden' – now clouds darken.
The Cree decreed, 'When the last tree has gone, last river poisoned, then money we cannot eat.'

Chorus
And, on the plains of Dakota, Hollow Horn Bear had prophesised:
'The Earth will cry tears of blood – and she will weep, she will weep.'

Verse Two
Goanna, possum, wallaby; the land is my mother; we are one.
Identity and Earth connected: Baada . . .. Toogee . . .. Pitjara.
From first sunrise to dried creek; dreamtime in the land we meet.
Walkabout through time and space; ancestors in our embrace.
Stories of mother earth woven with sun and moon; finger traced in stars and paint.

Chorus
Stolen from the land, a generation cries; The earth defiled so we will die.
Stolen from the land, a generation cries; The earth defiled so we will die.

Verse Three
Seas choke, smokestacks spew; it's corporate greed for the few.
Forests cleared, mass extinction rears; politicians stoking fears.
Racism wrapped in national flags; refugees in body bags.
Elites parade as ordinary man; ecocide disguised as consumer jam.
Extinction Rebellion rises, our Joan of Arc, Greta, mobilises. . ..

Chorus
And, on the plains of Dakota, Hollow Horn Bear had prophesised:
'The Earth will cry tears of blood – and she will weep, she will weep.'

Fast verse
Seas surge, Amazon burns.
Feel the heat; Take to the street.

Still mistaken, already forsaken?
Still mistaken, already forsaken?

The earth weeps, will you sleep?
The earth weeps, will you sleep?
The earth weeps, will you sleep?

Outro/Chorus

And, on the plains of Dakota, Hollow Horn Bear had prophesised:
'The Earth will cry tears of blood – and she will weep, she will weep.'
'The Earth will cry tears of blood – and she will weep, she will weep.'

A third song, *Jagannath*, is different again and this deliberately adopts a dramatic almost theatrical register filled with mythic allusions to different gods and spiritual traditions, as well as alluding to Thomas Hobbes' *Leviathan* and Anthony Gidden's prescient description of late modernity as an unstoppable 'Juggernaut' and 'runaway world'. The choruses are delivered in tongue-in-cheek humour, and the song overall is underpinned by driving, fast-paced, flamenco-ish guitar (similar to a flamenco Bulerias). The singer's persona playfully chides and goads the audience into reflecting on what they will do when the gods of destruction arrive. In this way, the song deals obliquely through a theatrical veil with our current world-in-crisis, whilst its high-octane delivery aims to register something of the impending urgency of our situation.

Jagannath

(Arabesque guitar introduction followed by fast furious rhythm)

Verse I
Jagannath's resurrected,
He's coming out to play.
The Juggernaut's on its way,
The World's runaway.

Chorus
What you goin to do?
Where you goin to go?
Images in the news
God almighty, what a view.

Verse II
Thanatos is at the helm,
Underworld bookings now.
Hypnos, God of sleep,
A merciful release.

Chorus
Will you stay?
Or will you run?
Book a flight maybe?
Watch TV, sit tight?

Verse III
Leviathan's brutish and mean,
English fields once sweet and green.
Kali and Shiva, Gods of destruction,
Yama's now the King of Ghosts.

Chorus
Will you faint?
Or will you fuck?
Will you live?
Or will you die?

Verse IV
Jagannath's resurrected,
He's coming out to play.
The World's runaway.
The World's runaway.

Chorus
Will you pledge?
Or will you pine?
Will you philosophise,
Or will you cry?

Verse V
Jagannath's resurrected,
He's coming out to play.
The World's runaway,
The World's runaway.

Chorus
Will you pledge,
Or will you pine?
Will you philosophise?
Or will you rise?

Ubuntu, in contrast to *Jaganneth*, is written and performed as an upbeat, uplifting and danceable song, that draws on the cultural flourishing of ideas and practices now coalescing in today's ecological awareness and sensibility as well as possible imagined futures. The term 'ubuntu' is an African communal term signalling that 'I am, because you are', or, in our interdependency, we can both be and thrive.

Ubuntu
(upbeat jazzy guitar)

You, me, nature, intwined:
A planetary community of fate.
Bio-diversity, cultural diversity
Nature/humanity one.
The 'human circle' still expanding,
History's 'moral arc' bending green.

Ubuntu: 'I am, because you are.
You are, because I am.' x4

Eco-anxiety, consciousness expanding;
Extinction Rebellion (XR) rising.
Biosphere the new public sphere;
Politicians forced to hear.
Global commons, imagined horizons;
Eco-battlefields of hope.

Ubuntu: 'I am, because you are.
You are, because I am.' x4

Indigenous wisdom in nature's embrace:
Nature's broken, Gaia's spoken.

Circular economies, deep ecology.
COP28, humanity's apology?
Precious Life, nature's delight.
Humanity and Nature one.

Ubuntu: 'I am, because you are.
You are, because I am.' x4

You, me, nature intwined.
A planetary community of fate.
Global awakening, our common fate.
Green awakening, never too late.
Everything's connected, nature's way.
The universe our sustainable guide.

Ubuntu: 'I am, because you are.
You are, because I am.' x4

And finally, one of Kahlo-After Frida's most direct and condemnatory songs perhaps, is written and performed through a persona that aims to embody something of the anger and active resistance felt and enacted by groups such as Extinction Rebellion and others in both the radical and growing moderate flanks of the climate and ecological movement.

Earth's Warming Blanket
(performed over pulsing/percussive Soleares, flamenco guitar)

Earth's warming blanket, woven in industrial time.
ExxonMobil lied and befuddled the public mind.
Corporate tobacco, big pharma the same.
Now planet Earth, not just us, is dying – who's to blame?

Still insatiable greed, corporate plunder.
Complacency and carbon chicanery taking us under.
Politician's empty words and broken promises.
'Fairy tales of eternal growth.'

Mass extinction Celsius: one point five (and soaring!);
Civil disobedience maths: three point five (system stalling?).
Planetary emergency, it's official, 'humanity's code red.'
Time to embrace inter-being . . . before we're dead.

The earth heaves, Greta's clarion cry:
'How dare you – how dare you!'
The planet shudders, Gaia moans:
You're killing me; I'll have your bones.

In their very different ways, each of these songs has sought to address today's world-in-crisis and do so in and through diverse music genres, different authorial/singer personas and various expressive registers and emotional appeals. Each is a written act of compression as well as register of semiotic symbolism. As a form they are closer to poetry than academic prose and pedantry. Curiously when writing them, the restrictions of form felt liberating. In their performance and reception, I like to think they have sometimes contributed to building a sense of communality with others, especially when performed at Green festivals (Chapter 7 by Muggeridge), and audience responses suggest that this is so. Though possibly this may also sometimes be helped along by an adjacent festival bar! And yes, sometimes as I say, they will have fallen on deaf ears too. But they have also played their part in rechannelling those daily feelings of despondency borne from the cognitive dissonance of living in a world that seems hell-bent on exponential growth and ecological exhaustion at the expense of human and planetary well-being. They have personally helped me in 'responding to the situation' and have done so through musical 'experimenting', 'inter-relating' with others, 'embodying' different emotional states and 'self-recognising' (Parlett, Chapter 18).

In their performance they have reminded me that amidst the cacophony of communicative voices, one's own internal voice also needs to be listened to and occasionally let loose. If nothing else, I hope these few indulgent personal reflections will have encouraged you to find and/or express your own voice in this world-in-crisis, and in whatever way(s) you feel most compelled and/or comfortable to do so. It is through the widening cracks of a world-in-crisis that our part in the web-of-life, paradoxically, is thrown into sharper relief – as well as the necessity for regenerative planetary responses. This is not only a struggle over perception and imagination, but fundamentally communication.

References

Albrecht, G. (2019) *Earth emotions*. Ithaca: Cornell University Press.

Capra, F. and Luisi, P.L. (2014) *The systems view of life*. Cambridge: Cambridge University Press.

Cottle, S. (2013) 'Journalists witnessing disasters: From the calculus of death to the injunction to care', *Journalism Studies*, 14(2), pp. 1–17.

Cottle, S. (2023) 'Reporting civilisational collapse: Research notes from a world-in-crisis', *Global Media and Communication*, 19(2), pp. 269–288.

Ghosh, A. (2016) *The great derangement*. Chicago, IL: University of Chicago Press.

Hanh, T.N. (2013) *Love letter to the earth*. Berkely: Parallax Press.

Kimmerer, R. (2013) *Braiding sweetgrass*. London: Penguin.
Lent, J. (2021) *The web of meaning*. London: Profile Books.
Macy, J. (2021) *World as lover, world as self*. California: Parallax Press.
Macy, J. and Johnstone, C. (2021) *Active hope*. California: New World Library.
McGilchrist, I. (2022) *The matter with things*. London: Perspective Press.
Raworth. K. (2017) *Doughnut economics*. London: Penguin.
Rifkin, J. (2022) *The age of resilience*. London: Swift Press.
Saito, K. (2021). *Marx in the Anthropocene*. Cambridge: Cambridge University Press.

NOTES ON CONTRIBUTORS

Simon Cottle (PhD) is Professor Emeritus, Media and Communication, in the School of Journalism, Media and Culture (JOMEC) at Cardiff University where he was formerly Deputy Head and Head of School. Simon is the author of 14 books and over 150 chapters and articles, many on global crisis reporting, and is the Series Editor for the *Global Crises and the Media Series* for Peter Lang Publishing. He is currently writing and lecturing on journalism and our world-in-crisis, performs as a guitarist and writes songs on ecology and the state of the planet. He can be contacted at CottleS@cardiff.ac.uk. (https://profiles.cardiff.ac.uk/emeritus/cottles)

Bridget Backhaus (PhD) is a Senior Lecturer in journalism and communications at Griffith University, Australia. A former community radio journalist and producer, her research explores the role of community media in social and environmental change with particular focus on issues of voice, listening, identity, and participation. Her work employs critical and participatory methodologies to explore the impacts and interconnections of community media. B.Backhaus@griffith.edu.au.

Victoria Fielding (PhD) is a Lecturer in Strategic Communication at the University of Adelaide. Victoria's research investigates the media's representation of political, social and industrial contestation and the influence of media reporting on democracy. She can be contacted at Victoria.Fielding@adelaide.edu.au.

Kerrie Foxwell-Norton (PhD) is an Associate Professor at Griffith University, Gold Coast. Her research interests focus upon environmental communication, media and journalism. She has engaged with many communities throughout Australia, exploring environmental and climate change communication in this age of ecological crises where impacts on local people and environments is her focus. She has worked with and for First Nation's communities and brings cultural awareness and respect to her daily life and work. K.Foxwell@griffith.edu.au.

César Jiménez-Martínez (PhD) is Assistant Professor in the Department of Media and Communications at the London School of Economics and Political Science. His research examines the mediation of nationhood, paying particular attention to phenomena such as nation branding, digital nationalism, and more recently protests at the nation-state level. César has received several awards, including the 2021 Anthony D. Smith award in nations and nationalism, and the 2023 ICA award in public diplomacy. His email is C.A.Jimenez@lse.ac.uk.

Michelle Johnston (PhD) is a senior lecturer at Curtin University in Perth, Western Australia where she teaches Screen Arts. Her research and creative practice are informed by participatory action research that has produced many hours of media, a documentary and a book on cross-cultural collaboration. She recently completed another feature documentary called *Earthship Freo* with co-producer Dr Mignon Shardlow in which she was also principal camera and editor.

Ron Johnston has a PhD in Ecology and Environmental Science. He was Subject Leader for Science and Sustainability Education on graduate and postgraduate teacher training programmes with the University of South Wales (2002–2016). Following this (2016–2018) he was sustainability science consultant with UNESCO supporting teacher research groups in Sikkim in Himalayan India embedding sustainability awareness within state science syllabuses. He has published widely on embedding sustainability issues into teaching and learning practise: https://www.ronjohnstonsustainablefutures.com/publications.

Simon Kerr (PhD) is a musician, songwriter and producer of the multimedia show Music for a Warming World. He trained in political ecology, teaching social sciences for several years before moving into University Management roles. He is currently Program Manager of the Murray-Darling Basin Water and Environment Research Program, an Honorary Research Fellow and adjunct member of the Climate Adaptation Lab at La Trobe University. He writes on environment, climate change and music. s.kerr@latrobe.edu.au.

Jenny Kidd (PhD) is a Reader in the School of Journalism, Media and Culture at Cardiff University. She researches in the interdisciplinary fields of Digital Heritage and Digital Culture. Jenny has led applied research projects with a range of practical and other outputs including two immersive experiences, a series of reports for industry, and many publications. She is author of *Museums in the New Mediascape* (2014) and *Critical Encounters with Immersive Storytelling* (2019).

Jeremy Lent is an author and speaker whose work investigates the underlying causes of our civilisation's existential crisis, and explores pathways toward a life-affirming future. His award-winning books, *The Patterning Instinct* and *The Web of Meaning,* trace the historical underpinnings and flaws of the dominant worldview, and offer a foundation for an integrative worldview that could lead humanity to a flourishing future. He is founder of the online global community the Deep Transformation Network.

Pippa Marland (PhD) is a Lecturer in Liberal Arts and English at the University of Bristol. She has published widely on Ecocriticism and contemporary literature, including as co-author of *Modern British Nature Writing, 1789–2020: Land Lines* (CUP 2022) and author of *Ecocriticism and the Island* (Rowman and Littlefield 2023) and the forthcoming *The Pen and the Plough: The Farm in British Nature Writing of the Long 20th Century*. She can be contacted at pm0035@bristol.ac.uk.

Mignon Shardlow (PhD) is Senior Lecturer in Journalism at the University of Notre Dame Australia in Fremantle, Western Australia. Recently Mignon co-produced a documentary with Michelle Johnston that told the story of a community of activists squatting in strategically located houses in Fremantle to prevent the destruction of important trees. The documentary explored themes of sustainable living, activism and the potential of documentary as a catalyst for change. Mignon can be contacted at mignon.shardlow@nd.edu.au.

Kingsley Marshall (PhD) is Head of the School of Film and Television and a research lead for the Sound/Image Cinema Lab, at Falmouth University. Kingsley's academic research focuses on cultures of film and television production, sound design and music, and the representation and use of artificial intelligence technologies in film. At his own company Myskatonic, he develops and produces music video, documentary, and feature films. He was an executive producer on *Enys Men* (Director: Mark Jenkin).

Troy Meston (PhD) is a Gamilleroi Senior Research Fellow in the Griffith Centre for Social and Culture Research. His work employs critical Indigenous studies and decolonial praxis to investigate the intersections between education, technology and Indigenous studies. He has amassed a diversified body of work, constructed curriculum, and industry outputs across the areas of Indigenous sport, financial literacy, cognitive science, Indigenous health, media and education. T.Meston@griffith.edu.au.

Steve Muggeridge is a Trustee of the Green Gathering charity and a Director of its production company that produces the international award winning, annual, Green Gathering at Chepstow. Steve has been involved with festivals since the Free Festivals of the early 1980s. Over decades, he has witnessed the evolution of Green philosophies and protest within the festival movement and mainstream. Currently engaged with pre-production of the 2025 Green Gathering. He can be contacted at stevemuggs3@gmail.com.

Malcolm Parlett (PhD) has enjoyed a long career as an independent psychologist, visiting professor in four universities, editor, writer, therapist, organisational consultant, and international teacher within the gestalt professional community. Following doctoral work in experimental psychology at Cambridge, Malcolm investigated teaching and learning at MIT and Edinburgh University; helped establish gestalt psychotherapy in Britain; and focusing on human development published *Future Sense* in 2015. He works as a coach and heads the Whole Intelligence Research Fellowship. malcolm.parlett@myphone.coop.

Chris Paterson (PhD) is Professor of Global Communication and Director of Taught Postgraduate Studies at Leeds University. He teaches in the areas of international journalism and climate communication and directs a research programme examining how rural communities in East and West Africa learn about climate change.

Salsabilla Sakinah is a PhD student in the School of Journalism, Media and Culture (JOMEC) at Cardiff University. Her PhD research focuses on how and why museums communicate the issue of environmental crisis through in-gallery digital media, and how visitors engage with and respond to it. Before doing the PhD, Salsa worked as a museum consultant in Indonesia. She can be contacted at SakinahS@cardiff.ac.uk.

Belinda Tyrrell is a research associate at the University of Liverpool's Heseltine Institute. A former policy and programmes officer at Liverpool City Council, Belinda worked on the performance monitoring of externally funded programmes including Neighbourhood Renewal Fund, and Housing Market Renewal Initiative, and was part of the Project Liverpool Team which mapped and tracked the value of Area Based Initiatives within the City of Liverpool.

Niina Uusitalo (PhD) is a Postdoctoral Research Fellow in the Faculty of Social Sciences at Tampere University, Finland. Uusitalo's background is in media and communication studies. Currently she is working at the intersection of visual studies and waste studies. Her theoretical interests lie in politics of aesthetics, eco-philosophy and more-than-human methodologies. In her work she explores theoretical concepts through photographic practices. She can be contacted at niina.uusitalo@tuni.fi.

Ruth Wallen, www.ruthwallen.net, is an artist and writer whose work fosters dialogue around ecological concerns and social justice. Her interactive installations, nature walks, web sites, artist books, performative lectures, and writing have been widely exhibited. She is emeritus core faculty and former chair of the MFA in Interdisciplinary Arts Program at Goddard College. Her current work bears witness to massive die-offs of trees, provides space for collective mourning, and advocates for healing of the life web.

Elke Weissmann (PhD) is Reader in Film and Television at Edge Hill University. She has published widely on television, in particular on *Transnational Television Drama* (2012, 2024). She is also editor of *Critical Studies in Television*, and head of Edge Hill University's Television Studies Research Group. Her recent research focuses on questions of governance and public value in relation to television, local communities and climate change.

Carrie Westwater (PhD) is a Lecturer in Creative and Cultural Industries, in the School of Journalism, Media and Culture (JOMEC) at Cardiff University. As an artist with an academic agenda, she considers the use of film and theatre as tools for navigating complex issues around trauma and the representations of such. She can be contacted at WestwaterCA1@cardiff.ac.uk.

Wilcannia River Radio, established in 2009, is owned and operated by Wilcannia locals. The station provides a voice for the community and is a service where local information can be disseminated. Wilcannia River Radio broadcasts community news, events and meeting information, job vacancies in the Wilcannia community, requests and cheerios. The station provides a great service in more ways than one; by bringing the community together, creating employment opportunities, building confidence, social inclusion and letting their voices be heard.

INDEX

A

L

M

N

O

P

R

S

T

U

V

W

Y

Simon Cottle, *General Editor*

The *Global Crises and the Media Series* provides a forum for academics and others engaging with the communication of some for the most pressing global challenges to humanity and the planet today. From the climate emergency to bio-diversity loss and the sixth mass extinction; from global financial meltdowns, forced migrations and zoonotic pandemics to world poverty and food, water and energy insecurity; from major wars and protracted conflicts to weapons of mass destruction, and the denial of human rights, these and other crises represent the dark side of our globalized planet. We live in increasingly turbulent times of overlapping, systemic and deepening crises. Each book in the series, whether a research-based monograph or edited or co-edited collection, provides an authoritative, theoretically informed and empirically engaged understanding of the global crisis in focus. And by this means each book seeks to stimulate wider academic study and public debate about the most pressing global crises that together constitute today's world-in-crisis.

For further information about the series and submitting manuscripts, please contact:

Professor Simon Cottle,
School of Journalism, Media and Culture, Cardiff University,
Two Central Square, Central Square, Cardiff CF10 1FS.
United Kingdom.
CottleS@cardiff.ac.uk

To order other books in this series, please contact our Customer Service Department at:

peterlang@presswarehouse.com (within the U.S.)
orders@peterlang.com (outside the U.S.)

Or browse online by series:

www.peterlang.com

Printed by
CPI books GmbH, Leck